Advance Praise for

One Hundred Years of Women Debating the Equal Rights Amendment

"*One Hundred Years of Women Debating the Equal Rights Amendment* provides an engrossing and thorough account of the multifaceted struggle for the ERA. With an impressive array of primary sources and editorial commentary, Melody Lehn and Camille Lewis foreground the diverse women who shaped the public debate around the century-long fight for the ERA. *One Hundred Years* will be a crucial resource for students, instructors, and anyone interested in gender equality."

—Rebecca DeWolf, author of *Gendered Citizenship: The Original Conflict over the Equal Rights Amendment, 1920–1963*

"Comprehensive and sweeping, this book is a tremendous achievement. Through women's debates over the Equal Rights Amendment, Lehn and Lewis expertly reconstruct a century of women's self-definitions and advocacy. In these pages, we meet familiar and surprising figures whose arguments ground a deeper, richer understanding of equality: that basic American value whose meaning has been anything but simple. The book offers the timely reminder that women have been both unequal citizens and essential drivers of the democratic process. The questions explored here remain as pressing as ever: what do women need to live in America on their own terms, and what will it take for that nation to live up to its own founding ideals of equality and justice?"

—Katherine Turk, author of *The Women of NOW: How Feminists Built an Organization That Transformed America*

"For too long, the women who made constitutional meaning and history have been ignored. Melody Lehn and Camille Lewis enable us to hear these women's diverse voices and to experience their brilliance, courage, and complexity as the uncertain fate of the Equal Rights Amendment continues to unfold."

—Julie C. Suk, author of *We the Women: The Unstoppable Mothers of the Equal Rights Amendment* and *After Misogyny: How the Law Fails Women and What to Do about It*

One Hundred Years of Women Debating the Equal Rights Amendment

One Hundred Years of Women Debating the Equal Rights Amendment

An Anthology, 1923–2023

Edited by
Melody Lehn and Camille K. Lewis

PETER LANG
New York - Berlin - Bruxelles - Chennai - Lausanne - Oxford

Library of Congress Cataloging-in-Publication Data

Names: Lehn, Melody, editor. | Lewis, Camille K., editor.
Title: One hundred years of women debating the Equal Rights Amendment : an anthology, 1923–2023 / Melody Lehn, Camille K. Lewis (eds).
Description: New York : Peter Lang, 2024. | Includes index.
Identifiers: LCCN 2024021544 (print) | LCCN 2024021545 (ebook) | ISBN 9781636675046 (paperback) | ISBN 9781636675053 (hardback) | ISBN 9781636675022 (ebook) | ISBN 9781636675039 (epub)
Subjects: LCSH: Equal rights amendments–United States–History. | Women's rights–United States–History. | Sex discrimination–Law and legislation–United States–History.
Classification: LCC KF4758 .O54 2024 (print) | LCC KF4758 (ebook) | DDC 342.7308/50904–dc23/eng/20240521
LC record available at https://lccn.loc.gov/2024021544
LC ebook record available at https://lccn.loc.gov/2024021545
DOI 10.3726/b22067

Bibliographic information published by the Deutsche Nationalbibliothek. The German National Library lists this publication in the German National Bibliography; detailed bibliographic data is available on the Internet at http://dnb.d-nb.de.

Cover design by Peter Lang Group AG

ISBN 9781636675046 (paperback)
ISBN 9781636675053 (hardback)
ISBN 9781636675022 (ebook)
ISBN 9781636675039 (epub)
DOI 10.3726/b22067

Published by Peter Lang Publishing Inc., New York, USA
info@peterlang.com—www.peterlang.com

This publication has been peer reviewed.

Dedicated to:

The women who raised us, who loved us, and who inspired us to fight for our rights.

Anne Marie Smith Lehn
Florence Crosby Lehn
Stella Uzdzinski Potter

and

Lorraine Bernice Chciuk Kaminski
Władysława Źaczek Kaminski
Stefania Bielatowicz Chciuk

Table of Contents

Section VI The Debate Persists: 2016–2023

Acknowledgments

If someone were to ask either of us to describe the process of completing this book, we agree that the word "joyful" best captures the experience. Our work began during the early months of the coronavirus pandemic in 2020. Like those who we write about in the introduction, we locked down, reconfigured our classes into remote offerings, binge-watched *Mrs. America*, and talked about the show with friends, family, students, and—importantly—each other. Out of those conversations came an idea that blossomed into this collaboration, which provided a bright spot as we navigated the new challenges posed by the pandemic.

Elizabeth Howard at Peter Lang championed this project from our earliest conversations. We are indebted to her and her team for exemplifying steadfast support, swift responsiveness, and sound advice in shepherding this manuscript through revision and publication. We also thank Tim and Joanna Smolko for their editorial help and enthusiastic support of our work.

Given the restrictions on in-person travel during the pandemic, archivists invaluably aided us as we brought our ideas to fruition. They did so under difficult and unprecedented conditions, yet generously responded to our queries and helped us to remotely acquire many of the texts we have included. Readers will find acknowledgments for archives and archivists within the notations of entries.

We also have individual thanks to offer.

Melody: This book would not exist were it not for wise teachers, mentors, and advocates. At Furman University, courses in the Women's Studies (now Women's, Gender, and Sexuality Studies) program opened my eyes to new ways of seeing, thinking, and knowing. I am profoundly grateful to Savita Nair, Lynne Shackelford, Elizabeth Smith, Courtney Tollison, Victoria Turgeon, and Diane Vecchio for their indelible impact on my professional trajectory. In Sean O'Rourke's classroom, I first encountered the study of women's speeches and found my vocational calling amid uncertainty about what to do with my life. At the University of Memphis, Janann Sherman taught me that women's histories matter if we are to understand the significance of their rhetorical choices, while Sandy Sarkela's commitment to recovering women's speeches endures in my classroom and across the pages of this book. In this vein, Jamie Capuzza, Wanda Fenimore, and Lori Stallings have served as incredible sounding boards who share the view that recovering and circulating women's rhetoric matters.

My Sewanee students are an inspiration for this book. A special thanks to Anna Day and Quinn Needham, who continued conversations about women's rhetoric and the ERA long after they left my classroom. I also thank Quinn, Nellie Fagan, and Pate Simmons for the kind invitation to participate for their "Feminist Fiends and Quarantine Queens" podcast, which focused on the *Mrs. America* episode "Phyllis." Preparing to "spill the tea" in this interview prompted me to more closely examine how the show represented the ERA debate.

My partner Adam Hawkins showed me kindness when I initially interviewed at Sewanee. That kindness now infuses our beautiful life together. I am especially grateful for his care and understanding during my mother's illness, which gave me much-needed time to complete this manuscript. I also wish to thank Karen Hawkins, Jerry Collins, Lois Stuller, Conrad Hawkins, and Stacey Chapman for welcoming me into the fold.

Finally, I thank my dear friend and co-editor Camille Lewis. We have known each other for more than 25 years, tracing back to our (okay, my) denim jumper days in church choir. It is nothing short of miraculous that we came together in a shared vision to imagine and complete this book. I am proud and grateful to know you.

Camille: My parents, Hank and Lorraine Kaminski, regularly affirmed my humanity and my own intellectual autonomy—a radical act within our conservative Evangelical world. My older brother Steve was my first academic colleague, showing me long before college how words powerfully create worlds. I could not imagine this book and the questions it asks without them.

When I attended the ultra-fundamentalist Bob Jones University, any assertions of my autonomy were met with skepticism, except with my teacher, DeWitt Jones. He had been Steve's teacher, too, and he cultivated the same intellectual curiosity my family had begun. When he mentioned to me in my Master's program—"There's a book you should see. It's all early feminist arguments, *Man Cannot Speak for Her*. Here. Take my copy."—I was hooked. American women of faith could effectively and logically assert their rights in the public sphere. For Dr. Jones, I am thankful.

My professors at Indiana University deepened and broadened that intellectual inquiry. Those graduate school conversations with John Lucaites, Robert Ivie, Robert Terrell, James Andrews, and J. Michael Hogan are all woven throughout this book. After graduation, in the ups and downs of post-doc life, many colleagues have supported me—sometimes arguing, sometimes cheering, always encouraging. Gary Weier, Daniel Brown, David Worthington, Alena Ruggerio, Marty Medhurst, Elesha Coffman, Theon Hill, Darrel Wanzer-Serrano, Deborah Breede, and Wanda Little Fenimore, thank you.

I will always appreciate the collegial and uplifting friendship of my current Furman colleagues. I've been chattering about the Equal Rights Amendment for months now, and they are consistently affirming and optimistic. This book would not have been possible without their help and support. From Jeffrey Makala and Nashieli Marcano in the archives, to my cohort of Judith Williams and Kaniqua Robinson and Tuğçe Kayaal, your patience and expertise are invaluable. Janice Rowe patiently helped me through the trenches of the minutiae. Adam Richards, Brandon Inabinet, Cynthia King, Selena Dickey, Alyson Farzad-Phillips, Mai Xiong-Gum, Mary Sturgill, and Mac McArthur—thank you all for listening to my frustrations, critiquing my nascent ideas, answering my questions, and imagining the possibilities with me. You all are gracious and kind, and I will be forever thankful for each of you.

As I was digging and reading and writing, my students—past and present and future—have been nearby. As I see the sparkle of activism in my current Furman students, I am thankful for your persistence, your questions, and your creativity. My personal friends are part of this too. Ruth and Bryant Burroughs, Marcie and Jason Yon, and Josh and Kim Guilliams listened to my frustrations and prayed through them with me. Ruth Buchanan was an always-enthusiastic coach, reminding me of the marathon of book-writing. And Ruthie Hawkins, Joanna Smolko, Lisa Kraus, Jeannette Jones, and Rachel Lilly kept me on task with daily reminders and nudges and, of course, memes.

My sons Isaac and Gavin were my incredulous audience when I first mentioned this book idea. "What?!" they said, "that hasn't passed yet! Why not?" For you and yours, I want to document the possibilities of rhetorical strategies for your own activism. And my darling husband and ever-present sounding board, Grant, you've been alongside, through thick and thin, always listening, always discerning, and always supporting. You are my delight.

Melody, who would have thought that the first soprano on the front row and the second soprano in the back could ever get together in such a happy, not-really-musical way? You're a thoughtful and careful scholar with boundless enthusiasm. I'm honored to join with you in this book. You are a queen.

Abbreviations

AAUW	American Association of University Women
ACLU	American Civil Liberties Union
AFL-CIO	American Federation of Labor and Congress of Industrial Organizations
ASCE	American Society of Civil Engineers
AUAM	American Union Against Militarism
AWSA	American Woman Suffrage Association
BPWC	National Federation of Business and Professional Women's Clubs
CEA	Constitutional Equality Amendment
CWA	Concerned Women for America
CWC	Congressional Women's Caucus
EEOC	Equal Employment Opportunity Commission
ERA	Equal Rights Amendment
FMF	Feminist Majority Foundation
GFWC	General Federation of Women's Clubs
ILGWU	International Ladies' Garment Workers' Union
IWW	Industrial Workers of the World
JBS	John Birch Society
LDS	Latter-day Saints
LWV	League of Women Voters
NAACP	National Association for the Advancement of Colored People
NACW	National Association of Colored Women
NAWSA	National American Woman Suffrage Association
NCDURA	National Committee to Defeat the Un-Equal Rights Amendment
NCL	National Consumers' League

NCLR	National Council of La Raza
NCNW	National Council of Negro Women
NFRW	National Federation of Republican Women
NNC	National Negro Congress
NOW	National Organization for Women
NWP	National Woman's Party
NWPC	National Women's Political Caucus
NWSA	National Woman Suffrage Association
PCSW	President's Commission on the Status of Women
UPWA	United Packinghouse Workers of America
VAWA	Violence Against Women Act
VMI	Virginia Military Institute
WEAL	Women's Equity Action League
WPP	Women's Peace Party
WTUL	Women's Trade Union League
YWCA	Young Women's Christian Association

Introduction: A Rhetorical History of the Equal Rights Amendment Debate

The limited FX series *Mrs. America* debuted in April 2020 on the streaming service Hulu as an ambitious and, many would argue, long-overdue attempt to portray the contest over the Equal Rights Amendment (ERA) in the 1970s and early 1980s. Actress Cate Blanchett tackled the role of Phyllis Schlafly, the conservative firebrand and the ERA's best-known opponent. Among the ensemble cast was Sarah Paulson as the fictional housewife Alice Macray, a conflicted Schlafly ally whose character arc personifies a growing disenchantment with the militant opposition to both the ERA and the broader women's rights movement.[1]

Mrs. America arrived at a particularly salient cultural moment. Donald Trump's meteoric political rise in the Republican Party, despite his well-documented record of misogynistic language and behavior, mobilized women to rise up in protest, form a resistance, and run for political office in record numbers.[2] For those women and men hoping to better understand the threat to women's rights that Trump's election posed, *Mrs. America* provided much-needed historical context relevant to the present day. The series' release also coincided with the emergence of the global COVID-19 pandemic. Americans were stuck at home in a national lockdown as elected officials deployed stay-at-home orders, sick citizens went into quarantine, workers shifted to remote work, and students departed from their school campuses. House-bound viewers with more time than usual on their hands welcomed the escapism provided by the promise of new episodes each week. By the time that Hulu released the fourth episode, "Betty," viewers were consuming an average of 38 hours a week of "lockdown TV"—including *Mrs. America*, which went on to earn several awards as one of the most-watched series of the year.[3]

Although *Mrs. America's* showrunner Dahvi Waller sought to "humanize the women on both sides of the [ERA] debate," those portrayed on the show nonetheless voiced concerns about the final product.[4] Phyllis Schlafly's daughter Anne Schlafly Cori took issue with the representation of her mother, accused the show's creators of depicting conservative women as "racists," and speculated that the show's politically motivated creators sought to resurrect the ERA in the twenty-first century.[5] In response, Schlafly's still-active Eagle Forum posted a series of YouTube videos to tell "The Truth Behind Mrs. America." The website *mrsamerica.org* launched to further disparage the series and revive Phyllis Schlafly, who died in September 2016, as a venerable conservative icon for a new generation.[6] Right-wing pundits at *Breitbart* chimed in to suggest that the show's attempts to ridicule Schlafly backfired and that pro-ERA feminists came across as "radical" and "shallow backstabbers."[7] Pundits at *Breitbart*—as well as other right-wing outlets such as *The Federalist* and the online blog for the Concerned Women for America—attacked the show's creators for assuming an improperly biased stance against Schlafly and other conservatives, and for "inventing facts" about what really happened among those debating the ERA during this period.[8] A statement from the Clare Boothe Luce Center for Conservative Women chastened Hulu for creating a show that "viciously malign[ed] Mrs. Schlafly because she was not the leftwing ideologue feminists demand from the women they support"—an expected though ironic critique, since the organization's namesake worked with Alice Paul, marched for the ERA, and was one of the earliest Congresswomen to support the amendment.[9]

Anti-ERA conservatives and Schlafly allies were not the only critics of the series. *Ms. Magazine* founder Gloria Steinem and former National Organization for Women President Eleanor Smeal co-authored an editorial for the *Los Angeles Times* outlining a somewhat related set of concerns about what they called the "misinformation" perpetuated by the series. The creators of *Mrs. America* contacted Steinem early in the production process to invite her input. But after reading the initial scripts, Steinem declined to participate because she felt the series "comes off as a catfight among women rather than a battle between the ERA and economic interests." Smeal, in turn, worried that the heavy focus on Schlafly and other ERA opponents created a "false premise" that understated how widespread support for the amendment really was, particularly among women of color.[10] Some commentators agreed with Smeal that *Mrs. America* sidelined non-white ERA supporters. Alessa Dominguez of *Buzzfeed News* observed that "the fight over the ERA is represented as a conflict primarily between white middle-class women (like Schlafly and her supporters) and white celebrity feminists."[11] Notwithstanding the abundance of reviews that deemed *Mrs. America* "must-see television," Linda Holmes of *NPR* summed up the overarching critique that took hold among both pro- and anti-ERA factions alike: "there is something not quite complete about it."[12]

As educators who teach courses in women's rhetoric, persuasion, and argument, we watched *Mrs. America* with several questions in mind—questions not specifically raised by the show's supporters and critics, but which are related to their observations about the show's inevitable limitations. These questions are guided by our belief that, as Carole Spitzack and Kathryn Carter put it, "rhetoric can be studied not by asking *if* women say anything important, or *if* there are any great women speakers, but by asking what women say, how women use the public platform, how women speak."[13] Accordingly, we wondered: what did the ERA's supporters and opponents *actually* say? How did they argue for their positions? How did those positions and arguments develop over time? What evidence did they use? Did they ever change their minds about the proposed amendment and if so, why? Who were their listeners? What barriers to speaking did they encounter and navigate? And as to the important questions of representation, inclusion, and accuracy raised by the show's critics—who was included and excluded in the conversation, and why?

One Hundred Years of Women Debating the Equal Rights Amendment: An Anthology, 1923–2023 begins to answer these questions. December 13, 2023, marked the one-hundred-year anniversary of the ERA's[14] first introduction in Congress. The time is ripe for revisiting how women across generations have argued that gender equality will reshape and reimagine our democracy if enshrined in the United States Constitution. Ours is an edited collection of primary texts debating the ERA over the past century.[15] Historian Elizabeth Novara emphasizes that "the discourse during the first few decades after the amendment's introduction showcases the differing viewpoints held by labor feminists, African American women, and various women's organizations at that time."[16] Thus, in contrast to narratives that begin with passage of the Nineteenth Amendment and then propel us forward to the 1970s, this volume recovers and surveys women's arguments around the ERA from its inception through the present day. Together and apart, these texts reveal the nuanced, complicated, and sometimes contradictory ways that women have contemplated the question of whether we need an Equal Rights Amendment.

The ERA Debate as Rhetorical History

This collection treats the ERA debate as a multifaceted public controversy where many voices over an extended period of time have made arguments, tested claims, proffered evidence, defended positions, issued refutations, offered remedies for misunderstanding,[17] and called upon audiences to collectively think and act in certain ways about the proposed amendment. Our critical approach is what Kathleen J. Turner calls "rhetorical history": that is, we seek "to understand the context [of the debate] through messages that reflect and construct that context."[18] Rhetorical history, in this sense, reflects what David Zarefsky describes as "the study of historical events from a rhetorical perspective." It is an inquiry into "history as a series of rhetorical problems [and] situations that call for public persuasion to advance a cause or overcome an impasse."[19] The longevity and public attention surrounding the ERA debate make it especially well-suited for a rhetorical history project. This perspective excavates and catalogs primary texts about the Equal Rights Amendment that illuminate yet also disrupt the accepted wisdom about women's rhetorical contributions to the debate. And while this collection cannot be an exhaustive account of "the conflicting rhetorical worlds" co-created by the ERA's supporting, opposing, and undecided voices for the past one hundred years, it does offer a starting point that will invite engagement and, we hope, inspire further investigation into this enduring, multigenerational rhetorical struggle.[20]

The longevity of the controversy is not the only reason why the ERA debate is well-suited for a rhetorical history project. Debating the ERA has long provided women with a "route to rhetorical authority" on matters that affect their lives and the lives of their fellow citizens.[21] As legal scholar Julie C. Suk observes, if the Equal Rights Amendment is ever added to the U.S. Constitution, it would become "the only piece of our nation's fundamental law that was *written by women* after suffrage, *adopted by women* leading the way in Congress, *given meaning by women* lawyers and judges, and *ratified by women* lawmakers in state legislatures of the twenty-first century."[22] American women rhetors initiated and drove the ERA debate for more than a century—and they are still going. The very possibility of an Equal Rights Amendment provided an exigence for some of these women to publicly speak—and to claim the right to publicly speak—in the first place. In fact, many of the women in this volume devoted the greater part of their lives to seeing the amendment succeed or fail.

And yet, women's rhetorical contributions to the ERA debate have not been adequately gathered and made available in one place prior to now, despite the abundance of texts that we have found. Edited collections that do the important work of recovering and collating women's speeches, scholarly and popular alike, have included speeches about the Equal Rights Amendment either sporadically or not at all.[23] Digital speech archives such as *American Rhetoric*[24] and *Gifts of Women's Speech*[25] have limited holdings when it comes to the ERA. The *Voices of Democracy Project*, a terrific pedagogical resource that "promotes the study of great speeches and debates in U.S. history," only features two units on the pro-ERA testimony of Shirley Chisholm and Gloria Steinem, both delivered to Congress in May 1970.[26] Iowa State University's Archives of Women's Political Communication, as part of the Carrie Chapman Catt Center, impressively features pro-ERA speeches by Chisholm and Steinem along with Betty Ford, Betty Friedan, Sonia Johnson, Carolyn Maloney, Jackie Speier, and Mary Church Terrell, while Phyllis Schlafly represents the anti-ERA position with two texts. With the exceptions of Terrell, Chisholm, and Schlafly, these holdings currently privilege the voices of white, elite, pro-ERA speakers after 1970—a trend certainly not limited to this archive.[27]

How, then, can we explain the ERA's reduced, biased, and uneven status in these locations where the great American speeches and debates are publicly documented?

In part, the answer lies in the persisting problem of valuing and making women's rhetoric accessible at all. More than 55 years ago, Robert J. Brake surveyed the available popular speech anthologies to assess the status of women in an essay titled "Women Orators: More Research?" His findings were, for the time, discouraging but unsurprising. The anthologies in circulation included few or no speeches by women. Wayland M. Parrish and Marie Hochmuth's *American Speeches* (1954), A. Craig Baird's *American Public Addresses, 1740–1952* (1956), and Ernest J. Wrage and Barnet Baskerville's *Contemporary Forum: American Speeches on Twentieth Century Issues* (1962) included no women. Others, such as Houston Peterson's *A Treasury of the World's Great Speeches* (1954) and Robert T. Oliver's *History of Public Speaking in America* (1965), included only one or two women.[28] By 1967, when Brake published his survey, women had been passionately debating the Equal Rights Amendment—an historic issue—in a variety of public forums for over four decades.

Primary source anthologies about women began appearing in the 1970s. In 1988, Susan E. Searing discovered more than 50 such anthologies that tended to focus on the recurring themes of "Western ideas about women; the development of feminism; and the social history of U.S. women."[29] Today, teachers and students have access to an abundance of speeches and other primary texts by and about women reformers,[30] nineteenth-century African American women rhetors,[31] women rhetors in the civil rights movement,[32] women political leaders,[33] women rhetors in religious communities,[34] and twenty-first-century women rhetors,[35] along with collections of speeches and writings by individual women.[36] We have come a long way from Brake asking if—rather than insisting that—more research into women's rhetoric is needed. Even so, much work remains if we are to fill in the blanks where women's voices have been muted, erased, and forgotten.

Another reason why the Equal Rights Amendment debate has been neglected relates to persisting misconceptions that women, satisfied with the ballot, were rhetorically stagnant from the 1920s until the feminist movement of the 1960s and 1970s reenergized and refocused their efforts. Women's suffrage speeches are readily available in indispensable anthologies such as Karlyn Kohrs Campbell's *Man Cannot Speak for Her: Key Texts of the Early Feminists*, Sally Roesch Wagner's *The Women's Suffrage Movement*, and Susan Ware's *American Women's Suffrage: Voices from the Long Struggle for the Vote 1776–1965*.[37] However, no comparable collection exists for the Equal Rights Amendment. As rhetoric scholars Sandra J. Sarkela, Susan Mallon Ross, and Margaret A. Lowe explain in their introduction to *From Megaphones to Microphones: Speeches of American Women, 1920–1960*, "the nature and scope of women's public, political activism between 1920 and 1960 is often underestimated."[38] Historians of American feminism agree. Dorothy Sue Cobble, Linda Gordon, and Astrid Henry argue in the opening of *Feminism Unfinished* that "much writing about the women's rights movement conceives of it as coming to a halt after women won the right to vote in 1920, then reawakening fifty years later in the 1970s and evaporating in the 1980s." Instead, they assert, "there was no period in the last century when women were not campaigning for greater equality and freedom."[39] The Equal Rights Amendment debate constitutes an ongoing rhetorical site where women since 1923 have campaigned for greater equality and freedom related to a host of issues including, but not limited to, marriage law, divorce rights, equal pay, job security, safe workplace conditions, educational opportunities, economic mobility, reproductive rights, racial equality, LGBTQIA+ rights, religious liberty, and peace and justice—all issues that continue to affect the lives and livelihoods of American women (and men) today.

Finally, the divisiveness of the debate, or what historian David E. Kyvig describes as "the inflamed rhetoric of the battle," further sheds light on why women's rhetoric about the ERA has yet to get its due credit.[40] Women were (and still are) not only divided about the amendment itself but also remain divided on their respective sides about how best to achieve their goals. As

Gloria Steinem's contribution to this anthology suggests, the media played a significant role in amplifying and perpetuating a narrative of divisiveness that does not always portray women in the most favorable light. The media's proclivity for characterizing this divisiveness in terms of a "catfight" or a "women-against-women" framework, as Kimberly Wilmot Voss points out, "marginalized the concept of feminism and shaped the way journalists covered the battle."[41] Voss also correctly notes that this kind of framing neatly separated women into two camps of pro-ERA feminists and anti-ERA antifeminists, with no accounting for a robust middle ground where undecideds sought clarity before committing themselves to a position. In addition to relentless commentary about the appearances of the women debating the amendment, gendered framing also diminished the possibilities for regarding the debate as a healthy and cooperative, though certainly at times a contentious and even uncivil, exchange of ideas and arguments about an important matter of public policy.[42] A rhetorical history approach helps us to see the women involved in the debate not as screeching felines, but as capable citizens participating in the democratic process.

Six Facets of the ERA Debate

A rhetorical history of the Equal Rights Amendment debate reveals at least six facets that we invite readers to bear in mind. Some facets have to do with debunking myths and misconceptions about the debate. Others reveal themes and trends that recurred as we sought, found, studied, and edited the texts compiled in this collection.

First, women of differing backgrounds, identities, experiences, vocations, and beliefs have come together and debated the Equal Rights Amendment over the past century. In curating a plurality of voices and viewpoints to sketch the arc of the ERA debate, we have often been reminded of Robin E. Jensen's charge that "because women and minorities have had fewer opportunities to give great speeches or to publish influential writings, scholars must look beyond publicly celebrated rhetoric to piece together a comprehensive narrative of rhetorical history."[43] Many names of women speakers often deemed "great"—or at the very least "famous" and perhaps even "infamous"—will undoubtedly be familiar to readers. The principal figures Bella Abzug, Shirley Chisholm, Betty Friedan, Gloria Steinem, and Phyllis Schlafly are represented here because they were on the front lines of the ERA debate at its height in the 1970s and 1980s. But scholars of women's rhetoric have cautioned against the temptation to focus attention on a few "great women speakers" who are either among the "famous few" or a "newly-declared or newly-resurrected famous few."[44] Doing so leaves the impression that any "greatness" that arises from women's speech is an unusual happening and, to Jensen's point, tends to generate exclusionary scholarly practices. Moreover, focusing on individual luminaries leaves little space to account for the "extraordinary bipartisan cooperation" exhibited by women who shattered barriers and created alliances across the political aisle in this debate.[45]

Thus, we have intentionally sought out those overlooked and unsung women who were ERA campaigners, allies, and opponents since 1923. Among the women included in this anthology, both familiar and forgotten, are former suffragists, elected officials, factory workers, labor activists, socialist agitators, nurses, lawyers, judges, insurance agents, pilots, engineers, military veterans, homemakers, domestic violence survivors, clergy, church secretaries, teachers, journalists, poets, civil rights leaders, LGBTQIA+ activists, community organizers, first ladies, and Supreme Court Justices. We also feature women from across the political spectrum and have attempted to offer a balanced rendering of the debate from as many sides of the controversy as possible. Accordingly, we have mapped the many-sided arguments advanced by women approaching the ERA debate on different personal, professional, and political grounds.[46] In so doing, we have embraced Jacqueline Jones Royster and Gesa E. Kirsch's call for feminist scholars in rhetorical studies to "find more and better ways to listen to the multidimensional voices that are speaking from within and across many of the lines that might divide us as language users—by social and political hierarchies, geography, material circumstances, ideologies, time and space, and the like."[47]

Second, many of the women in this book have been remembered and celebrated for various accomplishments that do not always extend to their advocacy about the ERA—a fact this rhetorical history seeks to rectify. Crystal Eastman, foremother of the American Civil Liberties Union, co-authored the earliest iteration of the ERA with Alice Paul, yet is often not credited alongside Paul for this work. Nora Stanton Barney fought for equal opportunities as one of the nation's first women engineers. In a lesser-known part of her history, Barney publicly lent her support to the ERA by testifying before Congress nearly one hundred years after the historic first women's rights convention led by her grandmother Elizabeth Cady Stanton met in Seneca Falls, New York. Republican Gladys O'Donnell submitted testimony to Congress in favor of the ERA alongside Shirley Chisholm and Gloria Steinem at hearings in May 1970. That testimony has been eclipsed by O'Donnell's status as a pioneering woman pilot and close contemporary of Amelia Earhart. Congresswoman Barbara Jordan's 1974 statement at Richard Nixon's impeachment hearings and her address at the Democratic National Convention two years later are considered among the greatest speeches of the twentieth century.[48] Less remembered are Jordan's speeches about the ERA. The lived experiences of these women informed their stance on the ERA which can inform our contemporary understanding of what motivated them to support, denounce, or question the amendment.

Third, women's rhetoric about the ERA has appeared in both written and spoken discourse across a wide array of venues, in different rhetorical genres, and directed to diverse audiences. The texts in this anthology include not only public speeches and testimony but also pamphlets, newspaper editorials, magazine articles, journal articles, and blog posts. In written discourse, the women in this anthology circulated their arguments to a wide readership. For example, women have historically debated the ERA in publications created by, for, and about women. In the 1920s, Carrie Chapman Catt argued against the ERA in a League of Women Voters pamphlet, while Crystal Eastman argued in its favor for *Equal Rights*, the official publication of the National Woman's Party. A century later, Congresswoman Jennifer Carroll Foy took her case from the halls of the Virginia House of Delegates to the pages of *Marie Claire* just as Congresswoman Danica Roem and coauthor Kate Kelly turned to *Teen Vogue* as an outlet for condemning those who use the ERA debate to espouse anti-trans viewpoints.

Women have also put the ERA front and center in publications that are not exclusively concerned with women's issues. In so doing, they have both subtly and explicitly insisted that women's issues should concern *all* citizens regardless of sex, affiliation, or creed. Elizabeth Gurley Flynn denounced the "phony Equal Rights Amendment" in the Communist newspaper the *Daily Worker*, Dorothy Kelso Funn antagonized Mary Church Terrell by opposing the ERA in the National Negro Congress's magazine *Congress Vue*, Rebecca Stiles Taylor used her daily column in the *Chicago Defender* to share the concerns of women of color about the ERA, and Yolanda Orozco wrote in to her school newspaper at the University of California-San Diego to assert that the ERA was inconsequential to the needs of Chicana women in the United States. In contrast to these opponents, Jeanette Marks endorsed the ERA in the *General Federation Clubwoman* magazine, Virginia Mollenkott promoted the ERA in the protestant periodical *Faith/At/Work*, Marta Sotomayor argued that the ERA was central to the progress of Hispanic women in an article for *Agenda: A Journal of Hispanic Issues*, and Congresswoman Sylvia Garcia contributed an op-ed to the *Houston Chronicle* to support the ratification efforts in Virginia. Even more recently, LDS lawyer Michelle Quist penned a "conservative case for the ERA" in the *Salt Lake Tribune*, while Mormon professor Valerie M. Hudson countered a few weeks later that feminists should ask tough questions about ERA for the Church of Jesus Christ of Latter-day Saint's *Public Square Magazine*.

In spoken discourse, the women in this book have raised up their voices at hearings, meetings, rallies, conferences, radio appearances, and other events—many, but not all, led by and for women. These efforts have not been without risk. Take, for example, the ways that race and privilege both intersect and operate when women speak in "arenas in which white elite males have dominated historically."[49] Several of the speeches in this volume were delivered by women confronting Congressional committees comprised entirely of white men with the ability to make decisions about women's lives with the stroke of a pen or the simple utterance of a "yes" or "no" in a vote. A visiting white woman testifying in a legislative hall about the ERA had a different rapport with the white male decision-makers than a white woman elected as a peer of those decision-makers. For women of color entering a predominantly white space and navigating the dualities of gender and race, the power dynamics were vastly different whether they were visitors or elected officials. As the texts in this collection indicate, these savvy women rhetors were cognizant of the injustices of having to advance their arguments time and time again, and many used the occasion to speak directly to that injustice. We invite readers to engage these dynamics and others they identify.

With the advent of the internet and social media, women's rhetorics are even more available in the twenty-first century. The Eagle Forum has archived and recirculated Phyllis Schlafly's extensive rhetorical record until her death in 2016. Other Eagle Forum members continue to pen and publish anti-ERA articles for the web. The right-wing Concerned Women for America has similarly continued to disseminate anti-ERA arguments.[50] Meanwhile, White House staffer Tina Tchen used her position in the Obama administration to promote the ERA on the official White House website. Speeches from twenty-first-century political leaders, such as Congresswoman Ayanna Pressley, are readily available thanks to YouTube. National, state, and grassroots organizations maintain a growing presence on Facebook, Twitter, and Instagram, as do various individual women who use their public platforms to promote their views about the ERA. Numerous hashtags such as #EqualRightsAmendment, #ERA, #ERA100, #ERAcentennial, #ERAvote, #ERANow, #RatifyERA, #EnactERA, #RiseUp4ERA, #FaithforERA, #EqualMeansEqual, #ERAisEverywhere, #FreeTheERA, and #28thAmendment continue to gain traction, make connections, and introduce new audiences to the conversation. The examples we selected represent but a small sampling of the dearth of texts that the ERA debate continues to engender.

Fourth, women are not monolithic in their political beliefs nor are they always faithful to partisan tribes or denominational herds when it comes to the ERA. As a consequence, dissent has sometimes yielded rebuke. Some conservative women held firm in their support of the ERA during the anti-ERA Reagan years and, in some cases, bore hefty costs associated with bucking the party line. In this sense, the case of Congresswoman Margaret Heckler is instructive. A staunch pro-life Catholic, Heckler concurrently supported the ERA and was among the slate of pro-ERA speakers at the May 1970 hearings before the Senate Judiciary.[51] As a concession for opposing the ERA, Ronald Reagan listened to Heckler and other Republican women who persuaded him to appoint the first woman to the Supreme Court, which he did with the pro-ERA moderate conservative Sandra Day O'Connor in 1981.[52] With waning support for the ERA in the Republican Party under Reagan and without the support of pro-choice women's groups like NOW due to her staunch antiabortion beliefs, however, Heckler ultimately lost her Massachusetts Congressional seat in 1982 but never gave up her pro-ERA position.

Heckler was not alone in her fate. Republican National Committee co-chair Mary Dent Crisp expressed dismay when her party dropped the ERA from its platform in 1980. Crisp, who had joined forces with Heckler to request Reagan appoint a woman to the Supreme Court, declared in a speech that "the rejection of the Equal Rights Amendment was heartbreaking to many Republican women who believed in the great traditions of the Republican party."[53] For her efforts, she endured a stunningly public censure about party disloyalty from Reagan on the floor of the party's national convention. The pro-choice feminist stayed a Republican but she was unceremoniously pushed out of leadership for not adopting the new anti-ERA party position.[54]

Women across faith traditions have similarly grappled with how to negotiate their religious beliefs with their views on the ERA. Beneth Jones, Lottie Beth Hobbs, Barbara Smith, Virginia Mollenkott, Elisabeth Elliot, Sonia Johnson, Maureen Fiedler, Michelle Quist, and Valerie M. Hudson all centered their understandings of the ERA within the logics of their respective faith traditions, yet reached differing conclusions about the amendment. Social media accounts on Facebook and Twitter such as "Republicans for the Equal Rights Amendment" (@GOP_4_ERA) and "Mormons for ERA" (@mormonsforera), as just two examples, bear further witness to how conservative and/or religious "ladies" do not necessarily oppose the ERA just as not all politically progressive "libbers" have supported it throughout history.

Fifth, women have, at times, changed their minds about the ERA with the passage of time, shifting cultural attitudes, and gains or losses in their political progress through new legislation and policies. Dorothy Kenyon's 1953 editorial expressed an unambiguous anti-ERA position, though she changed her view about the amendment later in life. Sandra Day O'Connor faced political attacks from conservatives for her pro-ERA stance during her 1981 Supreme Court confirmation hearings. However, the 1970 speech from O'Connor we found conveyed her earlier doubts about whether the ERA was even necessary when other legal options might be more effective. A 1973 pro-ERA speech from labor activist and union leader Addie Wyatt openly admitted her change of heart on the amendment. Relatedly, women's positions on the ERA do not always fall on a clear "for/against" side. While supportive of the ERA's merits, lawyer Ethel Krepps concluded it would do little to change the status of Native American women. Given the evidence, we consciously reject neat and unrepresentative either/or paradigms that limit women's voices to a single or consistent side of the debate. For this reason, we have chosen to arrange these texts chronologically in six sections rather than divide them into "for/against" categories.

And finally, women debating the ERA have advanced arguments that are, in fact, harmful to women's dignity and prospects. Just as historian Rebecca DeWolf cautions against automatic assumptions that pro-ERA women are liberal and anti-ERA women are conservative, the rhetorical record discloses that not all women who opposed the Equal Rights Amendment opposed women's rights or equality between the sexes. As it happens, many—especially in the early decades of the debate—worried that the ERA presented a potential barrier to legislative gains women had already achieved. These opponents critiqued the "broad," "vague," or "unknown" nature of the effects passing the ERA might generate, rather than contesting the idea that women needed further protection under the law. Their anti-ERA rhetoric could hardly be categorized as anti-woman.[55]

That said, we have for purposes of inclusivity and accuracy included speakers who fomented divisiveness and disinformation to attack their opponents, to mischaracterize their opponents' positions, and to promote faulty reasoning, insufficient evidence, and outright lies in their own arguments. Some of these speakers advanced ideologies and stereotypes that are detrimental to women's progress—ideologies and stereotypes with which we certainly do not agree, which warrant close scrutiny, and which demand resolute censure. To this point, Royster and Kirsch offer sage advice. They note that it is "neither easy nor common … to study those with whom we disagree, whose values we don't share, whose worldviews might be foreign to us." But rather than deny and ignore these voices, we must engage them and responsibly strive "to attend to our own levels of comfort and discomfort, to withhold quick judgment, to read and reread texts and interpret artifacts within the contexts of the women's chronologies, to interrogate the extent to which our own presence, values, and attitudes shape our interpretations of historical figures and periods."[56] And to those voices that do harm about the ERA and all else, we must name, expose, and counter that harm with our own *parrēsia*—commonly understood as "fearless or frank speech"—to create good faith arguments that are both eloquent and ethical.[57]

Overview of the Book

We have arranged this anthology of 65 texts into six sections divided chronologically by periods where the ERA debate ebbed and flowed—but never fully subsided. The first section begins with Alice Paul's June 1923 announcement of an "approaching anniversary"—the seventy-fifth anniversary of the first women's rights convention in Seneca Falls. By the end of that year, the ERA had been introduced in Congress. Section I, "The Debate Begins: 1923–1939," charts the early years when pro-ERA emancipationists and anti-ERA protectionists set the parameters and terms of the debate. The next section, "The Debate Expands: 1940–1959," tracks the debate during and following the war years as the emancipationist and protectionist arguments developed to accommodate new concerns about and opportunities for women's civic participation. Section III, "The Debate Shifts: 1960–1971," sees the debate stretch beyond the familiar emancipationist and protectionist exchanges as the burgeoning women's rights movement prompted advocates and opponents to reconsider the ERA anew. In Section IV, "The Debate Splits: 1972–1982," we account for the ten-year ratification period as the ERA debate intensified as it never had before.

Once the 1982 extension deadline passed without the requisite number of states having ratified, the debate did not simply end or disappear. Section V, "The Debate Continues: 1983–2015," shows that some women still viewed the ERA as a vital and attainable political goal—representing hope for some and danger for others. As women reflected on the causes and implications of the ERA's defeat, they simultaneously sought to forge a path forward for the amendment's revival and, in some cases, sought to ensure the ERA's permanent exclusion from the U.S. Constitution. The ERA debate took on new urgency in the twenty-first century as the #MeToo Movement arrived and Donald Trump won the U.S. presidency. In Section VI, "The Debate Persists: 2016–2023," we conclude with a series of texts that show the ERA debate is alive and well. With the new ratifications in Nevada, Illinois, and Virginia, the ERA still provokes strong reactions among the women who have fought for and against it, as well as the undecided citizens who nonetheless have a vested interest in the debate.

Each of the six sections is preceded by a concise introduction that situates the texts within a broader historical context. Likewise, each individual text is preceded by a short rhetorical history that blends historical description with biographical information contextualizing the rhetor's advocacy for women's rights and noting her affiliation with the ERA. Unless otherwise indicated, each text is published in its entirety. Editorial changes are noted, minor, and only appear occasionally in cases of grammatical or factual errors we discovered. Readers can judge—and perhaps even debate—how well each speaker makes her case, uses evidence and different kinds of proof, adapts her message to the audience, and meets the need of the occasion. And as the ERA debate endures beyond the one-hundred-year mark, readers can contemplate the lessons that these exchanges teach us about our roles and responsibilities as speaking, listening, and thinking citizens.

Certainly, the texts in this collection can be read chronologically. Spanning the entire volume, readers will see these women rhetors debate the ERA's meaning and purpose, the very need for a constitutional amendment, its potential effects, the procedural aspects of ratification, and the motives of those who support or contest the ERA. Over time, some consistent themes will become evident, as do the moments when new questions, areas of focus, and lines of argument arise.

But in the true spirit of deliberation, texts can also be read in pairs and groups to disclose the implicit and explicit ways that these rhetors understand, address, reinforce, and refute each other. Some connections are apparent in the proximity of their couplings and groupings. The arguments of early twentieth-century pro-ERA women (Alice Paul, Crystal Eastman, Lavinia Dock, Anita Pollitzer, Grace Hoffman White, Jeanette Marks, and Nora Barney) and anti-ERA women (Carrie Chapman Catt, Ethel M. Smith, Florence Kelley, Edith Valet Cook, and Maida Springer Kemp) naturally correlate to one another. Mary Church Terrell crafted her pro-ERA arguments as a direct rebuttal to Dorothy Kelso Funn's anti-ERA article. Paige Comstock Cunningham's testimony opposing Ruth Bader Ginsburg's appointment to the Supreme Court countered Ginsburg's testimony, which affirmed that she still supported the ERA. Tina Tchen's blog post on the White House website disputed Terry O'Neill's charges that the Obama administration—and Democrats in general—were not fighting hard enough to pass the ERA.

Other textual connections can be forged by speakers' shared traits and identities, such as race, sexuality, religion, political affiliation, professional experience, and/or organizational memberships. The presidents of the

National Organization for Women—among those represented by texts in this anthology are Betty Friedan, Aileen Hernandez, and Terry O'Neill—have historically used their platform to endorse the ERA from the 1960s onward. First lady Eleanor Roosevelt opposed the ERA until her death in the 1960s, yet her successors Lady Bird Johnson, Pat Nixon, Betty Ford, and Rosalynn Carter all supported it in the 1970s and 1980s—and they did so on different grounds, with different kinds of appeals, and with varying levels of enthusiasm. Republican rivals Phyllis Schlafly and Gladys O'Donnell moved in the same political circles and vied for the same leadership positions, yet Schlafly—the more conservative of the two—launched STOP ERA not long after O'Donnell endorsed the ERA alongside feminists Shirley Chisholm and Gloria Steinem in 1970. Yolanda Orozco insisted that Latina women did not need the ERA in 1976, but a year later Marta Sotomayor countered that they did. Fundamentalist Beneth Jones advised that the ERA was incompatible with Christianity, although queer theologian Virginia Mollenkott—an alumna of the Southern school bearing the Jones name—strongly disagreed, as did Maureen Fiedler, the Catholic nun inspired by Mollenkott's teachings. The 2019 exchange between Michelle Quist and Valerie M. Hudson provides glimpses into the contrasting positions held by Mormon women—an exchange reminiscent of the earlier exchange between Mormon leader Barbara Smith and excommunicated Mormon Sonia Johnson more than 40 years earlier. Readers might compare and contrast texts to identify points of common ground, areas of departure, and instances of argumentative originality.

The women in this collection also focus their ERA arguments around particular topical issues that make for some provocative juxtapositions. Reproductive rights, for example, is a central topic that recurs across many of these texts. In 1999, Cuban-American Republican politician Ileana Ros-Lehtinen worried about the ERA's potential effects on abortion and characterized her pro-life position as decidedly "feminist." A year later, Phyllis Schlafly's anti-feminist Eagle Forum circulated a memo arguing that to resurrect the ERA in the next century paved the way for taxpayer dollars to fund abortion. Another recurring topic is the role of American women in wartime. After World War II, insurance agent and former suffragist Caroline Katzenstein maintained that "democracy is fighting for its very life" and that passing the ERA had never been more urgent to America's standing in the world. New York Congresswoman Carolyn Maloney made a similar argument 55 years later after the September 11 attacks in her home state. In a related vein, New York Congresswoman Bella Abzug focused her 1971 Congressional speech on the ERA's implications for women's military service. Thirteen years later, Assistant Secretary of the Air Force Antonia Handler

Chayes provided testimony to Congress that the ERA—now two years past its ratification deadline—could help reinforce the nation's line of defense amid the threat of nuclear war. Whether reproductive rights, America's global reputation, or national defense, the ERA debate intersects with a plethora of other subjects and ongoing debates of civic importance.

However readers choose to engage the 65 speeches and writings in this book, our hope is that they will find what follows as instructive and inspiring as we have. *One Hundred Years of Women Debating the Equal Rights Amendment: An Anthology, 1923–2023* is an extraordinary story of American women's rhetorical leadership, ingenuity, and courage. The risks these women took are our rewards and our roadmap as the ERA debate continues to unfold in its second century.

Notes

1 Sam Adams, "Sarah Paulson on Playing a House Wife Who—Well, We Won't Spoil It," *Slate*, May 20, 2020, https://slate.com/culture/2020/05/mrs-america-sarah-paulson-interview-episode-8-houston.html.

2 Susan Chira, "Donald Trump's Gift to Feminism: The Resistance," *Daedalus, the Journal of the American Academy of Arts and Sciences* 149, no. 1 (2020): 72–85.

3 John Koblin, "Lockdown TV Loses Some of Its Audience After Peaking in March," *New York Times*, May 2, 2020, B4.

4 Ellise Shafer, "'Mrs. America' Cast and Creators on Portraying Historical Figures With Accuracy and Empathy," *Variety*, August 19, 2020, https://variety.com/2020/tv/news/cast-creators-mrs-america-cate-blanchett-1234740150/.

5 Anne Schlafly Cori, "A Miss on Mrs. America," *Eagle Forum*, December 8, 2020, https://eagleforum.org/a-miss-on-mrs-america.html.

6 "Our Mrs. America: Phyllis Schlafly," https://mrsamerica.org/mrs-america/; "Eagle Forum," https://www.youtube.com/user/EagleForum.

7 David Ng, "FX's Anti-Phyllis Schlafly Series 'Mrs. America' Paints Feminists as Shallow Backstabbers," *Breitbart*, April 16, 2020, https://www.breitbart.com/entertainment/2020/04/16/hulu-phyllis-schlafly-series-mrs-america-paints-feminists-as-shallow-backstabbers/.

8 Warner Todd Huston, "FX/Hulu Caught Fabricating Quotes in 'Mrs. America' Scene of Real-Life Phyllis Schlafly Debate," *Breitbart*, April 30, 2020, https://www.breitbart.com/entertainment/2020/04/30/ed-martin-fact-checks-fxs-fabricated-mrs-america-scenes-with-real-phyllis-schlafly-debate-footage/; Peter Burns, "Four Years After Her Passing, Feminists Are Still Losing to Phyllis Schlafly," *The Federalist*, June 2, 2020, https://thefederalist.com/2020/06/02/four-years-after-passing-feminists-still-losing-phyllis-schlafly/; Toni DeLancey, "4 Things You Should Know about *Mrs. America*, Hulu's Series on Phyllis Schlafly," *Concerned Women for America*, April 24, 2020, https://concernedwomen.org/4-things-you-should-know-about-mrs-america-hulus-series-on-phyllis-schlafly/.

9 "An Open Letter to Hulu about its 'Mrs. America' Series," Clare Boothe Luce Center for Conservative Women, April 2020, https://cblwomen.org/2020/04/an-open-letter-to-hulu-about-its-mrs-america-series/; Joanne Ostrow, "Luce: Women's Progress Slow," *Washington Post*, April 25, 1982, https://www.washingtonpost.com/archive/business/1982/04/26/luce-womens-progress-slow/2062c0b1-ffb5-4295-b0fa-f5d929e91ed5/; Martha Weinman Lear, "Clare Boothe Luce, She Who Is Behind 'The Women,'" *New York Times*, April 21, 1973, https://www.nytimes.com/1973/04/22/archives/on-harry-and-henry-and-ike-and-mr-shaw-clare-boothe-luce-she-who-is.html.

10 Eleanor Smeal and Gloria Steinem, "What 'Mrs. America' Misrepresents; Two Feminist Leaders Write that the FX Miniseries Is Wrong About Who Has Really Thwarted the ERA," *Los Angeles Times*, July 30, 2020, E1.

11 Alessa Dominiguez, "Hollywood Casts a Very Flattering Light on Right-Wing White Women," *Buzzfeed News*, April 14, 2020, https://www.buzzfeednews.com/article/alessadominguez/mrs-america-cate-blanchett-fx-conservative-women.

12 Linda Holmes, "'Mrs. America': A Star-Studded Cast Puts the ERA in the Spotlight," *NPR*, April 15, 2020, https://www.npr.org/2020/04/15/830814315/mrs-america-a-star-studded-cast-puts-the-era-in-the-spotlight.

13 Carole Spitzack and Kathryn Carter, "Women in Communication Studies: A Typology for Revision," *Quarterly Journal of Speech* 73, no. 4 (1987): 401–23, quotation on 407.

14 Throughout this volume, we refer to the "Equal Rights Amendment" or "the ERA." In some cases, our contributors have used a lower-case version of "equal rights amendment." A handful of women use "equal-rights amendment." Some simply use "ERA" with no "the" to mark the noun. We have retained the original language of speakers across the volume.

15 Given the political reverberations of the national ERA debate, along with the abundance of texts we discovered, we elected to focus this anthology on the proposed federal amendment to the U.S. Constitution. We would, however, point readers to study the debates—many still continuing today—in individual states to add equal rights amendments to their constitutions. Many of these state-level debates overlapped with the national debate, and readers will see speakers in this anthology cite the status of various state constitutions to make their cases. See Chrisi West, "State Legislators on the Front Lines in Fight for Equal Rights Amendment and Equal Protections on the Basis of Sex," *ERA Coalition*, March 22, 2023, https://eracoalition.blog/2023/03/22/state-legislators-on-the-front-lines-in-fight-for-equal-rights-amendment-and-equal-protections-on-the-basis-of-sex/; "State-Level Equal Rights Amendments," *Brennan Center for Justice*, December 6, 2022, https://www.brennancenter.org/our-work/research-reports/state-level-equal-rights-amendments.

16 Elizabeth Novara, "The Centennial of the Equal Rights Amendment (ERA): Origins and Early Debates," Library of Congress, July 27, 2023, https://blogs.loc.gov/manuscripts/2023/07/the-centennial-of-the-equal-rights-amendment-era-origins-and-early-debates/.

17 In *The Philosophy of Rhetoric*, I.A. Richards argues that "the study of rhetoric should be a study of misunderstanding and its remedies." See I.A. Richards, *The Philosophy of Rhetoric* (London: Oxford University Press, 1936), 3.

18 Kathleen J. Turner, "Rhetorical History as Social Construction: The Challenge and the Promise," in *Doing Rhetorical History: Concepts and Cases*, ed. Kathleen J. Turner (Tuscaloosa: University of Alabama Press, 1998), 2.

19 David Zarefsky, "Four Senses of Rhetorical History," in *Doing Rhetorical History: Concepts and Cases*, ed. Kathleen J. Turner (Tuscaloosa: University of Alabama Press, 1998), 30.

20 Sonja K. Foss, "Equal Rights Amendment Controversy: Two Worlds in Conflict," *Quarterly Journal of Speech* 65, no. 3 (1979): 275–88, quotation on 288.

21 Bonnie J. Dow, "Authority, Invention, and Context in Feminist Rhetorical Criticism," *Review of Communication* 16, no. 1 (2016): 60–76, quotation on 61.

22 Emphasis hers. Julie C. Suk, *We the Women: The Unstoppable Mothers of the Equal Rights Amendment* (New York: Skyhorse Publishing, 2020), 3.

23 Among those we surveyed are Judith Anderson, ed., *Outspoken Women: Speeches by American Women Reformers, 1635–1935* (Dubuque, IA: Kendall/Hunt Publishing, 1984); Victoria L. DeFrancisco and Marvin D. Jensen, eds., *Women's Voices in Our Time: Statements by American Leaders* (Prospect Heights, IL: Waveland Press, 1994); Miriam Schneir, ed., *Feminism: The Essential Historical Writings* (New York: Vintage Books, 1994); S. Michele Nix, ed., *Women at the Podium: Memorable Speeches in History* (New York: HarperCollins, 2000); Joy Ritchie and Kate Ronald, eds., *Available Means: An Anthology of Women's Rhetoric(s)* (Pittsburgh: University of Pittsburgh Press, 2001); Jennifer A. Hurley, ed., *Women's Rights: Great Speeches in History* (San Diego: Greenhaven Press, 2002); James Daly, ed., *Great Speeches By American Women* (Mineola, NY: Dover Publications, 2008); Anna Russell, ed., *Great Women's Speeches: Empowering Voices that Engage and Inspire* (London: White Lion Publishing, 2019); Shari J. Stenberg and Charlotte Hogg, eds., *Persuasive Acts: Women's Rhetorics in the Twenty-First Century* (Pittsburgh: University of Pittsburgh Press, 2020); Monica Lunin, *What She Said: The Art of Inspiring Action Through Speech* (Melbourne, Australia: Wiley, 2022). A notable exception is Mary Ellen Snodgrass's two-volume *American Women Speak: An Encyclopedia and Document Collection of Women's Oratory* (Santa Barbara: ABC-CLIO, 2017), which features a handful of speeches about the ERA including Congressional testimony by Caroline Bird, Martha Wright Griffiths, Aileen Hernandez, and Gloria Steinem.

24 As of this writing, a search for "Equal Rights Amendment" yields limited results on *Americanrhetoric.com*, an online speech bank. Shirley Chisholm's 1970 Congressional testimony is the only speech fully devoted to the ERA available in this database, while speeches by Geraldine Ferraro and Edward Kennedy mention the ERA. Chisholm's speech is ranked the ninety-first greatest American speech of the twentieth-century. See Michael E. Eidenmuller, *AmericanRhetoric*.com, Tyler, Texas, https://www.americanrhetoric.com/.

25 *Gifts of Women's Speech*, an online database of speeches by women around the world, only features pro-ERA Congressional testimony by Mary Church Terrell and Shirley Chisholm, and a speech by Eleanor Smeal that discusses the ERA, at the time of this writing. See Liz Kent Leon, *Gifts of Women's Speech: Women's Speeches from Around the World*, Sweet Briar, VA, http://gos.sbc.edu/.

26 Diane M. Blair, "Shirley Anita St. Hill Chisholm, 'For the Equal Rights Amendment' (10 August 1970)," *Voices of Democracy* 3 (2008): 50–62, https://voicesofdemocracy.umd.edu/shirley-chisholm-for-the-equal-rights-amendment-10-august-1970/;

Jill M. Weber, "Gloria Steinem, 'Testimony Before Senate Hearings on the Equal Rights Amendment' (6 May 1970)," *Voices of Democracy* 3 (2008): 162–81, https://voicesofdemocracy.umd.edu/gloria-steinem-testimony-before-senate-hearings-on-the-equal-rights-amendment-6-may-1970/.

27 At the time of this writing, a handful of other speeches in this database mention the ERA, but do not develop extensive arguments about the amendment. See "Carrie Chapman Catt Center for Women and Politics," *Archives of Women's Political Communication*, Ames, IA, https://awpc.cattcenter.iastate.edu/.

28 Robert J. Brake, "Women Orators: More Research?" *Today's Speech* 15, no. 4 (1967): 20–22.

29 Susan E. Searing, "Primary Source Anthologies for Women's History: Selected Books in Print," *Women's Studies Quarterly* 16, no. 1/2 (1988): 129–37.

30 Anderson, *Outspoken Women*.

31 Shirley Wilson Logan, ed., *With Pen and Voice: A Critical Anthology of Nineteenth-Century African-American Women* (Carbondale: Southern Illinois University Press, 1995); Shirley Wilson Logan, *"We Are Coming": The Persuasive Discourse of Nineteenth-Century Black Women* (Carbondale: Southern Illinois University Press, 1999).

32 Davis W. Houck and David E. Dixon, eds., *Women and the Civil Rights Movement, 1954–1965* (Jackson: University Press of Mississippi, 2009).

33 DeFrancisco and Jensen, *Women's Voices in Our Time*.

34 Elizabeth W. McLaughlin, ed., *Women's Voices of Duty and Destiny: Religious Speeches Transcending Gender* (New York: Peter Lang, 2019).

35 Stenberg and Hogg, *Persuasive Acts*.

36 See, for example, a sampling of those published just within the past 25 years: Suzanne Pullon Fitch and Roseann M. Mandziuk, *Sojourner Truth as Orator: Wit, Story, and Song* (Westport, CT: Greenwood Press, 1997); Carolyn DeSwarte Gifford and Amy R. Slagell, eds., *Let Something Good Be Said: Speeches and Writings of Frances E. Willard* (Chicago: University of Illinois Press, 2007); Ellen Carol DuBois and Richard Cándida Smith, *Elizabeth Cady Stanton, Feminist as Thinker: A Reader in Documents and Essays* (New York: New York University Press, 2007); Paula Doress-Worters, ed., *Mistress of Herself: Speeches and Letters of Ernestine L. Rose, Early Women's Rights Leader* (New York: The Feminist Press, 2008); Mario T. García, ed., *A Dolores Huerta Reader* (Albuquerque: University of New Mexico Press, 2008); Maegan Parker Brooks and Davis W. Houck, *The Speeches of Fannie Lou Hamer: To Tell It Like It Is* (Jackson: University Press of Mississippi, 2011); Christopher Densmore, Carol Faulkner, Nancy Hewitt, and Beverly Wilson Palmer, *Lucretia Mott Speaks: The Essential Speeches and Sermons* (Urbana: University of Illinois Press, 2017).

37 Karlyn Kohrs Campbell, ed., *Man Cannot Speak for Her, Vol. 2: Key Texts of the Early Feminists* (Westport, CT: Praeger, 1989); Sally Roesch Wagner, ed., *The Women's Suffrage Movement* (New York: Penguin, 2019); Susan Ware, ed., *American Women's Suffrage: Voices from the Long Struggle for the Vote 1776–1965* (New York: Penguin Random House, 2020).

38 Sandra J. Sarkela, Susan Mallon Ross, and Margaret A. Lowe, eds., *From Megaphones to Microphones: Speeches of American Women, 1920–1960* (Westport, CT: Praeger, 2003), 1.

39 Dorothy Sue Cobble, Linda Gordon, and Astrid Henry, *Feminism Unfinished: A Short, Surprising History of American Women's Movements* (New York: Liveright Publishing, 2014), xiv.
40 David E. Kyvig, "Historical Misunderstandings and the Defeat of the Equal Rights Amendment," *The Public Historian* 18, no. 1 (1996): 45–63, quotation on 46.
41 Kimberly Wilmot Voss, "The Florida Fight for Equality: The Equal Rights Amendment, Senator Lori Wilson and Mediated Catfights in the 1970s," *The Florida Historical Quarterly* 88, no. 2 (2009): 173–208, quotation on 176.
42 Susan J. Douglas, *Where the Girls Are: Growing Up Female with the Mass Media* (New York: Three Rivers Press, 1995), esp. Chapter 10 "The ERA as Catfight."
43 Robin E. Jensen, "Women's Rhetoric in History: A Process-Oriented Turn and Continued Recovery," *Quarterly Journal of Speech* 94, no. 1 (2008): 100–12, quotation on 101.
44 Spitzack and Carter, "Women in Communication Studies," 405.
45 Barbara Biesecker, "Coming to Terms with Recent Attempts to Write Women into the History of Rhetoric," *Philosophy & Rhetoric* 25, no. 2 (1992): 140–61.
46 That said, we recognize the challenges to recovering texts and voices that have not survived, or in some cases never saw the opportunity to make themselves known. In her anti-ERA 1970 Congressional testimony, for example, Myra Wolfgang stressed that achieving full representation of opposing voices was impossible since non-elite working-class women could not afford to take time off to advocate against ERA in Congressional hearings and elsewhere.
47 Jacqueline Jones Royster and Gesa E. Kirsch, *Feminist Rhetorical Practices: New Horizons for Rhetoric, Composition, and Literacy Studies* (Carbondale: Southern Illinois University Press, 2012), 4.
48 Brian T. Kaylor, "A New Law: The Covenant Speech of Barbara Jordan," *Southern Journal of Communication* 77, no. 1 (2012): 10–23.
49 Gesa E. Kirsch and Jacqueline J. Royster, "Feminist Rhetorical Practices: In Search of Excellence," *College Composition and Communication* 61, no. 4 (2010): 640–72, quotation on 641.
50 See, for example, Penny Nance, "The Equal Rights Amendment Is the Dems' Frankenstein Monster," Concerned Women for America Legislative Action Committee, February 13, 2020, https://concernedwomen.org/nance-the-equal-rights-amendment-is-the-dems-frankenstein-monster/; CWA Communications Team, "Don't ERAse Women with an Equal Rights Amendment," Concerned Women for America, February 26, 2023, https://concernedwomen.org/dont-erase-women-with-an-equal-rights-amendment/. We were unable to secure permission from the CWA to include a text from them in this volume.
51 *The "Equal Rights" Amendment: Hearings before the Subcommittee on Constitutional Amendments of the Committee on the Judiciary*, Day 2, 91st Congress (1970) (Statement from Margaret Heckler).
52 Marjorie J. Spruill, *Divided We Stand: The Battle Over Women's Rights and Family Values That Polarized American Politics* (New York: Bloomsbury, 2017), 289.
53 Spruill, *Divided We Stand*, 290.
54 Elaine Woo, "Mary Crisp, 83; Quit GOP Post in Clash with Reagan Over Abortion Rights, ERA," *Los Angeles Times*, April 24, 2007, https://www.latimes.com/archives/la-xpm-2007-apr-24-me-crisp24-story.html.

55 Rebecca DeWolf, *Gendered Citizenship: The Original Conflict over the Equal Rights Amendment, 1920–1963* (Lincoln: University of Nebraska Press, 2021).
56 Kirsch and Royster, "Feminist Rhetorical Practices," 652.
57 Arthur E. Walzer, "*Parrēsia*, Foucault, and the Classical Rhetorical Tradition," *Rhetoric Society Quarterly* 43, no. 1 (2013): 1–21, quotation on 1–2.

Section I The Debate Begins: 1923–1939

After the Nineteenth Amendment passed in 1920, suffrage leader Alice Paul initiated a collaborative equal rights campaign with legal scholars, reformers, and members of the National Woman's Party (NWP). Their purpose was to draft the Lucretia Mott Amendment, named in honor of the abolitionist and women's right's advocate of the same name. Paul and her militant allies strongly believed "that even though the Nineteenth Amendment had removed sex as a permissible reason for withholding the right to vote, it had failed to fully unseat the centuries-old legal foundation that had given men authority over women in law and in custom."[1] The original Equal Rights Amendment read: "Men and women shall have equal rights throughout the United States and every place subject to its jurisdiction. Congress shall have the power to enforce this article by appropriate legislation."[2] Accordingly, the ERA's architects hoped the amendment would offer a "clean sweep" that would guarantee women equal rights with men in all personal, professional, and civic areas of life. Or, as one newspaper headline glibly summarized, "women's party after still more equality."[3]

In December 1923, Senator Charles Curtis (R-KS), future Vice President of the United States, and Representative Daniel R. Anthony, Jr. (R-KS), nephew of nineteenth-century women's rights leader Susan B. Anthony, first introduced the proposed federal amendment in Congress. A delegation of women representing the NWP sat in both the Senate and House galleries as the amendment was introduced.[4] The NWP was not a political party, but rather was a "feminist pressure group organized to lobby Congress, to educate other women about discrimination against them, and to attempt to convince the Democratic and Republican parties to include the Equal Rights Amendment in their platforms."[5] White, educated, upper-middle-class women largely constituted the NWP's membership, which also boasted affluent women allies with useful social connections and time to devote to the cause. Many of these women shared common traits and experiences, such as a background in settlement work, uncommon professional success in male-dominated fields, and geographic ties to the Northeast.[6]

The NWP advanced the ERA as the best hope for eradicating any remaining legal discriminations against women. A federal amendment, they hoped, might offer at least three advantages if successful: permanence, if passed; expedience, if costly state-by-state campaigning could be avoided; and accountability, if politicians were required to admit outright whether they supported or opposed the ERA and, thus, supported or opposed equality for women.[7] Representative Winnifred Huck (R-IL), the NWP's Political Council Chair and only the third woman (and the first wife and mother) elected to Congress, made a cautiously optimistic appraisal upon the ERA's initial introduction: "We hope it will pass before the next election. But if it does not, we shall endeavor to elect a large number of women to the next congress so that we shall have sufficient strength to pass the measure without any further delay."[8]

Huck perhaps could not imagine that the ERA would encounter formidable resistance that would indefinitely stall its progress for more than a century. Throughout the 1920s and 1930s, Congress held a series of hearings on the amendment, but none resulted in any committee reports or concrete action toward meaningfully pushing it forward—thanks to both the "inconsistent defensive effort" of the ERA's supporters and the well-coordinated lobbying efforts of the ERA's persuasive challengers.[9] As historian Rebecca DeWolf explains, the rival views about American women's citizenship status carried over from the long campaign for national woman suffrage to shape the early debates about the ERA. DeWolf calls these two views "emancipationism" and "protectionism." The fundamental difference between these two views has to do with whether women should be treated equally with men under the law (emancipationism) or whether the law should apply specific sex-based standards to ensure women's fair treatment (protectionism).[10] NWP leaders Alice Paul, Crystal Eastman, Lavinia Dock, Anita Pollitzer, and Grace Hoffman White led the pro-ERA emancipationist side using any rhetorical means available to them, such as lobbying, letters, newsletters, journals, public testimony, and radio addresses. To their thinking, the ERA was a natural and necessary progression of the work their foremothers had already begun. Passing the ERA became the sole pursuit of the NWP following passage of the Nineteenth Amendment, which isolated Paul and her allies from other women's organizations of the time.[11]

But not all who fought for national woman suffrage saw the Equal Rights Amendment as a good and essential next step. Whereas ERA supporters hoped for a "clean sweep," the emerging opposition—comprised of both conservative and liberal voices—perceived "too blunt an instrument" in a federal amendment approach.[12] Liberally-minded protectionists such as Carrie Chapman Catt, Ethel Smith, Florence Kelley, and Edith Valet Cook countered emancipationist efforts by forming their own coalition of former suffragists, reformers, social feminists, and labor activists—many of whom joined Catt's League of Women Voters, a rival, nonpartisan national organization that staunchly opposed the ERA. These anti-ERA protectionists were not anti-women, nor did they believe the ERA was unnecessary because women had already achieved full legal and political equality. In fact, protectionists believed that the ERA posed a serious danger that could jeopardize the incremental gains women had already achieved through existing legislation, such as maternity laws and pensions for mothers. In a related vein, many middle-class protectionists worried that a federal amendment would naively and narrowly privilege the experiences of wealthy white women. And while protectionists conceded that the ERA might benefit some "exceptional skilled workers or professionals," they believed it would inevitably leave working-class and poor women with no relief.[13]

Rather than promote a single federal "blanket" amendment to emancipate women from legal discrimination, protectionists advocated for a sex-based "specific bills for specific ills" approach. Women needed this protection, they reasoned, due to their important roles and responsibilities as mothers who found themselves entering the workforce as wage earners. Protectionists forged strong alliances, and the list of organizations that came out against the ERA early on was long indeed. Under the banner of what historian Cynthia Harrison calls the "Women's Bureau coalition" were the League of Women Voters, the National Consumers' League, the Women's Trade Union League, the Charity Organization Society, the Girls' Friendly Society, the National Council of Catholic Women, the Council of Jewish Women, the National Association for Labor Legislation, the Women's Christian Temperance Union, the American Association for Organizing Family Social Work, the National League of Girls' Clubs, the Parent Teacher Association, the National Federation of Federal Employees, and the National Council of Mothers.[14] All were among those listed in the *New York Times* as the formidable army of dissent against the ERA.[15] With this many women's groups opposed to the ERA, public opinion largely favored the protectionist position in the 1920s and early 1930s.[16]

As women grappled with the meaning and potential consequences of the proposed amendment, their arguments did not always easily fall into either emancipationist or protectionist camps. For example, nurse Lavinia Dock had close affiliations with protectionists, yet advocated for an emancipationist position suggesting that any "special" protections granted to women might be better conceived as protections extended to *both* sexes to improve what she called "the health of the race." Author Edna Kenton made a similar point in a 1926 article for *Harper's Weekly*:

> Put eighteen clear words into the Constitution and settle the matter for all time. What the laws happen to be to-day we don't particularly care. What does concern us is that, whatever they are, they shall apply equally to every adult human being, man or woman, married or single. Where a law now predominantly favors men, let women share in that favoritism. Where a law predominantly favors women, let that favor be extended to men.[17]

Women like Dock and Kenton quite clearly articulated a nuanced, middle-ground approach that sought to improve conditions for women and men alike.

The arguments emerging from these competing perspectives, as readers will see, had both merits and failings. Historian Nancy F. Cott provides clarity in *The Grounding of Modern Feminism*:

> Those who advanced sex-based laws were looking at the labor market as it was, trying as best possible to protect women in it, and thereby contributing to the perpetuation of existing inequalities. Those who opposed sex-based "protections" were envisioning the labor market as it might be, trying to ensure women the widest opportunities in that imagined arena, and thereby blinking at existing exploitations.[18]

For the women debating the ERA at its inception, it was to be a slow and difficult rhetorical contest over the definition of American womanhood, the nature of citizenship rights, and the meaning of legal and political equality.

Notes

1 Rebecca DeWolf, *Gendered Citizenship: The Original Conflict over the Equal Rights Amendment, 1920–1963* (Lincoln: University of Nebraska Press, 2021), 73.
2 DeWolf, *Gendered Citizenship*, 74.
3 "Women's Party After Still More Equality," *Sunday Morning Star*, June 22, 1923, 23.
4 "Equal Rights Bill Offered in House," *Evening Star (Washington, District of Columbia)*, December 15, 1923, 9.
5 Susan D. Becker, *The Origins of the Equal Rights Amendment: American Feminism Between the Wars* (Westport, CT: Greenwood Press, 1981), vii.
6 Becker, *Origins*, vii.
7 Becker, *Origins*, 20.
8 "Equal Rights or Woman Congress," *Hinton Daily News (Hinton, West Virginia)*, December 11, 1923, 1; see also "Winnifred Sprague Mason Huck," U.S. House of

Representatives, History, Art & Archives, n.d., https://history.house.gov/People/Detail/15397.

9 DeWolf, *Gendered Citizenship*, 87.

10 DeWolf, *Gendered Citizenship*, 2.

11 Amelia Fry, "Alice Paul and the ERA," in *Rights of Passage, the Past and Future of the ERA*, ed. Joan Hoff Wilson (Bloomington: Indiana University Press, 1986), 13–16; Cynthia Harrison, *On Account of Sex: The Politics of Women's Issues 1945–1968* (Berkeley: University of California Press, 1988), 10.

12 Becker, *Origins*, 125.

13 Nancy F. Cott, *The Grounding of Modern Feminism* (New Haven: Yale University Press, 1987), 127.

14 Harrison, *On Account of Sex,* 7–8.

15 Silas Bent, "The Women's War," *New York Times*, January 14, 1923, 4.

16 DeWolf, *Gendered Citizenship*, 87.

17 Edna Kenton, "The Ladies' Next Step: The Case for the Equal Rights Amendment," *Harper's Weekly*, Volume CLII (December 1925–May 1926), 366–74.

18 Cott, *Grounding*, 136.

An Approaching Anniversary

Article for The Christian Science Monitor

ALICE PAUL
June 2, 1923[1]

No name is more closely associated with the early twentieth-century national campaign for woman suffrage than that of Alice Stokes Paul (1885–1977), a Quaker activist from New Jersey who endured jail and forced feedings so that American women could exercise the constitutional right to vote. Inspired by the militant tactics employed by the British suffragettes while studying abroad, Paul and her friend Lucy Burns returned to the United States and split from the National American Woman Suffrage Association (NAWSA). The two formed the Congressional Union for Woman Suffrage in 1913, which eventually morphed into the National Woman's Party (NWP) in 1916.[2] The NWP focused attention on promoting a federal suffrage amendment as opposed to the state-by-state approach favored by the NAWSA. The various protest activities that Paul and the NWP employed profoundly amplified the cause. Among their activities were public speaking and writing, songs and signs, rallies and marches, parades and pickets by the stoic "Silent Sentinels" in white dresses with their bright purple and gold banners outside of Woodrow Wilson's White House, not to mention the imprisonment and dangerous hunger strikes in protest. In no small part, Alice Paul's efforts directly led to the victory achieved by passage of the Nineteenth Amendment in 1920.[3]

After winning the vote, the women who had fought so tirelessly faced the impending question of "what next?" In response, Paul drafted the Lucretia Mott Amendment—known familiarly as the "Equal Rights Amendment"—with the help of Crystal Eastman and many others in 1923. At the historic site in Seneca Falls on the 75th anniversary of the first woman's rights convention,

Paul rose to introduce the amendment: "We shall not be safe until the principle of equal rights is written into the framework of our government."[4]

Alice Paul devoted the rest of her life to the ERA, though she did not exclusively focus on the amendment. During World War II, she moved to Europe, founded the World Woman's Party to extend the work of gender equality beyond U.S. borders, and covertly helped feminist leaders escape German-occupied territories. After returning to her homeland, Paul revised the ERA in 1943 to read: "Equality of rights under the law shall not be denied or abridged by the United States or by any state on account of sex." That language persists today. Unlike many of her contemporaries, Alice Paul lived long enough to see 35 states ratify the amendment. She died at age ninety-two in 1977 at the height of the renewed ERA debate.[5] The article below, published in the *Christian Science Monitor*, explained Paul's rhetorical strategy and anticipated the dueling factions that would form around the amendment in the decades to follow.

July 20 will mark the anniversary of the first conference for equal rights for women, which met seventy-five years ago at Seneca Falls, New York. Women from every part of the land will assemble at Seneca Falls on that date to do honor to the pioneers who first raised the banner of equal rights in the United States.

The memorable Seneca Falls meeting seventy-five years ago outlined a bold program for raising the status of women. It demanded equal rights in the franchise, in education, in industry, in the professions, in political office, in marriage, in personal freedom, in control of property, in guardianship of children, in making contracts, in the church, and in the leadership of all moral and public movements. In short, the conference of 1848 protested against every form of subjection of women and instituted a campaign to establish equal rights between men and women.

Today—after seventy-five years—only one of the objects set forth in the 1848 resolution has been completely attained. This one is equal rights in the franchise. The National Woman's Party, which played a considerable part in winning suffrage, is now dedicated to carrying to victory the remainder of the 1848 program. To this end it is working, as stated in its declaration of fundamentals, "that woman shall no longer be in any form of subjection to man in law or in custom, but shall in every way be on an equal plane in rights, as she has always been and will continue to be, in responsibilities and obligations."[6] More concretely stated, the campaign of the Woman's Party is striving to win for women:

> Equal control of their children;
> Equal control of their property;
> Equal control of their earnings;
> Equal right to make contracts;
> Equal citizenship rights;
> Equal inheritance rights;
> Equal control of national, state and local government;
> Equal opportunities in schools and universities;
> Equal opportunities in government service;
> Equal opportunities in professions and industries;
> Equal pay for equal work;
> Equal authority in the church;
> Equal rights after marriage to their own identity; and an
> Equal moral standard.

The Woman's Party activity has been confined, up to the present, to the state legislatures. This campaign has already been instrumental in obtaining equal rights legislation for over 13,000,000 women. Among the measures secured in the various states are jury service for women, the right of a mother to equal guardianship of her children, the right of married women to choose their own residence, equal inheritance rights for women with men, the opening of public offices to women, and the giving to a wife of greater rights over her property.

While this progress has been made, the complete achievement of equal rights is still to be won and the experience of the past two years with the legislatures seems to have convinced the workers for equal rights of the wisdom of turning to Congress, just as they finally turned to Congress in the suffrage struggle. It is understood that the Seneca Falls Conference of this coming July, in addition to celebrating the meeting of years ago, will probably vote to introduce in Congress an equal rights amendment to the national Constitution. The leaders of the Woman's Party are proposing an amendment reading:

> No distinction between the rights of men and women shall exist within the United States or any place subject to its jurisdiction.

As precedents, they refer to the constitutions of Austria, Czechoslovakia, Danzig, Estonia, Germany, and Lithuania, all of which declare, in one form of wording or another, complete equality for all citizens before the law.

If the Seneca Falls Conference this summer decides to bring the United States Constitution into line with the constitutions of these newer republics, it will mean that the Seneca Falls meeting of 1923 will be as epoch making—viewed in the light of history—as was the conference which it is called to celebrate.

The equal rights movement has not by any means attained as yet the general support which was accorded the basic idea of suffrage for women. The philosophy of equality is at war with the philosophy of special protection and privilege for women. On the one side stand the little band who met at Seneca Falls seventy-five years ago and their descendants, the Woman's Party of today, demanding equality. On the other side stand the women who ask for protection instead of equality.

The warfare of these two philosophies is finding vigorous expression at the present moment over the question of labor laws for women. The equal rights group insist on equality in industry as in all other fields. The Woman's Party platform on this subject reads:

> Women shall no longer be barred from any occupation, but every occupation open to men shall be open to women, and restrictions upon the hours, conditions, and renumeration of labor shall apply alike to both sexes.

The Woman's Party demands that in the field of labor no restrictions shall be placed upon women alone, because, it claims, such restrictions make it more difficult for women to compete with men in earning a livelihood. It points out that women have always performed the unpaid labor of the world, with no protest from anyone as to whether it may be beyond their strength. It points out that it is only in the field of paid labor that one finds this interest in the welfare of women, and it contends that this interest is largely, unconsciously perhaps, in protecting the jobs of men and not in protecting the welfare of women.

The Woman's Party says that if various restrictions are considered good for the individuals concerned and good for the race, they should apply to all workers in any industry. In this way, it contends, the individuals concerned will benefit, and the race will benefit—and women will not be injured by being subjected to any additional handicap in competing with men.

This warfare between equal rights and protection is not local to the United States. The Woman's Party brings evidence to show that it is in the more advanced countries and among the younger women of these countries that the theory of equal rights receives the most support. It also calls attention to the support given to the fundamental of equal rights in industry by the delegates from various European countries at the international congresses of women.

No one can foretell today whether the program of complete equal rights between men and women, as outlined in 1848 by Lucretia Mott, Elizabeth

Cady Stanton, and their co-workers, and as striven for in this generation by the Woman's Party, is destined to realization. Only time will disclose this. But in contemplating the fundamental of equal rights as against the fundamental of special privilege and protection, one cannot but feel that time is on the side of equal rights.

Notes

1 Alice Paul, "An Approaching Anniversary," *Christian Science Monitor*, June 2, 1923, 1. Public Domain.
2 Nancy F. Cott, *The Grounding of Modern Feminism* (New Haven: Yale University Press, 1987), 53–59.
3 "National Woman's Party," Alice Paul Institute, https://www.alicepaul.org/nwp/.
4 Lindsley Armstrong Smith and Stephen A. Smith, "Keeping Hope Alive: A Case Study of the Continuing Argument for Ratification of the ERA," *Frontiers: A Journal of Women's Studies* 38, no. 2 (2017): 173–207, quotation on 197.
5 J.D. Zahniser and Amelia R. Fry, *Alice Paul: Claiming Power* (New York: Oxford University Press, 2014), 322.
6 "Declaration of Sentiments," Seneca Falls and the Start of Annual Conventions, July 1848, Library of Congress, https://www.loc.gov/exhibitions/women-fight-for-the-vote/about-this-exhibition/seneca-falls-and-building-a-movement-1776-1890/seneca-falls-and-the-start-of-annual-conventions/declaration-of-sentiments/.

I Am Opposed to the So-Called Blanket Equality Bill

Article for League of Women Voters Pamphlet

Carrie Chapman Catt
January 1924[1]

Carrie Chapman Catt (1859–1947) became deeply aware of women's political inequality at age 13, when she realized that her mother could not vote in the 1872 presidential election.[2] As one of only six women in her class at Iowa State Agricultural College,[3] Catt first got involved in the suffrage cause by making speeches and organizing campus debates.[4] By 1887, Catt had joined the Iowa Woman Suffrage Association. Her gifts as an orator, writer, lobbyist, and organizer helped her ascend in the leadership of the National American Woman Suffrage Association (NAWSA), which united the National Woman Suffrage Association (NWSA) and the American Woman Suffrage Association (AWSA) in 1890. Catt succeeded Elizabeth Cady Stanton and Susan B. Anthony as the NAWSA's third president from 1900 to 1904 and served again from 1915 until her death in 1947. For 40 years, Catt led the national campaign for suffrage and pursued the same goals—though less militantly—as Alice Paul's NWP.[5]

With sex finally removed as a barrier to voting, Catt and Maud Wood Park guided NAWSA members to join the newly formed League of Women Voters (LWV). Paul and the NWP turned to the next pursuit—a federal amendment for equal rights—while Catt, as the LWV's honorary president, spearheaded the opposition.[6] Catt believed that women should not form their own political party, but rather should integrate into existing parties and exercise influence from within those parties. After Paul, Crystal Eastman, and the NWP unveiled the ERA, but before it was formally introduced in Congress, Catt published a warning against the dangers of the proposed amendment in an August 1922 editorial for *Woman's Home Companion*, a monthly magazine and precursor to the *Ladies' Home Journal*. Gertrude Battles Lane edited the *Companion* and by the 1930s, it reached some three-and-a-half million readers.[7] The LWV recirculated a briefer version of Catt's editorial among the emerging voices of other women leaders opposed to the ERA, including Wood Park and Florence Kelley, in its January 1924 pamphlet "Specific Bills for Specific Ills."

I am opposed to the so-called blanket equality amendment because it will not insure equality. Instead, it threatens to deprive women of some of the rights they have already gained.

Women of other countries, when they have secured the vote, have sponsored blanket equality bills. But the situation is entirely different in the United States. Other countries have a single code of laws, which govern all the people. The United States has forty-eight codes of law, one for the people of each state.

During the eighty years that women campaigned for the ballot, they appeared before state legislature after state legislature. The legislatures could not give women the vote; they could only submit the suffrage question to [referendums], but the men in those legislatures, stirred by the appeals of the women, made various concessions which were written into the civil code.

A blanket amendment, designed to remove all remaining discriminations against women in the United States, would run counter to many of these laws already on the statute books, and would be certain to cause litigation.

Notes

1 *Specific Bills for Specific Ills: The Legislative Policy of the League of Women Voters: Opinions of Eminent Jurists and Other Authorities in Support of This Method*, compiled by the League of Women Voters, Washington, D.C., January 1924, 7–8. Public Domain.

2 Kristin Thoennes Keller, *Carrie Chapman Catt: A Voice for Women* (Minneapolis: Compass Point Books, 2006), 9–10.

3 Iowa State students, alumni, and community members have long debated having a campus building named for Catt. The controversy stems from documented remarks Catt made later in life about how woman suffrage would strengthen white supremacy. On August 31, 2023, a review committee made an initial recommendation to retain Catt's name on the building. For a more in-depth review of the controversy, see Catt Hall Review, Initial Report, August 31, 2023, https://iastate.app.box.com/s/kqe216kd1z8j5vrfs4kijo4jhaictur0.

4 Jacqueline Van Voris, *Carrie Chapman Catt: A Public Life* (New York: The Feminist Press, 1987), 8.
5 "Carrie Chapman Catt (1859–1947)," Iowa State University Carrie Chapman Catt Center for Women and Politics," https://cattcenter.iastate.edu/home/about-us/carrie-chapman-catt/.
6 Elaine Weiss, *The Woman's Hour: The Great Fight to Win the Vote* (New York: Penguin Books, 2018), 330.
7 David E. Sumner, *The Magazine Century: American Magazines Since 1900* (New York: Peter Lang, 2010), 49.

The Trickery of Words

Article for Life and Labor Bulletin

Ethel M. Smith
February 1924[1]

Ethel Marion Smith's (1877–1951) interests in women's equality inside and outside of the workplace trace back to sex discrimination she faced in civil service when male co-workers with less experience routinely won promotions and raises over her. The Illinois-born Smith eventually resigned from her job to devote her full-time energies to the suffrage cause and labor reform. She served as secretary of the NAWSA's Congressional Committee, where she voiced strong disapproval for Alice Paul's militant methods and "heckling" strategies.[2] By 1918, Smith had joined the Women's Trade Union League (WTUL), where she lobbied, lectured, and wrote articles in the interest of an eight-hour workday, a minimum wage, better working conditions, unionization, and more representation of women's interests at the Department of Labor.[3]

From the beginning, Smith was among the most vocal and influential opponents of Alice Paul's proposed amendment. Smith was particularly concerned that the ERA would threaten minimum wage legislation for working women. While she did not support a blanket federal amendment, Smith did support state equal rights bills and legislation, which she believed could successfully address specific concerns on a case-to-case basis.[4] Paul opposed this view and felt that existing women's labor laws did not go far enough. Ignoring warnings from Smith and others that the ERA "offered working women an empty promise of equality," Paul proceeded with her campaign.[5] The initial terms of the debate were set in these early exchanges. Smith's article for the WTUL's *Life and Labor Bulletin*, a rival counterpart to the NWP's *Equal Rights*, recorded how Smith and other labor activists mobilized and presented their case for protectionism directly to President Calvin Coolidge in early 1924. When the NWP sent its own delegation led by Alva Vanderbilt Belmont to the White House later that year, a charmed Coolidge announced that he found it "a very impressive demonstration" and did not have "the slightest doubt that Congress will respond favorably" to the ERA proposal.[6] The second part of Smith's article, reprinted here, developed her position in light of the NWP's pro-ERA lobbying efforts and relied on legal opinions assembled by men to build her case.

The meaning of the terms depends upon who use[s] the terms and what the users intend.

"Open Shop," an employers' term, sounds well to the uninitiated public. Organized labor knows that it means in practice a shop closed to trade unions.

"Equal rights" sounds even more alluring. The principle is one upon which organized labor has always stood—equal rights for all mankind. But labor laws seek to establish equal rights by limiting the right of the contract. Employers who oppose these laws do so for that reason, wishing to retain their superior bargaining power. Where labor laws apply to women only, they limit women's right of contract, but not the right of men. Employers who oppose such laws do so because in women's labor, just so long as the right of contract is unlimited, there exists a great reserve of "cheap" (because unstandardized) labor by means of which wages can be kept down and the 8-hour day avoided.

The National Woman's Party proposes a constitutional amendment requiring that "Men and women shall have equal rights throughout the United States and every place subject to its jurisdiction," which would destroy the labor laws for women merely because they do not apply to men, and in order to give women unlimited right of contract, taking away the right to an eight hour day, for example, or their legal right to a living wage, to give them "equal rights" with men.

Or if the proposed "equal rights" amendment would not destroy the women's labor laws outright, it would throw them into the courts for endless litigation. Its language, lawyers say, if enacted into law, would support the legal profession in affluence for generations to come. For what are "rights" in terms of law? What are "equal rights?" Nobody knows finally until the courts decide in each case.

As to the probable effect of the Woman's Party amendment upon women's labor laws, however, a considerable body of legal opinion has been assembled. Among the constitutional authorities who have expressed themselves are George Wharton Pepper, United States Senator from Pennsylvania;

Roscoe Pound and Felix Frankfurter of Harvard University; Ernst Freund of the University of Chicago; William Draper Lewis of the University of Pennsylvania; Albert H. Putney of the American University; and a number of others. They agree that the courts would probably construe the amendment as invalidating such laws. An especially clear statement on the subject is made by Edgar A. Bancroft, of the law firm of Scott, Bancroft, Martin and MacLeish of Chicago, in a letter to the national legislative chairman of the National Women's Trade Union League, under the date of January 9, 1924. Referring to the large body of state laws for the protection of women and girls in industry and business, that are based solely on sex, Mr. Bancroft writes:

> All these distinctions in the laws rest upon actual and fundamental differences between the sexes; and the power of the State legislatures to deal with these subjects is now practically unlimited. The adoption of the proposed Amendment would certainly invalidate some of this legislation and render most of it of doubtful validity. It would thus impede and postpone similar enactments for the benefit of women and girls in backward States, and delay further progress in such legislation. In my judgment, there are no rights or benefits to women that can possibly result from this Amendment that begin to equal those which it is certain to jeopard[ize] and may destroy. It would be needless and hazardous limitations upon the general police powers of the States.

W. H. Holly, of the firm of Darrow, Sissman, Holly and Carlin of Chicago, when asked for an opinion on the new draft of the Amendment, replied:

> I am still of the opinion that the proposal is a dangerous one, and that it should not be adopted. Labor laws limiting the hours and otherwise attempting to protect labor as the weaker party in industrial contracts, have been held to be in conflict with the due process clause of the Federal Constitution cause, as it was argued, they interfered with the freedom of the laborer to enter into such contracts as he might choose. Other statutes which were limited in their operation to women workers have been held valid because of the special necessity of protecting women. If this amendment is adopted, the danger is great that it will be held that the government may no more interfere with woman's right to contract than with a man's, and that all such legislation will be held to be void.

Notes

1 Ethel M. Smith, "Labor's Position Against the Woman Party's Amendment," *Life and Labor Bulletin*, Vol. II, No. 6 (February 1924): 1–2. Public Domain.
2 "Suffrage Ire Aroused," *Washington Post*, June 6, 1915, 9.
3 Amy E. Butler, *Two Paths to Equality: Alice Paul and Ethel M. Smith in the ERA Debate, 1921–1929* (Albany: State University of New York Press, 2002), 12–17, 25.
4 Butler, *Two Paths*, 91, 106.

5 Rebecca DeWolf, *Gendered Citizenship: The Original Conflict over the Equal Rights Amendment, 1920–1963* (Lincoln: University of Nebraska Press), 60, 63.

6 "Coolidge Assures Women of Victory," *New York Times*, November 18, 1923, 22.

Equality or Protection

Article for Equal Rights

Crystal Eastman

March 15, 1924[1]

Crystal Catherine Eastman (1881–1928) grew up in Elmira, New York with suffragist parents who both also happened to be ordained ministers. Eastman matriculated to Vassar College with other budding suffragists, earned a Master's degree in sociology from Columbia University, and studied law at New York University. After law school, Eastman struggled to find employment as a practicing attorney and moved into labor reform. She led the first-ever inquiry into industrial accidents, breaking new ground and informing the creation of much-needed workers' compensation laws in the Northeast. During World War I, Eastman joined forces with labor activists Jane Addams and Lillian Wald to form several women's peace groups, including the Women's Peace Party (WPP) and the American Union Against Militarism (AUAM). Eastman was well-suited to the work of lobbying, speaking, writing, and organizing debates and forums for antimilitarists who deployed their arguments against war and imperialism to the American public.[2] Under Eastman's leadership, the AUAM's National Civil Liberties Bureau continues today as the American Civil Liberties Union (ACLU), which champions free speech, political equality, and human rights. Eastman is considered the "ACLU's founding mother" when she is properly credited.[3]

Eastman joined the NWP during the suffrage campaign and continued to pursue the Equal Rights Amendment. Her name has at times evaded inclusion among the names of her fellow ERA luminaries of this period, in part because she was living in England as the ERA debates unfolded in Congress and in part because of her premature death at the young age of 46. And yet, in the five years between the ERA's introduction to Congress and her death, Eastman split with her labor colleagues Jane Addams and Florence Kelley to endorse the call for a federal equal rights amendment.[4] In fact, Eastman helped draft the earliest iteration of the ERA with Alice Paul—though she often does not receive acknowledgment for doing so.[5] Eastman believed, as her below article for the NWP's journal *Equal Rights* (formerly *The Suffragist*) indicates, that a protectionist approach to women's rights would detrimentally protect them from the very rights they sought to claim.

A good deal of tyranny goes by the name of protection. For example, there is a law in Connecticut, one of the eastern American states, which reads:

> No public restaurant, café, dining-room, barber shop, hair-dressing or manicuring establishment or photograph gallery shall employ any minor under sixteen years of age or any woman, between the hours of 10 o'clock in the evening and 6 o'clock in the morning.

Classification of Women

For a woman engaged in these pursuits there may be as much insult and injury in such a law as there was for all women in the pre-suffrage classification of minors, idiots, criminals, and women as persons denied a voice in democratic government. And this law is not peculiar to the State of Connecticut nor to the United States of America. It is quite usual to prohibit night work for women in advanced industrial countries. It is one of the most commonly advocated industrial "reforms." Yet it is not maintained that women's lungs are more susceptible to the night air than the lungs of men, or that women's eyes are more injuriously affected by artificial light than the eyes of men. If this were true, we must begin by legislating against the full work-basket which the working-class mother takes up by lamp-light after her children are asleep and the dishes of the last meal are washed and put away.

Dangers of the Dark

No, the implication of such laws is really a moral one—women must not be allowed to work after dark lest they succumb to the dangers of the midnight streets. Although it must be obvious that in the agitation preceding the enactment of such laws the zeal of the reformers would be second to the zeal of the highly paid night-workers who are anxious to hold their trade against an invasion of skilled women.

To this sort of interference with her working life the modern woman can have but one attitude: *I am not a child.* I will have none of your protection.

But all the so-called protective legislation for women is not so indefensible. A great deal can be said for minimum wage laws and laws limiting the hours of labor for women on the ground that woman's labor is the least adapted to organization and therefore the most easily exploited and most in need of legislative protection. Less can be said for the type of law which prohibits certain trades to women on the ground of their physical inferiority. The danger that women will rush in large numbers into trades for which they are by constitution manifestly unfit is not so great as the danger that such a principle of sex prohibition once admitted in the law will be used by the influence of powerful unions to keep women out of trades for which they are manifestly fit.

Equality Versus Protection

Sooner or later in every industrial country where women have won the franchise, this vexed question of equality versus protection is bound to arise. The good suffragist, after she has won her vote, takes one long night's rest, awakes refreshed and eager, and begins to look around for equal opportunities in every field of human endeavor. On the very first corner she meets the earnest reformer, who stops her, saying, "My dear, you must not ask for Equal Rights in industry. If you do, what will become of this whole body of labor law which I have built up by years and years of patient effort to protect a weaker sex from the extreme rigors of industrial competition? Is all my work to be wasted?"

The Equal Rights Amendment

This is no idle rhetorical question. It is a very real question indeed. To meet it and answer it with courage and consistency and yet with sympathy and sound practical human judgment may well be the major concern of feminists for the next decade. In America, with the introduction in Congress last December of the Lucretia Mott amendment—(*Men and women shall have Equal Rights throughout the United States and every place subject to its jurisdiction*)—a battle royal has commenced. The amendment, sponsored, of course, by the younger and more militant element led by Alice Paul and the Woman's Party, was hardly 24 hours old before every member of Congress received a letter protesting in the strongest terms against it, signed by the official representatives of seven other national women's organizations, all of the more solid, more established, more distinctly humanitarian type.

The leading spirit in this opposition is Florence Kelley, founder and secretary of the National Consumers' League, known the world over as a passionate advocate of protective laws for women and children in industry, an exceedingly forceful, almost violent personality, a born fighter, and a leader as devoted and able in her generation as Alice Paul in hers. Thus at its beginning the battle is dramatized in the figures of these two lionhearts.

The Claim of the Opposition

To the claim of these seven opposing societies that the amendment is not supported by any national organization except the one that proposed it, the Woman's Party replies: "When Susan B. Anthony introduced the National Suffrage amendment in 1878, few women supported it." To the objection that the Equal Rights Amendment "would endanger existing statutes providing a 48-hour week, eight or nine or ten-hour day and other industrial standards governing the employment of women," the reply is:

The Answer to the Opposition

"The Equal Rights Amendment would not affect existing labor legislation, except to establish the principle that industrial legislation should apply to all workers, both men and women, in any given occupation and not to women workers alone. Examples of states where labor legislation already applies to both sexes are Oregon, where there is a 10-hour law for both men and women employees in mills, factories and manufacturing establishments, and Florida, which requires seats for both men and women employees in stores."

Time on the Side of Equal Rights

"It may be," the official organ concludes, "that the Woman's Party now stands alone for the Equal Rights Amendment—but time is on our side and as the principle of Equal Rights in the suffrage field has at last prevailed, just as surely will the principle of Equal Rights for men and women be established in every field."

It behooves us to watch carefully the contest of these two ideals in American legislation. For the issue will be raised before long on this side. The time will come when British women will have to do some hard thinking and declare their faith in the matter.

Notes

1 Crystal Eastman, "Equality or Protection," *Equal Rights*, March 15, 1924, 37. Reprinted in Blanche Wiesen Cook, *Crystal Eastman on Women and Revolution* (New York: Oxford University Press, 1978), 156–59. Public Domain.

2 Cook, *Crystal Eastman*, 6–7, 11–13.

3 Susan N. Herman, "Crystal Eastman, the ACLU's Underappreciated Founding Mother," *ACLU*, July 12, 2019, https://www.aclu.org/issues/free-speech/crystal-eastman-aclus-underappreciated-founding-mother.

4 Cook, *Crystal Eastman*, 31.

5 Julie C. Suk, *We the Women: The Unstoppable Mothers of the Equal Rights Amendment* (New York: Skyhorse Publishing, 2020), 22–26.

The Health of the Race

Address to the Subcommittee of the Committee on the Judiciary of the United States Senate

LAVINIA LLOYD DOCK
February 1, 1929[1]

The "nurse suffragist" Lavinia Lloyd Dock (1858–1956) embarked on a medical career at age 26 after happening upon a magazine article about Bellevue Hospital of Nursing in New York. Once on Bellevue's staff, Dock channeled her expertise and experience into creating curricular materials for nurses. Her groundbreaking 1890 *Materia Medica for Nurses* became a go-to training resource, and she brought the taboo topics of birth control and venereal disease into public conversation among medical professionals.[2] After a stint as Superintendent of Nurses at Johns Hopkins Hospital in Maryland, Dock joined the staff of the Henry Street Settlement in New York, got involved with the WTUL, participated in workers' strikes, and came to regard herself as a socialist. Dock's internationally recognized approach to medical care imagined a holistic view of patient health that accounted for socio-economic realities—an inclusive and rare approach for the time, especially insofar as it concerned the health of workers.[3]

Dock partnered with the NWP after initially finding community with Harriot Stanton Blatch's Equality League for Self-Supporting Women, a suffrage organization comprised of various trade-union women's groups. Dock had been briefly arrested after attempting to vote in an 1896 election in New York City and later served two jail terms in 1917 for picketing the White House and refusing to pay the fine for "obstructing traffic."[4] Dock was also among the five suffragists who made an arduous pilgrimage on foot from New York City to

Albany five years earlier as a public demonstration for the ballot. The 170-mile "suffrage hike" over 12 cold December days drew press coverage, with papers focusing on how the feet of "Surgeon Dock" blistered so badly that she had to cut off the front of her shoes.[5] By the time of her death in 1956, Dock had left an indelible mark on both the annals of nursing history and the history of women's suffrage.[6]

When the Judiciary Committees of the House and Senate convened for hearings on the ERA in 1929, Dock testified in her capacity as Pennsylvania Chairman of the Nurse's Council of the NWP. Although Dock retained her abiding connections with women's labor groups, she was anguished to be divided from former allies on the ERA question. How painful, she wrote in 1924, to find herself "separated from old associates in the woman movement, and hard to differ from trade union friends, when one is still heart and soul in sympathy with labor."[7] Dock's pro-ERA statement here, succinct as it is, modeled a nuanced approach to the debate. Her arguments were very much in keeping with her lifelong concerns about the health of the race and, more broadly, reflected a position held by many NWP members: that "good labor laws should be extended to *both* sexes" and "bad ones simply expunged."[8]

I only wish to make a brief statement, not particularly addressing myself to sex justice but on the point of the health of the race. I would like to see that with reference to all persons, to both sexes.

The opposition to the equal rights amendment is based upon the apprehension that existing "welfare" laws affecting women will be lost. The National Woman's Party holds that welfare laws as they are at present work hardship on many women by making it more difficult for them to earn a living. Conditions should be made better for all workers without regard to sex. Industry should be humanized. The health and welfare of potential or actual fathers should be regarded as important as that of mothers.

For myself, I cannot believe that the advancing and strengthening of woman's legal, social, and economic status will make her weaker in the world of industry or lessen her ability to care for herself and the young of the race. In the midst of a perplexing world, I feel sure of one thing and that is that the complete emancipation of women from old badges of inferiority will work for greater good for humanity than anything we can gain without such emancipation.

I thank you.

Notes

1 *Joint Resolution Proposing an Amendment to the Constitution of the United States Relative to Equal Rights for Men and Women, Hearings Before a Subcommittee of the Committee on the Judiciary*, Day 2, 70th Congress (1929) (Statement of Lavinia Dock). Public Domain.
2 Janet Wilson James, "Lavinia Lloyd Dock," in *Notable American Women: The Modern Period: A Biographical Dictionary*, ed. Barbara Sicherman, Carol Hurd Green, Ilene Kantrov, and Harriette Walker (Cambridge, MA: Harvard University Press, 1980), 195–98.
3 Deborah Philips, "Healthy Heroines: Sue Barton, Lillian Wald, Lavinia Lloyd Dock and the Henry Street Settlement," *Journal of American Studies* 33, no. 1 (1999): 65–82.
4 Susan Ware, *American Women's Suffrage: Voices from the Long Struggle for the Vote 1776–1965* (New York: Penguin Random House, 2020), 531.
5 Tiffany Lewis, "Mediating Political Mobility as Stunt-Girl Entertainment: Newspaper Coverage of New York's Suffrage Hike to Albany," *American Journalism* 36, no. 1 (2019): 99–123, quotation on 114.
6 Mary Lou Schwartz, "Lavinia Dock: Adams County Suffragette," *Adams County History* 3, no. 5 (1997): 71–79.
7 Susan D. Becker, *The Origins of the Equal Rights Amendment: American Feminism Between the Wars* (Westport, CT: Greenwood Press, 1981), 200.
8 Emphasis added. Cynthia Harrison, *On Account of Sex: The Politics of Women's Issues 1945–1968* (Berkeley: University of California Press, 1988), 18.

Whose Rights Are to Be Equal?

Address to the Subcommittee of the Committee on the Judiciary of the United States Senate

FLORENCE KELLEY
February 1, 1929[1]

A daughter of Philadelphia born into an Irish-Quaker family, Florence Moltrop Kelley (1859–1932) rose to prominence when she became involved in the settlement movement alongside white middle-class contemporaries including Jane Addams, Lavinia Lloyd Dock, and Lillian Wald.[2] Kelley served as secretary of the National Consumers' League (NCL), an association committed to creating "humane and enlightened" conditions for American workers through labor legislation, fair living wages, an eight-hour workday, and protective workplace practices.[3] The Illinois governor appointed Kelley to serve in the new post of Chief Factory Inspector in 1893. In that role, she oversaw a staff and budget that supported her examinations of factory working conditions in tenements and sweatshops across the state. Two years later, she added a law degree from Northwestern University to her arsenal of resources for exposing untenable labor conditions and fighting for workers' rights.[4] Kelley devoted the entirety of her adult life to speaking and writing about labor form, gender equality, and racial justice.[5]

Kelley appeared before the Subcommittee of the Committee on the Judiciary of the United States Senate just three years before her death in 1932. Her singular goal, evidenced by this selection from her testimony, was to represent the NCL's interests on the question of adding an Equal Rights Amendment to the Constitution. As a one-time member of the NWP's "inner circle" during the suffrage campaign, Kelley participated in early conversations about the subsequent campaign for equal rights. We must avoid "loosely drawn laws," she initially warned NWP member Elsie Hill.[6] But Kelley later came to regard Alice Paul as a "fiend" and the ERA, in its proposed version, a dangerous threat to women.[7] Kelley subsequently emerged as a leader of the protectionist opposition to the ERA. To her and other social feminists, the best path forward was not through a federal amendment, but through specific labor laws that would challenge sex discrimination and ensure women's economic, social, and political empowerment.

The organization I represent has headquarters in New York City, with 20 branches in 17 States. We shall celebrate our thirtieth anniversary next November.

We have had a great deal of experience in defending legislation for wage-earning men, women, and children. That is our important work. We have had other work besides that.

The two Oregon laws which were referred to, one having a limitation on their working hours for women alone, and the other on the hours of both men and women, were successfully defended by the National Consumers' League, Mr. Brandeis, now Mr. Justice Brandeis, acting as our counsel before the United States Supreme Court.[8]

We have opposed this so-called equal rights amendment from the very beginning. We pointed out the hardships which would be wrought if it were adopted, and constantly urged the point dwelt upon so impressively by the chairman, that the amendment would inevitably wipe out the power of the States.

The question that puzzles me is with reference to equal rights: Equal rights among whom? Everyone has talked about equality, but no one seems to have dwelt much upon the people concerned.

For instance, considering the amendment as a short cut. Ask the black women in Mississippi how much their enfranchisement has been expedited by the passage of the suffrage amendment!

Whose rights under the equal rights amendment are to be equal?

If we look at the future, immediately following the passage of this amendment the question becomes clearer. There are now roughly about 12,000,000 colored people in this country. Is it not reasonable to suppose that about 3,000,000 constitute the proportion of them who will acquire voting privileges? Their white sisters have them.

Does this amendment mean that there will be wholly and absolutely equal rights between the black and white? Does it mean that a black woman will have the same rights as a white man? Does it mean that there will be equality between a black woman in Mississippi and a white man in New York City? Who is to be equal and what is the equality to be? Is it to be solely political; is it political and economic? What kind of equality is it to be and among whom?

I submit that this question has never been answered. Although I have written articles addressed to the Woman's Party and requiring answers, I have had only one answer, and that from an individual not authorized to speak for her organization.

No one of us can know what the amendment is going to do. My father was 30 years in Congress. He voted for the reconstruction amendments. Many times he expressed his permanent amazement at the unforeseen consequences of the amendments.

Experience teaches that before supporting fundamental changes we should strive to know what will happen after. The only attempted answer to my question already referred to is this: We believe that this amendment will confer upon groups of people equal rights, equal rights of black women with black men and of white women with white men, of married women with married men, of wage-earning women with wage-earning men. That does not answer my question: Who will be equal with whom? That is a question of a good deal of importance and should be given serious study.

Notes

1 *Joint Resolution Proposing an Amendment to the Constitution of the United States Relative to Equal Rights for Men and Women, Hearings Before a Subcommittee of the Committee on the Judiciary*, Day 2, 70th Congress (1929) (Statement of Florence Kelley). Public Domain.
2 Kathryn Kish Sklar, "Hull House in the 1890s: A Community of Women Reformers," *Signs: Journal of Women in Culture and Society* 10, no. 4 (1985): 658–77.
3 Florence Kelley, "Aims and Principles of the Consumers' League," *American Journal of Sociology* 5, no. 3 (1899): 289–304.
4 Kathryn Kish Sklar, *Florence Kelley and the Nation's Work: The Rise of Women's Political Culture, 1830–1900* (New Haven: Yale University Press, 1995), 237–64.
5 Louis L. Athey, "Florence Kelley and the Quest for Negro Equality," *Journal of Negro History* 56, no. 4 (1971): 249–61.
6 Rebecca DeWolf, *Gendered Citizenship: The Original Conflict over the Equal Rights Amendment, 1920–1963* (Lincoln: University of Nebraska Press, 2021), 55–56.
7 Christine A. Lunardini, *From Equal Suffrage to Equal Rights: Alice Paul and the National Woman's Party, 1910–1928* (New York: New York University Press, 1986), 162.
8 Emma Wold, an attorney from Oregon and the legislative secretary of the National Woman's Party, testified about these laws at the same hearings.

The Principle of Liberty for Men and Women

Address to the Subcommittee of the Committee on the Judiciary United States Senate

ANITA POLLITZER
January 6, 1931[1]

South Carolina Lowcountry native Anita Lilly Pollitzer (1894–1975) spent her summer breaks supporting the suffrage cause by designing posters, selling lemonade, and debating anti-suffragists on the street. Pollitzer moved to Washington, D.C. after high school, where she met Alice Paul and joined the NWP. Pollitzer quickly rose in the ranks of NWP leadership. She took her case for suffrage to 39 states and was arrested—but did not serve jail time—for picketing the White House. Pollitzer's contributions were perhaps most crucial in East Tennessee, where she canvassed, raised funds, and personally lobbied legislators to help push the Nineteenth Amendment over the finish line. While history books would remember the mother of Representative Harry T. Burn (R-TN) for persuading her son to cast the final vote, it was Anita Pollitzer who laid the groundwork with the reluctant young legislator before that historic day.[2]

As Ethel Smith and Florence Kelley shored up support against what they viewed as an impending "blanket amendment," Pollitzer remarked, "One would really think that instead of attacking an amendment not yet finally drafted, all women interested in women would endeavor to help in the framing."[3] When Alice Paul announced a constitutional amendment for equal rights at Seneca Falls in November 1923, Pollitzer seconded and the other NWP attendees unanimously adopted the proposal.[4] Pollitzer succeeded Paul as chair of the NWP by 1945, after serving as the organization's national secretary and vice chairman.[5]

Like Paul, Pollitzer lived long enough to see the ERA fight taken up by a new generation of women's rights activists. She died in 1975 hopeful that the amendment would come to pass. In 1931, Pollitzer appeared as vice chairman of the NWP before a Subcommittee of the Committee on the Judiciary United States Senate hearing on the ERA. Her testimony framed the amendment as a guiding principle that if—enshrined in the Constitution—would not only guarantee women equality under the law but also make the United States a shining beacon of liberty for the rest of the world.

Mr. Chairman, our point is that in no respect should the rights of women be left to the whims of individuals, legislatures or organizations, but, just as men are citizens of this land, knowing that all their rights, privileges, and duties are guaranteed them by law, so we feel that they should be established for women.

To those of us who, ever since we have been adults, have worked for suffrage, equal rights seems a very logical sequence to the suffrage amendment. It seems so right that we really resent having to come to ask for our rights. We are not asking for any special rights. We are not asking for anything but the same opportunity to be human beings in this land of ours. Now, we have injected nothing into this equal rights movement that apparently has not been there from time immemorial. The leaders of men from the very earliest days have spoken in terms of equality.

We stand, as you know, for the equal rights amendment which reads, "Men and women shall have equal rights throughout the United States and every place subject to its jurisdiction." Now, we worked in the first days of the equal rights movement just as we did in the first days of the suffrage movement, state by state. We worked amassing our data. That is done now. It has taken more than 10 years in New York State to try to get the first dent made in jury service. It will take ten times six years and more and more to get these infinitesimal laws removed from the statute books of the State. It is not only these laws that confront us. There will be crises affecting the lives of women always, as long as we allow our law and our customs, and in the minds of men and women, this accepted and expected rule that there will be a difference in their treatment.

I remember, in the District of Columbia, several years ago, I went to practically every printing shop I could find to find out what had happened to women when the 8-hour law went through, and employer after employer said that he had dismissed women and had taken on men because he said, "We do have certain days that are rush days and on those days we have to use our people, and it is too much trouble to have our books opened, and so forth, and the other is the easier way." I think that is so simple to understand.

Our point is simply that women shall be as free as men to decide for themselves, when they will work and how they will work. It is almost incredible that they will take the thing least advantageous if they have that chance.

When we think of the time, energy, money and lives that women poured into establishing the suffrage amendment, that simple act of justice, we resent it, and we think all men and women should resent it. We come now with exactly the same proposition, not any small thing, but enunciating a great principle, the principle of liberty for men and women.

We need leaders tremendously. It seems to me [that] a handful of Senators and Congressmen who really and truly believe in the advancement of women could do more than they ever realize to help put through this great principle for human freedom.

It is not given to us often to be in a position to help in these great things. A few Presidents, a few Congressmen and Senators have had the opportunity to take part in such movements. It is this of which we are speaking, something that will for all time write into the law of our land this principle, this doctrine which will be like a great abiding faith, something to which we can turn in the council of nations. We feel very powerless when in international things other nations are ahead of us. We are lagging behind. Since the war the new democracies that have crept up have adopted this equal-rights principle in their constitutions.

Women are, of course, divided. Has there ever been a movement that we were not divided on? Nothing ever passes Congress or goes to the President that men and women are not divided on, but the National Woman's Party stood always for the passage of the suffrage amendment by constitutional amendment and stands for the establishment of equal rights by constitutional amendment. It is not a question of great interest to us how the adjustments are made. That we can work out. Every state can make its own decision as to how it wants its laws to apply to men and women, but we do ask that we have one principle for human beings and that men and women shall have equal rights and equal opportunities. It seems to us it is not too much to ask that for women in the United States in 1931.

Notes

1 *Joint Resolution Proposing an Amendment to the Constitution of the United States Relative to Equal Rights for Men and Women, Hearing Before a Subcommittee of the Committee on the Judiciary United States Senate*, Day 3, 71st Congress, (1931) (Statement of Anita Pollitzer). Public Domain.

2 Elaine Weiss, *The Woman's Hour: The Great Fight to Win the Vote* (New York: Penguin, 2018), 162–64; "Anita Pollitzer, Suffragist, Dies," *New York Times*, July 5, 1975, 16.

3 Nancy F. Cott, *The Grounding of Modern Feminism* (New Haven: Yale University Press, 1987), 124.

4 "Anita Pollitzer (1894–1975)," Turning Point Suffragist Memorial, https://suffragistmemorial.org/anita-pollitzer-1894-1975/.

5 Though gendered to our contemporary ears, this is the term listed in the Congressional transcript.

All Women Must Wake Up

Radio Address for Station WICC

GRACE HOFFMAN WHITE
August 23, 1935[1]

Grace Hoffman White (1859–1937) was once described as the "most hospitable of poets and friends."[2] She was born Virginia Grace Hoffman to the Rev. Cadwallader Colden Hoffman and his second wife Caroline Hogan, both Episcopal missionaries to Liberia.[3] Little else has been recorded about White's life prior to her 1885 marriage to John Jay White in Manhattan. When the Whites relocated to Washington, D.C., Grace—often referred to as "Mrs. J. J. White" in news reports—devoted herself to various political causes. She found camaraderie among the suffragists in the NWP and advocated for the Women's International League for Peace and Freedom, leading the New York branch from 1930 to 1931. Five years later, White and Alice Paul traveled to Geneva and presented an equal rights treaty to the League of Nations Assembly.[4] All the while, White maintained a demanding creative schedule—she published poems, staged plays, gave public readings, and led fundraising campaigns for the arts. The *New York Times* printed her "Sonnet to Jane Addams" as a tribute to her friend and fellow peace activist of Hull House fame.[5] The headquarters for the General Federation of Women's Clubs (GFWC) can be found in Grace and John White's former Washington, D.C. mansion, where it has lived since the 1920s.[6]

Seventy-six-year-old Grace Hoffman White took her case for the Equal Rights Amendment to the airwaves just two years after Adolf Hitler's appointment as chancellor of Germany. The invention of the radio opened up new possibilities for the ERA's supporters and opponents to plead directly with the American people, who could engage the debate without leaving their living rooms. As the threat of war hung over Europe like a storm cloud and economic depression devastated the home front, White represented the pro-ERA position at Station WICC in Bridgeport, Connecticut. White's remarks displayed her policy acumen as a longtime NWP member, while also drawing from her literary sensibilities to make the appeal her own. The vivid metaphor of "waking up" guided White's depiction of the stakes at hand and forecasted global ramifications should the women of America remain asleep.

"Never before in our history has the moment seemed so fraught with peril to the economic freedom of women. Never before have the advances we have made seemed so near being taken from us in the guise of misguided and unjust legislation."

These words of our National Chairman, Mrs. Florence Bayard Hilles, should awaken the interest and lively consideration of every thinking woman and bring before her the vital necessity of having embodied in the Constitution the glorious principle of equal rights for men and women.[7] That men and women shall have equal rights throughout the United States and every place subject to its jurisdiction—this is the aim and object of the National Woman's Party, a nonpartisan organization.

It has been said that "Democracy works best when the people know exactly how their representatives vote on important matters." Connecticut holds a very important position in the accomplishment of having this Amendment adopted. Our able Congressman-at-large, Mr. Citron, is on the Judiciary Committee of the House of Representatives at Washington.[8] This committee holds the proposed Amendment in its keeping, with power to vote it out to the House-at-Large. This speaks for itself. I am sure if the women of this state would write, asking him to push forward the Equal Rights Amendment, it would greatly aid in its immediate adoption and settle for all time equality before the law for men and women, equality of opportunity, equality of property rights, equality in the guardianship of children, and the equal right to sell their labor on the same terms as men. There are other examples too numerous to mention.

I ask you, must we go on having restrictive labor laws under the guise of protection, that apply to women and not to men? I do not believe there is an industrial state in the Union where women have not fought valiantly against such laws. The women of the United States are in great danger of losing their rights, for this is exactly the way the suppression of women began in Europe. The first ones to be deprived of opportunity were the married women, then the professional women, then the women in paid work of every kind.

All women must wake up and think what it means when seven of our industrial states, Connecticut among them, have entered into a compact to regulate the minimum wage paid to women and children. Why are we bracketed again with children? We must protest against the ratification of such conventions by writing to our Senators and Representatives and asking their support of the Equal Rights Amendment to the Constitution of the United States.

The California Businesswomen's Legislative Council, an organization of 30,000 affiliated women, are awake to the situation for they left at the White House, early in March, petitions of 6,000 signatures, urging the President to use his power to put over the Equal Rights Amendment. The Affiliated Teachers' Organization of Los Angeles, representing 10,000 teachers, have gone on record for it. In eight states, including the District of Columbia, the Federation of Women's Clubs endorse it; the Democratic Club of New York and Colorado are with us, and now the National Association of Women Lawyers support the Equality Campaign. The Bindery Women's Union, Local 66, is also with us—so you see what wide-awake company we are in and this is not all.

Isn't it time you do your part? Be alive to your responsibilities, seize every opportunity to get your clubs and organizations to pass resolutions, urging their Senators and Representatives to report the Equal Rights Amendment favorably; urge representative people to write letters to them, give them a regular letter shower and see how it works.

The assurance that the passing of the Equal Rights Amendment to the Constitution would give to men and women alike would make them able and ready to stand behind [the] government with indomitable power and to hold up their hands in any good cause until the battle is won.

Alice Paul, our former National Chairman, rightly says: "We must keep the gains that have been made here and we must press forward until we have won complete equal rights in our own land. Our country will then serve as an inspiration to women all over the world."

I beg you to remember that equality is the leaven of truth which increases the measure of life.

Notes

1 Grace Hoffman White for The National Woman's Party, "Radio Broadcast, Station WICC," August 23, 1935, Alice Paul Papers. National Woman's Party. Programs: ERA campaign: National Woman's Party speeches, interviews, statements, 1910s–1930s. MC 399, folder 1106. Schlesinger Library, Radcliffe Institute,

Harvard University, Cambridge, Mass. Reprinted with permission from WICC Radio/Connecticut.

2 Harriet Monroe, "Again, New York," *Poetry* 32, no. 3 (June 1928), 150–58, quotation on 153.

3 Peter R. Rodgers, "Hoffman, C(adwallader) Hoffman," in *Biographical Dictionary of Christian Missions*, ed. Gerald H. Anderson (Grand Rapids, MI: William B. Eerdmans Publishing Company, 1998), 297–98.

4 "Mrs. John Jay White, A Peace Advocate," *New York Times*, July 19, 1937, 15; "Miss Paul to Urge Equal Rights Pact," *New York Times*, February 9, 1936, 37.

5 "Sonnet to Jane Addams, Written by Grace Hoffman White of the Women's Peace League," *New York Times*, December 11, 1931, 22.

6 Marian St. Clair, "Arts, Culture, and the Clubwomen," *WHRC News* (Winter 2021), https://www.gfwc.org/whrc-news-winter-2021/.

7 Suffragist Florence Bayard Hilles (1865–1954), a longtime NWP leader from Delaware and daughter of U.S. Secretary of State Thomas F. Bayard, was among the Silent Sentinels arrested for protesting outside of the White House.

8 Representative William Michael Citron (D-CT) served in the House of Representatives from 1935 to 1939.

There Is No Single Formula for Equality

Address to the Senate Judiciary Committee

Edith Valet Cook
February 8, 1938[1]

Once described as a rare woman who "seems to have solved the problem of combining a professional career with the job of being a wife and mother," Edith Valet Cook (1892–1992) walked door-to-door with petitions and marched in suffrage parades with her mother in New York City.[2] When Cook and her husband settled in Connecticut after World War I, she organized for the Children's Home Commission in Waterbury and served as secretary for the Connecticut Child Welfare Association for more than half a century. Cook's failed bid to become Mayor of New Haven in 1957 came between two stints as a Republican in the State General Assembly. In concert with her welfare work and legislative career, Cook helped found the Connecticut League of Women Voters. A Yale Law graduate, she lectured and wrote extensively on topics such as jury duty, employment, and legal rights for married and divorced women. Her 1936 pamphlet "The Married Woman and Her Job" likened backlash against the employment of married women to "that philosophy of government which we now know as Fascism."[3] Cook spent her final years in California doing income tax work and died at the ripe age of 100 years old.[4]

Until the 1970s, the LWV opposed the Equal Rights Amendment. "We got the vote way back in 1920," Cook argued in 1934: "If women really want to change the conditions, they can do so in their States by simply exercising the right to vote."[5] Although the LWV later reversed course on the ERA, Cook retained her skepticism about the amendment well into the 1980s. No doubt, her privileged status as a white middle-class woman informed this view. "I've never been particularly for it, and I haven't, probably from my own experience because

I never had any trouble," she admitted to a historian in 1982.[6] In contrast, Cook's opposing testimony nearly 45 years earlier developed a policy-based argument in opposition to the amendment.

The National League of Women Voters represents the opinion of women in all sections of the country. It is an established, working organization composed of 550 branches, urban and rural, in 33 states in the North, East, South and West. It has behind it 18 years of unremitting effort to advance the position of American women by the removal of hampering legal and administrative discrimination, as well as by training them for responsible participation in government as citizens and voters. It is therefore from no amateur's point of view that we appear today to oppose the proposed amendment.

In the first ten years after women received the vote members of the League were especially active in removing discriminations against women in the law, and they successfully supported many state and federal enactments equalizing women's opportunities, beginning with the Cable Act of 1922 which gave independent citizenship to married women and helping to place in the law the principle of equal pay for equal work in the 1923 Act reclassifying Civil Service, their efforts then extending through their state legislatures into such fields as office-holding, admission to public employment, jury service, guardianship of children and property rights. In the last half dozen years' progress, although still steady, has been a good deal slower and for very good reason. First, the outstanding and obvious legal discriminations against women have, with a few significant exceptions, been removed. Second, most of the discriminations which remain are either of a type which do not bear oppressively on many women or are not possible of removal by a single simple formula. They are in the realm of domestic and family law concerning which there is no general agreement as to precisely what change would be desirable. Then, too, most women aware of the realities of present economic and political conditions have been turning their attention to more general solutions to these problems along human rather than strictly feminist lines.

Some legal discriminations do remain and call for solution. Typical of these are, for example, laws concerning the property rights of married women where, as has been pointed out, no one formula for effective equality has been agreed upon nor can be expected to meet constantly changing social and economic situations. Our experience in the League convinces us that the removal of even the simplest discriminations calls for several distinct and careful steps which include a study both of the laws and of the actual operation of these laws in a particular state, careful drafting of proposed changes, and work for the desired change. We have found that specific measures state by state are necessary to correct specific ills. In the more complex fields of family and property law, lack of care in drafting legislation may easily result in hardships more severe than those caused by discriminations removed.

To proceed effectively in the removal of remaining discriminations, it is our conviction that federal and state legislatures alike within their respective fields should be free to pass laws to meet the changing conditions, to repeal these later, if necessary, in general to keep the laws abreast of changing customs and social conditions without being limited by new and untried constitutional restrictions upon their powers. We believe also that women through the vote have now the means of correcting laws that are discriminatory against them whenever they agree that they are in fact discriminatory, and that they favor making changes in laws that affect their own status with precision and care, rather than through some glittering generality about equal rights. There is neither any need nor in any substantial sense any demand for an amendment to the Constitution of the United States for this purpose.

But to say that comparatively few laws remain to be changed is not to agree that women do not still suffer from discriminations which spring from custom and prejudice. Clearly these discriminations are not amenable to law. For instance, the handicaps that business and professional women must still overcome result in no way from legal discriminations, for laws controlling entrance into the various professions now apply equally to men and women. Such obstacles in the way of woman's advancement result from prejudices inherited from the past, from habits and traditions which are not usually changed by high-sounding phrases in the Constitution.

The League of Women Voters is opposed to the so-called Equal Rights Amendment because:

1. It would be completely ineffective—it would do none of the things that are claimed for it, since even after it became a part of the Constitution state legislation would still be necessary;
2. It would be dangerous—it might do irreparable harm by nullifying much legislation which does not treat men and women identically before the law but which has been designed to give the millions of wives who are economically dependent effective equality with their husbands. Moreover, it would assuredly cause legal chaos in every state by casting doubt on those laws which are different for men and women.
3. It is entirely unnecessary—it would do nothing that could not be done without it by the tried method of specific legislation state by state which is the only sure and certain way of changing laws to meet specific handicaps.

One state League of Women Voters taking a bird's-eye view of their state laws which treat men and women differently have put the thing in a nutshell as follows:

> "Shall we pass the EQUAL RIGHTS AMENDMENT and give up:
>
> 1. Allowance for support of widow for one year after death of husband,
> 2. Increase in widow's inheritance tax exemption from $3500 to $5000,
> 3. Sole liability of father for support of illegitimate child,
> 4. Support from husband for wife and minor children.
>
> In order that women may be employed as 'bell-hop, taxi driver, gas or electric meter reader, ticket seller at hours before six a.m. or after ten p.m. in mines, blast furnaces . . . or in pool-rooms or bowling alleys having only men patrons.'"

The opposition of the League of Women Voters to the proposed amendment is based also upon its interest in the structure and functioning of our constitutional form of government. We, therefore, oppose the amendment regardless of the possible adverse effect on laws equalizing unequal opportunities of women. We are interested not only in a particular need, but in what governmental procedures are best adapted to meet that need. The Constitution is not a recital of general principles, it is the law of the land, and such vague and uncertain generalities have no place in it. The language of the Constitution should, to be sure, be in broad and general terms, but certainly not in such vague and uncertain language that it cries aloud to the Supreme Court to interpret it. Furthermore, to incorporate into the Constitution a proposal for equality of the sexes with its implication not only of present, but of probable future, inequalities just at the time when we were hoping that women were on the road to being treated as citizens rather than women is to "freeze" into the fundamental law through court interpretation based on present traditional ideas a concept which women are bending all their efforts to eliminate.

Ninety years ago, when the first woman suffrage convention was held "equal rights" was an exciting battle-cry. Then women's position was so far below men's in every field that equality with men was a goal worthy of their best efforts. The recital of their grievances against men beginning with the statement, "He had never permitted her to exercise her inalienable right to the elective franchise through the complaint that he has monopolized nearly all the profitable employments to the crowning indignity that he has denied her the facilities for obtaining a thorough education all colleges being closed to her"—this complaint indicates that in those days equal rights were something to work for. Today to accept as an end equality with men is a backward step. Wider opportunities, social, economic, political, and cultural are needed so that women may advance all along the line. As a matter of fact, the League's experience through eighteen years indicates that the large majority of women throughout the country realize this and have gone far beyond the demands for mere equal rights. They understand that the real battle for equal rights was won in 1920 when women secured in the vote the tool with which they may make their desires effective in law whenever enough of them choose to do so.

Mr. Chairman, and members of the Senate Judiciary Committee, we have appeared here today that you may have evidence that women deeply concerned with, and widely experienced in, advancing the status of women, do not favor the proposal before you. Indeed, we represent a distrust of that proposal that extends far beyond our membership. Expressions of it have come to us during the past few days from every side, and we have been particularly interested in the opinions that have come from many learned lawyers, and in their expressions of confidence that upon its merits the proposal will not find favor with your committee. We, too, leave this matter in your hands with confidence, knowing that you realize that the mischievous character of the proposed amendment to the Constitution outweighs every other possible consideration.

Notes

1 Edith Valet Cook, "Statement of the National League of Women Voters in Opposition to the Proposed Equal Rights Amendment," Presented to the Senate Judiciary Committee, Equal Rights Amendment folder 1935–1947 (League of Women Voters Records box 4 folder 9), Maine League of Women Voters, the University of Maine, https://digitalcommons.library. umaine.edu/maine_women_archival_all/2/. Public Domain.
2 Carole Nichols and Joyce Pendery, "Pro Bono Publico: Voices of Connecticut's Political Women, 1915–1945," *Oral History Review* 11 (1983): 49–74, see 56.
3 "Danger to Jobs Seen for Married Women," *New York Times*, May 24, 1936, N6.
4 "Obituary for Edith Valet Cook," *Press Democrat (Santa Rosa, California)*, December 4, 1992, B2.
5 "Vote League's Campaign Seeks Human Rights," *Washington Post*, December 27, 1934, 12.
6 Edith Valet Cook, interview by Joyce Pendery, January 4, 1982, in Healdsburg, California, University of Connecticut Library Archives & Special Collections, http://hdl.handle.net/11134/20002:860496760.

Section II The Debate Expands: 1940–1959

Throughout the 1940s and 1950s, emancipationists and protectionists continued to make their appeals in statements and testimony at Congressional hearings, as well as in public speeches, radio addresses, newspaper editorials, magazine commentary, and journal articles. The women of the NWP persuaded the Republican Party to add the ERA to its platform at the June 1940 national convention in Philadelphia, 17 years after the amendment was first introduced in Congress.[1] To the dismay of ERA opponents, the Democratic Party followed suit at its July convention in Chicago four years later, in large part thanks to the tireless lobbying (and at times questionable tactics) of Pennsylvania party insider Emma Guffey Miller.[2]

Even so, the Democratic Roosevelt administration favored the protectionist approach. "He is not with us and never has been," counseled NWP member Harriot Stanton Blatch about Franklin Delano Roosevelt in 1935.[3] Like her predecessors Florence Harding and Lou Hoover, first lady Eleanor Roosevelt affiliated with the League of Women Voters. In keeping with the LWV's position, Roosevelt subscribed to the view that the ERA "would wipe out any protective legislation now in force for women."[4] She pointedly did not host the NWP at the White House, even though many other women's organizations were invited during her tenure.[5] Secretary of Labor Frances Perkins, the first woman to hold a presidential cabinet post, opposed the amendment as well. Perkins told a Congressional committee in 1945 that the ERA would enable male employers to exploit women workers and would give "women the freedom to ruin their health in places unsuitable for their physical structure."[6] Protectionists greatly appreciated the reliable allyship of high-profile women in the Roosevelt administration, especially as emancipationist arguments began to take further hold.

The political endorsements of the ERA coincided with rising support for the amendment during World War II. The departure of the nation's fathers, sons, and brothers drew record numbers of women out of the home and into the labor force. Between 1940 and 1944, the number of working women increased from 13 million to more than 19 million.[7] By 1955, more women worked outside the home than had worked during the war.[8] Consequently, the Women's Bureau coalition formed the National Committee to Defeat the Un-Equal Rights Amendment (NCDURA)—later renamed the National Committee on the Status of Women (NCSW)—in September 1944 to counter increased backing for the ERA. The NCDURA circulated materials attacking the ERA on as many grounds as possible, deeming it impractical, vague, legally unsound, confusing, unnecessary, misleading, and dangerous.[9] In May 1945, NCDURA Secretary Margaret Austin Stone implored the Chair of the House Judiciary Committee, Representative Hatton W. Sumners (D-TX), to regard the ERA as so "controversial" that the House table it until the end of the war.[10] Nevertheless, the House Judiciary Committee issued its first-ever favorable report on the ERA just two months later.[11]

While protectionists sought to ensure that women workers were not exploited or undervalued during wartime, emancipationists doggedly pushed their ERA agenda forward. Alice Paul revised the amendment's language in 1943 to read: "Equality of rights before the law shall not be denied or abridged by the United States or any State on account of sex."[12] That same year, queer English professor and NWP member Jeanette Marks drew from her poetic repertoire to craft a literary case for the ERA. At Congressional hearings two years later, white emancipationist Nora Stanton Barney and Black protectionist Maida Springer Kemp guided a public rendering of the debate, asking whether the ERA reflected a continuance of the ideals set forth at the 1848 Seneca Falls Convention or constituted a treacherous generalization that would undermine those ideals.

For Black women like Kemp, entering the ERA debate proved fraught with complexities related to both gender and race. Protectionists within the Women's Bureau coalition were inclined to include Black women in their efforts and even, on occasion, fought against racism. Because of this inclusion and advocacy, Black women were more likely to be found alongside protectionists opposing the ERA in the 1940s. Between 1944 and 1947, Kemp, Dorothy Kelso Funn, and Rebecca Stiles Taylor expressed anxieties of varying kinds about how the ERA might affect—or not affect—the political, economic, and legal status of Black women in the United States. But not all Black women aligned with protectionist arguments and coalitions. The white women of the NWP, as a rule, did not extend their lobbying to fight racism. Nor did they turn away known racists and segregationists who supported the ERA if they saw the prospect for securing more partners in the debate. Alice

Paul, as history has recorded, was known to utter "racist sentiments" and to exclude Black women in her crusade to combat sex discrimination.[13] For Mary Church Terrell, these realities were not enough to deter her from seeing possibilities in the proposed amendment. Terrell split with Funn, Kemp, Taylor, and Mary McLeod Bethune and posited that the ERA was an essential bipartisan step to neuter protectionist legislation that, in her view, actually disenfranchised the women of her race. These exchanges underscore the historically unrecognized stakes that women of color had in the early decades of the ERA debate.

By 1946, the ERA debate "dominated the politics of women's rights and opportunities in postwar Washington."[14] The Senate conditionally approved the ERA in August of that year. Over the next several years, the amendment moved forward with a series of divisive "riders"—or provisions—asserting that it would not affect existing protective legislation. On their face, such provisions appeared to seek compromise between pro-ERA emancipationists and anti-ERA protectionists. Senator Carl Hayden (D-AZ), the chief sponsor of the riders and a friend to the Women's Bureau coalition, was a known ERA opponent who many believed intentionally sought to foment further distrust between and among women's groups fighting for similar goals but through different means.[15] The ERA's opponents found another friend in Representative Emanuel Celler (D-NY), who chaired the powerful all-male House Judiciary Committee between 1949 and 1973. Celler consistently used his position to block the amendment's movement in the House.[16]

That is not to say, however, that all male politicians actively opposed the ERA. On the contrary, a long list of Republicans and Democrats alike endorsed the amendment during this period, though to limited degrees and with minimal effects. Seventeen Republican and eight Democratic governors voiced support for the ERA in 1944.[17] NWP leader and Washington socialite Perle Mesta was close friends with Bess Truman, who in turn persuaded her husband Harry to endorse the ERA while he was still a senator.[18] In turn, Truman became the first sitting president to endorse the ERA.[19] Dwight Eisenhower pledged in a 1956 address at Madison Square Garden to "do all in our power to make more secure, for all citizens, their civil rights. And, as a special item of this matter, we shall seek, as we promised in our Platform, to assure women everywhere in our land equality of rights."[20] Despite their lofty proclamations and promises about equal rights, neither Truman nor Eisenhower made the ERA a serious legislative priority during their administrations. In private, Truman thought the fuss over equal rights was "a lot of hooey," writing as much on a presidential appointment sheet after meeting with a women's group sponsoring the amendment.[21] Eisenhower summed up his own milquetoast efforts at a press conference in 1957: "I am in favor of [the ERA]. I just probably haven't been active enough in doing something about it."[22]

The support of male legislators and presidents, such that it was, did little to reassure labor activist Elizabeth Gurley Flynn and other skeptical protectionists who suspected hidden motives behind the "blanket amendment" and feared that Senator Hayden's rider would curtail the rights of women workers in the post-World War II era. Legally-minded protectionists like Dorothy Kenyon, an early target of Senator Joseph McCarthy, likewise worried that an amendment promising a "short road to freedom" would leave no room for new "differential legislation" that would further protect women's interests as workers and citizens.[23]

As both Flynn and Kenyon knew well, Joe McCarthy's witch-hunts contributed to postwar conservatism and, as a result, dramatically impacted civic life. The ERA debate did not remain untouched, as questions about women's proper roles shaped—and were shaped by—the national frenzy around anti-communism during these years. This frenzy fomented a national mood, historian Ruth Rosen argues, under which both marriage and motherhood became highly politicized as evidence of patriotic fidelity.[24] FBI Director J. Edgar Hoover, who had opposed woman suffrage, gave voice to this tendency by imploring women to marry young and produce children early to combat "the twin enemies of freedom—crime and Communism."[25] With their focus on homemaking and childbearing, this reasoning went, loyal American women would keep their focus on their households and on eradicating any Communist influences in their neighborhoods and communities. They need not be preoccupied with questions about their civil liberties, or with the so-called Equal Rights Amendment.[26]

The few women serving in Congress in the 1940s and 1950s, while not always in agreement about the nuances of the debate or the potential effects of the proposed amendment, cared deeply about civil liberties and fought to keep the ERA in the legislative spotlight. In 1943, Senator Hattie W. Caraway (D-AR) became the first woman in Congress to cosponsor the ERA. Clare Boothe Luce (R-CT), Margaret Chase Smith (R-ME), Winifred C. Stanley (R-NY), and Katharine St. George (R-NY)—whose 1957 speech appears in this anthology—all endorsed and sponsored the ERA. But the ERA only moved forward incrementally during these years, even as women continued to forcefully debate its merits and faults. The NWP soon fractured due to in-fighting—though members like former suffragist Caroline Katzenstein, now in her sixties, reliably continued to appear before Congress to testify on the ERA's behalf.[27]

At the close of the "original ERA conflict" in 1960, the protectionist frontlines had held strong despite Winnifred Huck's hopeful prediction that electing more women to Congress would help the amendment's prospects.[28] Not until 1959 did the League of Women Voters—"the last major hold-out"—stop actively opposing the ERA.[29] The 1960s, in turn, would see a new generation of advocates rewrite the terms of the debate as national movements for women's rights and civil rights commenced.

Notes

1 "Republican Party Platform of 1940," June 24, 1940, *American Presidency Project*, https://www.presidency.ucsb.edu/documents/republican-party-platform-1940.
2 "1944 Democratic Party Platform," July 19, 1944, *American Presidency Project*, https://www.presidency.ucsb.edu/documents/1944-democratic-party-platform; Susan Ware, *Beyond Suffrage: Women in the New Deal* (Cambridge, MA: Harvard University Press, 1981), 121; Rebecca DeWolf, *Gendered Citizenship: The Original Conflict over the Equal Rights Amendment, 1920–1963* (Lincoln: University of Nebraska Press, 2021), 157.
3 Susan D. Becker, *The Origins of the Equal Rights Amendment: American Feminism Between the Wars* (Westport, CT: Greenwood Press, 1981), 150.
4 Eleanor Roosevelt, "My Day," November 18, 1946, Eleanor Roosevelt Papers Project, George Washington University, https://www2.gwu.edu/~erpapers/myday/displaydoc.cfm?_y=1946&_f=md000498.
5 Paula F. Pfeffer, "Eleanor Roosevelt and the National and World Woman's Parties," *The Historian* 59, no. 1 (1996): 39–57.
6 Amelia R. Fry, "Conversations with Alice Paul: Woman Suffrage and the Equal Rights Amendment," *Part IV: The Equal Rights Amendment, Suffragists Oral History Project*, Online Archives of California, 1976, https://oac.cdlib.org/view?docId=kt6f59n89c&brand=oac4&doc.view=entire_text; "The Equal Rights Amendment," *Social Service Review* 19, no. 1 (1945): 111–12.
7 Cynthia Harrison, *On Account of Sex: The Politics of Women's Issues 1945–1968* (Berkeley: University of California Press, 1988), 4.
8 Ruth Rosen, *The World Split Open: How the Modern Women's Movement Changed America* (New York: Viking, 2000), 19.
9 Harrison, *On Account of Sex*, 20, 27.
10 "Defeat Un-Equal Rights Amendment," May 21, 1945, House of Representatives, https://history.house.gov/HouseRecord/Detail/15032436175.
11 Harrison, *On Account of Sex*, 21.
12 Christine A. Lunardini, *From Equal Suffrage to Equal Rights: Alice Paul and the National Woman's Party, 1910–1928* (New York: New York University Press, 1986), 172.
13 Harrison, *On Account of Sex*, 12.
14 Harrison, *On Account of Sex*, 15.
15 Harrison, *On Account of Sex*, 31.
16 DeWolf, *Gendered Citizenship*, 199–200.

17 Rebecca DeWolf, "The Equal Rights Amendment and the Rise of Emancipationism, 1932–1946," *Frontiers: A Journal of Women's Studies* 38, no. 2 (2017): 47–80, see 68.
18 Sara L. Sale, *Bess Wallace Truman: Harry's White House "Boss"* (Lawrence: University Press of Kansas, 2010), 71.
19 DeWolf, "The Equal Rights Amendment," 155.
20 Harrison, *On Account of Sex*, 36.
21 David McCullough, *Truman* (New York: Simon & Schuster, 1992), 471.
22 "The President's News Conference," August 7, 1957, *American Presidency Project*, https://www.presidency.ucsb.edu/documents/the-presidents-news-conference-305.
23 See Kenyon's speech in this volume.
24 Rosen, *The World Split Open*, 13.
25 Christopher Lydon, "J. Edgar Hoover Made the F.B.I. Formidable with Politics, Publicity and Results," *New York Times*, May 3, 1972, 52.
26 Michelle Nickerson, "Women, Domesticity, and Postwar Conservatism," *OAH Magazine of History* 17, no. 2 (2003): 17–21.
27 DeWolf, *Gendered Citizenship*, 154.
28 DeWolf, *Gendered Citizenship*, 216.
29 Lunardini, *From Equal Suffrage*, 170.

On Account of Sex

Article for the General Federation Clubwoman

Jeannette Marks
November 1943[1]

Mount Holyoke College English professor Jeannette Augustus Marks (1875–1964) was born in Chattanooga, Tennessee and attended various boarding schools before landing at Wellesley College, where Mary Emma Woolley taught Biblical literature and where Marks studied English literature at both the undergraduate and graduate level. Twelve years apart in age, the two women formed an intimate bond at Wellesley—one that continued with Woolley's appointment to Mount Holyoke College's presidency in 1901 and, consequently, continued with Marks' appointment to the English faculty there. The two women built a lifelong partnership together—"a mutual declaration of ardent and exclusive love," as their surviving correspondence reveals—until Woolley's death in 1947.[2] When Woolley's tenure as Mount Holyoke's first female president ended in 1937, the Board of Trustees eagerly replaced her with a "family man" who would perform the role more conventionally. Woolley had run afoul of the male-dominated Board by pressing for more faculty rights, trying to limit Board influence, and continuing a relationship with Marks.[3]

Although Woolley's name is more recognizable today, Marks lived an impressive life in her own right. She founded the Laboratory Theater at Mount Holyoke and her plays, *Merry Cuckoo* and *Welsh Honeymoon*, won her the Welsh National Theater prize. The subjects of her books and articles ranged in topic from English pastoral drama to drug addiction.[4] Along the way, she found time to curate and publish *The Life and Letters of Mary Emma Woolley.*[5] Today, the Jeannette Marks Cultural Center (familiarly known as "The Marks") stands proudly on the campus of Mount Holyoke as a queer-friendly gathering hub for LGBTQIA+ students, faculty, staff, and allies.[6]

Marks' 1942 play *Laughter* traced the history of the women's movement and won high praise with the ladies of the Alva Belmont House, who turned out to hear a dramatic rendering of the lives of Lucretia Mott, Elizabeth Cady Stanton, and Susan B. Anthony. A review of the play published in the *Washington Post* noted that Marks, an NWP member, was an "ardent worker for the equal rights amendment."[7] The magazine article for *General Federation Clubwoman* published here underscores this fact. The General Federation of Women's Clubs (GFWC), founded in 1890, served as an international umbrella organization for various women's clubs devoted to volunteerism and service. Although it trended conservatively in comparison to some other women's groups promoting the ERA at the time, the GFWC endorsed the amendment in 1944 because its members "recognized the necessity of paid employment for many women and the skills and talents qualified women had to offer in public life."[8] The year prior, Marks revisited the lives of those nineteenth-century luminaries from her play to suggest that their work remained unfinished so long as the Nineteenth Amendment stood as the final word on women's rights in the United States. Her literary style informed a decidedly unique entry in the ERA debate, as Marks wove together imagined conversations and historical facts to develop her position.

There is pleading on the face of the young woman who bends over some paper on which she is writing these dedicatory words: "To M. Talleyrand-Périgord,[9] Late Bishop of Autun."[10] Then she begins:

"Sir, the following are the words of Jean Jacques Rousseau which I, a woman, dare to challenge: 'The education of women should always be relative to that of men. To please US, to be useful to US, to make US love and esteem them, to educate US when young, and to take care of US when grown up . . . to render OUR lives easy and agreeable; these are the duties of women at all times, and what they should be taught in their infancy' . . ."

She paused to listen to her child humming in an adjoining room. Lovely this young woman was, with a face both tender and noble. With disgust she turned back to the sentence she had just copied from Rousseau and then went on:

"Sir, I plead for my sex—not for myself—for Justice to one-half the human race. Independence I have long considered the basis of every virtue . . . A character as a human being should belong to every woman, regardless of the distinction of sex . . ."

It was some one hundred and fifty years ago that Mary Wollstonecraft in England and Condorcet[11] in France urged that the inequality of the sexes should be abolished in order to raise the level of morality, believing as they did that inequality had been ruinous to the sex it favored, and had led to the use of force by men and to the degradation of women. Even then did they know that the moral armament of the future could be assured only if the justice of human equality were substituted for the injustice of discriminations on account of sex.

It is the year 1825 and thirty-three years have passed since Mary Wollstonecraft wrote her *Vindication* on behalf of women. The place is not England, but Johnstown, New York. Little Elizabeth Cady, the Judge's ten-year-old daughter, is pleading with her father to save the farm of the poor old woman, her friend, who is in the office with them. It is evident that this handsome, kindly man is disturbed.

"Even for you, Libby," he said, "I can't set aside the law, for Blackstone, the greatest of all lawyers, wrote in his *Commentaries* of the 'defect of sex' under the shadow of which all women, their children and their work, live."[12]

"Father," she protested, her cheeks as red as her pretty flannel dress, and her head held as high as the white starched ruff around her neck, "Father, are Flora and I 'defects of sex'?"

"As Blackstone said," the Judge explained apologetically, "all females live under the shadow of 'defect of sex'."

"Father, do boys have what you call sex?"

"Yes, child, yes. Don't you remember what the Bible says? 'Male and female created he them and . . .' "

But Libby was not interested in the Bible. She was interested in the persecution of her parent, and she broke in: "Father, do boys have what you call a 'defect of sex'?"

"No, child, boys live under no such shadow."

"I see. Then 'cording to Blackstone a girl is not as good as a boy!"

If she suffered from a "defect of sex," neither the child nor the woman ever suffered from any defect of wit. Elizabeth Cady became Mrs. Stanton. She had many children, themselves unusual. In 1848 she and James and Lucretia Mott, Martha Wright, their sister, and others, called the Convention at Seneca Falls to read in public their Declaration of Sentiments modeled on the Declaration of Independence. With time she won fame as a speaker for suffrage.

At Lincoln, Nebraska, in the discussion following her suffrage talk, she was heckled by a pompous man who drew his chair up in front of the platform and said:

"Madam, do you not think that the best thing a woman can do is to perform well her part in the role of wife and mother?"

"Sir," answered Mrs. Stanton, "I am the mother of seven children."

"Delightful, Madam, delightful!" retorted the man. "My wife has presented me with eight sons! Is not this a better life work for a woman than that of exercising the right of suffrage?"

Surveying him quietly from head to foot, Mrs. Stanton answered, "Sir, I have met few men worth repeating eight times."

"Where Liberty is, there is my country!" wrote Benjamin Franklin. To this, as he urged internationalism and asked for mercy to animals and justice to women, Tom Paine had replied: "Where Liberty is NOT, there is my Country!" Tom Paine's Country without Liberty, except for the women of China, Russia and New Zealand, is still the country of all women today. In the United States the only equal constitutional status so far gained by women is the right to vote. And in our day there is no more absurd record in legal history than the fact that on the statute books of the states of the United States there are 1,041 laws discriminating against women because they are "female," whereas on those same statute books there exists *not one law* discriminating against men because they are "male."

When in 1872, because of her attempt to cast her ballot in 1871 in Rochester, New York, Susan B. Anthony was tried at Canandaigua, Judge Hunt snarled: "Miss Anthony knew that she was a woman, the said Susan B. Anthony being then and there a person of *Female sex* and well knowing it!"[13]

In 1917, forty-five years after the trial and conviction of Susan B. Anthony, and because women continued to ask for the right to vote, the spiritual descendants of the great leaders of the past were being kicked and beaten, spat upon, arrested, tried, imprisoned and manacled in prisons in Washington and that neighborhood.

It was not Susan B. Anthony, with her splendid physique who faced the judge but a small, elderly woman, Mrs. Mary Nolan,[14] up from the South, lame and frail, who, before she was sent to prison, spoke these words in court:

"Sir, I have a nephew fighting for democracy in France. I should be ashamed if I were not here with these brave women in their fight for democracy in America. If we are guilty, it is because there is guilt in a demand for freedom ... I am willing to do or suffer anything to bring victory to the long courageous struggle ... There is not one of us left here this noon who will not fight on to the end."

Among the hundreds arrested were such women as Florence Bayard Hilles, daughter of our first ambassador to Great Britain; Mrs. Lewis, sister of the world-famous cancer expert, Dr. Howard Kelly; Betty Gram, the wife of Raymond Gram-Swing; and Alice Paul, the quiet, passionate Quaker girl from Swarthmore College, under whose leadership the right to vote was finally won—the only right so far gained in woman's struggle for equal constitutional status. For a century and a half, from revolution to revolution, from the 18th century down to our own day, multitudes of women and many men have dedicated themselves, and continue to dedicate themselves, in a "spirit of consecration" to the cause of freedom for women.

And now in conclusion—in February 15, 1943, the place the House of Representatives, Washington, D.C. Already the Lucretia Mott Amendment—equality of rights before the law shall not be denied or abridged by the United States or by any state on account of sex—is currently under consideration by the Sub-Judiciary Committee of the House. But the event on this day is the House celebration of Susan B. Anthony. Man after man has risen to his feet to pay tribute to her memory. At the close of the celebration Mr. Kefauver of Tennessee[15] used his own words to emphasize her spiritual power: "I go in the strength of right to make the right triumphant on the earth . . . I go in the name of the forgotten justice to make it remembered in high places and in low; I go in the name of the silent and the silenced ones to give them voices."

Then, as he ends, come these words of his own: "Let us take her bequest to do this unfinished work, that her dreams may be realized—to establish the new justice and equality of right!"

Notes

1 Jeannette Marks, "On Account of Sex," General Federation Clubwoman, November 1943, 11, 22. Reprinted from Doris Stevens Papers. National Woman's Party, 1916–1958. General, 1916–1946 (#46.1-46.15, Mem.1-Mem.2, OD.3m). Equal Rights Amendment, 1942–1944. MC 546, folder 46.14. Schlesinger Library, Radcliffe Institute, Harvard University, Cambridge, Mass. Reprinted with permission from Mount Holyoke College Archives and Special Collections. A special thanks to archivist Deborah Richards for her assistance.

2 "1930s: Pinnacle of Achievement and Controversy," Mary Woolley and Jeannette Marks: Life, Love, & Letters," Digital Exhibition, Mount Holyoke, https://commons.mtholyoke.edu/marywooleyjeannettemarks/mary-and-jeannette/; see also Leila J. Rupp, " 'Imagine My Surprise': Women's Relationships in Historical Perspective," *Journal of Lesbian Studies* 1, no. 2 (1997): 155–76, esp. 159–60.

3 For an extensive account of the controversy over Woolley's successor, see Ann Karus Meeropol, *A Male President for Mount Holyoke College: The Failed Fight to Maintain Female Leadership, 1934–1937* (Jefferson, NC: McFarland & Company, 2014).

4 "Jeannette Marks, Educator, Was 88," *New York Times*, March 16, 1964, 31.

5 Jeanette Augustus Marks, *Life and Letters of Mary Emma Woolley* (Washington, D.C.: Public Affairs Press, 1955).

6 "Cultural Center," Mount Holyoke, https://www.mtholyoke.edu/student-experience/community-and-belonging/cultural-centers/jeannette-marks-cultural-center.

7 "Jeanette Marks Reads Her Play at Women's Meeting Here," *Washington Post*, November 13, 1942, 4.

8 Paige Meltzer, "'The Pulse and Conscience of America': The General Federation and Women's Citizenship, 1945–1960," *Frontiers: A Journal of Women Studies* 30, no. 3 (2009): 52–76, see 57.

9 Marks had his name spelled incorrectly in the manuscript. We have made the correction here.

10 Charles Maurice de Talleyrand-Périgord was a French diplomat who authored a pamphlet arguing that women did not need access to education. Feminist thinker and writer Mary Wollstonecraft dedicated her 1792 magnum opus, *A Vindication of the Rights of Woman: with Structures on Political and Moral Subjects*, to Talleyrand-Périgord.

11 French mathematician and philosopher Marie-Jean-Antoine-Nicolas de Caritat, Marquis de Condorcet, supported equal rights for women in his works. See "The History of Feminism: Marie-Jean-Antoine-Nicolas de Caritat, Marquis de Condorcet," *Stanford Encyclopedia of Philosophy*, January 11, 2022, https://plato.stanford.edu/Entries/histfem-condorcet/.

12 Sir William Blackstone published his influential four-volume legal treatise *Commentaries on the Laws of England* between 1765 and 1769.

13 The presiding judge in this case was Judge Ward Hunt of the New York State Court of Appeals. See Martin Naparsteck, *The Trial of Susan B. Anthony: An Illegal Vote, a Courtroom Conviction and a Step Toward Women's Suffrage* (Jefferson, NC: McFarland, 2014).

14 Mary A. Nolan, an NWP suffragist, was the oldest protester arrested and imprisoned during the "Night of Terror." See Judith Poucher, "The Evolving Suffrage Militancy of Mary Nolan," *Florida Historical Quarterly* 95, no. 2 (2016): 221–45.

15 Carey Estes Kefauver served as a Democrat representing Tennessee, first in the House from 1939 to 1948 and then in the Senate from 1949 until 1963.

The Legislative Front: The Equal Rights Amendment

Article for Congress Vue

Dorothy Kelso Funn
February 1944[1]

Dorothy Kelso Funn (1903–1974) taught in Brooklyn city junior high schools from 1923 to 1943. She had graduated from Girls High School in Brooklyn in 1920 and earned her teaching certificate from the Maxwell Teaching School in 1922. After 20 years in education, however, and after engaging in local community activism in Brooklyn, she accepted an administrative post within the National Negro Congress (NNC) in Washington, D.C. which she held until 1946. Consistently, hers was a staunch and public voice for equality.[2]

However, Funn's public life is a curious roller coaster. In 1941, white administrators forced her to transfer to a different school for what the *New York Age* called "persecution ... due to her vigorous protest whenever racial issues which she considered unfair reared their ugly heads."[3] Throughout her community involvement in both Brooklyn and in the Capitol, she advocated for public ceremonies remembering Frederick Douglass during "Negro History Week," critiqued public derision of the Black press, and supported the United Nations.[4] At the beginning of World War II, she testified before the House Judiciary Committee revealing racial discrimination in hiring among defense contractors. Historian Erik Gellman records that she was "petite, vivacious, [and] dauntless." Along with Black female labor activists Jeanne Pastor, Maude Jett, and Ruth Jett, Funn started publishing the *Congress Vue* to reinvigorate the Negro Congress and to "link . . . progressive Negroes throughout the country."[5] Her arguments in the *Vue* are assertive and unwavering and even familiar to contemporary ears. Her tireless rhetorical strategy persists in all her public rhetoric—including her critique of the Equal Rights Amendment in 1944.

Yet Funn's final public activism requires explanation and nuance. In 1953, she testified before the House Un-American Activities Committee on the same day as band director Artie Shaw. Her testimony came four years after Black activist and entertainer Paul Robeson had been blacklisted as a Communist and after Jackie Robinson, too, was called before the Committee. In her two-hour testimony in May 1953, Funn named 65 people as Communists, including over 20 of her co-workers in the New York public schools. The media coverage of her statements exploded across front pages around the country. She claimed to have grown disillusioned with the *Congress* before she resigned, asserting that it was nothing more than a Communist front. As if the House testimony wasn't enough, Funn appeared again in 1956 naming Communist colleagues before the Eastland Committee in the Senate. It seemed to be her brand.[6]

How can we, decades after Funn's testimony and her death, assess her political activism for Black civil rights, labor, and feminism? The high Black turnover rate in the NNC across the United States reveals that Funn was not alone in her disillusionment, but she might have been alone in the conclusion that the group was nothing but a "front" for Communism. With Robeson portrayed as the icon of a "bad Negro," many Black Americans felt compelled to demonstrate that they personally were "good" by proving their patriotism to the Committee.[7] So nearly a decade before her naming her friends to the House and the Senate, Funn made the case against the Equal Rights Amendment in the NNC organ, *Congress Vue*.[8]

One of the chief pieces of legislation upon which the Republican party is depending in making a frantic bid for votes—especially the important war time vote of American women—is the much discussed "Equal Rights Amendment." It is necessary now to make a complete analysis of the proposed legislation and to show why all progressive forces must UNITE TO DEFEAT IT.

Past History of the Bill

As early as 1923, Republican senator Charles E. Dawes, later vice president under Herbert Hoover, introduced a bill giving "equal rights to women throughout the United States and everywhere subject to its jurisdiction." The bill was defeated and again in 1943, Republican forces got it favorably through the Senate Judiciary committee but failed to get the House Judiciary committee to report it favorably. Now this 20-year-old, twice-defeated Bill is being offered by the Republicans—with no amendments—as a "sop" to American womanhood.

What Does the Bill Contain?

It specifies that everywhere in the United States, men and women shall have (for all purposes, regardless of special circumstances and other factors) equal rights.

What Effect Would Passage of the Bill Have?

Because, in its present state, this measure lays down the principle that there is absolutely no difference between the sexes, and there should be none, its passage would have the effect of canceling all progressive, protective legislation for women which has been fought for and won throughout the years. Though it is true that in some states, all the laws which deny certain civil rights to women still exist, many of these same states have, through recognition of NATURAL differences between men and women, passed laws which are necessary and essential for the protection of American women.

Since much of this legislation affects working women mainly, and since passage of this "Equal Rights Amendment" would nullify these laws, the bill is essentially ANTI-LABOR. As women more and more must, during war time and in the peace to follow, take your places along with men as wage earners in industry, the protective laws in the various states become more and more important. THESE LAWS MUST NOT BE NULLIFIED.

Who Supports the Bill?

Loudest among the proponents of the "Equal Rights Amendment" are members of the "National [Woman's] Party." Made up of wealthy, powerful, non-working, women of leisure, who are in reality the feminine counterparts of the most reactionary men in both parties, this group is unable or unwilling to see how laws limiting the hours of women's work, banning night work, regulating wages, providing rest periods and maternity leave, introducing safety measures etc., must be maintained and not destroyed by a blanket amendment which takes none of these things into consideration. In Congress, the forces which are most often anti-labor are speaking out in favor of the bill.

Who Opposes the Bill?

Leading women trade-unionists and those closest to labor are unalterably opposed to the "Equal Rights Amendment." Unable to get the sponsors of the bill even to consider amending it in any way, women leaders of the CIO auxiliaries, the A.F. of L. auxiliaries, the National Women's Trade Union League, the YWCA, the National League of Women Voters, the American Association of University Women, the National Council of Jewish Women, the National Council of Catholic Women, the National Maritime Union Auxiliary, the Director of the Women's Bureau, Department of Labor, Mrs. Eleanor Roosevelt and others are strong in their public opposition to the measure.

What Can You Do?

Whenever a piece of legislation works a hardship on people in general, the Negro people specifically suffer most. This is true with a proposed "Equal Rights Amendment" and we must see that it does not pass.

1. Organizations of Negro women particularly, must speak out forcibly against the "Equal Rights Amendment."
2. Individuals, white and Negro, must unite with the forces opposing the bill and must clarify the issues everywhere to those who may be misled by its name and the connotation.
3. Members of the House Judiciary Committee must receive at once, WIRES, LETTERS, RESOLUTIONS from all progressive organizations to prevent this bill from reaching the floor for a vote.

Notes

1 Dorothy K. Funn, "The Legislative Front: The 'Equal Rights' Amendment," *Congress Vue* 1, no. 9, February 1944. Public Domain.

2 "141 Graduates at Girls' High," *Times Union,* June 25, 1920, 9; "Teachers Graduate at Teaching at Training School," *Brooklyn Daily Eagle,* June 28, 1922, 8.

3 Alfred A. Duckett, "Dorothy Funn Transferred: Authorities Call Her 'Red,'" *New York Age*, March 29, 1941, 7.

4 "National Negro Congress Delegation Visits Fred Douglass's Grave," *New York Age,* February 22, 1941, 7; Dorothy K. Funn, "Follows Hitler's Pattern," *Pittsburgh Courier*, May 16, 1942, 5; "National Negro Congress Supports United Nations," *Weekly Review*, July 7, 1945, 7; "Dorothy Funn, Brooklyn Educator, Makes Report

on Defense Bias for Legislators," *New York Age*, July 26, 1941, 7; Joseph H. Short, "Anti-Russian Talk Blamed," *Baltimore Sun*, June 13, 1945, 7.

5 Erik S. Gellman, *Death Blow to Jim Crow: The National Negro Congress and the Rise of Militant Civil Rights* (Chapel Hill: University of North Carolina Press, 2012), 169.

6 Williams Edwards, "Reds Control Super-Lobby, Probers Hear," *Chicago Tribune*, May 5, 1953, 1, 10; Peter Kihss, "Asserts Union Lobbyists 'Red,'" *Des Moines Register*, May 5, 1953, 2; "Red Probers Stir Hot Exchange in Quizzing I. L. W. U. Attorneys," *Honolulu Star-Bulletin*, December 6, 1956, 2.

7 For further discussion of these contrasting terms, see Gregory Mixon, "'Good Negro'—'Bad Negro': The Dynamics of Race and Class in Atlanta During the Era of the 1906 Riot," *Georgia Historical Quarterly* 81, no. 3 (1997): 593–621.

8 Lawrence S. Wittner, "The National Negro Congress: A Reassessment," *American Quarterly* 22, no. 4 (1970): 883–901; Andrea Friedman, "The Strange Career of Annie Lee Moss: Rethinking Race, Gender, and McCarthyism," *Journal of American History* 94, no. 2 (2007): 445–68.

Why We Need the Equal Rights Amendment

A Response to Dorothy Kelso Funn

MARY CHURCH TERRELL

1944[1]

Mary Eliza Church Terrell's (1863–1954) remarkable life spanned the middle of the Civil War to the beginnings of the Civil Rights Movement. Terrell left her home city of Memphis, Tennessee to study classics at Oberlin College and earn a Master's degree—becoming one of the first Black women in the United States to do so. Because married women were not permitted to teach, Terrell was forced to give up her teaching career. Therefore, she became a writer, lecturer, and reformer—along with fellow Memphian and journalist Ida B. Wells-Barnett—on issues of lynching and racial equality. Terrell co-founded and led the National Association of Colored Women (NACW) and served as a charter member of the National Association for the Advancement of Colored People (NAACP) upon its founding in 1909.[2] In Washington D.C., she debunked myths that the nation's capital was "the colored man's paradise" and—well into her eighties—boldly entered white-only establishments with other Black activists to test the legal limits of segregationist policies that were hardly limited to Southern states.[3] She lived just long enough to see the Supreme Court decide *Brown v. Board of Education*, the landmark 1954 decision that made it unconstitutional for public schools to racially segregate students.

Terrell saw many similarities between the disenfranchisement of women and Black citizens in the United States. A friendship with Susan B. Anthony yielded invitations to address meetings of the NAWSA, and Terrell later joined Alice Paul, Lucy Burns, and other NWP members in the picket line outside the White House. Even so, participating in the suffrage cause often proved difficult for Terrell who, like other Black suffragists, confronted indifference and cruel racism in many of her white sisters. As just one example, Paul dismissed Terrell's appeals that the NWP investigate the disenfranchisement of Black women in the South, characterizing it as a "race issue" rather than a "women's issue."[4]

Unsurprisingly, then, Black women were sharply divided about the ERA to the extent that they were even included in the conversation in these early years of the debate. Mary McLeod Bethune's National Council of Negro Women (NCNW) took the protectionist position and opposed the amendment. Yet, Terrell—like the white women of the NWP—saw the ERA as a necessary next step for ensuring all women's progress and, accordingly, rallied for support within the NACW.[5] Like many of her contemporaries, she took her case to the Senate Judiciary.[6] The text below, however, is Terrell's emphatic and disapproving rebuttal to Dorothy Funn's anti-ERA arguments (also included in this volume). It remains unclear where, how, or even if Terrell delivered or published her response, which drew on her ethos to document her concern that the ERA's opponents were increasingly casting it as divisive, partisan legislation.

I have read with great disappointment the article written by Dorothy K. Funn. Miss Funn, I am told, is a professional lobbyist for the National Negro Congress.

I am deeply grieved that any colored woman would oppose any legislation providing equal rights along any line of human endeavor. I am convinced that Miss Funn has never made a real study of the Equal Rights Amendment and what it entails. Her failure to inform herself of the facts in the case extends even to her ignorance of the National Woman's Party, its history, and its purpose.

Let me say first of all that I helped organize the National Association of Colored Women in 1896; I was its first president, and I was later named its honorary president for life. This organization has many thousands of members and has a state federation in almost every state. I am sure they are all interested in equality. I have worked consistently for the welfare of colored women, and no one can have their interests closer to their hearts than I. Everyone that knows me knows that I would never champion anything that would hurt my people and that I will spare no effort to advance any measure that would help them.

But colored women must realize that the so-called protective laws introduced under such a humanitarian title do not protect the colored woman. The ten o'clock law has not helped the charwoman who must scrub on her knees till five or six o'clock in the morning. No one worries about their morals because their jobs are not wanted by men. It is in the newspaper offices, in restaurants where tips are largest at night, and in jobs where overtime work commands extra pay that women are banished. Men push the protective idea to protect their own jobs. They "protected" the high-paid woman right out of their jobs but left the poor charwomen right on their knees.

May I correct Miss Funn's statement that the National Woman's Party is made up of "wealthy, powerful, non-working women of leisure." There is a large and active group of women in industry in the National Woman's Party who look to this organization to secure their fair deal in the industrial world. There is also a large group of business and professional women, of civil service women, of physicians, dentists, and lawyers who will compare quite as favorably in their concern about working women's problems as the League of Women Voters, the American Association of University Women, and others of that ilk.

The National Woman's Party was organized in 1913 for the one purpose of working for full equality for women. It realized that women in industry, as well as in any other class of women, needed the power of the ballot to establish their rights. This party originated the idea of securing suffrage through a federal amendment instead of the slow process of state-by-state legislation.

After suffrage was won, the National Woman's Party concentrated its efforts on securing for women full equality before the law—the equality asked for by the first organizers of the woman movement in 1848. This party made the first comprehensive survey of all laws in the United States concerning women and listed all discriminations that work to the disadvantage of women. Very soon it became convinced that many so-called protective laws were a handicap to women in industry—women actually in industry and not organizers or welfare workers. These women have time and again cited the difficulties they encountered in competition with men.

The National Woman's Party and its 26 allied national organizations which support the Amendment do not oppose legislation that will improve the conditions of working people. It only contends that the laws should be harmonized so that men and women alike will benefit by those restrictions, as in the Fair Labor Standards law approved by both the CIO and the AF of L, which places men and women on an equal basis on all interstate commerce.

The Equal Rights Amendment is not Anti-Labor, it is Anti-Unfair-Labor. Miss Funn writes, "As women more and more must, during wartime and in the peace to follow, take their places along with men as wage earners in industry, the protective laws in the various states become more and more important." True. That is why their opportunities must be equalized now while there is a demand for their labor. After the war, employers may find it too easy to shove women back into their inferior jobs because it is too expensive to keep them and because men, who can work any hours they please and can work overtime, can be secured.

Miss Funn attempts to place the responsibility for the Amendment upon Republican shoulders and presents it as an exclusively Republican measure. Certainly, the Democrats in Congress will not be pleased about that disposal. The Amendment is not a political party measure. Just as many Democrats as Republicans support it. Senator Gillette/Democrat of Iowa introduced the Amendment in the Senate, and sixteen Democrats and seven Republicans joined him as co-sponsors of the bill.[7] Another Democrat, Representative Ludlow of Indiana, introduced it in the House and joining him were twenty-one Democrats and twenty-two Republicans.[8] To be sure, the Judiciary Committee defeated it in the House by three votes, but another Democrat, Representative Cannon of Florida, initiated a discharge petition to take it out of the committee and bring it directly to the floor of the House for debate.[9] On the introduction of this petition, five Democrats and four Republicans spoke in support of it.

I agree with Miss Funn that we "must clarify the issues." If negro women will study the Equal Rights Amendment and understand why it is needed and what it will do for them and for all women, they cannot intelligently oppose it. It is humiliating to me to find that any of my people can be so misled on the question of equality.

Notes

1 Mary Church Terrell Papers: Speeches and Writings, 1866–1953; Undated; "Why We Need the Equal Rights Amendment," Library of Congress, Manuscript Division. Public Domain. We estimate that Terrell drafted this rejoinder to Funn at some point in 1944.

2 Karlyn Kohrs Campbell, "Mary Church Terrell," in *Women Public Speakers in the United States, 1925–1993: A Bio-Critical Sourcebook*, ed. Karlyn Kohrs Campbell (Westport, CT: Greenwood Press, 1994), 108–19.

3 Mary Church Terrell, "What It Means to be Colored in the Capital of the U.S.," 1906, Oberlin College Archives, Mary Church Terrell Papers, Series VII, Speeches by Mary Church Terrell, Box 6, http://dcollections.oberlin.edu/cdm/singleitem/collection/p15963coll16/id/566/rec/1.

4 Elisabeth Griffith, *Formidable: American Women and the Fight for Equality, 1920–2020* (New York: Pegasus Books, 2022), 41. For an in-depth study, see Evette Dionne, *Lifting as We Climb: Black Women's Battle for the Ballot Box* (New York: Viking, 2020).

5 Alison M. Parker, *Unceasing Militant: The Life of Mary Church Terrell* (Chapel Hill: University of North Carolina Press, 2020), 261.

6 Mary Church Terrell Papers: Speeches and Writings, 1866–1953; 1948, March 10, *Testimony Before the House Judiciary Committee on the Equal Rights Amendment*, Library of Congress Manuscript/Mixed Material, https://www.loc.gov/item/mss425490507/.

7 Democrat Guy M. Gillette represented Iowa in the U.S. House of Representatives for two terms and later served two non-successive terms in the U.S. Senate between 1936 and 1955.

8 Democrat Louis Leon Ludlow represented Indiana in the U.S. House of Representatives between 1929 and 1949.

9 Democrat Arthur Patrick "Pat" Cannon represented Florida in the U.S. House of Representatives between 1939 and 1947.

Those Great Pioneers of 1848

Address to the Senate Judiciary Committee

NORA BARNEY
September 28, 1945[1]

As the first woman to earn a degree in Civil Engineering from Cornell University, English-born Nora Stanton Blatch Barney (1883–1971) continued the work begun by her grandmother, Elizabeth Cady Stanton, and her mother, Harriot Stanton Blatch. Barney was the first woman admitted to membership in the American Society of Civil Engineers (ASCE) and later unsuccessfully pursued a lawsuit to overturn the association's policy to only admit women as junior members. While the policy did not change for another decade, the ASCE did award Barney with posthumous Fellow status in 2015 to honor her contributions to the field of engineering.[2] Barney's first husband, engineer Lee De Forest, divorced her in 1911 and publicly attributed the dissolution of his marriage to "the fact that his wife . . . had persisted in following her career as a hydraulic engineer and an agitator for the cause in which her grandmother, Elizabeth Cady Stanton, was a pioneer, after the birth of her child."[3] Barney's second husband, naval architect Morgan Barney, seemed more confident in his wife's ability to balance motherhood with her career, which extended to architecture and real estate development until her death in 1971.

Although less remembered than her famous relatives, Nora Barney championed gender equality in her own right. Perhaps this work is best embodied in Barney's 1946 pamphlet *Women as Human Beings*, which challenged how protectionist arguments against the ERA relied upon certain conceptions of "femininity" to "stop a woman in her chosen field."[4] In 1892, Elizabeth Cady Stanton appeared before the all-male House Judiciary Committee to deliver her swansong address "The Solitude of Self" on behalf of women's rights. The speech was both a culmination of her advocacy and a call to action for the next generation to pick up the torch for women's equality.[5] More than 50 years later, Stanton's granddaughter did just that when she appeared before the same committee of all-male legislators to argue for the Equal Rights Amendment. Barney's testimony highlighted the irony that the most controversial part of the Seneca Falls Convention platform—the elective franchise—had already passed, yet all other resolutions connected to women's equality remained unsettled until the ERA passed.

Members of the Judiciary Committee, I want to take you back a moment, about 98 years ago, to the Seneca Falls Convention of 1848. Many resolutions urging that women be given complete equality with men were passed at that convention, at which Lucretia Mott and my grandmother, Elizabeth Cady Stanton, and Frederick Douglass were present.

Some of the members of the convention fell by the wayside due to the storm of opposition the next day, but those three and many others stood firm. I am happy to say that in the presence of Mrs. Terrell, a member of the national advisory committee of the National Woman's Party. She is honorary president of the National Association of Colored Women; she typifies the presence of Frederick Douglass and the spirit of Frederick Douglass with us here today.

Now, strange as it may seem, the ninth resolution that was passed at Seneca Falls was the only one that was not passed unanimously. That resolution called for votes for women. So it is strange, isn't it, that 25 years ago we passed the suffrage amendment about which there was disagreement at Seneca Falls, and only now are we advocating an amendment which would cover the other resolutions adopted there about which there was no disagreement.

One of those resolutions read that all laws which prevent a woman from occupying such a station in society as her conscience shall dictate or which place her in a position inferior to that of man are contrary to the great precepts of nature, and therefore of no force or authority.

Now, that is all the equal rights amendment is.

Nothing could have been broader than what those great pioneers of 1848 asked for. There is one other thing I want to mention, namely we want to get the cobwebs out of our minds in regard to the effect of this amendment on the marriage relationship and the relationship of parents to children.

There was one great [woman] who pronounced her opinion on this subject. I came across it in my grandmother's diary of November 13, 1880. Mrs. Stanton wrote:

> A few days before Lucretia Mott died, she sent this sentiment with her autograph to Clara Spence, head of the Great Clara Spence School in New York: "In the true marriage relation the independence of the husband and wife is equal, their dependence mutual, and their obligations reciprocal."[6]

What finer sentiment could one have; and that is all the equal rights amendment stands for.

One moment before I sit down because this subject has not been touched upon. Our opponents asked us to carry through these measures state by state. I tried that. I practically commuted to Albany for many years before the equal rights amendment was introduced in Washington. I commuted to Albany at the request of the women printers, the women proofreaders, the women elevator operators, the women waitresses, and the women transportation workers.

Did we find these organizations that are opposing the equal rights amendment helping us at Albany? No. The Women's Trade Union League, the Consumer's League, the heads of the unions, stood there and shook their fists in the face of the working women members, paying members of those unions who came and asked for equality and threatened to take their union cards away from them for daring to go against the edict of the head of the union. These groups that are opposing the equal rights amendment today have been the ones that opposed us state by state in our demands for justice for women.

Notes

1 Equal Rights Amendment, *Hearings on S.J. Res. 61, Before the Committee on the Judiciary*, 79th Cong. (1945) (Statement of Nora Stanton Barney). Public Domain.

2 Ben Walpole, "ASCE Recognizes Stanton Blatch Barney; Pioneering Civil Engineer, Suffragist," *ASCE News*, August 28, 2015, https://news.asce.org/asce-recognizes-stanton-blatch-barney-pioneering-civil-engineer-suffragist/.

3 "Lee De Forest Says Women Sacrifice Wifehood in Devotion to a Cause," *New York Times*, July 28, 1911, 18.

4 Elizabeth Cady Stanton Papers: Miscellany, 1840–1946; Speeches; Barney, Nora Stanton, "World Peace Through a Peoples Parliament," 1944 and "Women As Human Beings," 1946, Library of Congress, Manuscript/Mixed Material, https://www.loc.gov/item/mss412100160/.

5 Elizabeth Cady Stanton, "'The Solitude of Self': Speech to the House Judiciary Committee," February 18, 1892, https://voicesofdemocracy.umd.edu/the-solitude-of-self-speech-by-ecs-to-the-house-judiciary-committee-speech-text/.

6 See Elizabeth Titus, "Clara B. Spence: Ahead of Her Time," *Ms. Magazine*, March 6, 2015, https://msmagazine.com/2015/03/06/clara-b-spence-ahead-of-her-time/.

The Danger of This Generalization

Address to the House Judiciary Committee

MAIDA SPRINGER KEMP
September 28, 1945[1]

Dressmaker and labor activist Maida Stewart Springer Kemp (1910–2005), born in Panama, got her start with the International Ladies' Garment Workers' Union (ILGWU) organizing strikes and protests against dangerous working conditions, low wages, long hours, and obstacles to unionization. In the Local 22 chapter of the ILGWU, she honed her leadership skills and in 1945, she represented the American Federation of Labor and Congress of Industrial Organizations (AFL-CIO) in England to meet with women workers, observe their working conditions, and gather information for the U.S. Office of War Information Exchange.[2] The *Chicago Defender* reported that Kemp and the other three women delegates were guests of Queen Elizabeth II at Buckingham Palace, where they discussed wartime labor issues. This venture cemented Kemp's reputation as an international labor activist. Until her death, Kemp applied her talents as a transnational educator who lectured, consulted, participated in relief initiatives, and established training programs in union organizing across the African continent.[3]

The same year as her England trip, Kemp testified to the House Judiciary subcommittee in opposition to the ERA. Much like other progressive groups of this period, those in the ILGWU and other labor organizations feared the ERA would strip away hard-earned protections for women workers already achieved. Women workers, they worried, would be especially vulnerable to an amendment many viewed as specifically intended to advance the interests of white middle-class women. With these concerns in mind, the ILGWU's leadership elected Kemp to speak on behalf of the organization to an audience entirely made up of white male Congressmen.[4] A year later, the Senate defeated the ERA by a razor-thin margin of 38–35 votes. Several prominent labor organizations, including those to which Kemp belonged, did not formally support the ERA until the 1970s. The AFL-CIO did not endorse the ERA until 1973, nearly 30 years after Kemp's testimony.

Mr. Chairman, my remarks, of necessity, are going to be brief because the hour is late, but, coming from several minorities as I do—a woman, a Negro, and a few others—I represent an organization of 325,000 members—the International Ladies' Garment Workers' Union. Eighty-five percent of that membership is female. Those of us in that organization who have helped and who have come into the organization and benefited by much of the legislation protective to women—the social gains, the economic gains—are certainly very definitely opposed to the equal rights amendment.

On the other hand, aside from my organization affiliations, I listened this morning raptly to many of the ladies here who so eloquently went down the line on democracy.

Now, democracy is a phrase carried on in principle. There is no more beautiful document than the Declaration of Independence, but in actual practice it falls short.

To me, a generalization of another bill—this equal rights amendment—can have the beautiful flowery language, but the practical application, no.

We fight so very hard for each individual and specific gain we make that I am one of those, along with the hundreds and thousands—yes, millions—of women, of industrial women particularly, in America, who do not want to see a generalization of the law take us back many, many years.

We industrial people who work for a living, who know what a factory means, who also know, as minorities, what our economic plight can mean, are against this amendment, and hope, in your considered judgment, gentlemen, since you do know the law so well, and since you do know how bitterly we fight for each individual gain we make, that you see the danger of this generalization in the equal rights amendment.

Notes

1 *Joint Resolution Proposing an Amendment to the Constitution of the United States Relative to Equal Rights for Men and Women, Equal Rights Amendment, Hearing Before a Subcommittee of the Committee on the Judiciary*, Day 1, 79th Senate (1945) (Statement from Maida Kemp). Public Domain.

2 Yevette Richards, *Maida Springer: Pan-Africanist and International Labor Leader* (Pittsburgh: University of Pittsburgh Press, 2000), 57–76.
3 George Padmore, "Women Trade Unionists Visit Queen of England," *Chicago Defender*, April 7, 1945, 6.
4 Richards, *Maida Springer*, 67.

The "Un-Equal" Rights Amendment

Editorial for the Chicago Defender

REBECCA STILES TAYLOR
March 8, 1947[1]

Rebecca Stiles Taylor (1879–1958) hailed from Savannah, Georgia as a trailblazing and unsung African American journalist, educator, lecturer, and social worker. She grew up under Southern segregation and graduated in 1896 from Savannah's Beach Institute, a school established at the end of the Civil War to educate freed slaves.[2] For nearly 30 years, Taylor taught English and grammar at Cuyler Junior High School and later took her pedagogical expertise to Bethune-Cookman College, where she served as the school's Dean of Women. In 1918, Taylor founded the Savannah chapter of the Federation of Colored Women's Clubs and two years later with Mary McLeod Bethune, she expanded her efforts to form the Southeast Association of Colored Women's Club.[3] Their efforts were part of the broader NACW Club Movement seeking to combat lynching and segregation, as well as to create opportunities for women of color to organize and discuss other issues of vital importance to them.[4] Taylor used her journalistic platform to call "upon the women to take their rightful places in the vanguard of civilization and not be satisfied with duties in the home, the church, and the local clubs."[5] Her great niece, the Rev. Saundra Stiles Thomas, remembered Taylor fondly in 2015: "A lot of people were afraid of Aunt Rebecca, because she didn't play."[6]

In 1937, the *Chicago Defender* hired Taylor as a columnist. The *Defender* was founded in 1905 as the premier national newspaper written by and for African Americans. Taylor's column largely focused on amplifying the purpose, beliefs, and activities of the Black women's club movement. Her 1947 editorial detailed the position of the Congress of American Women on the ERA. The Congress, founded in 1946 and disbanded in 1950, was an integrated coalition of members committed to women's liberation. Because of its Communist ties, the Congress eventually came under fire at the hands of Senator Joseph McCarthy's House Un-American Activities Committee.[7] As Taylor's column conveyed, the Congress's members widely believed that the ERA would erase the differences between the sexes. Accordingly, the women of the Congress proposed their own version of a federal amendment focused on ending sex-based discrimination.[8]

Every woman knows that she is a human being and wants the rights, and to be treated with the dignity of a human being. Yet, according to the laws in the various states of our nation, woman when she marries ceases to exist as a person.

Principles of Common Law

There are still hangovers of the feudal common law theory that marriages destroy a woman's identity. These are some of the principles of common law: Personal property of a woman becomes the property of her husband. The duty imposed on a wife is to render service to her husband, [and] her earnings from services to third persons belong to him. She is unable to engage in trade or business in her own name. The wife's wearing apparel and personal ornaments during marriage are the property of her husband. The proceeds of the industry of husband and wife belong to the husband. The husband has the right of recovery for injury to the wife for the resulting loss of her earning power and assistance. The father is the natural guardian of the minor child and has the sole right to appoint a guardian. On marrying, a woman loses her own domicile and acquires that of her husband. The will of a woman is revoked by her marriage and a married woman cannot make a valid will. Women may not become administrators or guardians after marriage. Women are not qualified to sit on either grand or trial juries.

The Fight for Women's Freedoms

In 1848, the first woman's rights convention was held. It began the struggle against the restrictions imposed upon women by the COMMON LAW. As a result, the married woman today does not live under the complete legal blackout created for her by the ancient feudal system. The struggle goes on today because in all states some of the old common law restrictions exist. In fact, there were in 1946 still about 1,000 state laws that discriminate against women. For example, 17 states discriminate against women as jurors: In 41 states the private domicile of a married woman depends on that of her husband. Only if dissolution of the marriage becomes necessary, are her separate existence, interests and rights recognized.

Four states limit the general contracts of a married woman. Five states make void the wife's conveyance of her separate real estate. Eight states give the husband control during marriage of all the common property without regard to the wife's contributions. Five states require a married woman to have court authorization to conduct a business of her own account. Three states require the husband's consent for the wife to engage in business and for her to keep her earnings from it. Six states include the personal earnings of the wife in the common estate, which is by law under the husband's control. Fifteen states give women a right to separate property but do not define personal earnings as separate property when living with her husband. Five states restrict appointment of women as administrators or guardians. Six states restrict such appointments of women upon their marriage. In three states the will of a woman is revoked by her marriage. In one state a husband may recover the value of her services for injury to a married woman's person.

Other Common Laws

There are, however, in all states acts for which even a woman who is something less than a human being, is capable and can be held responsible, that is, committing a crime. If she commits it in the presence of her husband, it is presumed that she did it under constraint by him and he is presumably punishable.

Secondary Human Beings

As long as these anti-woman laws exist in any of the states of our country, they perpetuate the theory that women are secondary human beings. As long as women lack freedom to control their own earnings in Georgia, the women of Pennsylvania are not free. Elimination of these laws is, therefore, a basic step toward women's rights to be a free and equal human being. Elimination of these laws is necessary, so that women can pursue the paths which lead to usefulness and honor, and so lay the basis for full economic, political and social freedom.

Beneficial Laws

It must be stressed, however, that there are many laws in the states that protect women, beneficial labor laws that have been fought for by labor and by women since 1847 when the first maximum hours law was passed. Laws in the states regulating hours, wages, and other working conditions of women are essential and vital factors in raising the economic status of women. These important women's laws would be wiped out completely if the so-called "EQUAL RIGHTS" Amendment were passed. The "UNEQUAL RIGHTS" amendment of the National Woman's Party is a direct attack on the working women. It seeks to end all differentiations between the sexes.

Congress of American Women

The Congress of American Women seeks to end only the discriminations against women. The "UNEQUAL RIGHTS" amendment is based on the unscientific and fallacious assumption that women are men. By this amendment, for example, any legislation giving maternity aid to women would be illegal because there is no maternity aid for men.

BE IT RESOLVED: That the Congress of American Women offer a new amendment to the Constitution of the United States which would provide the following: "There shall be no discrimination against women because of sex or marital status economically, legally, politically and socially in the United States of America and in territories subject to its jurisdiction. Nothing in this article shall be so construed as to invalidate or prevent the passage of legislation improving the condition of women in their work or in their family status."

Notes

1 Rebecca Stiles Taylor, "Federated Clubs," *Chicago Defender*, March 8, 1947, 17. Reprinted with permission from Reverend Saundra Stiles Thomas.
2 "Timeline," Beach Institute, https://www.beachinstitute.org/timeline.
3 "Georgia Women of Achievement Posthumously Honors Rebecca Stiles Taylor," *Savannah Tribune*, March 26, 2014, https://www.savannahtribune.com/articles/georgia-women-of-achievement-posthumously-honors-rebecca-stiles-taylor/; "Rebecca Stiles Taylor," Georgia Women of Achievement, https://www.georgiawomen.org/rebecca-stiles-taylor.
4 "About NACWC," National Association of Colored Women, https://www.nacwc.com/history; Stephanie J. Shaw, "Black Club Women and the Creation of the National Association of Colored Women," *Journal of Women's History* 3, no. 2 (1991): 11–25.

5 "Mrs. Rebecca Stiles Taylor Hurls Challenge to Women," *Alabama Tribune*, August 3, 1951, 4.

6 Emily Jones, "Forgotten Women Part 7: Rebecca Stiles Taylor," *Georgia Public Broadcasting*, December 8, 2015, https://www.gpb.org/news/2015/12/08/forgotten-women-part-7-rebecca-stiles-taylor.

7 Kate Wiegand, *Red Feminism: American Communism and the Making of Women's Liberation* (Baltimore: Johns Hopkins University Press, 2001), especially Chapter 3.

8 "Rebecca Stiles Taylor," Georgia Women of Achievement.

Democracy Is Fighting for Its Very Life

Address to the House Judiciary Committee

CAROLINE KATZENSTEIN
March 10, 1948[1]

When he wrote about suffragist Caroline Katzenstein (1888–1968) in 1916, journalist David J. Galter concluded that "some day when the story is written of the struggle of women of the Keystone State for their enfranchisement, due credit will be given to her who has done more for that cause than all her Jewish sisters in the state, and almost as much as the most active among non-Jewish workers."[2] Born in North Carolina, Katzenstein was heavily involved in the national suffrage campaign from 1910 to 1920 in Pennsylvania, first as a member of the NAWSA and then later as Executive Secretary of the NWP. Katzenstein, Alice Paul, and Lucy Burns organized Philadelphia's first open-air suffrage meeting without a police permit; thus, they faced the prospect of arrest—or worse. "We came, we saw, we conquered!" Katzenstein declared when the July 1911 event proceeded peacefully and some 300 people gathered.[3]

Despite Paul's appeals, Katzenstein did not enjoy public speaking for the suffrage cause.[4] She preferred to spend her time organizing unsanctioned meetings, engaging in nonviolent protest, and using her connections to solicit sympathetic press coverage of suffrage activities at both the state and national levels.[5] Katzenstein was among the Silent Sentinels outside the White House, though she was never arrested there or for burning President Wilson's effigy in the 1919 NWP Watchfire Demonstrations.[6] Among her greatest contributions to the suffrage cause was her vivid and comprehensive documentation of the violent treatment endured by the jailed suffragists, which she later published in 1955 as *Lifting the Curtain: The State and National Woman Suffrage Campaigns in Pennsylvania As I Saw Them.*[7]

For nearly 50 years, Katzenstein fought for the Equal Rights Amendment, though far less is known about her advocacy on this front in comparison to her suffrage work. During the 1950s and 1960s, she juggled her insurance career with a letter-writing campaign to politicians and presidents of both parties who either opposed the ERA or who supported the amendment without doing much of consequence to advance it. Harry Truman, Dwight D. Eisenhower, John F. Kennedy, Richard Nixon, Senator Robert A. Taft (R-OH), and Senator Joseph S. Clark Jr. (D-PA) all received letters from Katzenstein.[8] A quarter century after the ERA was introduced in Congress, the former suffragist testified in its favor. Her 1948 testimony struck a balance between flattering and shaming the male decision-makers, and her frustration at the ERA's shaky status in postwar America was palpable. The allure of the ERA, she insisted, was that it stood poised to elevate the nation's global standing and calm lingering fears that democracy remained under assault.

I hope, gentlemen, you realize that we feel genuinely humiliated in having to come to you, representatives of the leading democratic country in the world, to ask that unfair discrimination be removed from half of the citizens of the country. It should not be necessary to have to ask this, should it?

Not only are the women of the United States looking to you to give their plea for justice your needed support, but the eyes of women all over the world are focused upon you at this critical time. What you do for the equal rights amendment will be an historic record, one that may, I hope, add luster to your name in the future annals of our country.

It is, I believe, because I am in a way a small link between the yesterday and the today of our present campaign that I have been asked to take part in this hearing. It was in 1910 that the women of Pennsylvania opened in the center of Philadelphia their first woman suffrage headquarters and I had the privilege of serving as its executive secretary.

Now, to come to the present, we are living in an unhappy time. Greed, prejudice, misunderstanding, and fear stalk the world. We hear discussed openly the possibility of a third World War, and it has been suggested that in case of such an emergency it would be necessary to conscript not only men, but women and children as well.

In other words, democracy is fighting for its very life, and the tools of war today are so terrific that their use might mean the destruction of all civilization. In a desperate effort to save the democratic way of life, the United States is spending millions of dollars in foreign countries. Would not this work be more effective and our arguments more convincing if we could also show these countries that we practice what we preach and that we have written into our own Constitution full and complete equality for all, women as well as men.

In the struggle ahead of us we need the best that each citizen can give. I beg of you to relieve us of the necessity to spend more precious time, energy, and money on our campaign for equality of opportunity for women.

Over long years we have shown what patience, determination, and courage women have and we now ask you to release this energy for other effective work that now cries out to be done. We are ready to do our share of the world's work, too. I ask that you not keep us waiting.

Thank you.

Notes

1 *Equal Rights Amendment to the Constitution and Commission on the Legal Status of Women, Hearings Before a Subcommittee on the Judiciary*, Day 1, Eightieth Congress (1948) (Statement of Caroline Katzenstein). Public Domain.
2 David J. Galter, "Jewish Immigrant Girls Praised for Suffrage Work," *American Jewish Chronicle*, vol. 1, no. 25, November 3, 1916, 797.
3 J.D. Zahniser and Amelia R. Fry, *Alice Paul: Claiming Power* (New York: Oxford University Press, 2014), 120; see also Caroline Katzenstein, *Lifting the Curtain: The State and National Woman Suffrage Campaigns in Pennsylvania As I Saw Them* (Philadelphia: Dorrance & Company, 1955), 45.
4 Zahniser and Fry, *Alice Paul*, 121.
5 "'Lift the Curtain': Suffrage Leader Seeks Equal Rights," *Philadelphia Inquirer*, August 14, 1955, 10.
6 Melissa R. Klapper, *Ballots, Babies, and Banners of Peace: American Jewish Women's Activism, 1890–1940* (New York: New York University Press, 2013), 47; Susan Ware, *American Women's Suffrage: Voices from the Long Struggle for the Vote 1776–1965* (New York: Penguin Random House, 2020), 533.
7 Katzenstein, *Lifting the Curtain.*
8 Caroline Katzenstein Papers, Historical Society of Pennsylvania, November 2008, 3, https://hsp.org/sites/default/files/legacy_files/migrated/findingaidam8996katzenstein.pdf.

The Phony Equal Rights Amendment Again

Editorial for the Daily Worker

ELIZABETH GURLEY FLYNN
March 9, 1950[1]

The career of "Rebel Girl" Elizabeth Gurley Flynn (1890–1964) spanned more than a half century. Radical activism was in the blood of this New Hampshire-born labor leader, whose forward-thinking parents embraced socialism and feminism. In 1907, Flynn joined the newly formed Industrial Workers of the World (IWW), an international worker-led labor organization still going strong today. She helped found the ACLU in 1920 and joined the Communist Party a decade later. All the while, she spoke and wrote prolifically. She later estimated that she had delivered some 10,000 speeches—sometimes several within a single day—across her career.[2]

Flynn's extensive rhetorical and political activities led to several run-ins with the law throughout her life. Her troubles began with charges of sedition and espionage during World War I and culminated in a two-year prison term for charges of violating the Alien Registration Act of 1940, which rendered it illegal to participate in any activities designed to overthrow the U.S. government. During the lengthy trial, Flynn represented herself and delivered impassioned orations in her own defense. Flynn continued her affiliation with the Communist Party and served as its first woman national chairperson beginning in 1961. She died in Moscow, where she was honored with a state funeral. Even in death, Flynn remains a controversial figure. In 2023, Republicans in Concord, New Hampshire balked at a roadside marker installed to honor Flynn. The marker was swiftly removed.[3]

This editorial from Flynn appeared in the *Daily Worker*, the official Communist newspaper that reached upwards of 50,000 readers at its circulation peak. For several years, Flynn regularly penned a popular column for the *Daily Worker* and used this platform to publicize her messages about labor, women's rights, and freedom of speech.[4] As to the ERA, she opposed it on several grounds, including fears that women might be required to pay alimony to their ex-husbands, concerns that elderly women would face financial discrimination if they had never worked, and worries about how the amendment would affect penalties for rape. Like many other protectionists of this era, Flynn preferred unionization as the best mechanism for ensuring women's equality.[5] In keeping with her "rebel" style, Flynn's entry provides an unabashedly cynical take on the ERA and the motives of those behind it.

Plain words like "free," "open," [and] "equal" have clear meanings to honest people. But in the mouths of employers and politicians they become double talk, like free enterprise, open shop, equal rights. This is true of the misnamed equal rights amendment which annually pops out of the hopper of Congress.

Platitudes 27 years old are repeated by reactionaries posing as progressives, and Dixiecrats exposing their insulating Jim Crow chivalry. Lawmakers who turn a deaf ear to legislation on health, housing, and education become ardent champions of the ladies. God bless them.

They are all engaged in an attempt to pass a blanket amendment which will wipe out all protective labor legislation for women workers; all social legislation beneficial to women as wives, mothers, or widows; and this under the hypocritical guise of equality.

This equal rights amendment has from the birth been endorsed by the Republican Party, the National Manufacturers Association, by big employers like the Du Ponts, by state's righters. There have been 26 hearings on this bill since 1923. Its direct sponsor is the National [Woman's] Party, an extreme feminist group, which believes even rape laws should apply equally to both sexes. It is endorsed by the National Federation of Business and Professional Women's Clubs and similar middle- and upper-class groups. It has been opposed by the AFL and CIO and by every progressive women's organization, as well as by the Women's Bureau of the Department of Labor and 21 leading law schools.

That it is introduced voluntarily by reactionaries every year without any public demand, makes it suspect. With the heat on Congress through tremendous mass pressure to repeal Taft-Hartley,[6] to guarantee civil rights, to pass FEPC,[7] or to abolish the poll tax, these same Senators show no such sense of haste nor public duty. Incidentally, Senator Wiley, who favors the Mundt bill, is a loud advocate of the equal rights amendment, and Senator Kefauver (who presented a good substitute for it) is rumored to be opposed to the Mundt bill, if he does not weaken.[8]

Early in the session on January 25, Senate Joint Resolution 25 reintroduced the equal rights amendment. It passed 63 to 19. The opposition, ably voiced by Senators Lehman, Morse, Neely, and Hayden, resulted in the acceptance, by a vote of 51 to 31, of the Hayden amendment, providing that "no rights, benefits, or exemptions, now or hereafter conferred, on women shall be impaired."[9] This was opposed by sponsors of the blanket amendment and angrily criticized by the National [Woman's] Party, which said that all forthright supporters would be alienated by such a rider. This speaks for itself. They are not interested so much in giving women future rights as they are to deprive women of present real benefit and protections guaranteed by existing laws, which their amendment would nullify.

The case against the blanket equal rights amendment was ably set forth by a statement of the National Committee on the Status of Women. It contended that every law dealing with the manifold relations of women to society would be forced to run the gauntlet of attack on constitutional grounds, as, for instance, legal provisions for widow's allowances, family support, grounds for divorce, annulment of marriage, and maximum hours for women in protected industries.

"Many laws protecting safety and welfare of women in industry would necessarily fall," it points out. "Protective legislation would be declared invalid as denying women equal right to work or as denying men equal protection under law, as either could claim exact equality."

It sums up that "the basic fallacy in the proposed amendment is that it attempts to deal with complicated and highly concrete problems arising out of a diversity of human relations in terms of a single and simple abstraction." They label it as "hopelessly inept as a constitutional standard," and prophesy that "an era of regrettable consequences is highly probable. Extreme confusion in constitutional law is a certainty."

The legislation now goes to the House. The danger is that the Hayden amendment will be chopped off there or disappear in the final agreement on proposed legislation between the two legislative bodies. Senator Hunt let the cat out of the bag when he said: "During the war many barriers were dropped entirely. Do not allow them to return."

In other words, this equality is part of the cold war, in preparation for a hot war. Labor laws relative to women were suspended during the war and employers want that suspension made permanent. Warmongers want women equal to be able to draft them into the Armed Forces, for civilian defense, or for compulsory labor.

These are the hidden motives behind the equal rights amendment. We must not rely on the passage of the Hayden amendment, although it sounds well intentioned. Progressive men and women are opposed to all forms of discrimination against women or men. But to classify labor and social legislation as discrimination against women benefits only employers and all who exploit women.

Let your congressman hear from you in plain words rebuking this double talk in relation to equal rights and demanding the defeat of this phony bill.

Notes

1 At the request of pro-ERA Emma Guffey Miller, Flynn's 1950 article was included in the transcripts of *Hearings Before a Subcommittee of the Committee on the Judiciary, United States Senate, Proposing an Amendment to the Constitution of the United States Relative to Equal Rights for Men and Women*, Day 2, 84th Congress (1956) ("The Phony Equal Rights Amendment Again"). Miller's purpose was to illustrate that the anti-ERA position had troubling Communist backing. Public Domain.

2 Mari Boor Tonn and Mark S. Kuhn, "Elizabeth Gurley Flynn," in *Women Public Speakers in the United States, 1925–1993: A Bio-Critical Sourcebook*, ed. Karlyn Kohrs Campbell (Westport, CT: Greenwood Press, 1994), 221–37.

3 Remy Tumin, "New Hampshire Honored a 'Rebel Girl.' Then It Found Out She Was a Communist," *New York Times*, May 17, 2023, https://www.nytimes.com/2023/05/17/us/elizabeth-gurley-flynn-marker-communist.html.

4 Lara Vapnek, *Elizabeth Gurley Flynn: Modern American Revolutionary* (Boulder, CO: Westview Press, 2015), 128.

5 Helen C. Camp, *Iron Her Soul: Elizabeth Gurley Flynn and the American Left* (Pullman: Washington State University Press, 1995), 176.

6 The Taft-Hartley Act, or the Labor-Management Relations Act, controversially passed in 1947 and imposed cumbersome restrictions on labor unions that included stifling certain free speech activities such as boycotting, picketing, and striking. See Dale Mineshema-Lowe, "Taft-Hartley Act of 1947 (1947)," *Free Speech Center*, Middle Tennessee State University, September 19, 2023, https://firstamendment.mtsu.edu/article/taft-hartley-act-of-1947-1947/.

7 President Franklin D. Roosevelt established the Fair Employment Practices Commission (FEPC) in June 1941 to abolish discrimination practices related to race, religion, and nationality that might interfere with war work. Flynn refers here to the ultimately unsuccessful efforts to make the FEPC permanent after the end of World War II. Sex was noticeably absent from the wartime FEPC. See Eileen Boris, "Fair Employment and the Origins of Affirmative Action in the 1940s," *NWSA Journal* 10, no. 3 (1998): 142–51.

8 Here, Flynn criticizes Senator Alexander Wiley (R-WI), an ERA supporter, by noting his support of the "Mundt bill," otherwise known as the "Subversive Activities Control Act." Proposed in 1948 by Representatives Karl Mundt (R-SD) and

Richard Nixon (R-CA), the controversial bill required Communist Party organizations to register with the U.S. government as a protective measure against suspected "un-American" activities. Some viewed the bill as a vital and urgently needed measure to protect the country against Communist infiltration, while others—like Flynn—read it as a deeply troubling violation of civil liberties.

9 On its face, Senator Carl Hayden's (D-AZ) proposed 1950 "rider" (or provision) promised that no existing protective legislation for women would be harmed, compromised, or erased by ERA. And yet, many ERA opponents interpreted the rider as not only an unreliable attempt to mollify them in the short-term, but also—more seriously—as a divisive strategy meant to impede further investigation into the consequences of the amendment if passed. See Mary Frances Berry, *Why ERA Failed: Politics, Women's Rights, and the Amending Process of the Constitution* (Bloomington: Indiana University Press, 1986), 60.

There Is No Short Road to Freedom

Editorial for Civil Liberties

DOROTHY KENYON
April 1953[1]

A family trip to Mexico as a young woman exposed Judge Dorothy Kenyon (1888–1972) to the dire living conditions of the locals and sparked in her a life-long commitment to public service. The Smith College and New York University Law School alumna led a distinguished life as a suffragist, legal scholar, and formidable advocate for equal rights. Between 1938 and 1940, Kenyon served on the League of Nations Committee on the Legal Status of Women and later served as the first U.S. delegate to the U.N. Commission on the Status of Women. Kenyon made history when she submitted the "first resolution ever on equal pay for women to be introduced in the United Nations"—a resolution that drew "unanimous support" from all representative countries.[2] For more than 40 years, Kenyon labored on the National Board for the ACLU, to which she lent her expertise by authoring legal briefs on sex discrimination, championing equal pay for women, and pushing for the ACLU to defend abortion and birth control.[3] Kenyon's work with the ACLU prompted Senator Joseph R. McCarthy to accuse her of Communist affiliations in 1950. But Kenyon did not take the charge sitting down and retorted that the Wisconsin Republican was "an unmitigated liar" and a "coward to take shelter in the cloak of Congressional immunity."[4] Unlike so many others, Kenyon emerged largely unscathed from the charges—no doubt due to her brilliant legal mind and bold language.

Like Florence Kelley and earlier protectionists, Dorothy Kenyon worried about the legal implications of the ERA, which led her to oppose the amendment for much of her professional career. In particular, she worried about the ambiguity of the word "equality" and the related question of what standards or criteria must be reached for equality to be achieved. Between the 1920s and

1950s, Kenyon campaigned against the ERA in several forums. She testified in opposition before the subcommittee of the Senate Judiciary Committee in 1929. She represented the anti-ERA position in radio debates for the National Federation of Business and Professional Women's Clubs. She spoke against the ERA at universities. And she penned anti-ERA editorials, such as the one for the ACLU's monthly publication *Civil Liberties* included here.[5]

By the 1960s and 1970s, Kenyon reversed course on the ERA. In 1969, the National Organization for Women (NOW) finally persuaded the Equal Employment Opportunity Commission (EEOC) to interpret Title VII of the 1964 Civil Rights Act—which prohibits discrimination against someone on the basis of race, color, religion, sex, and national origin—"as a measure that prohibited special labor laws for women only."[6] For protectionists like Kenyon and her colleague Pauli Murray, this proved a vital turn of events that shifted their thinking about the amendment's promise. More pointedly, Kenyon had grown discouraged after losing a series of sex discrimination cases with an innovative, yet unsuccessful legal strategy that drew upon the Equal Protection Clause from Section 1 of the Fourteenth Amendment. "It's worthy passing the equal rights amendment, if only to stir up the men," she wrote to a friend just two years before her death.[7]

"Fundamental freedoms for all, without distinction as to race, sex, language or religion"—(*from the Charter of the United Nations*).

Women have come a long way in their fight for equal freedoms. Segregated and snubbed at the London Anti-Slavery Conference over a century ago, they have turned the tables since then with a vengeance. Now, in the words of an optimistic Georgia court, while the husband is still the head of the household, like the King of England, he is largely a figurehead.

That court, however, is a shade too optimistic. There are still large gaps in our freedoms and none have been gained without a struggle. Women first won the right to vote in this country in Wyoming in 1869. Yet it was not until 1920 that universal suffrage was finally obtained.

The right to serve on juries is also glacially slow in coming. An obligation of citizenship no less than the right to vote, there would seem to be no possible objection to it, except the dead hand of habit and inertia. Yet six states still limit jury service to men—Alabama, Georgia, Mississippi, South Carolina, Texas and West Virginia—and more than half of those states which have granted jury service to women have made it permissive instead of compulsory, an unnecessary gallantry which might well be left to the judges. Since the legislatures of all the six states mentioned above meet in 1953, except Mississippi, it is hoped that some of them may see the light and join the procession.

Equal pay for comparable work is another right that, surprisingly enough, has to be fought for. While this country has a much better record in this respect than many of the European countries, it is nevertheless true that there prevails throughout the world a consistent pattern of payments to women for the same or comparable work at lower rates than to men. Six states now have equal pay laws, bills to that effect are now pending in six other states, and there is also a federal bill pending which would cover workers in interstate commerce and which would lodge enforcement powers in the U.S. Department of Labor.

Those who find this blow-by-blow method of progression toward freedom too slow are advocating, as they have for many years, [for] a so-called Equal Rights Amendment to the Constitution of the United States providing that "equality of rights under the laws shall not be denied or abridged . . . on account of sex."

While applauding the general objective, the ACLU has long opposed this particular amendment because of its fear that the amendment as phrased would freeze "mathematical" equality into the Constitution by depriving the government of the power to enact differential legislation if and when needed to achieve true equality. There are areas, particularly in the fields of support and labor laws, where differential legislation may at any given time effect more exact *actual* equality than any *mathematically equal* laws could possibly do.

While the matter is now of much less practical importance than it was a few years ago, when women were much more exploited in the labor market than they are today and when labor legislation for men was all too often declared unconstitutional, the distinction is nevertheless an important one and the police power worth preserving for the purpose. Differential legislation, non-discriminatory but on the contrary equalizing in its effect (such as the income tax law), can be a valuable tool for freedom and should not be lightly thrown into the discard.

Perhaps a better way of going about this particular amendment (if we must have an amendment at all) would be to import into the equal protection clauses of the Fourteenth Amendment some of the language of the U.N. Charter quoted above—"without discrimination as to sex," etc.

But basically, there is no short road to freedom, and this amendment is no exception to the rule. The greatest inequalities, the greatest discriminations against women, exist not in law but in habit and custom. Unequal pay is not a matter of right at all, and the amendment, limited as it is to "rights under the law," would not touch it. Service on juries may be a right but it is even more certainly an obligation. And so it goes. Blanket provisions may sound pleasant and give us hope, but for practical purposes are largely illusory.

The battle for women's rights is part of the larger battle of peoples everywhere for freedom. It will be waged and won partly by legislation, partly by constitutional amendment, but most of all by changing people's habits of thought. That process is well underway.

Notes

1 Dorothy Kenyon, "Equal Rights for Women," *Civil Liberties*, April 1953. Retrieved from Smith College, "Agents of Social Change: An Online Exhibit Displaying New Resources on 20th Century Women's Activism," Dorothy Kenyon, https://www.smith.edu/libraries/libs/ssc/agents/kenyon.html. Reprinted with permission from the Smith College Archives. Special thanks to archivist Elizabeth Myers for her assistance.

2 Deborah J. Vagins and Tyler Ray, "ACLU and the Equal Pay Act of 1963: Celebrating 50 Years of Advocacy," *ACLU*, June 6, 2013, https://www.aclu.org/news/womens-rights/aclu-and-equal-pay-act-1963-celebrating-50-years-advocacy.

3 Leigh Ann Wheeler, "Where Else but Greenwich Village? Love, Lust, and the Emergence of the American Civil Liberties Union's Sexual Rights Agenda, 1920–1931," *Journal of the History of Sexuality* 21, no. 1 (2012): 60–92, quotation on 68.

4 "Judge Dorothy Kenyon Is Dead: Champion of Social Reform, 83," *New York Times*, February 14, 1972, 32.

5 "Equal Rights Law Debated by Women," *Fort Worth Star-Telegram*, March 23, 1937, 4; "Women List Program of Legislation," *Democrat and Chronicle*, November 22, 1930, 12.

6 Rebecca DeWolf, *Gendered Citizenship: The Original Conflict over the Equal Rights Amendment, 1920–1963* (Lincoln: University of Nebraska Press, 2021), 226.

7 Julie C. Suk, *We the Women: The Unstoppable Mothers of the Equal Rights Amendment* (New York: Skyhorse Publishing, 2020), 103.

Equality: Nothing More, Nothing Less

Address to the House of Representatives

KATHARINE ST. GEORGE
July 19, 1957[1]

After her cousin Franklin won the presidency, Republican Katharine Delano Price Collier St. George (1894–1983) withdrew from the political arena as a gesture of respect, only to come out in adamant opposition to his third term. The English-born Congresswoman representing New York proved a conservative, complex, and sometimes contradictory figure during her 18 years in the U.S. House of Representatives. St. George rejected the "feminist label" even as she worked tirelessly on issues for women's political and economic equality.[2] She is even credited with coining the phrase "equal pay for equal work."[3] St. George seized the opportunity when Representative Howard W. Smith (D-VA), an ERA supporter and segregationist, proposed the addition of the word "sex" in the Equal Employment Opportunity Section (Title VII) of the Civil Rights Act of 1964 in the hopes of blocking it. "We outlast you, we outlive you, we nag you to death. But we are entitled to this little crumb of equality. The addition of the little, terrifying word s-e-x will not hurt this legislation in any way," she argued in a floor speech directed to her colleagues.[4] Smith's plan backfired and his amendment ultimately passed. Title VII now forbids sex discrimination, among other kinds of discrimination, in employment.

Throughout her career, St. George aligned with the NWP and used her legislative clout to promote the amendment in the divided House. She struggled, and ultimately failed, to get the ERA to a floor vote in the 1950s thanks to the unrelenting anti-ERA efforts of Representative Emanuel Celler. St. George held traditional, and at times curiously cynical, views of womanhood that seem incongruous with her vocal support for equal pay and the ERA. "Most women would rather lie in bed all morning and play bridge all afternoon," she once told a reporter, before claiming that "a good mother in the home is twice as effective as one at a meeting."[5] In her 1957 House floor speech for the ERA, however, there was no trace of these offending views.[6] St. George positioned her arguments as an extension of Susan B. Anthony's legacy for women's rights—even though Anthony did not actually attend the Seneca Falls Convention and James Mott, husband of Lucretia Mott, presided over the gathering.

Mr. Speaker, on July 20, 1848, just 109 years ago, Susan B. Anthony presided over a meeting at Seneca Falls, N. Y., "to discuss the social, civil, and religious condition and rights of women."[7] As a result of that meeting the 19th Amendment was adopted in 1920, giving women the vote.

Today there is an amendment pending before this House, proposing an amendment to the Constitution of the United States relative to equal rights for men and women.

In looking over the life of Susan B. Anthony we find that the *Revolution*, her magazine, had as its motto these words: Men their rights and nothing more; women their rights and nothing less.

We always find any philosophy best stated briefly, and the more talk and verbiage we get the less we understand, and the less, to be brutally frank, we know what we are talking about.

In these very simple words Susan B. Anthony and her friends epitomized what the so-called equal rights amendment would do, and also answers the objections of those who claim it would take away necessary protection and special legislation needed by women.

First, she speaks of the rights of men and women. That is exactly what the amendment does. The title of the resolution reads: Proposing an amendment to the Constitution of the United States relative to equal rights for men and women.

Next, she wants both sexes to have their rights, nothing more and nothing less. These rights we spell out as being equality under the Constitution, nothing more or nothing less.

It is the fashion in some quarters to say: "Oh, I am all for equal pay for equal work." Well, you will never get it until you have full equality under the Constitution and under the law. You will never get it as long as you have second-class citizens, be they men or women, under the Constitution.

For those of us who are interested in and working for the equal rights amendment, the present session of Congress is bound to be somewhat frustrating.

As the sponsor of the amendment in the House of Representatives, I am always glad to find that the amendment is still a constant source of humorous writings on the part of many columnists and friends.

We are constantly told that the women of our country have all the money, all the power in the world, and that the American male is an unfortunate worm who toils ceaselessly for the female of the species without reward and without apparently even a kind word or a pat on the head. We are told that he will welcome the amendment or should—this is considered perfectly hilarious—because it would give him some rights and some semblance of equality which he does not now possess.

Well, the supporters of the amendment believe in equality, nothing more, nothing less. The opening sentence of the amendment reads: Equality of rights under the law shall not be abridged by the United States or by any state on account of sex.

If it is true that the women of America are so powerful and do control most of the wealth of the Nation, surely they should assume full responsibility and stop asking for special and unwarranted privileges. I do not happen to know many women who want or need these special privileges, and when we come to the matter of special legislation for the protection of special groups in the United States, the amendment will not change that at all. We have always had special groups who were protected under the law, notably our veterans, also the blind, the aged, the infirm, infants and others, so that argument is one of the most puerile of all.

The real problem is that, in my opinion, we will never get equal pay for equal work for women in this country until we have women acknowledged as citizens under the law and under the Constitution. It was Samuel Gompers who said in 1913: The industrial problems of women are not isolated but are inextricably associated with those of men.[8]

It is too bad that our modern labor leaders, many of them, do not appreciate the fundamental truth of this statement.

A very short time ago we passed a bill on the floor of this House to ensure the constitutional rights of some of our citizens, and a torrent of oratory is being poured out in the other body on the subject of second-class citizens.

Well, until a man's or a woman's rights are recognized under the Constitution and before the law, they are second-class citizens.

As to the question of special legislation for special persons or special categories of our citizens, we have always had it and always will have it, and the amendment will in no way interfere with it any more than the 19th Amendment did.

Notes

1 Katharine St. George, "Debate on Equality of Rights," Congressional Record—House, July 19, 1957, 11070. Public Domain.
2 Andrew Glass, "Katharine St. George Was Born, July 12, 1894," *Politico*, July 14, 2013, https://www.politico.com/story/2013/07/this-day-in-politics-094039.
3 Elisabeth Griffith, *Formidable: American Women and the Fight for Equality 1920–2020* (New York: Pegasus Books, 2022), 110.
4 "St. George, Katharine Price Collier," U.S. House of Representatives, https://history.house.gov/People/Listing/S/ST--GEORGE,-Katharine-Price-Collier-(S000764)/; Charles W. Whalen Jr., "Unlikely Hero: Judge Howard Smith Helped Give Women Equal Pay—Without Meaning To," *Washington Post*, January 2, 1984, A21.
5 Betty Beale, "Not a Woman's Country—Congresswomen," *Nashville Tennessean*, August 27, 1961, 56.
6 We have published the speech in its entirety up until St. George lists, at length, the full co-sponsors of the ERA in the House at this time.
7 See Women's Rights Convention, Lucy Stone and National American Woman Suffrage Collection, *The First Convention Ever Called to Discuss the Civil and Political Rights of Women, Seneca Falls, N.Y., July 19, 20, 1848*. Retrieved from the Library of Congress, https://www.loc.gov/item/27007548/.
8 Longtime activist and labor leader Samuel Gompers was "one of the architects of the labor movement." He served as the first president of the American Federation of Labor (AFL) beginning in 1886. See "Samuel Gompers," AFL-CIO, https://aflcio.org/about/history/labor-history-people/samuel-gompers.

Section III The Debate Shifts: 1960–1971

Nearly 40 years after its introduction to Congress, the Equal Rights Amendment remained in legislative limbo. For the first time since 1944, the amendment was conspicuously absent from the 1960 Democratic Party Platform thanks to urging by the well-organized protectionist opposition. A more open-ended endorsement of "legislation which will guarantee to women equality of rights under the law" appeared in its place.[1] The election of Massachusetts Senator John F. Kennedy did little to improve the ERA's standing. Kennedy aligned with the anti-ERA Women's Bureau coalition, in contrast to his Republican challenger Richard Nixon, who had issued a lukewarm endorsement of the ERA.[2] Kennedy also disappointed Democratic Party women by appointing only men to visible and important cabinet positions, despite precedents for doing so under the Roosevelt and Eisenhower administrations. In total, women held only 2.4% of the appointed positions in Kennedy's administration. Several initiatives between 1961 and 1963—such as legislation that supported creating day-care facilities and legislation that removed statutory limitations on women serving as military officers—nevertheless increased women's opportunities under Kennedy's all-to-brief tenure.[3] With their prospects concretely improving, many American women wondered if the ERA was merely a symbolic relic of yesteryear.

At the urging of his Assistant Secretary of Labor, former union lobbyist Esther Peterson, Kennedy appointed an historic President's Commission on the Status of Women (PCSW) in late 1961. The bipartisan PCSW was the Kennedy administration's principal effort to identify women's issues, improve their status, and promote their accomplishments. Accordingly, the persisting ERA question could not be ignored. The 26 commission members contemplated how the divisive amendment might shape their activity and, in turn, affect public perception of that activity. Peterson and Eleanor Roosevelt, two of the ERA's most prominent opponents, led the commission. A delegation of NWP members requested an audience with Kennedy, but Peterson dismissed the NWP as a "paper organization with no standing in substantial women's organizations." She advised that if Kennedy did agree to meet the delegation, he should remain "noncommittal" to endorsing the ERA outright.[4] In a sense, Peterson was correct. The NWP had stopped publishing its journal *Equal Rights* in 1954 and membership had seriously dwindled, leaving the ERA stranded with no organized campaign. In the end, the PCSW's final report advocated that protectionist laws for women be strengthened and took the position of "not now" on the ERA.

The report angered NWP members, and, thus, they dismissed the idea that any meaningful compromise had been reached on the ERA. Representatives Katharine St. George and Margaret Chase Smith, who launched a bid for the presidency in 1964, aired frustrations about the report's failure to prescribe solutions for sex discrimination.[5] Smith took aim at both the women who refuse to "give up special women's privileges in return for receiving equal rights" and the many "legislators [who] give lip service to the Equal Rights Amendment but do not support it when the chips are down."[6] Had Smith's candidacy been successful, the ERA's status may have improved. But her election as the first woman president was not to be. Lyndon Johnson ensured the amendment stayed out of the 1964 Democratic Party platform and Republicans dropped the ERA from the 1968 platform.[7] For the time being, protectionists seemed to have again prevailed.[8]

And yet, important legal and cultural changes lit a fire under the women of America and shifted the ERA's trajectory as the decade progressed. The Food and Drug Administration made oral contraception, known as "the Pill," accessible to women across the nation beginning in 1960. The Women's Equal Pay Act (which failed to muster the necessary support to pass in 1945) remerged as the Equal Pay Act of 1963, the first federal legislation to forbid sex-based discrimination in employment. Smith College alumna and former journalist Betty Friedan surveyed her graduating class to gauge their level of satisfaction as housewives. Friedan published the results in a groundbreaking 1963 book called *The Feminine Mystique*, naming the dissatisfaction middle-class white women felt with domestic life. The book launched a national women's movement and breathed new life into the ERA debate.

The next year, Lyndon Johnson signed into law comprehensive civil rights legislation. Title VII of the 1964 Civil Rights Act established that employers could not discriminate on the basis of sex along with race, color, religion, and national origin. Title VII also established the Equal Employment Opportunity Commission (EEOC) to ensure this promised equality in employment came to fruition. Aileen Hernandez, the first woman to serve on the EEOC, eventually resigned due to the commission's slowness to handle the sex discrimination part of its charge. Women were especially aghast in 1966 when the EEOC upheld a status quo that permitted sex-segregated employment advertisements to continue. For these reasons, Hernandez and others looked for alternate ways to improve women's lives.[9]

An opportunity came when Betty Friedan and a diverse group of women—some from Kennedy's PCSW and nearly all strangers to one another—gathered in a hotel room and founded the National Organization for Women (NOW) in June 1966. NOW, as these women imagined it, would be a new, women-led pressure group guided by a radical founding principle: "to organize and advocate for all women by channeling their efforts into one association that sought to end male supremacy."[10] NOW's second national conference in 1967 was a remarkable, multigenerational gathering. Alice Paul, now in her eighties, and "two rows of elderly dignified women" representing the NWP arrived to ensure that this bold new women's organization embraced the ERA as part of its agenda.[11] They had, in fact, joined NOW to promote the amendment—a crucial fact, since there were young women in the room who had never heard about the ERA. NOW endorsements of both the ERA and abortion proved controversial. A few protectionist hold-outs exited the meeting in frustration, taking with them NOW's vital access to office space, printing, and mailing made available through the United Auto Workers.[12] But in the end, 82 members of NOW endorsed the ERA, with only three "no" votes and six abstentions. This new generation of feminists issued a resounding denunciation of the view that the time for the ERA was "not now." Unlike the single-minded NWP, however, NOW would pursue a broader agenda for achieving women's total and complete emancipation.[13]

Despite overdue legislative victories and new organizations, women understood that the long-standing, sex-based cultural attitudes underlying their unequal treatment in society could not be wiped away by a gathering, vote, or stroke of a pen. A young lawyer named Ruth Bader Ginsburg came to realize that the Equal Pay Act of 1963 had "passed, but it didn't sink in."[14] Rutgers School of Law hired Ginsburg in 1963 as one of only two women on the faculty. She still earned less than her male colleagues because her husband, a prominent tax attorney, had a well-paying job. Younger women like Ginsburg, as well as the older guard of women's rights activists, came to understand that the "decades-old bargain—in which women received modest access to political power as long as their methods were polite and their demands incremental—seemed like a bad deal."[15]

And so, unsatisfied with unfulfilled promises and limited advances, women demanded more. Might the ERA warrant new consideration? Some protectionists began to think so. By the end of her life, Eleanor Roosevelt had retreated in voicing her opposition, citing women's advances in unionization for the change in position. Black civil rights leader and attorney Pauli Murray expressed misgivings about the amendment but later took a different view of the amendment and testified in its favor. Dorothy Kenyon followed suit.[16] By 1971, Esther Peterson had also changed her mind, telling Representative Martha Wright Griffiths (D-MI) in a private letter that after "much soul searching," she had come to the difficult "conclusion that the time for waiting for court action is past and the enactment of the equal rights amendment would be a constructive step."[17] Organizations such as the League of Women Voters, the American Civil Liberties Union, and the American Federation of Labor and Congress of Industrial Organizations reversed course as well and came out in support of the amendment.[18] Some women, however, still remained skeptical. Future Supreme Court Justice Sandra Day O'Connor spent her time in the Arizona state legislature fighting for the ERA throughout the mid-1970s but articulated lingering doubts about the ERA in an earlier speech.

A key turning point in the ERA's history came in 1970, nearly 50 years after Senator Curtis and Representative Anthony first introduced the amendment in Congress. In the House, Martha Griffiths shrewdly gathered enough signatures on a petition that at long last moved the ERA out of Emanuel Celler's Judiciary Committee. A new, bipartisan, and diversely constituted generation of elected women foregrounded and amplified Griffiths' efforts on behalf of the ERA in the halls of Congress. Among them were Griffiths, Bella Abzug (D-NY), Shirley Chisholm (D-NY), Florence Dwyer (R-NJ), Edith Green (D-OR), Margaret Heckler (R-MA), Louise Day Hicks (D-MA), Elizabeth Holtzman (D-NY), Barbara Jordan (D-TX), Catherine Dean May (R-WA), Patsy Mink (D-HI), and Charlotte Reid (R-IL). Holtzman, the young lawyer who challenged Celler for his House seat in 1972 and won, later led the successful campaign to extend the ERA's ratification deadline by three years. All of these women would be on the front lines of the ERA debate during and beyond the next decade.[19]

In the Senate, the Subcommittee on Constitutional Amendments held hearings over three days to consider the ERA after a 15-year period of no hearings on the amendment. Supporters dominated these May 1970 hearings with pro-ERA testimony. Among those submitting testimony was Republican Gladys O'Donnell, who had just a few years earlier tangled with an Illinois homemaker for leadership of the National Federation of Republican Women. O'Donnell won that contest, fomenting political smears and bitter cries of voter fraud from the losing side. The ERA was not yet on the radar of O'Donnell's more conservative challenger, a forty-three-year-old mother of six named Phyllis Schlafly, who went on to lose a race for the House seat representing her home state.[20] Opponents still had their say, however. Betty Finegan and Myra Wolfgang appeared on behalf of the Michigan Women's Commission to denounce the ERA amid the sea of passionate pro-ERA endorsements. Their arguments echoed those of earlier protectionists concerned with how the amendment might detrimentally reconfigure women's lives in both the home and the workplace.

In October 1971, the House passed the ERA with a 354 to 24 vote. The Senate followed in March 1972 with a vote of 84 to 8.[21] Only one woman in Congress—Representative Leonor Kretzer Sullivan (D-MO)—voted against the ERA, and she did so on increasingly unpopular protectionist grounds.[22] Three-fourths of states now had to ratify the amendment by March 22, 1979. The deadline was imposed, as law professor Julie C. Suk reminds us, to appease a "vocal minority of ERA opponents who had already established a reputation for filibustering civil rights legislation."[23] Consequently, many ERA advocates have long viewed the deadline as "artificial," "arbitrary," and in violation of Article V of the Constitution, which outlines the process for adding amendments and makes no mention of time limits.[24] With the ERA approved by Congress and a ratification deadline set, the debate had clearly and widely expanded. The ERA's prospects seemed, for the moment, to have exponentially increased.

Notes

1 "The 1960 Democratic Party Platform," July 11, 1960, *American Presidency Project*, https://www.presidency.ucsb.edu/documents/1960-democratic-party-platform.
2 Cynthia Harrison, *On Account of Sex: The Politics of Women's Issues, 1945–1968* (Berkeley: University of California Press, 1988), 116–17.
3 Cynthia Harrison, "A 'New Frontier' for Women: The Public Policy of the Kennedy Administration," *Journal of American History* 67, no. 3 (1980): 630–46, see 635, 643.
4 "Memorandum, Esther Peterson to Lee White," August 7, 1963, Papers of John F. Kennedy, Presidential Papers, White House Central Subject Files, HU: 3: Equality for Women: Executive, *John F. Kennedy Presidential Library and Museum*, JFKWHCSF-0374-013-p0001.
5 Elisabeth Griffith, *Formidable: American Women and the Fight for Equality 1920–2020* (New York: Pegasus Books, 2022), 138.
6 Pat Herman, "American Women Are Second Class Citizens!" *Sarasota Herald-Tribune*, April 12, 1964, 5.
7 Harrison, *On Account of Sex*, 183.
8 Rebecca DeWolf, *Gendered Citizenship: The Original Conflict over the Equal Rights Amendment, 1920–1963* (Lincoln: University of Nebraska Press, 2021), 200–201; Harrison, *On Account of Sex*, 183.

9 Renalia DuBose, "Compliance Requires Inspection: The Failure of Gender Equal Pay Efforts in the United States," *Mercer Law Review* 68, no. 2 (2017): 445–60; Ruth Rosen, *The World Split Open: How the Modern Women's Movement Changed America* (New York: Viking, 2000), 72–73.

10 Katherine Turk, *The Women of NOW: How Feminists Built an Organization that Transformed America* (New York: Farrar, Straus and Giroux, 2023), 8.

11 Marjorie J. Spruill, *Divided We Stand: The Battle Over Women's Rights and Family Values That Polarized American Politics* (New York: Bloomsbury, 2017), 20.

12 Maryann Barasko, *Governing NOW: Grassroots Activism in the National Organization for Women* (Ithaca: Cornell University Press, 2004), 41.

13 Harrison, *On Account of Sex*, 199, 205.

14 Ruth Bader Ginsburg and Amanda L. Tyler, *Justice, Justice Thou Shalt Pursue: My Life's Work Fighting for a More Perfect Union* (New York: Simon & Schuster, 2021), 36–67, 270.

15 Turk, *The Women of NOW*, 20.

16 DeWolf, *Gendered Citizenship*, 226.

17 Esther Peterson to Martha Griffiths, October 12, 1971, Esther Peterson Papers, 1884–1998, Box 54, Folder 1061, Schlesinger Library, Radcliffe Institute for Advanced Study, Harvard University, 2pp. Included in *How and Why Was Feminist Legal Strategy Transformed, 1960–1973.* Documents selected and interpreted by Serena Mayeri (Binghamton: State University of New York at Binghamton, 2007), https://documents.alexanderstreet.com/d/1000673539.

18 DeWolf, *Gendered Citizenship*, 226.

19 Julie C. Suk, *We the Women: The Unstoppable Mothers of the Equal Rights Amendment* (New York: Skyhorse Publishing, 2020), 114–17.

20 Suk, *We the Women*, 85.

21 Spruill, *Divided We Stand*, 31.

22 Suk, *We the Women*, 88.

23 Julie C. Suk, *After Misogyny: How the Law Fails Women and What to Do About It* (Oakland: University of California Press, 2023), 229–30.

24 "The Intertwining History of NOW and the ERA," National Organization for Women, https://now.org/the-intertwining-history-of-now-and-the-era/; Roxy Szal, "The ERA Has Been Ratified, Declares New Congressional Resolution," *Ms. Magazine*, January 31, 2023, https://msmagazine.com/2023/01/31/equal-rights-amendment-2/.

Women Under the Law

Excerpt from the Report of the President's Commission on the Status of Women

President's Commission on the Status of Women
October 11, 1963[1]

On December 14, 1961, John F. Kennedy announced Executive Order 10980 establishing the President's Commission on the Status of Women (PCSW), which placed women front and center on his legislative agenda. The duties of the PCSW were to issue recommendations to the president for action about employment policies and practices for women working in the Federal government.[2] PCSW member Pauli Murray labeled the commission "the first high-level consciousness group."[3] ERA opponent Esther Peterson, Kennedy's Assistant Secretary of Labor and head of the Women's Bureau, served as the PCSW's Vice Chair. Peterson invited former first lady Eleanor Roosevelt to lend her stature as chair, a position she held until her death the following November ("This may be the last thing I really do," Roosevelt told Peterson after agreeing to serve.[4]). The 26 women and men on the bipartisan commission included Attorney General Robert F. Kennedy, Radcliffe College president Mary Bunting, and civil rights leader Dorothy Height. Feminist lawyer and NWP member Marguerite Rawalt is often credited as being the only pro-ERA member of the commission, but at least two other members—Labor Department researcher Catherine East and Justice Department lawyer Mary Eastwood—were both "quietly pro-ERA."[5] Betty Friedan, enjoying her own newfound publicity, consulted with the PCSW as well.[6]

Given that only one member openly supported the ERA, it was no surprise that the PCSW established early on that its purpose was to "substitute constructive recommendations for the present troublesome and futile agitation about the equal rights amendment."[7] Even so, Peterson was cognizant of their responsibility to consider all possible ways to improve women's status, as well as the optics of the group ignoring or dismissing the ERA outright. Therefore, she promised a fair look at the amendment as part of making the commission's work legitimate and impartial. This task became especially important when the Senate Judiciary committee issued a positive report on the ERA in August 1962. The PCSW invited four groups—the NWP and the National Federation of Business and Professional Women's Clubs (BPWC) for the affirmative and the American Association of University Women (AAUW) and the American Nurses Association for the negative—to present their arguments. But the space created here for real deliberation did little to move the needle for the PCSW.[8]

Published under the title *American Women* by the U.S. Government Printing Office, the sixty-page report sold some 64 thousand copies when released on October 11, 1963, in honor of Eleanor Roosevelt's birthday. Historian Marjorie J. Spruill emphasizes that the report's publication and circulation "raised expectations that the government would take an active role in fighting sexual inequalities."[9] As to the ERA, the report made plain the commission's decision to "not take a position in favor of the equal rights amendment *at this time*."[10] Marguerite Rawalt's qualifying addition presented just a glimmer of hope. Rawalt recommended the language of "not now" be added to the final report about the amendment.[11] The section on "Women Under the Law" thus echoed the protectionist arguments from previous decades and reinforced the argument that women's equality was already covered in the Constitution, while still leaving the door open just a crack for the ERA to proceed.

Equality of rights under the law for all persons, male or female, is so basic to democracy and its commitments to the ultimate value of the individual that it must be reflected in the fundamental law of the land. The Commission believes that this principle of equality is embodied in the 5th and 14th amendments to the Constitution of the United States.

The 14th amendment prohibits any state from depriving any person of life, liberty, or property without due process of law and from denying to any person the equal protection of the laws. Essentially the same prohibitions apply to the Federal Government under the due process clause of the fifth amendment.

In the face of these amendments, however, there remain, especially in certain state laws and official practices, distinctions based on sex which discriminate against women. Both the States and the Federal Government may classify persons for the purpose of legislation, but the classification must be based on some reasonable ground. There exist some laws and official practices which treat men and women differently and which do not appear to be reasonable in the light of the multiple activities of women in present-day society.

The Commission considered various proposed methods of achieving greater recognition of the rights of women:

- Test litigation seeking redress from discrimination under constitutional safeguards looking to ultimate review by the U.S. Supreme Court.
- Amendment to the U.S. Constitution—the proposed equal rights amendment provides, in part, that *Equality of rights under the law shall not be denied or abridged . . . on account of sex.*
- State legislative action to eliminate discriminatory state laws.

Divergent viewpoints on these methods, particularly among national women's organizations and labor union groups, were made known in documents lodged with the Commission and in oral presentations at two hearings.

Constitutional Recognition

Since the Commission is convinced that the U.S. Constitution now embodies equality of rights for men and women, we conclude that a constitutional amendment need not now be sought in order to establish this principle. But judicial clarification is imperative in order that remaining ambiguities with respect to the constitutional protection of women's rights be eliminated.

Early and definitive court pronouncement, particularly by the U.S. Supreme Court, is urgently needed with regard to the validity under the 5th and 14th amendments of laws and official practices discriminating against women, to the end that the principle of equality become firmly established in constitutional doctrine.

Accordingly, interested groups should give high priority to bringing under court review cases involving laws and practices which discriminate against women.

At the same time, appropriate federal, state, and local officials in all branches of government should be urged to scrutinize carefully those laws, regulations, and practices which distinguish on the basis of sex to determine whether they are justifiable in the light of contemporary conditions and to the end of removing archaic standards which today operate as discriminatory.

The Commission commends and encourages continued efforts on the part of all interested groups in educating the public and in urging private action, and action within the judicial, executive, and legislative branches of government, to the end that full equality of rights may become a reality.

Notes

1 *American Women: Report of the President's Commission on the Status of Women*, 1963, Original from University of Michigan, https://babel.hathitrust.org/cgi/pt?id=mdp.39015016913678&view=1up&seq=3&skin=2021&q1=amendment. Public Domain.
2 John F. Kennedy, "Executive Order 10980—Establishing the President's Commission on the Status of Women," *American Presidency Project*, December 14, 1961, https://www.presidency.ucsb.edu/documents/executive-order-10980-establishing-the-presidents-commission-the-status-women#axzz1UU8oizn3.
3 Elisabeth Griffith, *Formidable: American Women and the Fight for Equality, 1920–2020* (New York: Pegasus Books, 2022), 137.
4 Esther E. Peterson, Oral History Interview—JFK#2, 1/20/1970, John F. Kennedy Presidential Library, 56, https://www.jfklibrary.org/sites/default/files/archives/JFKOH/Peterson%2C%20Esther%20E/JFKOH-EEP-03/JFKOH-EEP-03-TR.pdf.
5 Griffith, *Formidable*, 137.
6 Marjorie J. Spruill, *Divided We Stand: The Battle Over Women's Rights and Family Values That Polarized American Politics* (New York: Bloomsbury, 2017), 17.
7 Katherine Ellickson, "The President's Commission on the Status of Women: Its Formation, Functioning, and Contribution," 1976, Katherine Ellickson Papers, Walter Reuther Library, Archives of Labor and Urban Affairs, Wayne State University, Detroit, MI. Included in *Revisiting the President's Commission on the Status of Women through the Activism of Dorothy Height, and Her Part in the Emergence of New Forms of Women's Activism, 1961–1966*. Documents selected and interpreted by Kathryn Kish Sklar and Keisha N. Blain (Alexandria, VA: Alexander Street, 2022).
8 Cynthia Harrison, *On Account of Sex: The Politics of Women's Issues, 1945–1968* (Berkeley: University of California Press, 1988), 122, 126.
9 Spruill, *Divided We Stand*, 16.
10 Quoted in Rosalind Rosenberg, *Jane Crow: The Life of Pauli Murray* (New York: Oxford University Press, 2017), 261.
11 Rebecca DeWolf, *Gendered Citizenship: The Original Conflict over the Equal Rights Amendment, 1920–1963* (Lincoln: University of Nebraska Press, 2021), 215.

We Should Not Compromise: We Must Pioneer

Address to the Second National Conference of the National Organization for Women

Betty Friedan
November 18, 1967[1]

Bettye Naomi Goldstein Friedan (1921–2006) kicked off the second-wave feminism movement when she named "the problem that has no name" in 1963. That first bestselling book, *The Feminine Mystique*, documented a survey Friedan had conducted among her Smith College alumna classmates. She concluded that "the only way for a woman, as for a man, to find herself, to know herself as a person, is by creative work of her own."[2] Friedan identifying and naming the angst that countless (predominantly white) middle-class women felt in their post-World-War-II domestic-centered lives set off a loud cultural explosion that spurred on the women's movement of the 1960s and 1970s.

In 1966, Friedan co-founded the National Organization for Women (NOW), which today continues "to promote feminist ideals, lead societal change, eliminate discrimination, and achieve and protect the equal rights of all women and girls in all aspects of social, political, and economic life."[3] During its second meeting at the Mayflower Hotel in the nation's capital, Friedan introduced NOW's continued support for the Equal Rights Amendment, published in resolution form here. Friedan believed that the ERA and abortion "were and are the two gut issues of the women's movement essential to real security—and equality and human dignity—for all women, whether they worked outside or inside the home."[4] The meeting generated little fanfare. Only 100 members were present. The discussion that followed her reading of the resolutions shows some doubt among the members that the ERA could ever be ratified. As the women debated the exact phrases used as well as the religious arguments for and against women's reproductive freedom, Friedan never wavered: "We can't weaken NOW. We must get a statement that most people will agree on . . . We should not compromise—we must pioneer."[5] Friedan spent the rest of her life fighting for the ERA. She advocated for it in speeches and writings, testified favorably at the May 1970 ERA hearings, and famously debated Phyllis Schlafly in May 1973 at Illinois State University (Friedan's angry retort that she would like to burn Schlafly at the stake unfortunately did little to advance the ERA cause.[6]). Friedan died in 2006 widely regarded as the "the mother of feminism," although she remains a polarizing figure within the history of the women's movement.[7]

The purpose of this afternoon meeting is to discuss and vote upon two resolutions: A resolution urging the House and Senate Judiciary Committees to approve the Equal Rights amendment and to call the Ninetieth Congress to approve this amendment, for the submission to the states for ratification.

And a resolution endorsing the principle that it is a basic right of every woman to control her reproductive life, and that those laws preventing abortion should be repealed.

As a preliminary to discussion of the Equal Rights Amendment, an example of what the law would amend was introduced. If an Equal Rights Amendment was passed, job discrimination would be outlawed. As of now, women are discriminated against by state protective laws. If the Equal Rights Amendment was passed and enforced, if the fair practices section of the 1964 Civil Rights Act was enforced, state protective laws would be illegal.

An example of a job discrimination case NOW helped was the case of three women from Indiana who were denied higher paying jobs with the Colgate-Palmolive Company because of new weight-limit restrictions imposed on women workers. Georgiana Sellers, Ann Casey, and Lena Moore filed a complaint against the company for job discrimination, basing their complaint on Title VII of the Civil Rights Act.[8] In the state of Indiana there is no state protective law prohibiting women from lifting 35 lb. or more. To win the case, the company employers went beyond the borders of the state and enforced the protective law in their factory because in two other of their factories in different states they had the protective laws. The judge ruled in the company's favor. The case is on appeal . . .

The resolution calling for the ratification of the Equal Rights Amendment was passed out and read aloud:

Resolution

WHEREAS, the National Organization of Women (NOW) is incorporated for the purposes of taking action to achieve equal rights and responsibilities in all aspects of citizenship, public service, employment, education, and family life; and

WHEREAS, women have been unsuccessfully seeking equal rights under the Fifth and Fourteenth Amendments of the United States Constitution through litigation extending over a full century; and

WHEREAS, NOW is actively assisting women workers in seeking to invoke the protection of the United States Constitution to strike down statutes and official practices which deprive women of equal job opportunities; and

WHEREAS, other classes of women persons have been adjudged full recognition by the courts of complete equality without class distinction; and

WHEREAS, the Equal Rights Amendment would unequivocally secure the right to equal treatment under the law without differentiation based on sex; and

WHEREAS, opposition to the Equal Rights Amendment in the past was principally based on the presumed need for special "protective" labor legislation for women, the basis for which opposition Congress has removed by the enactment of the equal employment opportunity provisions of the Civil Rights Act of 1964; and

WHEREAS, there is now pending in Congress various joint resolutions, such as S.J. Res. 54 and H.J. Res. 52, which would amend the U.S. Constitution to provide that "Equality of rights under the law shall not be denied or abridged by the United States or by any state on account of sex."

BE IT RESOLVED THAT, NOW urge the House and Senate Judiciary Committees to immediately report favorably on the Equal Rights Amendment and call upon the Ninetieth Congress to approve this amendment, without qualification, for submission to the states for ratification.

Notes

1 "Minutes from the Second National Conference of the National Organization of Women," Washington, D.C., November 18, 1967, https://350fem.blogs.brynmawr.edu/1967/11/19/national-conference-of-now-minutes/. Public Domain.

2 Betty Friedan, *The Feminine Mystique* (New York: W. W. Norton, 1963), 472.

3 "About," National Organization for Women, https://now.org/about/.

4 Betty Friedan, *"It Changed My Life": Writings on the Women's Movement* (New York: Random House, 1976), 106.

5 "Minutes from the Second National Conference of NOW," *National Organization for Women*, Bryn Mawr College, https://350fem.blogs.brynmawr.edu/1967/11/19/national-conference-of-now-minutes/.
6 Rachel Shteir, *Betty Friedan: Magnificent Disrupter* (New Haven: Yale University Press, 2023), 184–85.
7 Marjorie J. Spruill, *Divided We Stand: The Battle Over Women's Rights and Family Values That Polarized American Politics* (New York: Bloomsbury Publishing, 2017), 96. For an in-depth study of Friedan's controversial tactics and beliefs, see Shteir, *Betty Friedan.*
8 For more on the "Colgate-Palmolive flush-in," see Shteir, *Betty Friedan*, 129–30.

Prejudice Against Women Is Still Acceptable

Address to the House of Representatives

SHIRLEY CHISHOLM
May 21, 1969[1]

"What does your husband think about all this?" This was the question posed to Shirley Anita St. Chisholm (1924–2005) on her very first day in office by male colleagues baffled that she had entered politics at all.[2] The New York Democrat, who famously ran on the campaign slogan "unbought and unbossed," was the first Black women elected to Congress. She grew up in Brooklyn and drew accolades as an accomplished debater—which would come in handy once she reached the nation's capital in 1969. In Congress, the former schoolteacher and New York Assemblywoman got to work straight away. Chisholm's very first floor speech in March 1969 strenuously denounced the Vietnam War. She co-founded the Congressional Black Caucus and the National Women's Political Caucus (NWPC) in 1971 with Bella Abzug, Betty Friedan, Gloria Steinem, and others. Chisholm also attended early NOW meetings with Black activists Septima Clark and Eleanor Holmes Norton. These and other women of color experienced the critique that future NOW president Aileen Hernandez raised about the initial lack of diversity represented in the organizational leadership, which was compounded by the differences in how white and non-white women understood and encountered oppression.[3] On her own terms, Chisholm launched an historic bid for the presidency in 1972 and did not seek reelection in 1982, the year that the ERA's ratification period expired.[4] She retired from political office, yet stayed engaged in politics, until her death in 2005.

Two months after her Vietnam speech, Chisholm again stood before her colleagues: this time, to reintroduce the Equal Rights Amendment. She sponsored the ERA even though she believed that "the law cannot do the major part of the job of winning equality for women. Women must do it themselves. They must become revolutionaries."[5] "Fighting Shirley," of course, embodied this very idea throughout her political career. As her speech emphasized, Chisholm was the first elected official in Congress able to give voice to what civil rights leader and fellow ERA supporter Pauli Murray called "Jane Crow"—the duality of discrimination against women of color on both gendered and racially prejudicial grounds.[6] By the next year, Chisholm's colleague Martha Wright Griffiths had masterfully activated an unusual strategy of a "discharge petition" to obtain the requisite number of signatures needed to finally move the ERA out of the House Judiciary Committee and bring it to the floor for debate.[7]

Mr. Speaker, when a young woman graduates from college and starts looking for a job, she is likely to have a frustrating and even demeaning experience ahead of her. If she walks into an office for an interview, the first question she will be asked is, "Do you type?"

There is a calculated system of prejudice that lies unspoken behind that question. Why is it acceptable for women to be secretaries, librarians, and teachers, but totally unacceptable for them to be managers, administrators, doctors, lawyers, and Members of Congress?

The unspoken assumption is that women are different. They do not have executive ability, orderly minds, stability, leadership skills, and they are too emotional.

It has been observed before, that society for a long time, discriminated against another minority, the blacks, on the same basis—that they were different and inferior. The happy little homemaker and the contented "old darky" on the plantation were both stereotypes produced by prejudice.

As a black person, I am no stranger to race prejudice. But the truth is that in the political world I have been far oftener discriminated against because I am a woman than because I am black.

Prejudice against blacks is becoming unacceptable although it will take years to eliminate it. But it is doomed because, slowly, white America is beginning to admit that it exists. Prejudice against women is still acceptable. There is very little understanding yet of the immorality involved in double pay scales and the classification of most of the better jobs as "for men only."

More than half of the population of the United States is female. But women occupy only 2 percent of the managerial positions. They have not even reached the level of tokenism yet. No women sit on the AFL-CIO council or Supreme Court. There have been only two women who have held Cabinet rank, and at present there are none. Only two women now hold ambassadorial rank in the diplomatic corps. In Congress, we are down to one Senator and 10 Representatives.

Considering that there are about 3½ million more women in the United States than men, this situation is outrageous.

It is true that part of the problem has been that women have not been aggressive in demanding their rights. This was also true of the black population for many years. They submitted to oppression and even cooperated with it. Women have done the same thing. But now there is an awareness of this situation particularly among the younger segment of the population.

As in the field of equal rights for blacks, Spanish-Americans, Indians, and other groups, laws will not change such deep-seated problems overnight. But they can be used to provide protection for those who are most abused, and to begin the process of evolutionary change by compelling the insensitive majority to reexamine its unconscious attitudes.

It is for this reason that I wish to introduce today a proposal that has been before every Congress for the last 40 years and that sooner or later must become part of the basic law of the land—the equal rights amendment.

Let me note and try to refute two of the commonest arguments that are offered against this amendment. One is that women are already protected under the law and do not need legislation. Existing laws are not adequate to secure equal rights for women. Sufficient proof of this is in the concentration of women in lower-paying, menial, unrewarding jobs and their incredible scarcity in the upper-level jobs. If women are already equal, why is it such an event whenever one happens to be elected to Congress?

It is obvious that discrimination exists. Women do not have the opportunity that men do. And women that do not conform to the system, who try to break with the accepted patterns, are stigmatized as "odd" and "unfeminine." The fact is that a woman who aspires to be chairman of the board, or a Member of the House, does so for exactly the same reasons as any man. Basically, these are that she thinks she can do the job and she wants to try.

A second argument often heard against the equal rights amendment is that it would eliminate legislation that many States and the Federal Government have enacted giving special protection to women and that it would throw the marriage and divorce laws into chaos.

As for the marriage laws, they are due for a sweeping reform, and an excellent beginning would be to wipe the existing ones off the books. Regarding special protection for working women, I cannot understand why it should be needed. Women need no protection that men do not need. What we need are laws to protect working people, to guarantee them fair pay, safe working conditions, protection against sickness and layoffs, and provision for dignified, comfortable retirement. Men and women need these things equally. That one sex needs protection more than the other is a male supremacist myth as ridiculous and unworthy of respect as the white supremacist myths that society is trying to cure itself of at this time.

Notes

1 "Equal Rights for Women," Hon. Shirley Chisholm of New York in the House of Representatives, Proceedings and Debates of the 91st Congress, First Session, May 21, 1969, 13380–81. Public Domain.
2 Shirley Chisholm, *Unbought and Unbossed* (New York: HarperCollins, 1970), 92.
3 Katherine Turk, *The Women of NOW: How Feminists Built an Organization that Transformed America* (New York: Farrar, Straus and Giroux, 2023), 112.
4 Shirley Chisholm, *The Good Fight* (New York: HarperCollins, 1973).
5 Chisholm, *Unbought*, 196.
6 Pauli Murray and Mary O. Eastwood, "Jane Crow and the Law: Sex Discrimination and Title VII," *George Washington Law Review* 34, no. 2 (1965): 232–56.
7 Lila Thulin, "Why the Equal Rights Amendment Is Still Not Part of the Constitution," *Smithsonian Magazine*, January 15, 2020, https://www.smithsonianmag.com/history/equal-rights-amendment-96-years-old-and-still-not-part-constitution-heres-why-180973548/.

Gentlemen, Women are Enraged

Address to the Senate Judiciary Committee

Aileen Hernandez
May 5, 1970[1]

As an undergraduate at Howard University, Aileen Clarke Hernandez (1926–2017)—the daughter of Jamaican immigrants—studied with future Supreme Court Justice Thurgood Marshall, joined the campus NAACP, and protested whites-only lunch counters with Howard law student Pauli Murray: all while maintaining an exemplary grade point average and graduating *magna cum laude* with a degree in political science and sociology.[2] Hernandez proceeded to study comparative government at the University of Oslo in Norway before returning to the United States and participating in a training institute for labor organizers through the International Ladies' Garment Workers' Union. She eventually moved west to work as a regional union organizer in Los Angeles and, by 1961, had advanced to the position of assistant director of the California State Division of Fair Employment Practices.[3]

Following passage of the 1964 Civil Rights Act, Lyndon Johnson named Hernandez to the new Equal Employment Opportunity Commission (EEOC) where she fought—as the lone woman on the commission—for the right of female flight attendants to retain employment after marriage.[4] Hernandez attended the inaugural NOW conference in 1966. Two years later, she succeeded Betty Friedan as president after openly criticizing NOW for not having enough racial diversity in its leadership or outreach to women of color. In her new role, Hernandez sought to more intentionally incorporate women of color within NOW's largely white, middle-class membership, though this work did not come easily.[5] She co-founded the Minority Women's Task Force and co-founded the NWPC alongside Bella Abzug, Shirley Chisholm, Betty Friedan, Dorothy Height, and Jill Ruckelshaus. After her presidential term with NOW ended in 1971 (she departed the organization in 1979), Hernandez taught and founded an urban consulting firm.[6] A Nobel Peace Prize co-nominee in 2005, Hernandez suffered from dementia in her later years and died in 2017 from complications at home in California.

Hernandez often said, "all issues are women's issues," in a nod to the philosophy of Eleanor Roosevelt, whom she greatly admired and met in the late 1940s through the ILGWU.[7] Unlike Roosevelt, Hernandez supported the ERA. Almost immediately after assuming the presidency of NOW, Hernandez appeared in the May 1970 hearings on the ERA to testify in its favor. Her primary strategy was to channel the anger of American women at the fact that the amendment had yet to pass.

My name is Aileen C. Hernandez, and I am the national president of the National Organization for Women, an organization whose acronym NOW expresses forcefully our concept of the timing for equality for women.

I and my sisters in this new feminist organization appear before you today with decidedly mixed emotions. We are infuriated by the cavalier manner in which the gentlemen of the Congress have treated the question of equality for women for 47 years since the Equal Rights Amendment to our Constitution was first introduced. We are saddened by the fact that an amendment is needed, because our male founders and male-dominated courts refuse to accept women as people in setting forth and interpreting the guarantees of freedom in the Bill of Rights.

We are also, however, somewhat indebted to you and to your predecessors in the Senate and the House, because without your dismissal of our petition to you for equality, NOW would never have been born.

In 1966, hundreds of women met in Washington, D.C., to submit and discuss their report on the status of women, reports carefully and intelligently developed in the years of study in the many commissions formed throughout the United States as a result of a gauntlet thrown down by then-President John F. Kennedy in his charge to the National Advisory Commission on the Status of Women, a charge to study and make recommendations on the nature and extent of discrimination against women in the United States. As those delegates attempted to implement their recommendations, they learned that action was not a part of their charge. Out of their frustration came NOW. A group of women met in the hotel room of Betty Friedan, who was then in the process of writing a second book, and decided that a civil rights organization for women was needed if women were to become first-class citizens in this society.

The rage of those women was translated into a program for action, which included as a high priority the passage of the long bottled up in Congress equal rights amendment for women and for men. NOW's program is very easily defined. We believe in equal rights and responsibilities for men and women, and our members, both men and women, are working to bring women into full participation in the mainstream of American society now.

In the short four years, or not quite four years, since NOW was formed and under the leadership of Betty Friedan, NOW has tallied many gains, chief among which is the fact that new feminists are on the march and that sex discrimination is no longer treated as an obscene joke.

Gentlemen, women are enraged. We are dedicated and we mean to become first-class citizens in this society. We really do not feel that these hearings are necessary. The Congress could and should vote immediately. The issue has been thoroughly defined. Either this Congress recognizes that women, like other oppressed people within our Nation, will wait no longer for equity, and with this recognition moves immediately to redress the many grievances, or like other oppressed groups, women will adjust their tactics to achieve their demands.

Others who testify after us, and some who have testified before us, will address themselves to the technical and legal arguments for passage. This panel for NOW addresses itself to the justness of the cause and the urgency of the demand. We demand the right to assume our roles in every aspect of this society. We demand the right to be heard on all the issues of concern: we demand inclusion in this society NOW so that we may bring all our considerable talents to bear to change those things which need changing in order to achieve full justice for all and to preserve those things which help us to achieve our goal.

Gentlemen, the challenge is directly to you; you have the opportunity to redress the obvious injustices against women by voting immediately to send the amendment to the floor of Congress and to work to achieve its passage in this session of Congress. If you miss this opportunity—and NOW sincerely hopes you do not—the women of America may well see fit to ensure in November that many of you and your colleagues never have another chance to insult the women of America by your failure to act.

Notes

1 *The "Equal Rights" Amendment: Hearings on S.J. Res 61, Before the Committee on the Judiciary*, Day 2, 91st Congress (1970) (Statement of Aileen Hernandez). Public Domain.

2 Carolina Alonso Bejarano and Kim LeMoon, "Aileen Clarke Hernandez: Advocate for Black Women's Leadership," in *Junctures in Women's Leadership: Social Movements*, ed. Mary K. Trigg and Alison R. Bernstein (New Brunswick, NJ: Rutgers University Press, 2016), 63.

3 Katherine Turk, *The Women of NOW: How Feminists Built an Organization that Transformed America* (New York: Farrar, Straus and Giroux, 2023), 60–62.

4 Ethel L. Payne, "LBJ Goes to Bat for Womanhood," *Chicago Daily Defender*, October 19, 1967, 4.

5 Carol Giardina, "MOW to NOW: Black Feminism Resets the Chronology of the Founding of Modern Feminism," *Feminist Studies* 44, no. 3 (2018): 736–65.

6 Turk, *The Women of NOW*, 298–99.

7 "NOW Mourns the Loss of Aileen Hernandez," *Now.org*, February 27, 2017, https://now.org/media-center/press-release/now-mourns-the-loss-of-aileen-hernandez/.

Nature Cannot Be Amended

Address to the Senate Judiciary Committee

BETTY FINEGAN
May 6, 1970[1]

Although pro-ERA testimony guided the May 1970 hearings before the Senate Judiciary Committee, the protectionist position had not fully waned. Elizabeth Ann "Betty" Dickson Finegan (1922–2019), then-chair of the Michigan Women's Commission, represented the commission's anti-ERA position at these hearings. In one of many state-level commissions inspired by President Kennedy's PCSW, the fifteen-member Michigan Women's Commission was created by statute in 1968 and tasked with six charges: (1) review and study women's status across the state; (2) focus attention on the distinct problems women face in various home and workplace roles; (3) make recommendations about reducing discrimination against women in both public and private employment contexts; (4) offer educational resources for women's professional improvement; (5) create advisory committees across a variety of fields; and (6) highlight ways that women improve life in the state.[2]

While not as instantly recognizable as others who testified, Betty Finegan of Birmingham, Michigan, was no stranger to the state and national political scene. In high school, the Massachusetts native honed her speaking skills in dramatic and vaudeville clubs.[3] The "housewife," as press reports described her, later served on the resolutions committee at the 1960 Republican National Convention.[4] She worked on the successful governor campaigns for George W. Romney and William Milliken (incidentally, Michigan first lady Helen Milliken was a leading campaigner for the ERA in her state[5]). And as Governor Milliken's appointed chair of the Michigan Women's commission, Finegan pressed for equal pay and fought for limits on women's work hours.[6]

News reports noted that the anti-ERA position of the Michigan Women's Commission directly contradicted that of the Women's Bureau of the U.S. Department of Labor, which had changed course since the tenure of Frances Perkins. In contrast, Finegan explained the protectionist nature of the commission's opposition ahead of her Congressional appearance. "In certain areas, real equality can be obtained only by a difference in treatment," she argued in March 1970.[7] Union organizer and labor activist Myra K. Wolfgang followed Finegan with a lengthy speech informed by her work as international vice president of the Hotel and Restaurant Employees Union. Wolfgang stated that the woman she represented was not the privileged "bird in the gilded cage," but "Tillie the Toiler"—the woman "not burdened with the necessity of holding philosophical discussions on whether women should or should not be in the work force" because she already *was* in the work force.[8] Both Finegan and Wolfgang articulated lingering sentiments that Ethel Smith, Florence Kelley, Maida Kemp, and others had expressed decades earlier—concerns that the ERA's elite supporters were detached from the realities of the working woman's life, the amendment stood to decimate any gains women had already made, and ratification quashed any possibility for future labor reform.

I am Mrs. John Finegan, and I am chairman of the Michigan Women's Commission. Mrs. Wolfgang is a member of the women's commission, but is also representing the hotel and restaurant workers, in the State of Michigan.

The Michigan Women's Commission is a statutory body consisting of 15 members from all over the state plus four ex-officio members who are directors of the department of labor, education, social service, and civil service. Members are appointed by the Governor of the State.

Our charges are to study and review the status of women, strengthen home life, direct our attention to the critical problems facing women as homemakers, wives, mothers, and workers, and to secure appropriate recognition of the contribution women have made.

We are concerned with the multidimensional role women have as wives, mothers, homemakers, and workers in today's complicated society. We are concerned with women realizing their potential and we are seeking means to enable them to do this. We are concerned with utilizing more fully the huge resources of women power in this country. We want to have a choice in what course their lives will follow.

The Michigan Women's Commission has gone on record as opposing the equal rights amendment. Our opposition is fundamental and deals with matters that are basic to our social structure. There are real differences both physical and social between men and women. Nature cannot be amended. Women still bear children and will continue to give them the majority of care. They will still need maternity benefits and maternal care. Our society today still recognizes that the wife and mother is the center of the family. We firmly believe this should be so. The legal position of women cannot be stated in a single formula as their relationships are so varied. Absolute legal equality is impossible. Where there are real physical and social differences, identity of treatment is itself a form of discrimination.

Secondly, we believe women already have the protection of the laws because of the fifth and 14th amendments which guarantee to all persons due process and equal protection of the laws without arbitrary discrimination. We are confident that the courts today will interpret these laws to give full recognition to this principle.

Certainly, there are injustices in the treatment of women. We recognize the discrimination in employment, in promotions, in training opportunities, in admission to universities, in access to public accommodations, in the social security system and in many other areas. We wish to correct these inequalities by specific legislation. Orderly legislative revision, by means of specific legislations, is the practical way to erase such unwise discrimination as still exists in the laws. Discrimination exists in the laws relating to property, personal status, marriage and employment. Legal discriminations in state laws and constitutions will be changed as fast as enough women in those states want them changed.

Michigan's law limiting the number of hours a woman could be forced to work would be threatened. Unfortunately, our law applies to women only. Passage of the equal rights amendment would nullify it. And there is no guarantee that new legislation would be enacted to provide protection for both sexes. Therefore, there would be no protection for either sex. The women's commission has gone on record as favoring protective legislation for both men and women.

We want equal opportunities and responsibilities and equal status for women. We do not think the equal rights amendment will accomplish this.

It is our conviction that: First, the amendment is unnecessary. The 5th and 14th amendments guarantee to all persons due process and equal protection of the laws without arbitrary discrimination. Most of the inequalities about which its advocates complain are due to custom and tradition and not to law.

Second, the adoption of the amendment would nullify Michigan's labor laws for the protection of women. This legislation is perhaps more necessary than before because of the number and proportion of women in the labor force.

And finally, adoption of the amendment would cause great confusion in the wide field of laws relating to property, personal status, and marriage.

We ask the committee's consideration of the position of the Michigan Women's Commission.

Notes

1 *The "Equal Rights" Amendment: Hearings before the Subcommittee on Constitutional Amendments of the Committee on the Judiciary*, Day 2, 91st Congress (1970) (Statement of Mrs. Betty Finegan, Michigan Women's Commission). Public Domain.
2 "Michigan Women's Commission Act of 1968," Michigan Women's Commission, https://www.michigan.gov/mwc/about.
3 "Elizabeth Ann Dickson," *Winchester High School Yearbook*, Winchester, MA, 1939.
4 "County Republicans to Name Elliott Successor Thursday," *Birmingham (Michigan) Eccentric*, September 21, 1961, 8-A.
5 "Former Mich. First Lady Helen Milliken Dies at 89," *Politico*, November 16, 2012, https://www.politico.com/story/2012/11/former-mich-first-lady-helen-milliken-dies-at-89-083963.
6 Frank Angelo, "A Few Good Men Break a Barrier," *Detroit Free Press*, May 11, 1979, 11; "Commission of Women Is Formed," *News-Palladium* (Benton Harbor, Michigan), July 25, 1969, 5; "Women Pressure Lansing for New Equal Pay Law," *News-Palladium* (Benton Harbor, MI), June 29, 1971, 9; "Oppose Women's Work Hour Plan," *Traverse City Record Eagle*, September 19, 1968, 11.
7 Helen May, "Women's Group Opposes Rights Amendment," *Detroit Free Press*, March 19, 1970, IC.
8 *The "Equal Rights" Amendment: Hearings before the Subcommittee on Constitutional Amendments of the Committee on the Judiciary*, Day 2, 91st Congress (1970) (Statement of Mrs. Myra K. Wolfgang, Vice President, Hotel and Restaurant Employees and Bartenders International Union, AFL-CIO, [on] Behalf of the Michigan Women's Commission); "Myra Wolfgang," Jewish Historical Society of Michigan, https://www.jhsmichigan.org/mwwmd/2017/05/myra-wolfgang.html.

We Are Tired of Being the Silenced Majority

Address to the Senate Judiciary Committee

GLADYS O'DONNELL
May 5–7, 1970[1]

Although the name Phyllis Schlafly has gone down in the ERA's history, the name of Schlafly's one-time rival Gladys Livingston Berry O'Donnell (1904–1973) has received far less credit than deserved. By 1930, O'Donnell had acquired her pilot's license, won several transcontinental air race awards, and started the O'Donnell School of Aviation with her husband. She was among the founding 117 members of the "Ninety-Nine Club"—an international organization led by Amelia Earhart for licensed women pilots (otherwise known as "aviatrixes"[2]). During World War II, the O'Donnells served their country by training some eight thousand Army Air corps cadets.[3]

A devout Republican, O'Donnell served as state president of the California Federation of Republican Women and, later, as both secretary and vice chair of the state Republican central committee. The high—and low—point of O'Donnell's political career arrived with the 1967 contest for the presidency of the National Federation of Republican Women (NFRW). On the heels of Barry Goldwater's defeat, the Republican Party faced a growing fracture between deeply conservative and more moderately liberal factions. The NFRW Board worried that Goldwater's ardent supporter Phyllis Schlafly would steer them away from the pragmatic centrism needed to advance the party's interests. And so, party leaders recruited O'Donnell to run for president. After a highly contentious campaign, O'Donnell defeated Schlafly, who insisted the election was unfairly decided and called for investigations into "illegalities and irregularities."[4] When the election outcome did not change, Schlafly moved on to other pursuits and founded her anti-ERA Eagle Forum just four years later. O'Donnell relished her two terms as NFRW president and enthusiastically traveled the country—often in her own plane—to advance its interests and campaign for Republican candidates. A mere three years after her Congressional testimony, O'Donnell died of cancer having lived a groundbreaking life on earth and among the clouds.

O'Donnell represented the NFRW's pro-ERA position during the three-day hearings about the ERA before the Senate Judiciary Committee in 1970. Perhaps she was inspired by her lost friend Amelia Earhart, an active member of the NWP and an early supporter of the ERA who personally lobbied President Herbert Hoover to support the amendment in 1932.[5] O'Donnell submitted a full-throated, impassioned, and at times confrontational statement for the record. To make her case, she returned to a familiar historical appeal—the courageous legacy of the women who came before to fight for political enfranchisement.

On behalf of our Board of Directors and half million members I express appreciation for the opportunity to present the following statement for the National Federation of Republican Women.

The Equal Rights Amendment has long been supported by our organization and on January 23, 1970, to reemphasize our endorsement, it was again approved by a unanimous vote of our Board of Directors.

The extraordinary anachronism of this hearing is that it is taking place in the early twilight of the twentieth century; that it finds women still struggling for equality in an enlightened, libertarian society. One hundred and ninety-four years ago the Declaration of Independence set forth the philosophical tenets of a young nation—"we hold these truths to be self-evident, that all [men] are created equal, . . ."

Beyond all doubt the word "men" is used in its generic sense and women were not excluded, but we must admit that men are much more "equal" than women.

It has been my privilege to hear two days of testimony in this hearing. Witnesses established with professional skill and clarity the framework for legal and economic consideration of the Equal Rights Amendment. The women who made the presentations deserve profound admiration.

The hearings also provided an unbelievable defense of discrimination against women, first through Biblical quotations to prove their inferiority, and secondly by a slide presentation of chairs, tools, and other industrial devices to show that they are not suitable for women's anatomy. Neither quality nor excellence is a matter of size or shape. The opposite poles of this argument could be the late, great Babe Didrikson and Tiny Tim.

In this presentation it is my wish to approach the subject as a matter of the heart and spirit and then as a political reality.

This year we celebrate the 50th Anniversary of the 19th Amendment which gave American women the right to vote. Last year we honored the State of Wyoming which, as a territory, gave this recognition to women 100 years ago. Mrs. Esther Hobart Morris of South Pass, Wyoming, guided the victory.[6] Shortly thereafter she was appointed justice of the peace of South Pass, the highest honor the West could bestow for a quality it admires—true grit.

As we prepared a suitable tribute to the women pioneers who carried the crusade for the right to vote, we did considerable research. To know their story is to be acutely aware of the enormity of their legacy; the unwavering, single-minded purpose; the courage of heroic measure. Will we ever know women like this again—magnificent women who bring a lump to our throats?

The settlement of the west, or any other part of this country for that matter, owes more to the endless toil of these pioneer women than to all other factors in its history. A character in Edna Ferber's *Cimarron* tells it this way:

> You can't read the history of the United States, my friend ... without learning of the great story of those thousands of unnamed women ... women in mud caked boots and calico dresses and sunbonnets, crossing the prairie and the desert and mountains, enduring hardship and privation. Good women with a terrible and rigid goodness that comes of work and self-denial. Nothing picturesque or romantic about them, I suppose ... No, their story's never really been told, but it's there just the same. And if it's ever told straight, you'll know it's the sunbonnet and not the sombrero that's settled this country.

The greatest of all observers of the American scene mid-nineteenth century, Alexis de Tocqueville, said, "If I were asked ... to what the singular prosperity and growing strength of the United States ought mainly to be attributed, I should have to reply, 'to the superiority of its women.'"

The first national convention for women's suffrage was held in Seneca [Falls], New York, in [1848]. Seventy-two years later, in 1920, the 19th Amendment was passed. It was just a step in a long journey—the struggle continues.

Granddaughters and great-granddaughters of the pioneers are now in the forefront. Their quest is for the Equal Rights Amendment. It has been before Congress for 47 years. In this interim women have been more quiescent, but now the tide is rising and the mood changing. Predictably the old bromides and clichés are being dusted off. We have heard many of them at this meeting. There is a very special concern about legislation protecting women. If

I read the evidence correctly, there is a large question about *who* is getting the protection. Too often it turns out to be not protection but insulation—a buffer between women and opportunity, higher wages, faster promotion and positions of leadership.

This is not what women want. We reject it. Women want to be accepted as people, free independent human beings. As such we would have the coinciding benefits—equal opportunity, compensation, recognition and inclusion at policy-making levels. Collectively and individually we would like to be in on some of the take-offs since we are always at the crash landings.

Women do not desire to dominate what man has so long considered his private domain and which he is loathe to share. We just wonder why man needs so much defense of his masculinity. The great majority of women are happy as homemakers. But those of us who choose a career want to be accepted and treated as equals.

Women make up 40% of the workforce, represent 51% of the population. We have expanded beyond the four walls and roof that once defined our province and are escaping the psychological conditioning of inferiority that has been imposed upon us since time began.

Varying figures place the preponderance of women over men in the United States at 4½ to 7 million (voting age). These are politically significant figures, and it is ironic that we are here today endeavoring to justify a plea for an Equal Rights Amendment that we should have had long ago as a matter of simple justice. We are tired of being the silenced majority.

Looking back across the years since the 19th Amendment we can see where women erred. Winning the vote was accepted as an end in itself, which it was not. Having won political power, women have never used it. Therein lies our failure.

It is the opinion of many astute women in politics that we will not get any place until we elect more women to high office. This is a major goal of our Federation. We are urging State Federations to seek out qualified women of character, stability and training to become candidates. Once they have been nominated, either by primary election or convention, we will assist in every way in the general election.

Where we do not have women candidates, we will screen the potential men who are anxious to run and encourage those who are sympathetic in matters of concern to women. This is in the best political tradition—the way in which every group achieves its political objectives. It is time that women used a little of their abundant political moxie.

The proliferation of women's activist groups across the nation speaks eloquently and sometimes stridently for itself. Approaches vary widely, as at this hearing, but the goal is the same—equal rights and protection under the law, acceptance as persons, and recognition based on individual merit.

How little this is to ask after centuries of patient, enduring servitude and imposed inferiority.

Women can be a powerful force, acting collectively on an issue generating as much heat and polarization as the Equal Rights Amendment. A determined mood long absent from women's groups is spreading—its emotional logic is that nothing less than militancy is effective. We hope this is not true.

Years of experience and costly legal procedures have proved that the 5th and 14th Amendments and Title VII of the Civil Rights Act are not the answer to our need. The void in our Constitution concerning women should be bridged by an Amendment in clear, simple language which recognizes us as first-class citizens with equal rights and protection under the Constitution.

Favorable action on this simple request could bring historic distinction to this Congress and earn for it the lasting gratitude of American women. And how wise and ingenious it would be to magnanimously grant this recognition now—while there is still time!

In closing there should be no clearer summation than the objectives of proponents of the Equal Rights Amendment than the slogan of those early pioneers in the movement for women's right—"Principles, not policy; justice, not favor; men, their rights and nothing more; women, their rights and nothing less."

Notes

1 *The "Equal Rights" Amendment: Hearings on S.J. Res 61, Before the Committee on the Judiciary*, 91st Cong. (1970) (Statement of Gladys O'Donnell for the Record). Public Domain.

2 "Our History," Ninety-Nines, https://www.ninety-nines.org/our-history.htm.

3 E. J. Bachinski, "Gladys O'Donnell, Former Leader of GOP Women, Dies," *Washington Post*, May 10, 1973, B22.

4 Bachinski, "Gladys O'Donnell"; Donald T. Critchlow, *Phyllis Schlafly and Grassroots Conservatism: A Woman's Crusade* (Princeton, NJ: Princeton University Press, 2005), 142–43.

5 David Dismore, "Today in Feminist History: Amelia Earhart Fights for the Equal Rights Amendment (September 22, 1932)," *Ms. Magazine*, September 22, 2020, https://msmagazine.com/2020/09/22/feminist-history-september-22/; Susan Ware, *Still Missing: Amelia Earhart and the Search for Modern Feminism* (New York: W.W. Norton & Company, 1993).

6 Esther Hobart Morris (1814–1902) was an abolitionist and suffragist in Wyoming, where she broke precedent to serve as the first female justice of the peace in the nation. See Abby Dotterer, "Esther Hobart Morris, Justice of the Peace and Icon of Women's Rights," *Wyoming Historical Society*, September 4, 2019, https://www.wyohistory.org/encyclopedia/esther-hobart-morris-justice-peace-and-icon-womens-rights.

I Am Not Sure the Equal Rights Amendment Is Necessary

Remarks to the Associated Women Students at Arizona State University

SANDRA DAY O'CONNOR
May 7, 1970[1]

Sandra Day O'Connor (1930–2023), the daughter of cattle ranchers, enrolled at Stanford University at age 16 to study political science and then earned a law degree from there in 1952. After marrying John O'Connor III, she got involved in Arizona state politics and served as a moderately conservative Republican state senator in the legislature beginning in 1969. On July 7, 1981, President Ronald Reagan announced O'Connor as his nominee to the Supreme Court. The nomination proved divisive. The more socially conservative members of Reagan's party threatened "a nasty political protest" if he did not withdraw the nomination.[2] Among other things, those critics cited O'Connor's stance on the ERA as evidence of disqualifying liberal leanings during her Supreme Court confirmation hearings.[3]

Contrary to how her detractors portrayed her, O'Connor's position on the ERA evolved over time. Beginning in 1972, she fought for two years in the Arizona state legislature to ratify the ERA at the height of the national debate. Arizona's two Republican senators to Congress—Paul Fannin and Barry Goldwater—opposed the amendment. O'Connor wrote to both to change their minds even though neither man changed his opinion or vote. In 1973, O'Connor exhorted her colleagues to put the ERA into the hands of Arizona citizens. The next year, however, the measure failed in a 5-4 vote.[4] The 1982 ratification deadline came and went. Supreme Court Justice Sandra Day O'Connor, the first woman to serve in this capacity, had moved on to other things.

While the Senate Judiciary Committee heard testimony about the ERA in hearings held over three days in May 1970, O'Connor concurrently addressed the subject in remarks to the Associated Women Students at Arizona State University. Her speech focused broadly on women's equality in industry, equal pay, and childcare for working women—issues that closely aligned with those championed by pro-ERA feminists. O'Connor only briefly mentioned the ERA in this speech, yet her focus was on the very issues with which ERA supporters were concerned—women's equality in the professions and the civic sphere. She had not yet reached the resolve exhibited a few years later when she led the charge for Arizona to ratify the amendment.

I am very honored to be here tonight as your guest speaker for the conclusion of ASU's Women's Week.

It is very timely that you should concentrate on the role that women play in this country today. It will have been 50 years next August 26 since the suffragettes succeeded in obtaining final ratification of the franchise for women. Women in this country more or less settled back and relaxed after obtaining the franchise. Now, the great-granddaughters of the suffragettes are unpacking the banners and going forth again to claim equality with men—in law, in treatment, and in attitude.

Women's organizations throughout the land have formed to pursue these goals. There has been a President's Commission on the Status of Women since December 1961. Most states, including Arizona, have state Commissions on the Status of Women. Mrs. Kathryn Gammage is Chairman of Arizona's Commission on the Status of Women. In 1966, Betty Friedan formed the National Organization for Women (NOW). In New York, a group called the Feminists has been formed, the leaders of which advocate an end to the family unit as it now exists.

Other groups of long-standing, such as the YWCA, the BPWC, and the Association of University Women also are taking an active interest in issues relating to equality of women.

What is the situation today which prompts the concern with equality for women? A woman's place is in the home, but it is in other places too. It is in the professions, in government, in civic affairs, and in business, generally. When the good Lord handed out talent and ability, He didn't ask the parents whether they were to be given a boy or a girl. I, as a woman, feel equal, but am I? How do my sisters feel? Who suffers more from economic discrimination: women or blacks? The statistics are revealing. The U.S. Department of Labor has reported that approximately 30 million women are in the labor force in this country. This represents 37% of the nation's labor force and 42% of all women of working age. In Arizona, there are approximately 180,500 women in non-farmer employment, representing 35% of the state's labor force.[5]

For every dollar a man is paid, a woman gets only 58 cents. Three-fifths of all working women are married. Approximately 10.6 million are mothers with children under 18.

A woman with four years of college earns typically $6,694 a year, while her male counterpart earns $11,795. The gap is widening, and the more education a woman has the greater the gap between her and her male counterpart.

With respect to discrimination against women as compared to discrimination against blacks, the median family income of blacks was 60% of the median family income of whites in 1968. In the same year, the median income of a woman was only 58.2% of a man's.

The reason, according to the Women's Bureau of the Department of Labor, is usually not that women are paid less than men for doing the same work. The problem is that women, through discrimination, as well as choice and custom, tend to have lower-paying jobs. Women tend to have jobs as clerks, cosmetologists, typists, or low-paid technicians. They seldom work as painters, carpenters, truck drivers, and engineers. In Arizona, only 600 out of 18,900 in mining. 6,700 out of 28,300 in transportation and utilities. However, in finance and real estate, 14,600 out of 26,800. In education, 24,900 out of 49,000.[6]

Women graduates from the universities this June will be offered lower median starting salaries than male graduates, even though their educational qualifications are the same. For example, female graduates in accounting are being offered $746 per month, compared with $832 per month for male graduates. In liberal arts, women are being offered $631 per month, as compared with $688 per month for the men.

Title VII of the federal Civil Rights Act forbids discrimination in employment on the basis of sex, race, religion, color, or national origin. Arizona has similar laws. Even so, many states have laws regulating the number of hours women can work or the types of jobs they can do. These laws were originally designed to protect women. Today, they tend to discriminate against them and to cause them economic harm, because they make employers unwilling to hire women when the job might, on some occasions, require overtime. I am pleased to have successfully sponsored a bill this session in the Arizona Legislature, which has now been signed by the governor, repealing Arizona's 8-hour law for women's work.

There are other industries that women are still second-class citizens. The percentage of women on college faculties has been declining. There are fewer women in Congress than there were ten years ago. If we doubled the number of women in the U.S. Senate, it would bring the total number of female senators to two! The number of women in state elective office in this state, other than judges, has declined from two to zero, and from a total of nine in the Legislature to eight since 1968.

Many states still excuse women from sitting on juries solely because they are women. Many states, including Arizona, do not give women equal rights with their husbands to manage and dispose of their community property.

Recently, interest has been rekindled on a proposed "equal rights" amendment to the U.S. Constitution. It was first proposed in 1923 and hearings are now being held for the second time before a Senate Judiciary Committee. The equal rights amendment declares, "Equality of rights under the law shall not be denied or abridged by the United States or by any state on account of sex."

Frankly, I am not sure the equal rights amendment is necessary. I am inclined to believe that a few well-chosen cases brought before the federal courts would establish the equality of women under the equal protection clause of the 14th Amendment, and the Civil Rights Act, in a meaningful way.

We all tend to personalize our own experiences in looking at questions such as these and to fit ourselves into the statistics. When I attended Stanford University and then Stanford University Law School a good many years ago, at the University I experienced a feeling of equality of opportunity in terms of scholastic achievement. There were other benefits too. In Law School, there were only 10 women and 300 men.

Upon graduation from law school, I sought job opportunities with various law firms in California. Many firms declined to interview me, and those which did expressed no interest in putting a woman on their staff, even though my class standing was very high. My first employment was in government services as a deputy county attorney. Through the years (I have been out of law school 18 years), the situation has remained much the same. It has always been more difficult for me as a woman to obtain the employment I sought in the first instance, but once obtained, recognition for good performance has never been a problem. Discrimination against women is least in government service and is highest in the private sector. Fortunately, I like government service very much indeed, and it has been a very happy solution for me. Once a woman has gained some experience and earned a reputation as a capable person, she is in greater demand, at least in public and civic service.

Recently, I have entered into a new occupation—that of holding a political office as a member of the State Legislature. Anthropologist Margaret

Mead has stated, "I personally am surprised that more women are not going into politics. If women want real power and change, they must run for public office and use the vote more intelligently." I think Dr. Mead is absolutely right about this. One advantage to being a woman in politics is that while it is not too difficult to put your foot in your mouth in politics, it is a lot harder to do when you are wearing high heels. One of the unexpected little disadvantages of going into politics is that your age becomes a matter of public record, and you periodically gag as you see it there in black and white.

Do marriage, families, and careers for women mix? It depends, of course, on the personalities of the husband and the wife and the special needs of the children. For me, the answer has been emphatically "Yes." American wives have the greatest opportunity in the world to enjoy the freedom of choice as to their avocation. The ultimate happiness to me is the feeling of fulfillment which comes from doing constructive work for the good of society and mankind. Joy is love and work—work of one's choice. Those women who are fortunate enough to have husbands and other means to support them can truly enjoy the freedom of choice to select that work which is most satisfying to them, and to select work of a part-time or occasional nature. How lucky can one be to have both the pleasures of family life and children as well as a productive career! It is possible to achieve, and it makes a woman more interesting and a more dynamic individual to her family, as well as to others.

It helps to marry someone with the understanding and expectation of both partners that the wife intends to pursue her separate career. If this is clear at the outset, there is less likelihood of subsequent disappointment by the husband who experiences a greater share of responsibility for childcare as a result. Husbands today don't necessarily think their wives should not work or become active in politics. In fact, my own husband said when I went to the Senate, "I think it is a tribute to American democracy when a cook, who moonlights as a janitor, can be elected to high public office." I also overheard him remark to someone who asked him what it is like to be married to a Senator, "I've been trying to get next to a political figure for years, and I finally made it."

There is still another advantage to my husband as a result of my career. When I have become too verbose at home, he can remind me to save my remarks for the floor of the Senate where they are paid to listen to me.

I would urge you to consider pursuit of your potential careers and to consider making yourselves available for public office. The cold, hard fact is that the overwhelming percentage of men who would be desirable public officers or members of the legislature are unable to do so because it would be disastrous for their family finances or their normal careers. This leaves a great opportunity for us as women to participate.

There are some specific goals which we as women should also strive to meet in the near future. First, we must provide adequate day-care facilities throughout the nation for the children of women who want to or who must work. Far too little is presently being done in this state and elsewhere about this problem. Second, we must try to change our tax laws so as to allow as a deductible business expense the cost of childcare incurred as a result of employment. Third, we must persuade employers to recognize the value to themselves of providing part-time job opportunities for women at all levels of skill and responsibility. I was forced to work on a full-time basis for an employer until I had become sufficiently indispensable that my employer was then willing to hire me on a part-time basis (which I preferred) in order to continue to have my services. For mothers of school age children, a workday of 9:00 a.m. to 3:30 p.m. is often the only day possible for their continued employment. My work on the Arizona State Personnel Commission convinced me that a woman can often be fully as productive on a part-time basis as other employees are on a full-time basis.

Fourth, we must insist on equal pay for equal work, as well as equal opportunity for positions for which we are qualified. The statistics I quoted earlier show that we have a considerable way to go in this area before reaching our goal. Equal recognition will come of its own accord if we do our work well, and with grace, and dignity.

Fifth, we should support an amendment to Title VII of the Civil Rights Act to include employment of teachers and administrative personnel in education institutions.[7] In working for equality, we would do well to heed the words of John Stuart Mill: "The position which gives the strongest stimulus to the growth of intelligence is that of rising into power, not that of having achieved it; and of all resting points, temporary or permanent, in the way to ascendency, the one which develops the best and highest qualities is the position of those who are strongest enough to make reason prevail, but not strong enough to prevail against reason."

I hope we, as women, can soon achieve that happy state.

Notes

1 Sandra Day O'Connor, "Remarks to Associated Women Students at ASU," May 7, 1970, Arizona State Archives—State, County, and Local Government Records, Arizona Memory Project, https://azmemory.azlibrary.gov/nodes/view/119786. Reprinted with permission from Arizona State University, Archives and Public Records. A special thanks to Wendi Goen for her assistance.

2 Francoise Coste, "'Women, Ladies, Girls, Gals …': Ronald Reagan and the Evolution of Gender Roles in the United States," *Miranda* 12 (2016): 1–18.
3 Julia Malone, "New Right Strategy: Let's Drag Out O'Connor's Confirmation Hearing; Focus: Abortion, Women's Rights, School Prayer," *Christian Science Monitor*, September 3, 1981.
4 Joan Biskupic, *Sandra Day O'Connor: How the First Woman on the Supreme Court Became Its Most Influential Justice* (New York: Harper Perennial, 2005), 59–61.
5 The last sentence of this paragraph is hand-written in O'Connor's speaking copy of the text. She used abbreviations (e.g., "approx") that we have corrected.
6 Beginning with "In Arizona," the following statistics are hand-written in O'Connor's speaking copy. We have included them as written.
7 This fifth call to action is hand-written in O'Connor's speaking copy.

Equal Power and Responsibility for Women

Address to the Senate Judiciary Committee

Pauli Murray
September 15, 1970[1]

Anna Pauline "Pauli" Murray (1910–1985), originally from Baltimore, grew up with relatives in Durham, North Carolina, after her[2] mother died of a cerebral hemorrhage and her father was murdered by a white guard while committed to a mental institution. Murray was no stranger to protesting for racial equality. She mounted a well-publicized campaign to gain entrance to the University of North Carolina, which only admitted white students. In March 1940, Murray and friend Adelene McBean were briefly jailed in Virginia for refusing to comply with segregated seating on a bus—fifteen years before Rosa Parks was arrested in Montgomery, Alabama for the same transgression. Four years after the arrest in Virginia, Murray graduated with a law degree from Howard University as the only woman and first in class—an impressive feat since she achieved academic excellence while organizing other Howard students in a series of risky sit-ins in the nation's capital.[3]

The misogyny she encountered at Howard and in the broader civil rights movement prompted Murray, with Mary O. Eastwood, to coin the term "Jane Crow" to describe the duality of racist and sexist oppression faced by minority women of color.[4] Murray spoke and wrote about Jane Crow for the rest of her life—at Yale Law School while earning a doctorate, while teaching law in Ghana, at the founding of NOW alongside Betty Friedan, and in the legal briefs that inspired Ruth Bader Ginsburg's strategies for fighting sex discrimination through litigation under the Fourteenth Amendment. As if legal advocacy, coalition-building, and protest activities were not enough, Murray spent her later years training to become an Episcopal priest and became the first African American woman ordained in January 1977. The Rev. Dr. Murray died of cancer in 1985 and achieved sainthood in 2012.[5]

Murray joined the civil and political rights subcommittee on John F. Kennedy's Commission on the Status of Women at her friend Eleanor Roosevelt's invitation. At the time, Murray was among the majority of PCSW members who doubted the ERA could accomplish what litigation targeted at specific state laws that discriminated against women could do. At NOW's second national conference, Murray expressed another reason to oppose the ERA: her deep concern that NOW prioritizing the ERA would draw attention away from the plight of poor Black women.[6] But by 1970, Murray's position had changed.[7] Ahead of the May 1970 hearings on the ERA, Murray circulated a memorandum that urged her ACLU colleagues to "reexamine [their] position on the Equal Rights Amendment" and to *not* send any ACLU representative to "testify in opposition to the amendment."[8] Instead, Murray herself appeared to endorse the ERA before the Senate Judiciary Committee in September of that year. In this selection of her testimony, Murray provided a vital glimpse into her own journey in changing her mind on the amendment, leaving no ambiguity as to where she now stood on the ERA.

My name is Pauli Murray, and I am a professor of American Studies at Brandeis University. I am an attorney holding a degree of Doctor of Juridical Science from Yale University School of Law and my field of concentration for almost thirty years has been constitutional law in the field of human rights. Since 1962 when I served on the Committee on Political and Civil Rights of President Kennedy's Commission on the Status of Women, I have devoted my studies to the constitutional rights of individuals not to be discriminated against because of sex and have written extensively in this field. I have also joined with other attorneys in litigation before the Federal courts to test the constitutionality of laws and practices which make legal distinctions on the basis of sex.

As a Negro and a woman, I have labored under the double handicap of discrimination because of race and discrimination because of sex. Having spent nearly fifty years of my life trying to overcome the disabilities and sense of inferiority imposed upon me by reason of my race, I cannot afford another fifty years trying to overcome similar disabilities imposed upon me because of my sex. During the past ten years I have watched almost an entire generation of older women who were responsible for winning the long struggle for women's suffrage pass off the scene before they could win their lifelong struggle for constitutional equality. It is in memory of women like Mary McLeod Bethune, Eleanor Roosevelt, Elsie Hill, Betsy Graves Reyneau[9] and others that I urge the United States Senate to approve the Equal Rights Amendment as adopted by the House of Representatives without change, so that it may be submitted to the States for ratification.

My own life spans the second half-century of the Emancipation of Negroes and the first half-century of the political emancipation of women in the United States. My parents were born during Reconstruction; my grandmother was born in slavery, the progeny of rape by a white master of his octoroon[10] slave. For nearly sixty years I have carried the burden of proof as to my competence and proficiency in a society which has both explicitly and implicitly been dominated by the ideas that Blacks were inherently inferior to Whites and women were inherently inferior to men. My whole personal history has been a struggle to meet standards of excellence against barriers which were placed ever higher as fast as I overcame the last one.

When I graduated from Hunter College in 1933, I faced the barrier of unemployment and the stigma of WPA whom many referred to as "boondogglers."[11] I was among the last to leave the WPA rolls because Negroes were unable to find jobs in private industry. When I sought graduate training at the University of North Carolina in 1938—in the state in which I grew up and in which my family were taxpayers—my application was rejected because of race. My experiences with segregation and other manifestations of racism led me to seek a career as a civil rights attorney and in 1944 I graduated from Howard University School of Law, *cum laude*, first in my class and winner of a Rosenwald Fellowship which specifically stated "for graduate study in law at Harvard University."

When I applied to Harvard University, however, after the submission of my picture and records, I received a letter from the late Professor T. R. Powell, then Chairman of the Committee on Graduate Studies at Harvard Law School, stating, "Your picture and the salutation on your college transcript indicate that you are not of the sex entitled to be admitted to Harvard." Since Harvard Law School was one of the few major law schools in the country which offered a graduate program in law during World War II, I was compelled to travel across the country to the University of California, Berkeley, reduce my fellowship funds through unanticipated travel and out-of-state tuition fees, and instead of devoting my entire energies to graduate scholarship as the Fellowship grant had intended, I found it necessary to do part-time work as a waitress in order to recoup my financial deficit. Within these limitations I was not able to complete the work necessary to qualify for my doctorate, and it was not until twenty years later that I was able to achieve the J.S.D. degree at Yale University.

In short, although my motivation, energy, and effort to meet the highest standards of performance have been operative throughout my life, I have experienced numerous delays in my career, not for the traditional reasons given for the failure of women to develop on par with men in our society (marriage, child-rearing, etc.), but by a combination of individual and institutional racism and sexism—Jim Crow and Jane Crow.

Although today I am a university professor and member of the legal profession holding its highest academic degree, the road over which I have traveled is the experience of most Negro women in America. Born in genteel poverty, I have shared the experience of domestic workers, service workers, lower paid clerical workers, social investigators in the Department of Welfare in New York City and, as a former Consultant to the Equal Employment Opportunity Commission, have intimate knowledge of the problems of race and sex discrimination, particularly in employment opportunity ...

All that has been said about the frustrations and deprivations of American women generally because of discrimination by reason of sex can be said with special force about the position of Black women. If human dignity is the objective of the law which guarantees individual rights, then Negro women as a group historically have suffered the most violent invasions of that personal dignity and privacy which the law seeks to protect. During the slavery era in the United States, it was held by some courts that the rape of a black slave woman was not a criminal act but a trespass on and injury to the property of another person for which the master might recover damages. There was no recourse if the forcible rape was perpetrated by the owner of the slave woman ... The penalty for rape or attempted rape on any white female by a slave or a free Negro, however, was death ...

The relevance of this historical reference to the Equal Rights Amendment is that the Negro woman has suffered more than the mere addition of sex discrimination to race discrimination. She has suffered the *conjunction* of these twin immoralities which produced an aggravated condition of degraded status from which [she] has not yet recovered. For while slavery has been abolished and citizenship has been recognized by virtue of the Thirteenth and Fourteenth Amendments, the Negro woman remains on the lower rank of social and economic status in the United States. The black male, at least, can identify with and aspire to the dominance of this white counterpart. The black female has experienced neither the "protections" which the opponents of the Equal Rights Amendment are so zealous to preserve nor the idealizations of "womanhood" and "motherhood" which the society includes in its mythology . . .

The conjunction of race and sex discrimination directed toward a Negro woman has a special quality of virulence which becomes almost unbearable. My personal experience and observation lead me to believe that when the dominant white male is afflicted by racism and sexism, albeit unconscious, his hostility toward the Negro female who asserts her rights as a person is unbounded. It is as if his superior position is threatened on two fronts simultaneously, and he finds it necessary to resist with greater intransigence than if he were required to yield only a single symbol of dominance. In her struggle for survival with dignity, therefore, the Negro woman stands almost alone and must appeal to the fundamental law of the land to give her a footing upon which to build some semblance of stability for herself and for her children.

Moreover, unless and until the Black woman is accorded the respect of her personhood which is the natural birthright of every individual, the position of all women in the United States is compromised and threatened. There is hardly a member of this Congress who, if he has eyes to see, has not seen upon the face of an aging Negro woman domestic or service worker a look of quiet desperation, or sometimes of grim endurance, and upon the faces of younger, more militant Black women a fury which is almost unbounded. In my view, the tragedy of Angela Davis, is that she saw the hypocrisy of our male-dominated society and not its promise. She lacked the capacity to endure the thousands of crude as well as oblique indignities to which a Negro woman is subjected in the United States and which go unapprehended and unpunished . . . .[12]

I do, however, wish to state that for the past eight years I have been deeply involved in attempting to implement the constitutional rights of women through alternatives to the Equal Rights Amendment. In 1962, at the request of the President's Commission on the Status of Women and its Committee on Civil and Political Rights of which I was a member, I prepared an exhaustive memorandum entitled "A Proposal To Reexamine the Applicability of the Fourteenth Amendment to State Laws and Practices Which Discriminate on the Basis of Sex Per Se."[13] My study advanced the thesis that the principle of equal rights as declared in the text of the proposed Equal Rights Amendment could be established through proper judicial interpretation of the Fourteenth Amendment, provided that there was a reexamination of the doctrine of "sex as a valid basis for legislative classification" and a shift of emphasis from distinctions based upon sex per se to a functional analysis. The Commission adopted this approach in its Final Report in October 1963 and called for early judicial clarification of the constitutional status of women by the Supreme Court so that the principle of equality without regard to sex might be firmly established in our fundamental law. I annex hereto and incorporate as part of this statement the Memorandum.

Advocates of the Equal Rights Amendment who served on the Commission were persuaded to accept this view as a possible route to equal rights, and subsequently those of us who had advocated a reexamination of the Fourteenth Amendment as an alternative labored long and hard to vindicate the Commission's position.

The sad fact is that we have failed. In the seven intervening years, attempts to raise the issue of equality for women before the Supreme Court have been frustrated either through procedural roadblocks or because victories won in the lower courts were not appealed by the States' Attorneys' General. Federal judges resorted to judicial abstention through reluctance to review the *Muller* precedent of 1908 which has not yet been reexamined and overruled by the Supreme Court.[14] In the absence of a clarifying decision by that Court, the constitutional position of women remains ambiguous, and it is entirely understandable and justifiable that women and their attorneys, frustrated by continued judicial delays, now seek an unequivocal constitutional declaration of equality . . .

Finally, I appeal to this Committee and to the United States Senate to use the uniquely human gift of vision and imagination in a creative approach to the Equal Rights Amendment. Much of the testimony already presented has either emphasized the possible dire consequences or the grievances which have led to the urgent demand for the adoption of the Amendment. I suggest that what the opponents of the Amendment most fear is not equal rights but equal power and responsibility. I further suggest that underlying the issue of equal rights for women is the more fundamental issue of equal power for women. No group in power has surrendered its power without a struggle. Many male opponents of equal rights for women recognize the more fundamentally revolutionary nature of the changes which a genuine implementation of such an amendment would bring about. A society in which more than half of the population is absent from the formal authority and decision-making processes is a society in dangerous imbalance. Those who argue in support of the idea of fundamental differences between men and women only reinforce the compelling reasons why women should have access to equal power through the implementation of equal constitutional rights . . .

A Congress of the United States in which one-third or more are women (if one uses the formula of the percentage of the labor force who are women) and the unique experiences of this untapped resource are likely to accelerate our progress toward the solution of such massive problems as pollution, poverty, racism and war. Similarly, in all of the other public and private institutions of the United States, the introduction of women in greater proportion to their representation in the total population than presently exists would necessarily transform these institutions into more humane and inclusive instruments of human activity. The presence of women would also accelerate the presence of other groups in our heterogeneous population and bring into play a variety of human experiences and wisdom which would enrich the entire process. Women may well hold the key to the reconciliation of the races, the generations and the social and economic classes. The adoption of the Equal Rights Amendment and its ratification by the several States could well usher in an unprecedented Golden Age of human relations in our national life and help our country to become an example of the practical ideal that the sole purpose of governments is to create the conditions under which the uniqueness of each individual is cherished and is encouraged to fulfill his or her highest creative potential. The first step toward this goal of equality of right can be taken if the members of the United States Senate can make the great leap of faith and adopt the Equal Rights Amendment by the necessary two-thirds majority. It is the challenge and the opportunity of this Century, and your place in history may be determined by the decision you make upon the other half of the population.

Notes

1 Hearings Before the Committee on the Senate Judiciary, 91st Congress, (1970) (Statement from Pauli Murray). Public Domain.

2 Murray struggled with her sexuality and gender identity throughout her life and, at one point, sought medical attention. She was once married to a man and had relationships with women but did not identify as a lesbian. Murray's choice of a gender-neutral name and use of the phrase "he/she personality" in private correspondence has led to questions about the appropriate use of pronouns. We have followed Murray's biographer Patricia Bell-Scott and used she/her pronouns here. For further discussion, see "Pauli Murray as a LGBTQ+ Historical Figure," National Museum of African American History & Culture, https://nmaahc.si.edu/blog-post/pauli-murray-lgbtq-historical-figure; "Who Is Rev. Dr. Pauli Murray?" Pauli Murray Center for History and Social Justice, https://www.paulimurraycenter.com/who-is-pauli.

3 Patricia Bell-Scott, *The Firebrand and the First Lady: Portrait of a Friendship: Pauli Murray, Eleanor Roosevelt, and the Struggle for Social Justice* (New York: Alfred A. Knopf, 2016), 63.

4 Pauli Murray and Mary O. Eastwood, "Jane Crow and the Law: Sex Discrimination and Title VII," *George Washington Law Review* 34, no. 2 (1965): 232–56.

5 "Pauli Murray Named to Episcopal Sainthood," *Duke Today*, July 14, 2012, https://today.duke.edu/2012/07/saintmurray.

6 Rachel Shteir, *Betty Friedan: Magnificent Disrupter* (New Haven: Yale University Press, 2023), 121.
7 Julie C. Suk, "A Dangerous Imbalance: Pauli Murray's Equal Rights Amendment and the Path to Equal Power," *Virginia Law Review* 107 (2021): 3–20.
8 "Pauli Murray to ACLU Equality Committee," memorandum, 30 March 1970, Pauli Murray Papers: Series II, 1935–1984, Box 55, Folder 959, Schlesinger Library, Radcliffe Institute for Advanced Study, Harvard University, available at https://documents.alexanderstreet.com/d/1000688021.
9 Betsy Graves Reyneau, the first suffragist jailed for protesting against Woodrow Wilson, promoted civil rights through art. See "Betsy Graves Reyneau," *Michigan Women Forward*, https://miwf.org/timeline/betsy-graves-reyneau/.
10 This now offensive term refers to a person whose great-grandparent was of African descent.
11 WPA stands for President Franklin Roosevelt's "Works Progress Administration," a work-relief program. "Boondoggler" is a derogatory term that refers to useless activity that suggests the appearance of work, or doing nothing. See Nathan B. Silverstein, "Benefits Seen in New Deal; Payments to WPA Employees Viewed as Aids to Recovery," *New York Times*, September 4, 1936, 18.
12 See Meredith L. Roman, "'Armed and Dangerous': The Criminalization of Angela Davis and the Cold War Myth of America's Innocence," *Women, Gender, and Families of Color* 8, no. 1 (2020): 87–111.
13 Pauli Murray, "A Proposal to Reexamine the Applicability of the Fourteenth Amendment to State Laws and Practices Which Discriminate on the Basis of Sex Per Se," December 1, 1962, Box 8, Folder 62, President's Commission on the Status of Women Records, 1961–1963, Schlesinger Library, Radcliffe Institute for Advanced Study, Harvard University, https://documents.alexanderstreet.com/d/1000681163.
14 *Muller v. Oregon*, 208 U.S. 412 (1908) decided that the Fourteenth Amendment does not prevent the limitation of women's work hours.

The Price of Inequality Is High Indeed

Address to the U.S. House of Representatives

Bella Abzug

October 6, 1971[1]

Senator Edward Kennedy once described his colleague Bella Savitzky Abzug (1920–1998) as "a central figure in the politics of the country for twenty-five years—kind of a revolutionary."[2] Abzug's early career as an attorney had her representing people brought before the House Un-American Activities Committee. Within her caseload was the highly publicized case of Willie McGee, a Black man who many believed was falsely accused of raping a married white woman.[3] Abzug later won a seat representing New York in the House of Representatives from 1971 to 1977. "Battling Abzug," as she was called, used her political clout in the House to draw attention to a host of women's rights issues, including Title IX and the ERA, often while wearing one of her trademark hats. She helped found both Women Strike for Peace and the NWPC. Following the 1977 National Women's Conference in Houston, Jimmy Carter named Abzug as co-chair of the bipartisan National Advisory Committee for Women. But Abzug and Carter clashed, and after six months, Carter had her fired. Gloria Steinem called it the "Friday afternoon massacre" as other committee members resigned in protest.[4] Abzug spent her later years continuing to advocate for women's equality and died of breast cancer and heart disease in 1998.[5]

On October 6, 1971, Abzug addressed her colleagues at length on the House floor. In large part, her rhetorical task was to challenge a modification to the ERA proposed by Representative Charles E. Wiggins (R-CA), who believed that women should be exempted from the military draft because the Department of Defense allegedly told him that it would be "impossible for the military to operate" should the ERA be ratified. In this section of her address, Abzug masterfully laid out her arguments and refuted the claims of those who oppose the ERA on the basis of how it might adversely reshape the military. The House rejected the Wiggins amendment and finally passed the ERA by a 354 to 23 vote one week after Abzug's address. Alongside Shirley Chisholm, Margaret Heckler, and Patsy Mink, Abzug proudly voted in favor of the ERA, which then moved on to the Senate for approval.[6]

I rise in support of the Equal Rights Amendment in its original form, unfettered by the crippling Wiggins Amendment. Equal rights for over one-half of the population of the United States is unquestionably the most important piece of business before this Congress. An amendment proposing equal rights for women under the law was before Congress in 1923. Now, after almost 50 years of enduring repeated defeats, the women of the United States demand their ... equal treatment under the law, nothing more and nothing less.

If there remains in your minds a doubt concerning the need for such an amendment to assure women in this country their rightful equality, I ask you this question ... who, men or women, wield the power in this country?

In this legislative body, there are 12 women. Of 100 senators, one is a woman.[7] This token member has the formidable task of representing 51% of our population in the law-making branch of our federal government.

Once the laws are made, women, like men, must look to the courts for their interpretation. The courts remain an almost exclusively male stronghold. Only one of 97 U.S. Courts of Appeal judgeships is filled by a woman. Four of 402 federal district court judges are women. And the Supreme Court, the ultimate arbiter of those human rights so often denied women, has not one female justice. So much for the representation of women in the legislative and judicial branches of our government ...

Let me briefly review those arguments which opponents to the Equal Rights Amendment have offered. Perhaps the most serious charge, and one which is reflected in the Wiggins Amendment, is that the Equal Rights Amendment will destroy the "protective legislation," particularly labor legislation, which has so benefited women. My colleagues, the inferior position that women now occupy in the employment field is, in large part, the result of actions of male-dominated state legislatures and labor commissions that persist in enforcing anachronistic state laws restricting women in employment. What is the protection afforded by these laws? The protection has been to preserve the male prerogative which has been made virtually immune from assault by barring all females from the competition ...

An argument that has been voiced with the greatest frequency and vehemence in opposition to the Equal Rights Amendment is that women would be subject to the draft. My colleagues, I hope that my position on the draft is clear to you. I am unilaterally opposed to the draft! The draft is a terrible thing, and it is my belief that nobody, male or female, ought to be subject to compulsory military service. I am adamant and uncompromising in my opposition.

But I am equally adamant in my resolve not to stand by and see the Equal Rights Amendment weakened or defected by those who do not believe in the concept of full equality for America's women. And these foes of sexual equality have seized upon the issue of the draft as their best means of defeating this measure. It would be a mockery of justice to allow this issue to deny women their just rights.

This last tragic decade of war has made clear to us that the draft, so long as it persists, and I would hope that it would not continue another day, is without question the most serious and onerous feature of citizenship. A whole mythology, based on the concept of women's physical inferiority, has developed in connection with military service, and the result has been to reinforce women's status as sub-citizenship. The social stereotype persists that women should somehow be less concerned with the affairs of the world than men. In the Congress of the United States and in the political life of this nation, political choices and debate often reflect a belief that *men* who have fought for their country have a special right to wield political power and make political decisions. When women are limited by Armed Forces regulation to no more than a fixed percentage of the total Armed Forces, they are denied this right. And this right is no less than the right for a woman to be taken seriously as a citizen who shares equally with men all civic responsibilities and enjoys the full complement of privileges associated with citizenship. So long as this right and responsibility are denied women, they are denied the status of full citizenship, and the respect that goes with that status.

What are the arguments against making women subject to the draft? The only compelling argument in my view is that no one should be subject to the draft, but I confront much lesser points.

The first argument is that women are incapable of combat duty. My colleagues, history is replete with examples of women who have fought side by side with men in defense of their homes and country.

The second argument voices speculative concern for matters of discipline if men and women serve together in combat situations. And surely it is grossly insulting and unreasonable to suppose that persons, women and men, facing a situation fraught with danger will behave without courage and discipline.

The final argument raises the terrible prospect of women engaged in killing. I tell you now that all combat is degrading, dehumanizing, and dangerous. As between ritualizing our young men and our young women, there is little to choose. I voted against student exemptions from the draft on the grounds that special burdens should not be placed on the poor and those with minimal education. It is my belief that all young men were equally subjected to the draft. The move to end the draft would be immeasurably strengthened by the extension of personal interest. So too, I feel that making women subject to the draft would be one of the quickest ways to end this depressive regulation for all citizens.

The Equal Rights Amendment would make voluntary as well as compulsory military service available to women and men on the same basis.

Although it has long been recognized that the military service has served as the "poor boy's college," apparently no thought has been given to what has happened to the poor boy's sister while he has found a road out of his cycle of poverty and despair. The Equal Rights Amendment would insure that the real and substantial benefits available through military service are available to women on the same basis that they are available to men . . .

My colleagues, we are confronting an ironic situation. The cry has been against compulsory military service for women because they will be involved in combat. The truth is that only a very small percentage of men, 8%, presently serving in the Armed Forces are in combat zones. While the remaining vast majority fulfill their military obligations in non-combat positions, they are receiving valuable training and education, and they will continue to receive benefits from their military service after they have left service to return to private life. The Equal Rights Amendment would ensure that women who seek, or are subject to, military service receive the same training and benefits to which men are now entitled, but which are denied to women.

Fellow members of Congress, let us not forget that the Armed Forces is a very substantial employer with approximately 2.7 million employees. Women have a right to seek employment in the Armed Forces on the same basis as men, to receive the same training, and to benefit from the same privileges now accruing only to men. We cannot indulge in hypocrisy by allowing this sector of the federal government to discriminate in a manner, which, were the government covered as an employer under Title VII of the Civil Rights Act of 1964, is directly in violation of federal law.

The matter of sex discrimination in education is such an important matter that I feel I must touch on it, although I do not have the time to give it the full attention that it deserves. Why is sex discrimination in education such an important issue? The answer is two-fold: it is because sex discrimination is so pervasive in every level of our educational system, and because it shapes the aspirations of young girls when their personalities and expectations are most malleable. Females first learn in the classroom that they can aspire to no better than second-class citizenship. The message is clear in many ways . . . in textbooks, illustration, and teacher models. Girls can grow up to be nurses, but only boys can be doctors; girls can aspire to motherhood which consumes all their energies, while boys become fathers and master careers; girls can learn to take dictation, but boys can learn to dictate.

The formative influence on young minds of societal expectations cannot be exaggerated. Young girls who seek to achieve educationally rather than to assume the submissive, dependent, and deferential role that society has dictated for them are found by psychologists to suffer fear of social rejection should they succeed.

Sex discrimination in education extends beyond students into the teaching and administrative level to find its victims. Although men are only 12% of the elementary school teachers, they account for 78% of the elementary school principals. Of the 13,000 school district superintendents, only two are women, and education is traditionally a "woman's field"!

At the secondary school level, 1/2 of the teachers are women but only 4% of the high school principals are women.

One example can illustrate graphically the discrimination that women encounter in seeking admission to colleges and universities. In 1964, 21,000 women were turned down for college entrance in Virginia. During that same time, not *one* male applicant was rejected.

Even beyond the graduate level, women continue to suffer from academic myths. The myth is that there is a shortage of qualified female candidates for doctorates, but the fact is that a higher percentage of women with doctorates go into teaching than men with doctorates. And now that we are beginning to see a surplus of Ph.D.'s in some academic areas, we have begun to see the plight of women worsen, for women are often the "last hired" and the "first to be let go" in the academic community.

It is a revealing statistic that of the *2,700* charges filed by the Women's Equity Action League against colleges and universities for sex discrimination in employment of faculty, *none* has ever been refuted.

My colleagues, when young girls and young women are denied the right to an equal education, without regard to their sex, they are handicapped for their lifetimes.

The Equal Rights Amendment proposes to give equality of rights to women and men, so that sex is not a factor in determining what rights one enjoys. There are two qualifications to this general rule: The Equal Rights

Amendment will not preclude legislation, or official action, relating to physical characteristics unique to one sex, and will not preclude legislation respecting personal privacy. For example, laws providing maternity benefits would not be violative of the Equal Rights Amendment since only women can qualify as mothers. Similarly, laws regulating sperm donors would stand since only men can fulfill this function. This is not discrimination: It is simple recognition of a physical characteristic unique to one or the other sex.

A particularly frivolous argument opposing the Equal Rights Amendment is that men and women would be forced to use the same restrooms and bedrooms. The obvious solution is for the Supreme Court to extend the right of privacy recognized in *Griswold v. Connecticut*[8] to permit separate restrooms and sleeping quarters in public institutions …

My colleagues, I think that you should know something else which you may not know. The women of America know that polite society looks with ostensible horror at one who tells an ethnic joke, portrays racial stereotypes, or acknowledges religious prejudice. Yet, in this same society, women are the butt of crude jokes on the cocktail circuit, the object of gross discrimination in the employment and educational sector, and caricatured pawns in the advertising world. But the women of America will no longer content themselves with leavings and bits and pieces of the rights enjoyed by men.

Be assured that your vote will be recorded … whether you return to Congress or are defeated by the organized opposition of women to whom you have denied equal rights may be decided by this vote. This is a fact of political life in 1971. Equal Rights and equal responsibilities … we demand no more and will accept no less!

Notes

1 Bella Abzug, "The Equal Rights Amendment Statement of Congresswoman Abzug," October 6, 1971, Bella Abzug Papers 1970–1976, Series VII: Public Statements, Subseries VII: 4: Speeches and Remarks, October 6—Equal Rights Amendment (1971), Columbia University Rare Book & Manuscript Library. Public Domain. A special thanks to Tara Craig and Jonathan Jara at Columbia University Library's Rare Book & Manuscript Library.

2 Suzanne Braun Levine and Mary Thom, *Bella Abzug: How One Tough Broad from the Bronx Fought Jim Crow and Joe McCarthy, Pissed Off Jimmy Carter, Battled for the Rights of Women and Workers, Rallied Against War and for the Planet, and Shook Up Politics Along the Way, An Oral History* (New York: Farrar, Straus and Giroux, 2007), 111.

3 See further Bridgette McGee-Robinson, "My Grandfather's Execution," All Things Considered, *NPR*, May 7, 2010, https://www.npr.org/2010/05/07/126539134/my-grandfathers-execution.

4 Carole Ashkinaze, "It Was Bella Abzug's Strident Style, Not Substance, That Got Her Fired," *Atlanta Constitution*, January 20, 1979, 3B.
5 "Bella Savitzky Abzug," United States House of Representatives, History, Art & Archives, https://history.house.gov/People/Detail/8276.
6 Eileen Shanahan, "Equal Rights Amendment Passed by House, 354–23," *New York Times*, October 13, 1971, 1.
7 Margaret Chase Smith (R-ME).
8 *Griswold v. Connecticut* is a 1965 Supreme Court ruling that, on the basis of privacy, struck down a Connecticut law criminalizing the use of contraception by married couples. See "Griswold v. Connecticut," Planned Parenthood, https://www.plannedparenthoodaction.org/issues/birth-control/griswold-v-connecticut.

Section IV The Debate Splits: 1972–1982

The seven-year ratification period between 1972 and 1979—later extended by three years to 1982—represented the most intense, divisive, and publicized period of debate about the Equal Rights Amendment. The ERA's supporters continued to stretch across the political spectrum and generate new opportunities for bipartisan and multiracial collaboration. Concurrently, a number of new organizations formed to pursue the ERA's ratification in earnest.

At NOW, Betty Friedan, Aileen Hernandez, Wilma Scott Heide, Karen DeCrow, and Eleanor "Ellie" Smeal all prioritized the ERA during and well beyond their respective presidential tenures between 1966 and 1987.[1] On February 17, 1970, Heide led some 20 NOW members into a Senate subcommittee hearing, where they disrupted deliberations about lowering the voting age to insist that the ERA be given a fair chance to be heard. "I am not a 'bubble head' and I do not burn bras. I am a middle-class member of mid-America," Heide later testified.[2] Once Congress passed the ERA, the women of NOW felt confident about the ratification process—so much so that they only held one workshop about the ERA at their 1973 convention.[3] When NOW reached another key goal that year, the members were even more optimistic. The Supreme Court ruling in *Roe v. Wade* guaranteed women reproductive rights through access to safe and legal abortion services. *Roe* remained federal law for nearly 50 years.[4] By 1974, three out of every four Americans supported the ERA. Furthermore, the amendment enjoyed considerable support among political conservatives, religious fundamentalists, and housewives in these early years of the ratification period.[5]

Once it became clear that the ERA's path to ratification would not be smooth or inevitable, however, the women of NOW mobilized. With the deadline approaching, NOW leaders declared an "ERA Emergency" and called for boycotts in unratified states when planning vacations and gatherings.[6] This proved an effective and, as the U.S. Court of Appeals affirmed, perfectly legal method of exercising free speech.[7] Political scientist Maryann

Barakso has documented other creative rhetorical methods that NOW leaders and members employed during the ratification period.

> NOW ... conducted vigils in front of the White House (including one thirty-seven-day fast by eight members), door-to-door education campaigns, walkathons, marches dedicated to the memory of suffragists, and protests at Mormon temples (one of which involved activists chaining themselves to temple gates) and conservative churches.[8]

In the final years of the ratification period, NOW devoted a quarter of its budget to efforts in the hold-out states. Members left their jobs and even their home states to help the ERA in fiercely fought state campaigns.

The nonpartisan National Women's Political Caucus (NWPC), founded in 1971 to increase the number of women in office, also promoted the ERA during the ratification period. Members saw the amendment as a key priority for helping achieve better, more equitable political representation at national, state, and local levels. Comanche activist LaDonna Harris, Mexican American activist Lupe Anguiano, and African American civil rights activists Myrlie Evers, Fannie Lou Hamer, and Dorothy Height joined forces with a bipartisan alliance of pro-ERA feminists and politicians including Bella Abzug, Shirley Chisholm, Betty Friedan, Ann Lewis, Patsy Mink, Eleanor Holmes Norton, Jill Ruckelshaus, and Gloria Steinem to establish and expand the NWPC. Two NWPC members, liberal Texas Democrat Liz Carpenter and moderate Michigan Republican Elly Peterson, teamed up in 1976 to co-chair ERAmerica, a group devoted to securing the final ratifications needed to bring the ERA over the finish line through fundraising, lobbying, education, and public relations. Although ERAmerica struggled to achieve the high goals set by its visionary leaders, its very existence sent a strong signal that women of very different beliefs could unite for common causes.[9]

At the American Civil Liberties Union, lawyers Brenda Feigen and Ruth Bader Ginsburg advocated for the ERA on legal grounds as co-directors of the new Women's Rights Project. Harvard Law alumna and NOW member Feigen had not only testified at the May 1970 Senate hearings, but she had also arranged the pro-ERA testimony at the request of Senator Birch Bayh (D-IN). Ginsburg, who went on to become the second woman appointed to the U.S. Supreme Court, developed and tested legal strategies across numerous sex discrimination cases during her time at the ACLU. As strong ERA advocates, both women sought to ensure equal opportunities for women by generating educational materials for women about their legal rights and training other attorneys in how to better represent women under the law.[10]

In a precedent-shattering turn, former and current first ladies of this era departed from their predecessors who either opposed the ERA or stayed silent on the subject.[11] Lady Bird Johnson, Pat Nixon, Betty Ford, and Rosalynn Carter all came out in support of the ERA during the ratification period. An endorsement published under Nixon's name appeared in the 1972 Republican National Convention program. Republican Ford and Democrat Carter launched serious—and controversial—national advocacy campaigns that leveraged their influence with their husbands, their political parties, lawmakers, the press, and the public. When attacked for her advocacy, Ford boldly declared at the 1975 International Women's Year Conference in Cleveland, Ohio that "being ladylike does not require silence" on the ERA or anything else.[12] Johnson, Ford, and Carter sent a meaningful bipartisan message when they stood on stage together in 1977 to address the National Women's Conference in Houston. And in the final push to ratify, Johnson and Ford joined Ellie Smeal at a 1981 ERA rally in front of the Lincoln Memorial.[13]

But as partisan politics increasingly enveloped the ERA debate, Republican Nancy Reagan stood apart from her first lady contemporaries when it came to the ERA. She demurred that while she and her husband "both believe in equal rights, equal pay and all the things ... ['Ronnie'] just feels a better way to go about it is through legislation than that amendment."[14] Conversely, Maureen Reagan was an ERA loyalist who unsuccessfully tried to persuade her anti-feminist father to change his mind.[15] Reagan's Secretary of Transportation Elizabeth Hanford Dole tried as well, but reluctantly conceded at a 1984 press conference that the Republican president was not going to budge on this issue.[16]

All told, however, never before had the ERA enjoyed such widespread and institutional support, especially with visible backers in the White House for most of the ratification period. Thirty states ratified the ERA within the first year alone.[17]

For all the apparent harmony and coalition-building, the women's rights movement was not monolithic in its political strategies, prioritization of goals, achievements at inclusivity, and leadership philosophies—not unlike the differences between Alice Paul's NWP and Carrie Chapman Catt's LWV a half-century earlier. Betty Friedan balked at the idea of including the rights of lesbians in NOW's founding documents, famously coining the phrase "lavender menace" to encapsulate her belief that "man-hating" lesbians might compromise the case for women's liberation.[18] She was already behind the times. In 1955, Phyllis Lyon and Del Martin had founded the Daughters of Bilitis, the earliest lesbian organization in the nation. When police raided

New York's Stonewall Inn in 1969, a movement for gay liberation launched. That same year, Friedan ousted lesbians and lesbian allies in the New York NOW chapter, and women like Rita Mae Brown departed to found new organizations such as Radicalesbians to seek inclusion of lesbianism in feminist goals.[19] Gloria Steinem insisted that sexual preference should not preclude women from participating in the movement, and she correctly worried that division on this issue would empower anti-feminists to mobilize and form a strong opposition to feminist goals, including the ERA. Although NOW passed a resolution in 1971 making lesbian rights a "legitimate concern of feminism," the issue had already created the kind of opening that Steinem feared.[20]

Abortion was an intensely divisive issue as well. Antiabortion women left NOW in 1968 to create their own organization, the Women's Equity Action League (WEAL). WEAL took a different and less militant approach than NOW, hoping to entice conservative women into membership around three signature issues: education, employment, and tax inequalities. Though in sharp disagreement with NOW's endorsement of abortion in its Bill of Rights, the women of WEAL found common ground in NOW's commitment to seeing the ERA pass.[21] But the formation of new groups, often in competition with one another, hindered the ability for the ERA's supporters to have a truly unified front. Historian William H. Chafe summarizes the dilemma well: "The advantage was that women could enter into the movement in many places and feel comfortable. The disadvantage was that at times energies seemed divided, and disagreement rather than consensus prevailed over what needed to be done."[22]

Women's rights activists soon learned that having a unified front would be desperately needed, for a conservative cyclone was circling in the Midwest. In February 1972, Illinois activist Phyllis Schlafly published her usual kind of crank literature with a feminine touch in her newsletter, *The Phyllis Schlafly Report*. A master at self-publishing and a failed political candidate, Schlafly had been wielding her persona as an "underdog" against East Coast Republican "kingmakers" for eight years. Her popular 1964 book *A Choice Not an Echo* helped convince the GOP to reject Nelson Rockefeller and nominate Barry Goldwater for president. Her tropes were familiar to any far-right John Birch Society member: a persecution complex, a dystopic fantasy that powerful elites were conspiratorially in power, and an isolationist American exceptionalism.[23] Hers were, in other words, protectionist arguments of a rather different sort than previously seen.

But that early 1972 edition of Schlafly's *Report* launched the savvy homemaker into territory that would create her empire. Her arguments became the primary talking points for a certain group of conservative women across the United States who rose up to form a loosely aligned coalition of anti-ERA proponents. Called "What's Wrong with 'Equal Rights' for Women?" Schlafly argued that the "privilege" of American (white) womanhood was far better than any paltry rights "equality" might grant. Yes, American women were on a lovely pedestal, and on that pedestal, they must stay.

The article seemed to be just another easily-ignored newsletter from Schlafly. At least it was until one of her 5,000 subscribers, Ann Patterson from Oklahoma, called her up. Patterson had been mildly supportive of the ERA. Like most Republicans, she considered it a good thing—until she read Schlafly's article. Patterson phoned her Oklahoma state representative since the ERA was in deliberation. She, then, distributed reprints of Schlafly's article within the Oklahoma House before the vote. On March 29, the ERA faced its first defeat in the United States. The ERA's supporters were not especially worried; it was, after all, just *one* state.[24] But Schlafly could smell blood in the water. If she and her band of white, middle-class housewives could slow down the ERA's passage in Oklahoma, where could they go next? By May, the STOP ERA ("Stop Taking Our Privileges") campaign was born.

In Texas, a church secretary heard something different in the ERA. Lottie Beth Hobbs was a Church of Christ employee and a regular ladies' Bible study leader. She knew fundamentalist women. When she first heard about "equal rights," she marched off to the public library for information. The feminist books she checked out appalled her; so much that she hid them under her bed so that her nieces and nephews wouldn't see them and be tainted (Hobbs remained unmarried). Schlafly's original newsletter fell into her purview as well. And Hobbs lifted large portions of Schlafly's arguments with one key addition: what the ERA would do to "the church." In 1974, Hobbs took the text to a local printer and asked him to jazz it up with some clip art. "Ladies, Have You Heard?" included two women connected by a long, spiraled phone cord stretching around the border of the page. Pink was her choice to grab women's attention to "appeal to the appalled."[25] All over Texas hanging on front doorknobs and tucked inside church bulletins, Hobbs' "pink sheets" tapped into a market that Schlafly and Patterson really couldn't reach—fundamentalist women.[26] Hobbs found a way to infuse her pietistic evangelism with the separatist fears of one-world governmental takeovers and moral decline. These familiar tropes propelled the newly formed STOP ERA movement. Hobbs herself brought the Texas fundamentalist participation to nearly 60%.[27]

In sum, without fundamentalist women, STOP ERA would have never started or flourished the way that it did. The fear they fomented was easily peddled to small groups of women dotted across the country, meeting in Mary Kay parties, PTAs, and Bible studies. These women were alarmed at even the choice to leave their confining domestic pedestal. And whispering about these anxieties within accessible networks is an efficient method of persuasion.[28]

The merging of Catholics with fundamentalists was still tenuous, however. The rhetorical parallels between Schlafly's John-Birch-style conservatism and fundamentalist separatism were obvious. Both were afraid of the mythical "communist." Both saw themselves as underdogs over and against the power brokers of the Republican Party. Both considered their influence "grassroots." Both were able to frame themselves as allies of powerful white men rather than grasping for power themselves.[29] However, these two activist trajectories landed in opposite locations. STOP ERA was a gateway into politics; and Hobbs' politically-charged evangelism feathered her ecclesiastical nest apart from governmental intervention.

Meanwhile, Mormon women, who had long been at the forefront of the ERA debate, were outside this fundamentalist vs. mainline squabble. Before Congress passed the ERA, Mormons had generally supported a constitutional amendment for equality without controversy. LDS General Relief Society President Amy Brown Lyman and General Young Women's President Lucy Grant Cannon both endorsed the ERA in the 1940s. Judge Reva Beck Bosone, Utah's first Congresswoman, publicly supported the ERA until her death in 1983.[30] Capitalizing on Utah's perceived progressive history supporting woman suffrage, Mormon women of the 1970s could easily argue for equality's inclusion in the Constitution, as excommunicated ERA advocate Sonia Johnson articulated. Nevertheless, the LDS's patriarchal ethic cements a gender hierarchy. If Mormons are building a family for eternity, a complimentary or subjugated status for women must endure. Since the LDS origin story reinforces that the United States is exceptionally blessed by God, Mormon Barbara Smith easily defended a status quo that placed feminism—and, thus, the ERA—in opposition to the home, family, and church.[31] For many Mormon women, church opposition to the ERA constituted a profound betrayal of the legacy for women's rights established by their foremothers. As of 2023, Utah still has not ratified the ERA.[32]

More mainline religious voices, like Catholic nun Maureen Fiedler and feminist theologian Virginia Mollenkott, dominated the 1970s pro-ERA arguments. Fielder casuistically stretched the ERA to comport with Catholic primacy of pro-life arguments, and Mollenkott donned a professorial tone to alleviate the evangelical fears STOP ERA stirred. She used the evangelical hermeneutic in her article and stood in direct contrast with fundamentalist

ERA opponent Beneth Jones, whose husband called Mollenkott a "devil."[33] In a less contentious pairing, Johnson stood face-to-face with her fellow Mormon counterpart, Barbara Smith, whose argument was not as incendiary as the fundamentalists.

These counter arguments prompted Schlafly to adjust to the evangelical nomenclature. In 1977, she published the *Power of the Positive Woman.* Yet in 1981, the book was adapted to be the *Power of the Christian Woman* with the majority of changes in the first chapter to include many Bible verses. The book was essentially the same, but after the first chapter, the fundamentalist woman would be hooked.[34]

The STOP ERA identity remained irresistible. Always-poised, Schlafly specifically would boast about her ultra-femininity in order to, as we say in the twenty-first century, "own the libs." Irritating the "libbers" was Schlafly's chief rhetorical strategy, and her confidence inspired white conservative women. Since the Antis were unencumbered by political norms, they could be exasperatingly creative. They created a "Bread Day," for instance, and gave state legislators homemade bread—zucchini quick bread, by the way—along with this poem from Oklahoma fundamentalist, Beverly Findley:

> Women who want to be women
> Have made this bread for you
> Because they love being homemakers
> All the year through.
>
> It's an honor to be a homemaker,
> In this right we want to remain,
> But the ERA would take away our choice
> And have laws read: men, women, same.
>
> We cannot be the same as men,
> We're just not created that way.
> We have a place in life to fullfill [sic]
> And are content to leave it that way.
>
> So enjoy your bread,
> Appreciate it too,
> Because unless the ERA is stopped,
> The homemaker may be you![35]

The Antis' creativity won them media attention, while the political elites soldiered on with their persistent and expected support.

To listen only to the white political elites debating with the white political upstarts, however, misses the complete picture and reinforces aspects of what Gloria Steinem aptly called "The Catfight Theory of History."[36] That conflict was among cisgender, white, middle-class women fighting for the attention of white male officials. When we listen more deeply, we see rhetorical diversity at work. Civil rights activist Dorothy Height carried the argumentative torch from Mary Church Terrell into this era. Barbara Jordan and Patsy Mink were among the first women of color elected to the Congress. After protectionist arguments fueled the rhetoric of women of color in the earliest ERA debates, Jordan and Mink were clear that the amendment is necessary for "womankind" and "sisterhood" writ large. Latina scholar Marta Sotomayor agreed. Queer activists Midge Constanza, Virginia Mollenkott, and Sonia Johnson all added their full-throated endorsements. These women demand inclusivity while still critiquing ERA's opposition. They mapped a path forward for all American women—a path *through* the Equal Rights Amendment—while pending anti-equalitarian legislation still threatens their progress. They also expanded the significance and stakes of the debate.

Yet listen even more carefully. There are forgotten voices in this section that too many historians ignore. Addie Wyatt was the link between the protectionist arguments from the earliest debates among women of color and the 1970s. Wyatt is often listed as a feminist activist, but her voice is rarely highlighted.[37] Her speech was unusual because she normalizes changing one's mind when presented with new information and changing exigencies. Yolanda Orozco remained unimpressed with the promises of the ERA for Chicana women. Native American activist Ethel Krepps was completely unconvinced that so-called equality will change anything for her and for people like her. These critics stood both opposed to STOP ERA and apathetic to the ERA, countering easy classifications of the amendment's debaters as either strong supporters or staunch opponents.

Thus, women debating the Equal Rights Amendment in the decade after 1972 stretched the argumentative boundaries. The sides were never simply bifurcated in these ten years but multifaceted and intersectional. At times, ERA historians frame the STOP ERA movement as unlike any previous political movement. Marjorie J. Spruill summarizes that "for the first time in American history, leaders from these previously hostile religious groups seem to fear encroaching secularism as a threat posed by feminism more than they feared one another."[38] However, the postbellum Women's Christian Temperance Union and the 1920s and 1930s Ku Klux Klan galvanized the same women for a moral crusade: white, middle-class, pious, nostalgic, and religious. Both organizations, like STOP ERA, played to the same white fear of the marauder.[39] This was nothing new in the 1970s. Women coalesced around religious piety in the 1890s and the 1920s. In their earlier political activism, American white women frequently ignored women of color just as they did in the 1970s. We can correct that oversight by listening closely today.

Notes

1 "Past and Current Presidents," National Organization for Women, https://now.org/about/history/presidents/.
2 David M. Dismore, "Today in Feminist History: The E.R.A. in the Senate (September 15, 1970)," *Ms. Magazine*, September 15, 2020, https://msmagazine.com/2020/09/15/feminist-history-september-15/.
3 Maryann Barakso, *Governing NOW: Grassroots Activism in the National Organization for Women* (Ithaca: Cornell University Press, 2004), 63.
4 "The Intertwining History of NOW and the ERA," National Organization for Women, https://now.org/the-intertwining-history-of-now-and-the-era/.
5 Mark R. Daniels, Robert Darcy, and Joseph W. Westphal, "The ERA Won—At Least in the Opinion Polls," *PS*, 15, no. 4 (1982): 578–84.
6 Barakso, *Governing NOW*, 70–72.
7 Harold J. Logan, "NOW Says State Suits Show ERA Boycott's Impact," *Washington Post*, March 6, 1978, A2.
8 Barakso, *Governing NOW*, 80–81.
9 Marjorie J. Spruill, *Divided We Stand: The Battle Over Women's Rights and Family Values That Polarized American Politics* (New York: Bloomsbury, 2017), 27, 58; "The Long Road to Equality: What Women Won from the ERA Ratification Effort," Library of Congress, https://guides.loc.gov/american-women-essays/era-ratification-effort#note_29.
10 Brenda Feigen, *Not One of the Boys: Living Life as a Feminist* (New York: Alfred A. Knopf, 2000); Amy Leigh Campbell, "Raising the Bar: Ruth Bader Ginsburg and the ACLU Women's Rights Project," *Texas Journal of Women and the Law* 11 (2002): 157–243.
11 Jill Abraham Hummer, *First Ladies and American Women* (Lawrence: University Press of Kansas, 2017).
12 Betty Ford, "International Women's Year Conference, Cleveland, Ohio, October 25, 1975," Frances K. Pullen Papers, Box 3, Gerald R. Ford Presidential Library, https://www.fordlibrarymuseum.gov/library/document/0003/1069183.pdf.
13 Barbara Rodriguez and Orion Rummler, "The 19th Explains: What Is the Equal Rights Amendment and Will it Become Part of the Constitution?" *19th News*, April 27, 2023, https://19thnews.org/2021/03/equal-rights-amendment-19th-explains/.
14 "Nancy Reagan Denies Giving President Cue," *New York Times*, August 19, 1984, 29.
15 Spruill, *Divided We Stand*, 288–89.
16 "Elizabeth Dole Suspends Push for Rights Measure," *New York Times*, September 28, 1984, A22.
17 Julie C. Suk, *We the Women: The Unstoppable Mothers of the Equal Rights Amendment* (New York: Skyhorse Publishing, 2020), 82.

18 Ruth Rosen, *The World Split Open: How the Modern Women's Movement Changed America* (New York: Viking, 2000), 83.
19 Rory Dicker, *A History of U.S. Feminisms* (Berkeley, CA: Seal Press, 2016), 93–94.
20 Spruill, *Divided We Stand*, 22.
21 Rosen, *The World Split Open*, 83.
22 William H. Chafe, "The Road to Equality," in *No Small Courage: A History of Women in the United States*, ed. Nancy F. Cott (New York: Oxford University Press, 2000), 553–54.
23 Spruill, *Divided We Stand*, 112.
24 Chelsea L. Ball, "From Red Dirt to Red State: Oklahoma and the Equal Rights Amendment, 1972–1982," Master's thesis (University of Oklahoma, 2016); Ruth Murray Brown, *For a Christian America: A History of the Religious Right* (New York: Prometheus, 2013), 30.
25 Brown, *For a Christian America*, 107.
26 Brown, *For a Christian America*, 39, 51, 65.
27 Brown, *For a Christian America*, 75; see further Camille K. Lewis, *Romancing the Difference: Kenneth Burke, Bob Jones University, and the Rhetoric of Religious Fundamentalism* (Waco, TX: Baylor University Press, 2007).
28 Spruill, *Divided We Stand*, 107; Brown, *For a Christian America*, 35.
29 Spruill, *Divided We Stand*, 133–34, 138; Jerome Himmelstein, *To the Right: The Transformation of American Conservatism* (Oakland: University of California Press, 1992), 67–76.
30 Kelly Whited Jones, "100 Years Later, Women Are Still Fighting for Equality and the ERA," *Salt Lake Tribune*, July 22, 2023, https://www.sltrib.com/opinion/commentary/2023/07/22/kelly-whited-jones-100-years-later/; Gabi Price, "Reva Beck Bosone," Utah Women's History, https://www.utahwomenshistory.org/bios/reva-beck-bosone/.
31 Mary Jane Woodger and Carrie Taylor Anguiano, "Combating the 'Too Broad, Too Vague, and Too Non-Definitive, Blanket Approach' to Finding Solutions for Women's Issues: The Essential Barbara B. Smith in Defining the Role of Women in the LDS Church," *Journal of Mormon History* 43, no. 3 (2017): 122–44.
32 Becky Jacobs, "'Do Not Give Up': Utahns Rally at Capitol in Support of Equal Rights Amendment," *Salt Lake Tribune*, August 26, 2021, https://www.sltrib.com/news/2021/08/26/do-not-give-up-utahns/.
33 Penelope Green, "Virginia Mollenkott, 88, Dies; Feminist Found Liberation in the Bible," *New York Times*, October 31, 2020, https://www.nytimes.com/2020/10/26/books/virginia-mollenkott-dead.html.
34 Spruill, *Divided We Stand*, 131; Brown, *For a Christian America*, 71–72, 124.
35 Brown, *For a Christian America*, 63.
36 Eleanor Smeal and Gloria Steinem, "Why 'Mrs. America' Is Bad for American Women," *Los Angeles Times*, July 30, 2020, https://www.latimes.com/entertainment-arts/tv/story/2020-07-30/steinem-and-smeal-why-mrs-america-is-bad-for-american-women.
37 Spruill, *Divided We Stand*, 167–69, 347–49, 369–71, 377–79.
38 Spruill, *Divided We Stand*, 131.
39 Brown, *For a Christian America*, 128.

Republican Support of Equal Opportunity

ERA Endorsement in the Republican National Convention Program

PAT NIXON
August 1972[1]

When thinking about those who best symbolize the progressive woman of the 1970s, the name Thelma Catherine Patricia Ryan Nixon (1912–1993) rarely comes to mind. Pat Nixon is best remembered not as a lightning rod for the modern woman, but as emblematic of a true woman who stood silently beside her husband as he waxed poetic about her sturdy cloth coat in his famous "Checkers Speech" and, later, as he resigned from the U.S. presidency in disgrace. The nickname "Plastic Pat," uncharitably assigned by pundits, promoted a view of her as what one biographer describes as a long-suffering "Stepford wife, a robot, [and] Betty in Pleasantville."[2] But Pat Nixon was no shrinking violet and, in recent years, first lady scholars have made a strong case that her contributions have long been overlooked.[3] As first lady from 1969 to 1974, Nixon sat in on Cabinet meetings, wore a pantsuit in public (the first presidential spouse to be photographed doing so), privately lobbied her husband to appoint a woman to the Supreme Court, and traveled extensively around the world as a goodwill ambassador to 32 nations.[4] A stroke in 1976 permanently hindered Nixon's health in her post-White House years.

Pat Nixon expressed support for the Equal Rights Amendment as early as 1968, although she did not forcefully lobby for the ERA as her successors Betty Ford and Rosalynn Carter would do.[5] Once in the White House, Nixon's press secretary Constance Stuart relayed that the first lady supported the ERA.[6] In so doing, Nixon became the first presidential spouse of any party to publicly support the amendment. Nixon endorsed the ERA at a campaign stop in September 1972 and later reiterated that position at a press conference in Chicago. A month earlier, the letter included here appeared in the Republican National Convention Program under her name. Her argument aligned with the Republican Party platform and her husband's long-standing (though many would argue "tepid"[7]) support of the ERA throughout his political career. In other words, at least from this text, her words read as an affirmation grounded in party affiliation rather than personal conviction—though nonetheless, hers was an historic endorsement from a sitting first lady.

It is a special pleasure to greet the convention delegates as you embark on the historically significant sessions and decisions in the days ahead. This gathering of Republicans and concerned Americans gives us an opportunity to reflect with pride upon the progressive path our country has pursued in the past three and one-half years. Among these great strides forward, America has experienced greater legal and social encouragement of equal opportunity for women.

The Republican Party, having led the fight for women's suffrage in the 1900s, was the first national party to endorse the Equal Rights Amendment in 1940. Since that time, professional women in our federal government have been playing an increasingly important role in our national development through their perceptive talents and innovative contributions. The enthusiasm expressed by our Republican leaders has helped to set the stage for greater national acceptance of career women in a variety of fields and professions.

The President has given special support in this effort, setting new precedents in the hiring of women for positions in the federal government. During this Administration more women have been appointed or promoted to high-level government positions than ever before in history. During this past year alone, the number of women in top government posts has more than tripled, and more than 1,000 women have moved into middle-management jobs.

This support of equal opportunity for women is a substantive reflection of the Republican Party's blending of the precious ideals conceived by our forefathers with contemporary values flexible enough to adjust to the continually changing needs and demands of our maturing society. It is through this intense dedication to America's strongest and most meaningful traditions that we have willingly met the unprecedented international and domestic challenges that face us as a nation. We believe that this same indomitable spirit reflects the intrinsic mood of the American people and will lead us to a successful and rewarding campaign in 1972.

May I offer my warmest congratulations and gratitude for your contributions of long hours and tireless energy for a better America.

Notes

1 1972 Republican National Convention program, Helene and Jack Drown Collection, Box 8: 1972–1979, Republican Associates, Richard Nixon Presidential Library and Museum. Public Domain.
2 Conrad Black, *Richard M. Nixon: A Life in Full* (New York: PublicAffairs, 2007), 1049.
3 See Diana B. Carlin, Anita B. McBride, and Nancy Kegan Smith, *Remember the Ladies: The Legacies of America's History-Making Women* (San Diego, CA: Cognella Press, 2024), esp. 217–24.
4 Carl Anthony, "Pat Nixon and Women's Issues of the 70s," First Ladies' National Library, January 3, 2016, http://archive.firstladies.org/blog/pat-nixon-and-womens-issues-of-the-70s/; Carlin, McBride, and Smith, *Remember the Ladies*, 219; see also Melody Lehn, "'Mrs. Nixon's Goodwill Mission': The Great Peruvian Earthquake, Rhetorical History, and the Art of Personal Diplomacy," *Presidential Studies Quarterly* 52, no. 2 (2022): 290–312.
5 Anthony, "Pat Nixon."
6 Jill Abraham Hummer, *First Ladies and American Women: In Politics and At Home* (Lawrence: University Press of Kansas, 2017), 102.
7 Hugh Davis Graham, "Richard Nixon and Civil Rights: An Enigma," *Presidential Studies Quarterly* 26, no. 1 (1996): 93–106, quotation on 97.

I Was Opposed to ERA

Address to the Illinois Senate Executive Committee

Addie Wyatt
April 4, 1973[1]

The family of labor feminist and theologian Reverend Addie Cameron Wyatt (1924–2012) fled the Jim Crow South after her father got into a physical confrontation with his white employer.[2] Like so many other Black women in the United States, Wyatt faced intersectional discrimination in employment. Even though she qualified as a typist, her white employers assigned her to the factory floor as a canner with other Black women at the Armour and Company meatpacking plant. And so, in 1941, she joined a union.[3] By the early 1950s, Wyatt worked for the independent Illinois Meat Company, had connected with other union leaders including Maida Springer Kemp, and had joined the Local 56 chapter of the United Packinghouse Workers of America (UPWA), which eventually elected her vice president.

In 1955, Addie and her husband Claude Wyatt co-founded the Vernon Park Church of God in the South Side of Chicago. Wyatt's union became the very first to invite a young preacher named Martin Luther King, Jr. to the city. She proudly marched alongside King in Chicago and Selma, where they were briefly jailed together. Wyatt's labor activism and civil rights activities drew the attention of Eleanor Roosevelt, who helped secure a place for Wyatt on the Labor Legislation committee of the Kennedy Administration's Commission on the Status of Women.[4] Wyatt later helped co-found NOW alongside Betty Friedan and she was among those who resigned in a public show of solidarity when Jimmy Carter dismissed Bella Abzug from his National Advisory Committee for Women.[5] She spent her final years in ministry with her husband in their home church and died in 2012. Today, the Chicago-based Addie Wyatt Center for Nonviolence Training carries Wyatt's legacy forward for a new generation of civil rights leaders.[6]

As Wyatt indicated in her 1973 testimony before the Illinois Senate Executive Committee, she was among those labor activists who initially opposed the ERA but later changed her mind in the early 1970s. In the battleground state of Illinois, Wyatt lent her expertise to several pro-ERA organizations and initiatives including NOW, the Coalition of Labor Union Women, the League of Black Women, ERA-Central, and ERAmerica. Although Wyatt did not live to see Illinois ratify the ERA (that would not happen until 2018), she continued to fight after the 1982 ratification deadline passed. Wyatt's pro-ERA advocacy, along with her commitment to other women's rights concerns, was not without controversy. After the International Convention of the Church of God asked her to speak on Christian witness in 1980, at least two male ministers publicly demanded the invitation be rescinded since, they maintained, Wyatt's support of the ERA would "destroy Christian principles in the home and in the church."[7] But Wyatt explained in her address that the decision to support the amendment did not come lightly and reflected an acute awareness of the evolving and precarious legal landscape for women's equality.

My name is Addie Wyatt. I am Director of Women's Affairs of the Amalgamated Meat Cutters and Butcher Workmen of North America AFL-CIO. I appear here in that capacity on behalf of my union to urge you to support the proposed Equal Rights Amendment to the United States Constitution.

Several years ago, I was opposed to ERA because I was concerned about its effect on laws concerning employment of women—those laws commonly referred to as "Protective Legislation." Illinois had one protective law of general application. It dealt with hours of women workers, limiting their hours to 8 per day, 48 per week. Some of the women I represented liked this law because it gave them the right to decline to work overtime. Some of the women I represented did not like this law because it denied them the opportunity to work overtime and thus receive the time and one-half extra compensation by which male co-workers had been able to increase their income. But like it or not, in 1970 the hours law for women in Illinois became a moot point. The Southern District of Illinois Federal District Court held that the law conflicted with Title VII of the 1964 Civil Rights Act and was thus void. This decision was characteristic of decisions across the land which have systematically invalidated protective laws in all states where they existed.

With protective laws no longer a real issue, I realized that the substantial merit to and need for the Equal Rights Amendment required us in the labor movement to change our former position in respect to the Equal Rights Amendment. I am proud to have played a part in achieving endorsement of the ERA by the Amalgamated. Since that time, I have joined with many of my sisters and brothers in the labor movement to work actively for passage of the Amendment. It is in error to assume that all of "labor" is opposed to ERA. The Amalgamated Meat Cutters which represents over 500 thousand workers supports ERA as do TWENTY other International unions affiliated with the AFL-CIO as well as the UAW[8] and the Teamsters.[9]

We support the Equal Rights Amendment because it guarantees at the highest level of our law—the Constitution—that each citizen of our great land will be treated on her or his merits as a human being, rather than on any preconceived assumptions based on sex. Black people know how injurious stereotyping can be. Constitutional amendments and federal legislation have been enacted to break down barriers to the advancement of blacks. Now it is time to accord the same legal guarantees to the last segment of second-class citizens … women. We know that the Equal Rights Amendment is not a panacea and that it will not completely erase sex discrimination from our society any more than earlier laws have eliminated all race discrimination. However, the Equal Rights Amendment will at least be a step in the right direction in that it will announce to the nation and to the world that the United States of America has reaffirmed its belief not merely that all men are created equal, but that all PEOPLE are created equal.

On behalf of the Amalgamated Meat Cutters and the 110,000 women and 440,000 men it represents, I urge you to vote DO PASS on the bill to ratify the Equal Rights Amendment to the United States Constitution. Thank you.

Notes

1 Addie Wyatt, "Statement before the Illinois Senate Executive Committee Concerning the Equal Rights Amendment to the United States Constitution," Illinois State Executive Committee, April 1973, Springfield, Illinois, Harsh Research Collection, Chicago Public Library. Public Domain. A special thanks to Beth Loch and Cynthia Fife-Townsel at the Chicago Public Library's Vivian G. Harsh Research Collection.

2 Marcia Walker-McWilliams, *Reverend Addie Wyatt: Faith and the Fight for Labor, Gender, and Racial Equality* (Urbana: University of Illinois Press, 2016), 3.

3 Kim Kelly, "The Indomitable Rev. Addie L. Wyatt," *The Nation*, January 11, 2022, https://www.thenation.com/article/activism/addie-wyatt-labor/.

4 Dorothy Sue Cobble, "Labor Feminists and President Kennedy's Commission on Women," in *No Permanent Waves: Recasting Histories of U.S. Feminism*, ed. Nancy

A. Hewitt (New Brunswick: Rutgers University Press, 2010), 150–51; Joan McGann Morris, "Interview with Rev. Addie L. Wyatt," December 14, 2002, *Working Women's History Project*, https://wwhpchicago.org/the-reverend-addie-l.-wyatt.html.

5 Andrew Mollison, "Women Advisers Quit as Carter Fires Abzug," *Atlanta Journal-Constitution*, January 14, 1979, 1A.

6 Addie Wyatt Center for Nonviolence Training, https://www.addiewyattcenter.org/.

7 Walker-McWilliams, *Reverend Addie Wyatt*, 167–68.

8 United Auto Workers.

9 International Brotherhood of Teamsters.

The Mini-Amendment with Maxi-Consequences

Anti-ERA Pamphlet

BENETH PETERS JONES
July/August 1974[1]

Beneth Alice Peters Jones (1937–2019) was born in Albany, Oregon, but moved to Phoenix, Arizona where she graduated from the segregation academy, Phoenix Christian High School, in 1955. In her senior year, she won top honors as a speaker in a "Voices of Democracy" event in Phoenix.[2] Her choice for her undergraduate education would move her 2000 miles from home to Greenville, South Carolina. At Bob Jones University as a sophomore, she won the female lead in the annual campus theater production, unusual for her age. She played the ingénue Roxane in *Cyrano De Bergerac* against the male lead, grandson of the school's founder, Bob Jones III.[3]

Soon after she became Mrs. Bob Jones III, the first lady of Bob Jones University, with her vocation as always subordinate to her husband's educational enterprise. The Voices of Democracy speaker now spoke at Ladies' Bible studies, and the once yearbook editor now wrote short devotionals for the school's newsletter, *Faith for the Family,* under the name "Sunshine on the Soapsuds." Her folksy style was similar throughout the body of her writing. For example, as she stated in one women's ministry manual, "When Herkimer Husband uses a certain (irritating) vocal tone, Winifred Wife makes a hard left turn onto Stubborn Street regardless of what he's saying. Or when Rhonda Roommate indulges in an idiosyncrasy (of which she is unaware), Sally Servant abruptly swings onto Acid Avenue."[4] As Phyllis Schlafly fomented fear, uncertainty, and dread among the political conservatives around the passage of the Equal Rights Amendment, Beneth Jones was cast again in a new role: to warn the particular sect of Evangelical separatists in the Bob Jones University constituency.

But Jones was not plumbed for this kind of argumentative writing. Her compliant, complimentary persona contradicted any kind of assertive case-building. Perhaps an Illinois student on the staff of the Bob Jones University Press, Susan Linder, contributed the bulk of the writing work while Jones added the folksy title.[5] Compare this South Carolina fundamentalist version to Schlafly's original and Lottie Beth Hobbs' iteration in this volume. All worried about a husband's financial provision; this is a clue that they were not talking to any working-class women but rather addressed rising middle-class cisgender white women. All framed their argumentative opponents as unfeminine "libbers." All misused the 1971 *Yale Law Journal* article. And all imagined sinister Soviet standards as the future for American women.

This is the day of "minis"—the mini-camera, the mini-computer. Almost everything mini is in some way a marvel, packing tremendous capability into a tiny amount of space. Now we have the mini-amendment. And it, too, is a marvel—for it is actually a deadly mini-bomb—short, general, and innocuous-sounding, but dangerous. That is the ERA, the so-called equal rights amendment. Here are its 24 words: *Equality of rights under the law shall not be denied or abridged by the United States or by any state on account of sex.*

The ERA has been approved by both Houses of Congress, and as of March 1974, 33 states ratified the amendment. Approval by only five more states would make the ERA the law of the land. Supporters feel that Illinois, Florida, Louisiana, Oklahoma, and Missouri will soon ratify. The mini-bomb is about to go off.

The marching, shrieking women-libbers are more of a nuisance than a danger. They can be laughed at or ignored. But the ERA is not just another "women's lib stunt." As a national law, it could have dangerous implications for women and men. The phrase "equality of rights" will allow the courts broad interpretation—which could bring surprising results even to ERA's most vocal supporters. A Christian, who understands the privileges and duties for each sex outlined in God's Word, should fight this attack that seeks to bludgeon male and female into "equality."

You need to know the meaning behind those 24 words before you can begin to help defeat the ERA. Both friends and foes recognize an article in the *Yale Law Journal* of April 1971, as an accurate analysis of the amendment's consequences. The article points out that, under ERA, the state would not be able to require a husband to support his wife. Instead, the mate with the highest earning power would be the family breadwinner, regardless of sex. ERA supporters say that the husband's legal responsibility only has "psychological value," since the law is enforced only when a partner files for divorce or sues for non-support. But "psychological value" changed to a grim economic reality when a Washington judge awarded a husband in a divorce case the custody of his three children and ordered the mother to pay child support. The judge explained his decision by "the improved economic position of women generally in our society."

The laws for protection of women would be changed as drastically as those for their support. The *Journal* says that ERA would not permit "seduction [laws], statutory rape laws, laws prohibiting obscene language in the presence of women ... prostitution and 'manifest danger' laws." In other words, the ERA views sex crimes in sex-neutral terms, a practice already written into Illinois law.

Men have traditionally fought their country's wars while women have remained on the home front. The ERA would end this distinction by requiring women as well as men to register with Selective Service Boards. But "equality" of treatment by the Armed Forces would only begin with registration. In case the draft is renewed, a wife and mother would not be automatically deferred. The parent called first would be drafted. Once she joined the service, a woman would have to take the same physical test as men. According to the *Journal*, "neither the right to privacy nor any unique physical characteristic justifies different treatment of the sexes with respect to voluntary or involuntary service." Pregnant women would receive "only slightly different conditions of service." Women could even be put on the front battle lines, because "women are physically as able as men to perform many jobs classified as combat duty, such as piloting an airplane or engaging in naval operations."

Presently there are many state laws protecting women on the job. Some are especially appreciated by female factory workers, such as those requiring seats and rest periods. Women are allowed to work only a certain number of hours or lift a certain maximum weight; they cannot hold some jobs, such as mining. ERA would remove this protective legislation. Supporters say that only "discriminatory" laws would be annulled, and that protective legislation would simply be extended to male workers. But labor leaders point out that courts would be "far more hesitant to extend to the male majority a law originally passed to 'protect' a minority of female employees than to eliminate the 'benefit' for the women."

You may not care if the courts invalidate weight lifting regulations for women. But note this *New York Times* description of "equal rights" in the

Soviet Union: "women make up 50% of the workforce. Many typically female jobs are the least attractive: paving streets, picking up garbage, digging holes."[6] Obviously, the exchange of protection for "equality" often results in exploitation.

The Senate hearings on the ERA brought out the amendment's threat to the constitutional right of privacy. Professor Paul Freund of Harvard Law School testified that ERA "would require that there be no segregation of the sexes in prison, reform schools, public restrooms, and other public facilities." Senator Sam Ervin of North Carolina questioned Phil Kurland, editor of the *Supreme Court Review* and professor of law at the University of Chicago:

SENATOR ERVIN:	The law which exists in North Carolina and in virtually every other state of the union which requires separate restrooms for boys and girls in public schools would be nullified, would it not?
PROFESSOR KURLAND:	That is right, unless the separate but equal doctrine is revived.

Ervin described other ways privacy would be affected by ERA. Members of either sex will be able to perform police searches involving the removal of clothing, no matter who is being searched. Sleeping quarters in hospitals, prisons, and the armed forces would not be segregated by sex. Already the San Quentin prison in California has hired women guards to supervise male inmates. The women perform a guard's normal duties, including supervising showers and making body searches.

The strongest supporters of the ERA show us how really dangerous the amendment is. A *New York Times* News Service article describes ERA's attack on the home: "to give women full participation in society, they say, is necessary to overthrow ... Institutional marriage, which, they assert, enslaves women for economic reasons."[7] The article also implies that ERA supporters hope the new law lays the groundwork for the repeal of all abortion laws.

But the most frightening implications of ERA are its designs on the church. A 32-year-old Roman Catholic nun claims: "[R]eligious women are beginning to learn that God is not necessarily male, that Jesus wasn't a male chauvinist, and that Saint Paul's hang-ups about women are no more to be tolerated than those of Hugh Hefner."[8] The women's liberationists are angered by the refusal of some religious leaders to bow to their demands. Thus, they are trying to convert the woman in the pew to their viewpoint. Some reformers, such as Kenneth Woodward, religion editor of *Newsweek*, believe female church-goers are too complacent about "the second-class status that male dominated religion assigns them." To achieve "true liberation," says Woodward, feminists must "cut through the sexually charged myths of the Judeo-Christian tradition." In opposing Christianity, the liberationists are attacking the one influence which has allowed women to be treated with kindness and dignity.

Do you hear the ticking of the mini-bomb? You should—and you should start immediately to help block ratification of this amendment. Christians must pray earnestly and specifically against the ERA, believing God's promise: "If my people, which are called by my name, will humble themselves, and pray, and seek my face, and turn from their wicked ways; then I will hear from heaven, and will forgive their sin, and will heal their land" (II Chronicles 7:14).

In addition, Christians need to learn about the ERA. Ignorance is not neutrality; it can only help ERA's supporters. A good strategy is to look into the mind of the enemy itself. To start, go to your library and asked for the June 1971 issue of *McCall's*, and read the Betty Friedan article topped by the picture of a raised, clenched fist.

An excellent source for anti-ERA materials is the Phyllis Schlafly report (Box 618, Alton, Illinois 62002). Mrs. Schlafly is the chairman of the national STOP ERA campaign. Her monthly newsletter gives a clear analysis of the effects ERA could have, including testimonies by labor leaders and law professors. The report occasionally includes a column on "equal rights in action," sample cases in states that have already passed the amendment.

Once you understand your opponent, you'll be able to intelligently talk and write against the ERA. Let your state and federal congressman know—repeatedly—that you are against ratification. You need to make your voice heard over those who convinced Congress to pass ERA. One Republican Senator said: "I voted for it to get those militant women off my back, and I figured I'd leave it up to the states to decide." You can also participate in campaigns to oppose passage planned at state fairs this summer.

If your state has already ratified the amendment, urge a movement to rescind. Nebraska has already rescinded, and 14 other states have introduced measures to do so.

Whether you are a man or a woman, ERA could drastically change your life. It threatens your privacy, your home, and your church. The threat will become a reality, unless you act now to retain your God-given position over "equality of rights."

Notes

1 Beneth Peters Jones, "The Mini-Amendment with Maxi-Consequences" (Greenville, SC: Bob Jones University Press, 1974). Public Domain. A special thanks to Kathy Lafferty at the University of Kansas's Spencer Research Library.

2 "Voices of Democracy Event Winners Here Announced," *Arizona Republic*, November 30, 1954, 6.

3 Jeannie Putnam, "The Lives They Led: Beneth Jones," *Greenville Journal*, December 25, 2019, https://greenvillejournal.com/news/the-lives-they-led-beneth-jones/.

4 Beneth Peters Jones and Bobbie Yearick, *With Heart and Hand: A Manual for Women in God's Service* (Greenville, SC: Bob Jones University Press, 1992), 27.

5 After Jones' original article, BJU published "The Injustice of Equal Rights" by Susan Alice Linder. A member of the Bob Jones University Class of 1974 and an Illinois native, Linder worked at the BJU Press as a staff writer during that year after her graduation. Her arguments mimic Schlafly's, arguments she likely consumed as a politically conservative, female Illinoisian. Linder writes her identified article like a student debater—a parallel rhetorical form evident in Jones' article. Beneth Jones *never* writes that assertively. As a result, we think it is likely that Linder ghost-wrote—or at the very least heavily contributed to—Jones' text.

6 The article Jones quotes goes on to say, "Others, such as teaching, medicine and scientific work, are more gratifying, but even where women make up most of the workers, a man is usually in charge." See Bernard Gwertzman, "Woman's Role in Society Is Troubling Soviet, Too," *New York Times*, January 25, 1971, www.nytimes.com/1971/01/25/archives/womans-role-in-society-is-troubling-soviet-too-womans-role-in.html.

7 Jones quotes from Deidre Carmody, "Feminists Shifting Emphasis from Persons to Politics," *New York Times*, August 22, 1972, https://www.nytimes.com/1972/08/22/archives/feminists-shifting-emphasis-from-persons-to-politics-feminists-are.html.

8 Michael B. Adelstein and Jean G. Pival, eds. *Women's Liberation* (New York: St. Martin's Press, 1972), 135.

Ladies! Have You Heard?

Anti-ERA Pamphlet

LOTTIE BETH HOBBS
October 1974[1]

Lottie Beth Hobbs (1921–2016) was the eighth child born to Alonzo and Sallie Hobbs. She graduated from Abilene High School in 1938 and earned a B.A. from the Churches of Christ denominational school, Abilene Christian College, in 1943. She settled in Fort Worth, Texas as the church secretary for the sprawling Polytechnic Christian Church, conducting church meetings for women-only on the topics of "Religion in the Home," "Managing Your Emotions," and "Combatting Communism." At the same time, she was regularly speaking out for the conservative cause, publicly supporting Richard Nixon before his election and writing letters to the editor after his election.[2]

As soon as the Equal Rights Amendment passed the Senate and was sent to the states for ratification in 1972, Hobbs found her platform. In October 1974, she purchased advertisement space in the Clifton, Texas local newspaper with what appears to be a transcript of a speech she would later deliver at the Odessa College Auditorium. Her rhetorical form for her titles was consistent; she regularly began with a question: "Liberated Women . . . Are You Sure?" and "Ladies, Have you Heard?" Soon after, Hobbs formed an anti-feminist group whose name would morph from "Concerned Citizens for Feminine Freedom" to "Women Who Want to be Women" to "The Association of the Ws." When STOP ERA met in St. Louis in 1975, Lottie Beth Hobbs was listed as an "officer" in that national organization. She was the central antagonist to the ERA in Texas, especially among her own denominational sisters. By 1978, she's petitioning President Carter, and by 1980, she's speaking on the same platform with Ronald Reagan. By the time of her last endorsement for a local Texas politician in 1991, Hobbs had spoken out in favor of "states' rights," antiabortion politicians, men-only military, parental rights, creationism, private Christian schools, and even book burning. All in all, Hobbs was a consistent and vocal culture warrior.[3]

Her 1974 "Ladies, Have You Heard?" pamphlet made her famous. Hobbs duplicated this text on pink paper, a move that made Texas beauty entrepreneur Mary Kay Ash take notice. Ash even had her "Mary Kay Ladies" distribute Hobbs' pamphlet as they knocked on doors and conducted home make-up parties. Can you imagine? Sitting among your closest girlfriends, ready to wash your face, try a new "toner" and lipstick, while an amply-coifed saleswoman hands you a pink sheet with church-lady clip art in the header that asks a series of incendiary questions.[4] Judith N. McArthur and Harold L. Smith report that Hobbs lifted some paragraphs right from Phyllis Schlafly's Eagle Forum newsletter.[5]

DO YOU KNOW WHO IS PLANNING YOUR FUTURE FOR YOU? ARE YOU SURE THEY ARE PLANNING WHAT YOU REALLY WANT? IF NOT, IT'S TIME TO WAKE UP AND SPEAK UP! THE HOUR IS LATE!

ARE YOU SURE YOU WANT TO BE "LIBERATED"?
God created you and gave you a beautiful and exalted place to fill. No women in history have ever enjoyed such privileges, luxuries, and freedom as American women. Yet, a tiny minority of dissatisfied, highly vocal, militant women insist that you are being exploited as a "domestic drudge" and "a pretty toy." And they are determined to liberate you whether you want it or not! What is "liberation"? Ask women in Cuba. Castro "liberated" Cuba! Remember!

WHAT IS THE EQUAL RIGHTS AMENDMENT?
On March 22, 1972, the U.S. Congress passed the Equal Rights Amendment (ERA) and sent it to the states for ratification. If it is ratified by 38 states, it will become law, enforced by the federal government, superseding all state laws on related subjects. The Amendment reads: "Equality of rights under the law shall not be denied or abridged by the United States or by any states on account of sex." Simple, isn't it? BUT HAVE YOU LOOKED AT THE HOOK INSIDE THE BAIT!

THE MOST DRASTIC MEASURE
Senator Sam Ervin called the ERA "the most drastic measure in Senate history." Why? Because it strikes at the very foundation of family life, and the

home is the foundation of our nation. Can you possibly avoid being drastically affected by the ERA? NOT A CHANCE! Actually, it is a Loss of Rights Amendment. How will it affect YOU?

DO YOU WANT TO LOSE YOUR RIGHT NOT TO WORK?
If you are married, you may choose to work outside your home. But you may choose to stay at home, to rear your children, to be supported by your husband. The ERA will abolish this right. It will invalidate all laws which require the husband to support his family and will make the wife equally responsible for support. You can be forced to supply half the family support, or all of it, if you are a better wage earner (pp. 944, 945, *Yale Law Journal*, which was inserted in the Congressional Record by Senator Birch Bayh, leading proponent of ERA).[6] What about your children? You can be forced to put them in a federal day care center, if one is available. And to see that one is available is a major goal of the National Organization for Women (NOW)—leaders in the movement to ratify the Equal Rights Amendment. Under the ERA, if a wife fails to support her husband, he can use it as grounds for divorce (*Yale Law Journal*, p. 951). This can work a special hardship on senior women who have spent their lives rearing their families and are not prepared to enter the job market.

WILL THE ERA HELP DIVORCED WOMEN?
Divorced women will lose the customary right of child custody, child support, and/or alimony, and can be forced to pay child support and alimony, if her husband wins custody of the children (*Yale Law Journal*, p. 952).

WHAT ABOUT OTHER EFFECTS ON FAMILY LIFE?
Wife and children will not be required to wear the name of husband and father. They can choose any name they wish. Can you imagine the resulting confusion? According to leading law counsels, the ERA will permit homosexuals to "marry" and adopt children.

DO YOU WANT TO LOSE YOUR RIGHT TO PRIVACY?
The aim of NOW and other pro-ERA groups is to totally "desexigrate" everything. Professor Paul Freund, Harvard Law School, testified that ERA: "would require that there be no segregation of the sexes in prison, reform schools, public restrooms, and other public facilities." This includes all public schools, college dormitories, and hospital rooms.

DO YOU WANT YOUR HUSBAND TO SLEEP IN BARRACKS WITH WOMEN?
If your husband is in the armed forces, or a fireman, what can you expect under ERA? It will be illegal to have separate facilities—so your husband will be sharing sleeping quarters, restrooms, showers, and/or foxholes with women.

DO YOU WANT TO LOSE YOUR RIGHT NOT TO BE DRAFTED?
Some women are crying for "equal rights" in the armed forces. But do you want them to abolish your right NOT to be drafted? ERA will do this. All women will register at age eighteen, subject to all military duties including combat. If you have small children, "whichever parent was called first might be eligible for service; the remaining parent, male or female, would be deferred" (*Yale Law Journal*, p. 973). Do you want this for your daughters? Men, do you want your wives and daughters living in barracks with men? Going into combat with them?

DO YOU WANT PROTECTIVE LAWS AGAINST SEX CRIMES?
The ERA will abolish "seduction laws, statutory rape laws, laws prohibiting obscene language in the presence of women, prostitution and 'manifest danger' laws" and all laws against forcing women into prostitution (*Yale Law Journal*, pp. 954, 964).

WILL ERA PROVIDE BETTER PAY FOR WOMEN?
Not at all. Proponents of ERA incessantly sing the tune: "We want equal pay for equal work." They do not tell you that this is already guaranteed under:

(1) The Civil Rights Acts of 1964, Subchapter VI: Equal Employment Opportunities (42 U.S. Code 2000e-2).
(2) The Equal Opportunities Act of 1972 (Public Law 92–261).

So the "equal pay for equal work" argument is deceptive—merely a smokescreen to hide the real intent of the ERA.

WILL THE ERA HELP WORKING WOMEN?
As noted above, it will NOT provide higher pay or increased job opportunities. It will NOT cause a husband to do more work around the house. It WILL, however, very adversely affect women in industry, by invalidating ALL PROTECTIVE LAWS FOR WOMEN—laws regulating weight lifting restrictions, rest periods, excessive working hours, and maternity leaves. The ERA will do nothing for teachers. Their protection is already guaranteed by law. It WILL, however, adversely affect education by eliminating all single-sex schools—military schools, seminaries, or women's colleges.

HOW WILL THE ERA AFFECT CHURCHES?
The National Organization for Women (NOW) is demanding that women "be ordained in religious bodies where that right is still denied." To refuse to do this will be illegal under ERA. One goal of NOW is to abolish the tax-exempt status of all churches.

A WOMAN'S UTOPIA?

At women's lib rallies, Russia is proudly cited as a country where women have equal rights. Harry Trimborn, staff writer, *Los Angeles Times*, visited Moscow and described just how "great" it is (*L. A. Times*, December 23, 1970): "The women do the work and the men tell them how do to it. Like sweeping the streets, bricklaying, loading cargo ships, collecting garbage, building dams, digging ditches and mining coal . . . then she must spend at least 50% of her off-work time shopping and cooking. She can expect little help from her husband."[7] A Russian woman must put her baby in a state-operated child care unit. She (as well as men) can be jailed for refusing to engage in "socially useful labor" or for leading a "parasitic way of life." This is a living picture of "liberation"!

CAN A STATE REVOKE ITS RATIFICATION OF ERA?

Absolutely! When 38 states ratify the ERA, it will become the 27th Amendment to the U.S. Constitution. At one time, 33 had ratified. Nebraska and Tennessee have rescinded their ratification. "Clearly a state can change its mind either way before the amendment is officially declared to be ratified" (Prof. Charles L. Black, Jr., of Yale University Law School, Congressional Record, May 8, 1973, p. s8522).

WHAT CAN YOU DO ABOUT IT?

1. Find out where your state now stands on the Equal Rights Amendment.
2. Find out who your State Legislators are (you can call your local Democratic or Republican Headquarters.) Write them. Ask them to oppose ERA. Tell them that NOW does not speak for you, nor for most women. Ask your friends to write.
3. If possible, visit your representatives personally.
4. Work to inform as many people as possible.

TOO LONG WE HAVE BEEN THE "SILENT MAJORITY." IT'S TIME TO SPEAK UP! LET YOUR VOICE BE STRONG AND CLEAR!

Notes

1 Lottie Beth Hobbs, "Ladies? Have You Heard?" Fort Worth, TX, October 1974. Public Domain.

2 "ACC Graduates from 8 States, Land Overseas," *Abilene Reporter-News*, May 19, 1943, 17; "PTA Calendar," *Fort Worth Star-Telegram*, February 12, 1950, 37; "Church Symbol of What Few Can Do," *Fort Worth Star-Telegram*, June 4, 1955, 3;

"We Believe," *Fort Worth Star-Telegram*, November 4, 1960, 4; Lottie Beth Hobbs, "A Fine Editorial," *Fort Worth Star-Telegram*, November 22, 1960, 4; "'Variety' Subject Of Course," *Fort Worth Star-Telegram*, January 17, 1961, 10; "Miss Hobbs To Speak," *Fort Worth Star-Telegram*, October 14, 1961, 5.

3 Lottie Beth Hobbs, "Liberated? Are you Sure?" *Clifton Record*, October 31, 1974, 11; "Liberated? Are you Sure?" *Clifton Record*, November 11, 1974, 11; "Stop ERA Conference," *Altamont News*, October 16, 1975, 4; Nancy Weaver, "Pro-Family Activist Criticizes Feminist Philosophies," *Clarion-Ledger*, Jackson, MS, February 2, 1978, 15; "Cast a 'Know' Vote," *Fort Worth Star-Telegram*, August 11, 1980, 20; "Morris Matson," *Fort Worth Star-Telegram*, May 2, 1991, 153; Sara Fritz, "The ERA Fight 'May Go Right Down to the Wire,'" *El Paso Herald Post*, March 30, 1977, 26; "'Creationists' Challenge Darwin," *Journal Herald*, Dayton, OH, August 26, 1980, 21.

4 Stephen Harrigan, *Big Wonderful Thing: A History of Texas* (Austin: University of Texas Press, 2019), 763.

5 Judith N. McArthur and Harold L. Smith, *Texas Through Women's Eyes: The Twentieth-Century Experience* (Austin: University of Texas Press, 2010), 246.

6 Barbara A. Brown, Thomas I. Emerson, Gail Falk, and Ann E. Freedman, "The Amendment in Operation," *Yale Law Journal* 80, no. 5 (April 1971): 920–78.

7 Harry Trimborn, "Liberated?: Soviet Women Equal: They Do the Work," *Los Angeles Times*, December 23, 1970.

Receive the Gift Bestowed

Remarks at the University of Utah

Barbara B. Smith
December 1974[1]

Utah native and Latter-day Saints (LDS) church leader Barbara Bradshaw Smith (1922–2010) embodied the ideals of Mormon womanhood. "Sister Smith" lived out her belief that "motherhood is essential in the Lord's plan for saving souls" by marrying her high school sweetheart in the Salt Lake Temple and having seven children.[2] She served as the LDS Relief Society president for ten years, which gave her a significant amount of influence over Mormon women. Cornelius M. Lambi claims that her appointment to this leadership position in the LDS church was an intentional counter-statement to the women's movement, admiring how "her face and very embodiment became the image that LDS women clung to as the stable LDS role model. From her youth, she learned the value of womanhood and the gift it could be to the world, along with the immense capability women possessed to create and achieve."[3] Smith consistently reiterated these views in her own public testimonies and writings. Upon her death, the *Deseret News* remembered her as "a beacon of light" and example of kind selflessness.[4]

Departing from earlier pro-ERA Mormon women, Smith became the public face of LDS opposition to the ERA in the 1970s and 1980s. In early October 1976, Smith met with Phyllis Schlafly, and by the end of the month, the LDS church had officially come out against the ERA.[5] Church leaders now believed the ERA would threaten the family, subvert women's roles, promote abortion, and lead to women serving in the military. Those opposing Mormon women and men formed new groups, endorsed anti-ERA political candidates, developed and circulated anti-ERA arguments, wrote letters, and made calls. Their well-organized grassroots advocacy blossomed outside Utah and shaped other states' anti-ratification campaigns. Smith led these efforts and campaigned beyond the church's corridors as well. She served as a delegate to the 1977 Houston Conference, debated excommunicated Mormon Sonia Johnson on the *Phil Donahue Show* in 1980, and made her case in person to both Jimmy Carter and Ronald Reagan. Under Smith's leadership, the Relief Society trained Mormon women to become better civic actors familiar with the nuances of parliamentary procedure and equipped with an understanding of how to participate in public forums, such as the various women's conferences where the ERA took center stage.[6] Given the church's stake in the debate and its conservative views about women's submissive roles, it's no surprise that two LDS apostles, Gordon B. Hinckley and James E. Faust, "instructed" Smith "on what to say" when she spoke on the ERA in the selection of 1974's "Receive the Gift Bestowed" below.[7] The patriarchal ethic of Mormon doctrine comes through loud and clear in Smith's politics. If Mormons are building a family for eternity, then this persistent complementarian status for women—that they are "not less than men, just different"—makes sense.[8]

During this Christmas season do you often turn to the scriptures, as I do, and consider the gifts of God that are offered to all of his children?

1. Eternal life
2. The order of the universe
3. The uniqueness of each individual
4. The family unit

These all are priceless gifts, but how are they *received*?[9]

> For what doth it profit a man if a gift is bestowed upon him, and he receives not the gift? Behold, he rejoices not in that which is given unto him, neither rejoices in him who is the giver of the gift.[10]

The actuality of these gifts in *our* lives was from the beginning of this earth when God created two sexes and set up the pattern for the families of the earth. He blessed them and, as President J. Reuben Clark so eloquently stated:

> So began the Earth family from which we spring, the first unit organism on this earth that makes the perfect relationship between man and woman.[11]

He gave the man and woman joint and individual responsibilities. Together they were to *subdue and beautify* the earth and replenish it. To the man He gave the charge, "By the sweat of thy face shalt thou eat bread."[12]

And to the woman he said that she was to bear the children of the earth and it would not be easy, "In sorrow thou shalt bring forth children."[13] Recognizing that to function well all family units must have order and that order is brought about by a governing head. The Lord appointed Adam to that position, saying to Eve, "And thy desire shall be to thy husband, and he shall rule over thee."[14]

> And it came to pass that after I, the Lord God, had driven them out, [of the Garden of Eden] that Adam began to till the earth, and to have dominion over all the beasts of the field, and to eat his bread by the sweat of his brow, as I the Lord had commanded him. And Eve, also, his wife, did labor with him.[15]

From the scriptures we sense that in the *Garden of Eden*, Adam and Eve *began* a cherished companionship. Throughout their earth life they labored together for common goals. "Adam and Eve, his wife, called upon the name of the Lord, and *they* heard the voice of the Lord." Who heard it? They did—both Adam and Eve. "And he gave unto *them* commandments."[16] Later on an angel spoke to Adam. Adam shared the message with his wife:

> And Eve, his wife heard all these things and was glad, ... And Adam and Eve [together] blessed the name of God, and they [who?—they] made all things known unto their sons and their daughters.[17]

In the beginning, then, we see what apparently was a warm, close, mutually supportive companionship. *There were* separate and unique responsibilities, but obviously *there were* also many shared activities and interests, both spiritual and temporal.

The special gift of family life continues through history, and we are all partakers of this gift. Just as Eve was honored, as explained in the scriptures, so are, and were, many women, among them Deborah—a mother, a prophetess, a judge; Sarah; Miriam; Esther; Ruth; and Hannah—some honored for their great spiritual roles; others, such as Esther, for both spiritual greatness and political acumen. The angel Gabriel proclaimed Mary, "highly favoured, ... blessed ... among women."[18] Mary was highly favored and blessed among women because she had been chosen to be the mother of Jesus. She was offered the opportunity to bear, rear, guide, and direct the beloved son of God, which gift she humbly and gratefully received. Hers was an honored position of responsibility and fulfillment in a family unit, as has been that of women since the time of Eve.

Jesus, in his love, recognized the special gifts of women ... In our own period the Lord, Jesus Christ, has given gifts of counsel. Through the prophet Joseph Smith, as recorded in the 25th section of the Doctrine and Covenants, he taught women to live lives of virtue and to be a comfort to their husbands and delight in them, to remain meek (shall we say teachable), to expound the scriptures and exhort the Church when called upon to do so, and to learn much. In another section, he taught men to rule with persuasion, gentleness, meekness, long-suffering, kindness, knowledge, and love unfeigned.

The unique roles of men and women as delineated in the scriptures are clearly ones of love and caring for each other; they are mutually supportive and sharing—not one being superior or inferior, but with a balance of responsibilities . . .

This twentieth century has seen our nation struggle with new definitions of women's rights. Congress and state legislatures are being petitioned by women seeking redress.

What troubles them? We live in one of the most affluent societies of the world, where women have unprecedented opportunities for self-development. They can attend high schools, technical schools, colleges, universities, and professional schools. In comparison to some countries, our economic abundance has made it *possible* for women to devote their time to homemaking instead of being forced to work in the shops, fields, and factories with their husbands to provide the needed sustenance. True, some American women are compelled to support families, but many have the option and luxury of being full-time mothers and homemakers. In addition, they have the time to give volunteer and Church service, to seek further education, or to develop their personal talents. In spite of this, troubles are evident.

The last few decades have seen a multitude of surveys meant to shed light on the question of women's reported discontent in the face of this abundance and these opportunities. The result of an opinionnaire responded to by thousands of women indicated that hundreds of them had a sense of alienation, of despair, of frustration, and of dissatisfaction. However, in another in-depth survey on the attitudes of women involving 3,000 females, more than two-thirds of the women considered their homemaking as rewarding and as important as jobs held by men. Nonetheless, there are troubling issues of concern to women, and women desire that some the wrongs of the past be corrected. They enumerate such things as:

1. Unequal pay for equal work.
2. Unequal opportunity for promotions and advancements in paid employment; little voice in major public decision-making.
3. Guilt over failure to fit standardized or stereotyped roles.
4. Traditional deference to the concept of male supremacy.
5. Restrictions on the use of credit and credit cards.

6. The inability to obtain home loans and housing.
7. Discrimination against the administration of a child's estate.
8. Restrictive marital duties and parental obligations.
9. Restrictions on school entrance and activities.
10. Inequities in property rights, job benefits, and inheritance.

There are others.

In my opinion, many of these concerns are valid, and the efforts being made to correct injustices, and unfair practices, and attitudes are deserving of support. May I say that there has been much already accomplished by way of legislative action in the Congress and in the various state legislatures, and by means of presidential directives, and local ordinances in improving conditions for women . . .

Many of these organizations and many individual citizens, however, are pinning their hopes for betterment upon a single act—the adoption of an amendment to the United States Constitution—popularly called "The Equal Rights Amendment," which reads "Equality of rights under the law shall not be denied or abridged by the United States or by any state on account of sex." They feel the passage of this amendment will somehow be a panacea for all that remains to be accomplished.

It is my considered judgment that *the Equal Rights Amendment is not the way.*

Passage of the amendment may nullify all laws covering the gamut of domestic relations in such matters as financial liability of a father to support his wife and children, or the awarding of custody of children in divorce actions, which now provide favorable treatment for women.

It may be very distressing for women to find that the right of privacy as now provided in laws, rulings, and ordinances is no longer present. Military conscription of women may be interpreted to be a mandate of the act. They may find themselves "locked-into" a system which makes no allowance for the physical, biological, or emotional differences in the sexes.

It is my opinion that the amendment will not fulfill their hopes, but rather would work to the disadvantage of moral and social values which have produced strong people, strong homes, and a strong nation. By reason of the nature of the act itself, it seems unlikely that it can accommodate for the fundamental differences and appropriate roles of men and women. Once it is passed, the enforcement will demand an undeviating approach which will create endless problems for an already troubled society.

I want women to have social, financial, and legal rights; I want each woman to be a valued individual, creative and with many options as to how she will develop. I would like to eradicate laws and practices unfair to women *and* men, while still keeping laws that provide for *their special needs.* I want to see a woman learn much. I want her to become the best woman, the best citizen, responsible and participating, in both her own country and in the Kingdom of God; the best homemaker; the greatest individual she is capable of becoming. I want her to be self-confident, trained, a great participator and partner in life; but, I want to be *sure* that the laws enacted will provide for these things to happen. The Equal Rights Amendment is not the way. It is quite possible that it will bring in its wake a sea of troubles in which the needed special care and consideration for women will be lost.

The Declaration of Independence says, "We hold these truths to be self-evident: that all men are created equal . . ." It does not say all are identical—equal in life, liberty, and the pursuit of happiness, but not identical. God has created men and women with unique roles, women to bear children and men to father them. This will not change. It is a truth. No constitutional amendment will reverse this.

The Equal Rights Amendment is so broad that it is inadequate, inflexible, and vague; so all-encompassing that it is non-definitive. Paul A. Freund of the Harvard Law School says, "The choice resembles that in medicine between *a single broad-spectrum drug with uncertain and unwanted side effects* and a selection of specific pills for specific ills."[19] It appears to me that the Equal Rights Amendment is not only imperfect but even dangerous. The blanket approach of the Equal Rights Amendment is, in my opinion, a confused step backward in time, instead of a clear stride forward into the future. It will nullify the hard-won protections of women. It will create endless litigation in the courts in which legal decisions are made, which might create circumstances harmful to the solidarity of the family and the optimum protection of children.

Is there a law which is unfair to men? If so, change it by the necessary legislative process.

Is there a law which is unfair to women? If so, change it. Seek redress in the legislatures, in the courts, through presidential decree, or by group action. But make sure that *each* law is carefully considered individually. Insist on the enforcement of laws in an orderly process as exemplified by the greatest suffragette leaders of the past. As you do, make *sure* the uniqueness of the individual is protected and the family strengthened.

We can point to Utah women with pride in the woman's suffrage movement,[20] and we need to be grateful to women who have, down through the years, made us aware of the needs of women. But from my study of history, I do not believe that the Equal Rights Amendment is a continuation of the woman's suffrage movement that gave women the right to vote. *Equal rights* are not necessarily *woman's rights* and, indeed, indiscriminately applied *equality may abolish women's rights.*

Women's rights are part of my heritage. Strong active women have always been an important part of my life. My grandmother sought her right to be an individual in a day when it was far more difficult than now, and she became a professional woman in this country, a practicing physician, in a time when it was not only very unusual here, but almost impossible for a woman to be so educated. She was, at the time she received her medical degrees, a mother of three children. She set up her practice in her home so that she could be with her children and still minister to the sick and suffering of those in the neighboring communities.[21] ...

Let us respond to the gifts of God by spending our lives in strengthening the uniqueness of each individual. Let us further the greatness of the family and do nothing that will weaken it or join with anyone or any groups that might try to do so. Let us be watchful that nothing destructive happens to the family unit or the individual. Let us give attention to proposed laws, their implications, and their possible applications. Let us be thoughtful and use the past to give perspective to the present and the future ...

I testify to you that God lives, that he knew the end from the beginning when he organized our universe and created this beautiful world we are privileged to live in. He was and is fully aware of our individuality and the importance of strong family units that can bring to pass his eternal purposes for us, his children.

I pray that we may receive the gift bestowed, rejoice in it, and be one with him from whom it comes, I humbly ask in the name of Jesus Christ, Amen.

Notes

1 Barbara B. Smith, *Receive the Gift Bestowed* (Salt Lake City: Institute of Religion, 1974). Reprinted with permission from the Church of Jesus Christ of Latter-day Saints and Lowell V. Smith.

2 "Barbara Bradshaw Smith," Church of Jesus Christ of Latter-day Saints, https://www.churchofjesuschrist.org/callings/relief-society/relief-society-presidents/barbara-bradshaw-smith?lang=eng; "Barbara B. Smith," Brigham Young University, Provo, UT, https://speeches.byu.edu/speakers/barbara-b-smith/.

3 Cornelius M. Lambi, "Barbara B. Smith's Media Presence: Shaping the LDS Women Identity during the ERA Movement," *International Journal of Gender and Women's Studies* 4, no. 1 (June 2016): 23–31.

4 "Former Relief Society General President Barbara B. Smith Passes Away," *Deseret News*, September 14, 2010, https://www.deseret.com/2010/9/14/20140751/former-relief-society-general-president-barbara-b-smith-passes-away.

5 Martha Sonntag Bradley, *Pedestals and Podiums: Utah Women, Religious Authority, and Equal Rights* (Salt Lake City: Signature Books, 2005), 281–82.
6 "The Mormon Relief Society and the International Women's Year," *Journal of Mormon History* 21, no. 1 (1995): 106–67, quotation on 149.
7 D. Michael Quinn, "The LDS Church's Campaign against the Equal Rights Amendment," *Journal of Mormon History* 20, no. 2 (1994): 85–155, quotation on 106.
8 Christopher Smart, "LDS Women's Leader Who Led Anti-ERA Fight Dies at 88," *Salt Lake Tribune*, September 16, 2010, https://archive.sltrib.com/article.php?id=50283193&itype=CMSID.
9 Smith's manuscript had certain words and phrases underlined for emphasis. We have retained those rhetorical choices here using italics.
10 Joseph Smith, Jr., *Doctrine and Covenants of the Church of the Latter-day Saints* (Kirtland, OH: F.G. Williams & Company, 1835), 88: 33.
11 J. Reuben Clark, "Our Homes," *The Relief Society Magazine*, December 1940, 805.
12 Moses 4:25. "Moses" is Joseph Smith's translation of the first six chapters of Genesis. Unlike historically Christian translations, Smith's was idiosyncratic and broadly expanded.
13 Moses 4:22.
14 Moses 4:22.
15 Moses 5:1.
16 Moses 5:4–5.
17 Moses 5:11–12.
18 Luke 1:28.
19 Paul A. Freund, "The Equal Rights Amendment Is Not the Way," *Harvard Civil Rights—Civil Liberties Law Review*, March 1971, 6.
20 Because the male Mormon settlers in the Utah territory wanted to prove to outsiders that their polygamous lifestyle was not oppressive to women, women's suffrage was passed statewide in 1870 with little argument or fanfare. In sum, there was no women's suffrage movement of note in the state. So, for Utah women, suffrage was not only a matter of women's equality, but also Mormon branding. See Patricia Lyn Scott and Linda Thatcher, *Women In Utah History: Paradigm Or Paradox?* (Logan: Utah State University Press, 2005).
21 Smith's maternal grandmother was Caroline Amelia Daniels Mills Davis, known as a "pioneer woman physician" of Utah. See "Physician Dead," *Ogden Standard-Examiner*, August 25, 1934, 2.

La Chicana and "Women's Liberation"

Published in the UC San Diego Student Paper, Voz Fronteriza

YOLANDA OROZCO
January 5, 1976[1]

Yolanda Orozco (1951–present) had a long and notable career on the bench, serving the public and then practicing privately in commercial litigation before retiring in May 2023. After graduating from Stanford Law School in 1979, she became a trial lawyer for the Department of Justice and then a federal public defender. She was in private practice until 2010, when Governor Arnold Schwarzenegger appointed her to the Los Angeles California Superior Court.[2] Her most recent (and most controversial) decision was to call the *Daily Mail's* publication of U.S. Representative Katie Hill's (D-CA) nude photos "a matter of public issue or public speech," and, thus, protected under the First Amendment.[3]

Since her undergraduate days at the University of California, San Diego, Orozco has actively argued for Latinx rights in the civic sphere. She wrote for two student papers, *Prensa Popular* and *Voz Fronteriza*. In the former's April 1974 issue, Orozco confronted working-class Latinas' involvement in the women's movement despite its domination by middle-class whites. Articles on reproductive rights and equal pay concluded with a headline: "the Woman Question is a Class Question."[4] While no specific author is listed for any essay in that issue, the ideas are certainly an early form of this article Orozco wrote for the first issue of *Voz Fronteriza*, meaning "voice of the border." By 1976, the Equal Rights Amendment was clearly in her purview.

Lately, many Chicanas have made efforts to more clearly define our position within "*el movimiento.*" Chicanas have been organizing around issues arising out of our particular needs and problems. These issues are seldom treated within the context of the women's liberation movement. Yet, it is often the case that as soon as Chicanas begin to assert themselves in a particular situation we are labeled as "women's libbers." The implication being that we are followers of a women's movement and therefore we can be dismissed for all intents and purposes. How invalid the arbitrary application of such a label becomes evident upon a brief examination of what the women's liberation movement is all about.

The women's movement has in recent years evolved into a multifaceted political movement wherein exist diverse factions that often are in conflict with each other. Jo Freeman in *The Politics of Women's Liberation* divides the women's movement into two major groups. One, the "older group," consists mainly of women employed by the government who initiated the first task forces to examine the status of women in government agencies, and the founders of the National Organization for Women (NOW). The "younger group" is comprised of more "radical women," those who participate in the Civil Rights Movement or as members of the new left.[5]

The major distinction between the two groups is at once obvious. The former is characterized by a conservative approach; their goals have been to institute legislative reform and to have new laws passed with the hope that these in turn will effect changes in policy and create equality for women. The more progressive sectors of the women's movement recognize that true equality for women is not possible within this capitalistic structure that exploits not only women but also Third World people and members of the working class.

So, whereas the conservative element of the women's movement has shown some political clout as evidenced in the passage of various pieces of legislation to end sex discrimination in employment, provide maternity benefits, and the most recent struggle to have the Constitution amended by the Equal Rights Amendment the question concerning us is if, in fact, such legislation will benefit Chicanas. The answer is an unequivocal NO! While the women's movement can struggle and agitate for career and professional advancement, more facility in securing credit and property, the reality is that such demands are inconsequential to us. Many Chicanas do not even graduate from high school, fewer yet attend college. And although a majority of Chicanas are employed, they are relegated to the lower-paying jobs, as are Chicanos. The oppression of Chicanas cannot be divorced from the exploitation of La Raza, for to do so would be to fall prey to the system's divide-and-conquer tactics.

This is not to say that the women's movement has not had any effect on Chicanas at all. In a survey conducted at this campus dealing specifically with the Chicana and the women's movement, an overwhelming response was that the women's movement had affected their role as women in some way. The majority of Chicanas responding to the survey saw the movement as being a "consciousness raising one" resulting in more "self-confidence" and "assertiveness." The respondents also readily identified with certain issues raised by the women's movement, especially the right to legal abortions on demand and ready access to birth control. So it is that the women's movement struggle for the right of women to have control over their bodies is an issue that has influenced Chicanas. However, it is important only in so far as there is freedom of choice. For many Chicanas as well as for Black and Puerto Rican women who have been victims of forced sterilizations or who have served as guinea pigs for testing new methods of birth control, this freedom to choose is lacking.

Even though the majority of Chicanas responding to the survey could relate to certain issues of the women's movement, for the most part they saw it as being an elitist movement comprised of white middle-class women who see the oppressor as the males of this society. Their struggle becomes one of attempting to achieve relative equality with white males. But as Emily F. Gibson, a black writer, wrote in the *L.A. Times*: "Equality of opportunity with men simply loses its luster when survival is the dominant drive or when 'to be equal' to a black man still means to be discriminated against."[6] Thus, for Chicanas to demand equality with Chicanos is to ignore that together we are fighting for political and economic survival as an ethnic group and as a class.

It needs to be pointed out that if the women's movement has ignored the needs and priorities of Chicanas and therefore excluded us, then to some extent so has the Chicano movement that often confines Chicanas to stereotypic sex roles—in the kitchen or at the typewriter.

Sylvia Gonzales, professor at Sacramento State College, writes in an article in the *L.A. Times*: ". . . for the Chicana, the awakening of consciousness has also been prompted in part by the 'machismo' she encounters within the Chicano Freedom Movement itself."[7]

Of course, it must be recognized that often Chicanas, as well as Chicanos, perpetuate traditional social roles through our attitudes and actions. It is imperative that Chicanas and Chicanos recognize that sexist attitudes do exist on both sides. Out of this recognition should evolve a consciousness that will enable a restructuring of traditional male-female responsibilities and roles.

It is understood that we are necessarily reflections of the political and economic system that envelopes us. Nonetheless, where attitudes exist that divide Chicanas and Chicanos and as a result hinder our struggle, they must be eradicated at the individual level. Barbara Ehrenreich, in a speech given at the National Socialist Feminist Conference, illuminates this point well:

> . . . socialism means much more than a redistribution of wealth or a change in the ownership of the means of production. The revolution is not just something you read about in the newspapers; it is not just something which occurs in the realm of political economy. The revolution process extends into all aspects of life—including those which have been defined as "personal" and not "political." And the revolutionary transformation of the entire fabric of social relationships . . . socialist feminist thinking is characterized by an emphasis on the importance of subjective factors in revolutionary change. That is, we don't have to wait until "after the revolution" to transform ourselves as people—we know that transforming ourselves is part of making the revolution. From this point of view, the task of "consciousness raising"—uprooting deeply entrenched bourgeois, racist, and sexist attitudes—is central to political struggle.[8]

Notes

1 Yolanda Orozco, "La Chicana and 'Women's Liberation,'" *Voz Fronteriza*, Vol. 1: 1, January 5, 1976, 6, 13. Reprinted in Alma M. Garcia, *Chicana Feminist Thought: The Basic Historical Writings* (New York: Routledge, 1997). Public Domain.

2 "The Honorable Yolanda Orozco," *Trellis.com*, https://trellis.law/judge/yolanda.orozco.

3 "Judge Tosses Former Rep. Katie Hill's Suit Against Tabloid," *Californian*, April 8, 2021, A9.

4 *Prensa Popular*, April 9, 1974, https://library.ucsd.edu/dc/object/bb4506230k.

5 Jo Freeman, *The Politics of Women's Liberation: A Case Study of an Emerging Social Movement and Its Relation to the Policy Process* (Lincoln, NE: iUniverse.com, 2000).

6 Emily F. Gibson, "'Why Join, When Being Equal to a Black Man Offers No Advance?'" *Los Angeles Times*, September 15, 1975, 24.

7 Sylvia Gonzales, "'What Do Chicanas Have to Gain? What Help Do Anglos Give Us?'" *Los Angeles Times*, September 15, 1975, 24.

8 National Socialist Feminist Conference, Antioch College, Yellow Springs, Ohio, July 4–6, 1975; includes correspondence. Papers of Barbara Ehrenreich, 1922–2007 (inclusive), 1963–2007 (bulk), MC 565: T-300: Vt-119, 15.11–16.1., Box: 15; Box: 16. Schlesinger Library, Radcliffe Institute.

The Bible and the Equal Rights Amendment

Article in Faith/At/Work

VIRGINIA RAMEY MOLLENKOTT
February 1977[1]

Virginia Ramey Mollenkott (1932–2020) embodied all the contradictions possible for a white feminist theologian. She grew up in a single-parent home in the Plymouth Brethren church in Philadelphia. She attended, graduated from, and taught at Bob Jones University where a faculty member advised her to marry as the necessary "cure" for lesbianism. She married fellow BJU student Friedrich Mollenkott in 1954. Her studies at Temple University (M.A.) and New York University (Ph.D.) prompted her to read the Bible seriously and closely. And in reading John Milton, she found the resolve to divorce her husband for "incompatibility" in 1973. She wrote 13 books, including *Another Christian View* with Letha Scanzoni, *Omnigender: A Trans-Religious Approach*, and *Is the Homosexual My Neighbor?* She also taught English for three decades at William Paterson University in New Jersey, where she retired as an emerita professor of English in 1997.[2]

Mollenkott identified as an evangelical her whole life even after proving herself as a feminist theologian. Her strategic use of the term "evangelical" to describe her own identity as well as the organization she founded in 1975—the Evangelical Women's Caucus—contradicted the politically conservative ownership of that term. This creative casuistry with her identity and faith prompted the then-president of her *alma mater*, Bob Jones III, to call her a "devil" for "writing favorably about lesbianism" and to order other Christians to "pray for her destruction."[3] Despite the hate, Mollenkott was known among countless BJU alumni as a kind and gentle friend. One member of the BJU class of 2003,

Sandra Merzib, took a class at BJU called "Women in Christian Service" with Patricia Berg. Berg used Professor Mollenkott as the exemplar of the opposite of a "Christian woman." Merzib, however, was more curious than forewarned. She remembers that she

> found [Mollenkott's] email address and wrote to her. I was gay and scared and trying to figure myself out. I received a response from her around 3 years later. She said she waited to reply to me because she wanted to make sure I had graduated and that I could read her email safely. She did not want me to potentially get expelled. I appreciated her so much. I appreciated her discretion and her wise, kind words. I continue to appreciate her. She was one of the people who paved the way for me to come out and be who I am.[4]

Within this progressive Protestant periodical in 1977, Mollenkott used that same professorial persona to tame the fears that STOP ERA stirred up.

As an evangelical Christian, should I support the ratification of the Equal Rights Amendment? When I began to think this question through, I realized that for me the answer depended upon several factors: the wording and intent of the amendment in the context of modern American society and the guidance of Scripture. Obviously, I was not going to be able to find a chapter and verse which would tell me, "Thou shalt (or shalt not) support the ERA."

I was aware that a constitutional amendment must be ratified by three-fourths of the states (38) within seven years of its proposal by Congress. To date, 34 States have ratified. Four more must ratify by March of 1979 if the ERA is to become Federal law. The states which have not yet ratified are Alabama, Arizona, Arkansas, Florida, Georgia, Illinois, Indiana, Louisiana, Mississippi, Missouri, Nevada, North Carolina, Oklahoma, South Carolina, Utah, and Virginia. In some of the states which have already ratified, efforts are being developed to rescind ratification. In the midst of such urgent controversy, I felt that I must educate myself so that my influence, however small, might be utilized in accordance with biblical principles.

First, I had to study the text of the amendment. Its simplicity amazed me: just three sentences, saying in essence that "Equality of rights under law shall not be denied or abridged on account of sex." All around me I heard people making strong assertions about the hidden meanings of those simple words. But I soon discovered that the assertions were based on fear rather than facts. Reminding myself of Proverbs 18:13—"He that answereth a matter before he heareth it, it is folly and shame unto him"—I was determined to do some investigating.

Leviticus 25:10, speaking of the Year of Jubilee, provides some alleviation of Hebrew inequities by ordering that every 50th year the Hebrew people should "proclaim liberty throughout all the land unto all the inhabitants thereof." Although our founding fathers failed to include slaves, Indians, and women in their application of that idea, the fact that it was engraved on the Liberty Bell indicates that they thought the biblical principle of personal liberty should be basic to the American way of life. And the Declaration of Independence plainly and properly links liberty with equal opportunity. But I found that the *Congressional Record* of August 10, 1970, records Senator John Tower's admission that without passage of the ERA, American women will remain second-class citizens: Said Tower, "Adoption of an Equal Rights Amendment will be a historical marker and will formally state society's recognition of the full citizenship and rights of women."[5]

I discovered that in some states women cannot serve on juries, get a mortgage, start a business, or control their own property on the same basis as men. For instance, in some states a widow loses control of her own property until the entire estate she owned with her husband has gone through probate—but in the same states, a widower retains control of his share of the property through the whole probate process. The ERA is designed to end such inequities.

I found out that American schools currently spend ten times more on boys' sports programs than on those for girls. After passage of the ERA, equal opportunity and equal facilities would be required by law, without the current legal entanglements of trying to bring federal, state, and local laws into harmony with each other.

My studies convinced me that Psalm 82:3 is typical of the whole Bible in its insistence on human justice and fair dealings: "Defend the poor and fatherless: do justice to the poor and needy." I was also especially impressed with Isaiah 58:6–9 and Amos 5:21–24. The New Testament only intensifies the requirement of justice by requiring not only justice but also love: for instance, "by love serve one another" (Galatians 5:13; see also I John 3:16–17 and James 2:14–17). Since I like to be treated fairly and since I am told to treat others as I would like to be treated (Matthew 7:12), it is evident that I must expend my energy in the interest of social justice. I discovered that under the ERA, women would lose none of the legal protection now given to them, but the laws which currently protect women would be extended to afford equal protection to men. For instance, laws against rape would not be rescinded, but they would be extended to cover sexual abuse of either sex. That's justice.

I found that ERA would not interfere in private family decisions by requiring women to provide 50% of the family income. Instead, it would help ensure that women who do work outside the home will have the same opportunities and benefits as men who work. To my shock I discovered that although an Equal Pay Act was passed over a decade ago, between July 1973 and July 1974 alone, reports were documented of approximately 30,000 women workers who were underpaid by more than $18 million. ERA would speed up the eradication of such injustice by requiring the employer rather than the employee to carry the burden of proof and the legal fees. For that reason, and in order to save billions a year by continuing to evade equal payment for equal work, Big Business has allegedly provided generous funding to anti-ERA campaigns (for details, see *Ms.*, May 1976).

I knew that some evangelicals had been frightened by Phyllis Schlafly's assertions that ERA would promote immorality in various ways. But I found that Schlafly's charges cannot be substantiated. The ERA would in no way challenge the constitutional right to privacy, which guarantees the separation of the sexes in restrooms, sleeping quarters, and public areas where bodily privacy is an issue. Neither does it give the go-ahead to homosexual marriages, since marriage is legally defined as a union between a man and a woman. Neither does the ERA encourage unisex, since equality is not sameness. Neither does it undermine states' rights by eliminating state control over marriage and divorce laws, child custody, prison regulations, and the like, all of which would continue to be administered at the state level. Neither would the ERA give women a constitutional right to abortion on demand or otherwise encourage illicit sex; as Senator Sam Ervin remarked, the amendment "does not abolish abortion laws or make available safe birth control devices" (*Congressional Record*, March 20, 1972). Neither would it force women into the armed services, snatching them away from their children. Even if the draft were restored, women would be eligible for exemption for family responsibilities, just as men have always been. But the ERA would end the current practice of forcing female volunteers to meet higher standards than male volunteers.

Under ERA, I discovered, sexual discrimination in insurance rates would become illegal. We women would then have to pay more for life insurance than we currently do, but we would pay less for almost every other kind of insurance—health, pension, disability, and so forth—where the premiums are currently higher for women than for men. And the ERA would assist men by equalizing social security benefits. A widower would automatically be entitled to his wife's benefits at her death, just as widows currently are entitled to their husband's benefits.

In short, I found that the ERA is intended to correct the many inequities and injustices based on sex. If a law restricts rights, it will no longer be valid; if it protects rights, it will be extended to both men and women. Because I take the Bible seriously and could never argue that the Bible favors unjust and prejudicial treatment, I must do my best to bring about the passage of the ERA. As Micah 6:8 (NEB[6]) puts it, "What is it that the Lord asks of you? Only to act justly, to love loyalty, to walk wisely before your God."

Notes

1 Virginia Mollenkott, "The Bible and the Equal Rights Amendment," *Faith/At/Work*, February 1977, 32–33. Public Domain. A special thanks to David Stiver at the Flora Lamson Hewlett Library at the Graduate Theological Union for his assistance.
2 Ann Linstatter, "Virginia Mollenkott: Warrior in the Battle for Evangelical Acceptance of Gays (1932–2020)," *Religion Dispatches*, October 6, 2020, https://religiondispatches.org/virginia-mollenkott-warrior-in-the-battle-for-evangelical-acceptance-of-gays-1932-2020/.
3 Penelope Green, "Virginia Mollenkott, 88, Dies: Feminist Found Liberation in the Bible," *New York Times*, October 26, 2020, https://www.nytimes.com/2020/10/26/books/virginia-mollenkott-dead.html.
4 Sandra Merzib (speech pathologist) in conversation with editor Camille K. Lewis on September 20, 2020. Used with permission.
5 Senator John Goodwin Tower (R-TX) served from 1961 to 1985.
6 New English Bible.

Womankind

Address at the "Womankind" Conference

BARBARA JORDAN
June 25, 1977[1]

During the impeachment proceedings of Richard Nixon, a voice rose from the fray to display the character of the democratic process at work. Congresswoman Barbra Charline Jordan (1936–1996) of Texas—the first Black woman elected to represent the South in the U.S. House of Representatives—took her place as the most junior member of the House Judiciary Committee tasked with investigating the president. A rapt national audience tuned in to watch the live television coverage of the committee hearings. Jordan spoke with strength and conviction in favor of removing Nixon from office: "My faith in the Constitution is whole, it is complete, it is total. I am not going to sit here and be an idle spectator to the diminution, the subversion, the destruction of the Constitution," she declared.[2] It was a remarkable moment from a woman born into Southern segregation nearly 40 years earlier. A skilled debater and lawyer trained at Boston University, Jordan won a seat to the Texas State Senate in 1966—the first Black woman to do so. Six years later, Jordan successfully ran for Congress and served in the House until a multiple sclerosis diagnosis forced her to exit politics in 1979. She retired in Houston with longtime partner Nancy Earl and joined the faculty at the University of Texas-Austin. Jordan succumbed to complications related to leukemia and pneumonia in 1996.[3]

Although she did not claim the term "feminist" for herself, Jordan endeavored to advance gender equality.[4] She first sponsored the addition of an Equal Legal Rights Amendment to the Texas State Constitution while serving as a state senator. Once she reached Congress in 1972, Jordan helped the ERA move through state ratifications before the seven-year deadline expired in 1979. With several states left to ratify, Jordan argued for a three-year extension before her colleagues in May 1978. Her testimony helped to secure the ratification extension, which the House passed by a 233 to 189 vote on August 15, 1978.[5] Jordan delivered the following speech at a Pennsylvania women's conference held in Pittsburgh. The three-day proceedings at Duquesne University were part of a series of state and regional meetings—all told, some 56 in total—held in conjunction with the celebration of International Women's Year. Thirty-five hundred attendees participated in workshops, prepared reports on the status of women, and heard Jordan's keynote address. The time for consciousness-raising and passing the ERA is now, Jordan argued, because women's rights were already being rolled back, Congress did not always have women's interests at heart when legislating, and political change comes far too slowly.[6]

We meet at a time of uncertainty. The drive for passage of the Equal Rights Amendment is temporarily stalled. Its opponents publicly proclaim that ERA will never pass. In the courts, reverse discrimination cases continue to be won. Progress now comes slowly if at all; one step at a time rather than in leaps and bounds.

In some cases, we seem to be sliding backwards. Last week, the House of Representatives approved an amendment that would prohibit the use of federal funds for affirmative action programs. Some of our fellow citizens do not want to make the reality of our condition conform with the idea of equality that they accept in principle. They do not want to validate the principle of equality—to implement it—if they must change the way they think, change their hiring practices, and change the way federal funds are now allocated.

What seems to be the problem? Why are some people finding it difficult to accept the idea of equality that we espouse?

One reason is that the traditional societal taboos and prejudices that prevent women from achieving their full potential have not been discarded. Despite the progress that has been made, many Americans are not yet liberated from the confining thought pattern that women must assume only secondary and retiring roles.

Many men still believe that women should not compete with men in the job market. They assert that women are taking the jobs of men who are trying to support their families. Some people believe that women work not out of necessity but to satisfy their egos and their sense of equality. That is the myth.

The reality is that millions of women work out of necessity. Listen to these words from the Economic Report of the President in 1973: "Women work outside of the home for the same reasons as men. The basic reason is to get the income that can be earned by working ... Two-thirds of all women who work are single, separated, widowed, or have husbands who earn less than $7000 yearly ... Working women are paid 57 cents for every dollar a man earns." That is what the president's report said in 1973. Nothing has changed.

Those women who do work are the low persons on the totem pole in the job market. Almost half of the women who work are employed as salesclerks, secretaries, receptionists, and telephone operators.

Are those the types of jobs that satisfy the ego?

Are those the types of jobs that satisfy your sense of equality?

Women are partially to blame for their own inequality in the job market. Too many women believe in the myth that women are not as competent as men.

Last year, a Gallup Poll came out on women in America. Some of you may have read the findings. Mr. Gallup reported that it is the attitude of women about themselves that "most restrains them from breaking old stereotypes and ending discrimination." Sixty percent of all women would overwhelmingly, underscore overwhelmingly, prefer to work for a man as opposed to a woman.

How are we to change the stereotypes that now exist when so many women still believe in them? The problem in large part remains our own definition of ourselves. The problem is less legal than it is social and cultural. Laws and government initiatives by themselves cannot eliminate deeply-rooted prejudices overnight.

If we are to succeed in our equal rights campaign, our first task remains the winning over of other women to our point of view. Many women continue to be ill-informed.

We must develop a comprehensive national education program that discredits, once and for all, those myths that prevent women from understanding their true potential. Educate, inform, make women understand the true facts. We must use all the instruments available to us—television—radio—every instrument—to overcome the existing knowledge shortage. Develop a program of education that will raise the consciousness of all women. That is the first task of this convention.

The second task of this conference is to organize women politically. It is not enough to belong to a women's rights organization. More is required. If our ideas are to be legislatively influential, we must be organized at the precinct, county, and state level.

You have everything to gain by joining political organizations. If you are a precinct captain, a state representative has to come to you for votes. If you are a county committee leader, a state senator has to come to you for support.

I have been a state senator. I am now in Congress. I know that the men in those chambers respect political power. The merit of our cause is not the sole standard by which these men make their decisions. If you are not organized, you do not have political clout. If you do not have political muscle, you cannot build the coalitions necessary to pass legislation. If you can't form such coalitions, you offer nothing to your representatives in return for their votes. That's the way politics works. Organize!

It is important that we organize at this time. The country is shifting to the right on issues such as equal rights—affirmative action—and civil rights. Progress will not come as it did in the past.

There are attempts being made to gut existing laws that protect women. Earlier, I spoke to you about an amendment passed in the House of Representatives to prohibit the use of federal funds for affirmative action programs. What would be its effects? It will limit the enforcement powers of existing laws: The Executive Order which prohibits discrimination by federal contractors: Title VI of the Civil Rights of 1964; Title IX of the Education Amendments of 1972. This conference must take a stand against this amendment. Write your congressman. Write your senators this week.

The plight of young women on welfare also merits your special attention. Over nine million women are on welfare. Most are young and uneducated. If we are to demonstrate that women have compassion and common sense, let us help these young women. But even more importantly, let us take such action because it is right.

Outrage and compassion must exist somewhere. Someone must care. Outrage is difficult to sustain in the halls of Congress. No incorrigible children write graffiti on the walls. No litter fills the halls. Violence is not an imminent threat. We are well protected in Washington.

The 95th Congress is again trying to reform our welfare system. The president is proposing a reform package that will hit hardest those who need the most help—unwed teenage mothers. You must participate in that debate that is now beginning in Washington. If a guaranteed income program is ever to be enacted, we must work for its passage. We will not be giving these young women very much. If they do not have such a minimum income, they will never have the opportunity to get the education they need in order to get the jobs they want.

Other legislation is now pending in Congress that needs your support. Congress is holding hearings on a bill to amend Title VII of the Civil Rights Act of 1964. If passed this bill would undo the effect of the recent Supreme Court decision that allows companies not to cover pregnancy as a temporary disability.

Congress must also refinance and revise the social security system. In doing so Congress must fulfill the requirements of equity established by recent Supreme Court decisions. Married women who now work do not receive equal benefits. Next month the House Ways and Means Committee will hold hearings on bills that will assure women equal treatment in the development of a new social security plan.

The legislative process is slow and tedious. Compromise does not come easily. Congress does not always take women's issues seriously. All these impediments can be overcome if women accept the challenge to exert their political prowess.

The women's movement can be proud of its accomplishments. More has been accomplished in the last decade than in all the previous 117 years since women first met in convention at Seneca Falls. But we have not attained all of our goals. Let us devise a new set of tactics and a new strategy.

Our tactics—organized political pressure at every level of the political process. Regardless of your opinion of politicians, they can count. Those who don't will have lots of time for remedial work in arithmetic during their retirement which is mandated by election results.

Our strategy—different women working in different ways to raise the consciousness of all Americans—men and women.

Our goal—human rights and true equality for all Americans.

Notes

1 Barbara C. Jordan, "Womankind—June 25, 1977—Pittsburgh, Pennsylvania," June 25, 1977; University of North Texas Libraries, Portal to Texas History, https://texashistory.unt.edu/ark:/67531/metapth611115/. Public Domain. This copy appears to be Jordan's speaking copy. We have incorporated her minor hand-written changes—words added and lines crossed out—into this transcribed text to best capture the essence of Jordan's remarks as they were spoken.

2 Barbara Jordan, "The Constitutional Basis for Impeachment, U.S. House Judiciary Committee Impeachment Hearings, Washington, D.C., July 25, 1974," in *Barbara Jordan: Speaking the Truth with Eloquent Thunder*, ed. Max Sherman (Austin: University of Texas Press, 2007), 27–31.

3 J. Jennings Moss, "Barbara Jordan: The Other Life," *Advocate*, March 5, 1996, 43; see also Talia Lakritz, "Barbara Jordan Was One of the First Black and LGBTQ Women in Congress, But Her Relationship Was Kept Secret Until Her

Death," *Business Insider*, February 17, 2023, https://www.businessinsider.com/black-lgbtq-women-congress-black-history-month-pride-month-2023-2.

4 Mary Beth Rogers, *Barbara Jordan: American Hero* (New York: Bantam Books, 1998), 189.

5 Mary Russell, "ERA Deadline Extension Voted by House, 233–189," *Washington Post*, August 16, 1978, A1.

6 "Jordan Speaks on 'Womankind,'" *Pittsburgh Courier*, June 25, 1977, 13.

The Power of the Positive Woman

Speech to the Daughters of the American Revolution

PHYLLIS STEWART SCHLAFLY
November 14, 1977[1]

No other person gets more attention for stopping the Equal Rights Amendment than Catholic St. Louisan, Phyllis Stewart Schlafly (1924–2016). After graduating from two Catholic schools—Convent of the Sacred Heart and Washington University—as well as earning a Master's degree in Political Science from Radcliffe College, she married John Frederic "Fred" Schlafly, Jr. in 1949. While she joked that her interest in political science was piqued only because that class was at the late hour of 10:00 a.m., she was tenacious and politically active right from the start. In 1946, she helped Congressman Claude I. Bakewell's campaign, and she was the first woman to seek the Republican nomination in Illinois' 24th district in 1952 when her firstborn son was 15 months old.[2] She claimed that she was "tired of doing nothing but sitting around and criticizing" politicians. In other words, she wanted to do something "positive."[3]

Barry Goldwater's run for president, however, made Schlafly a household name as she backed the "hero of the GOP Right."[4] Inspired by his candidacy, she self-published 1964's *A Choice Not an Echo*, a book that cast aspersions on the East Coast "secret kingmakers" who controlled, she insisted, the GOP. As an alleged former member of the John Birch Society, Schlafly knew the way to stir up the fear, uncertainty, and dread necessary to activate comfortable conservatives.[5] She never stopped inflaming those fears, and her last publication—released the day after her death—was more of the same, *The Conservative Case for Trump*.[6]

In essence, Schlafly created and harnessed conservative outrage for the Equal Rights Amendment. All over the country, those recruited to the ERA opposition through Schlafly's deft skills in self-promotion and networking replicated, distributed, and copied the 1972 article "What's Wrong with 'Equal Rights' for Women?" from her newsletter, *The Phyllis Schlafly Report*. That was the text that started STOP ERA, the loudest anti-feminist organization resisting the passage of the ERA in the 1970s and 1980s. Early recruits were Goldwater campaigners and Schlafly loyalists from the earlier entanglement with Gladys O'Donnell over leadership of the National Federation of Republican Women. Members of the Daughters of the American Revolution, the National Council of Catholic Women, and Women for Constitutional Government (founded by Southern segregationist white women) soon followed. STOP ERA chapters sprung up all around the nation and members became the primary foil for pro-ERA activists and politicians.[7]

In 1977, Schlafly published *The Power of the Positive Woman*, which morphed into *The Power of the Christian Woman* in 1981. This selection from her speech is her oral adaptation of that book. Delivered to the feminine pillars of the white middle- and upper-class in the Daughters of the American Revolution, Schlafly demonstrated her consistent style. The same humor she used in 1952 to shrug off her political ambition—the class was just later than all the others—persisted in this speech. Notice that she ended nearly every paragraph with a particular kind of joke—self-effacing and umbrage-taking. But in that humor, said with a flirtatious wink and wry smile, is little more than a straw man fallacy. Just as she had explained in 1952, the conservative platform is "positive" in its retrograde nostalgia. And her opposites are simply "negative" and maladjusted.

Thank you very much for those kind words, Madame Regent, distinguished guests, and good friends. It's a very great pleasure to be invited to visit with you for a while this afternoon. And I would like also to thank my husband, Fred, for letting me come. I love to say that because it irritates the women's libbers more than anything I say.

I actually can't complain about my husband ever interfering with my civil liberties. Every time we have an argument, he always assures me of my constitutional right to remain silent. The phenomenon called the women's liberation movement has developed a certain picture of women, an image of women which I believe was best summarized in an advertisement developed by the National Organization for Women and run as spot announcements on many television stations and as ads in many newspapers and magazines. This advertisement shows a darling curly-headed child, and the caption over the picture is, "This normal healthy child was born with a handicap. It was born female."[8]

Now this is the starting assumption of the women's liberation movement. That somebody—it isn't clear who, God or the establishment or a conspiracy of male chauvinist pigs—has dealt women a foul blow by making us female. And it is up to society and the Constitution and legislation to remedy these centuries of oppression, of injustice. And so they go about the country telling women that they've been kept in serfdom. That is a favorite expression of Congresswoman Martha Griffiths.[9] They tell women that we've been oppressed for the last 200 years. They tell women that you're just second-class citizens in America. And worst of all, you're not even a person . . .

And yet they go abroad and up and down the country proclaiming this myth, the myth of the mistreatment of women. Now you may think that this is so far removed from reality that we need not concern ourselves with what they're saying, but the women's liberation movement has had a tremendous impact on our society . . .

The second dogma of the women's liberation movement is that of all the examples of injustice to women and oppression of women the greatest is that women get pregnant, and men don't get pregnant. And obviously if women are going to have their full equality, their full fulfillment in our society, we have got to make them equal in the right and ability not to be pregnant. And that is why the women's liberation movement is compulsively oriented into abortion on demand, funded by the government, accepted by our people as just simply another operation like a tonsillectomy or an appendectomy. They see in this is the only way that women can achieve their full equality.

And then the next dogma of the women's liberation movement is that the second example of oppression of our women is that society expects mothers to take care of their babies. And this is so unequal, this is so degrading, this is so confining, so oppressive. If women are to achieve their full equality in our system, if they are to have their full fulfillment and identity as a person, then obviously they must be relieved of this oppressive burden of being expected to take care of their babies. And we must make childcare the obligation of society, of the government, of the taxpayers, of anybody except the mothers because it is so unequal . . .

Then the fourth dogma of the women's liberation movement is that there really isn't any difference between men and women except those obvious differences. And all those other differences that you think you see are just due to societal restraints and stereotyped education. And we're going to change all that by having a gender-free educational system. We're going to change all that by ending roles and ending stereotypes and giving equal funding to women's sports and all that sort of thing . . .

Now I don't think for most people we need to go into much detail on fallacies in these dogmas. As far as your own self-image, as the ability to have babies, or the obligation to take care of babies, it's a matter of your attitude toward life. Most women, most mothers look upon the ability to participate in the creation of new life as the great privilege that God has given to women. This is something to be looked at in a positive way, not a negative way. And when you look at the task of taking care of babies, surely it has its drudgery, but it's certainly better than most of the jobs of the world. And you've got something to show for it after 20 years. You've got something living and breathing that returns your affection. Certainly, a factory machine and a typewriter don't return your affection. You've got a new citizen that you brought into the world . . .

The women's liberation movement based on their dogmas have, then, developed five commandments to guide their tactics and what they're after in society today. Some of us may have ten commandments to live by, but they have developed five which determine what they do, their activities, and their goals. The first is that we must build a gender-free society. They want to make a society in which you are not permitted to have any reasonable differences of treatment or assignment of one sex to a particular occupation and not the other, etc. They want to end stereotypes. They want to induce role reversals in the schools so that the girls and the boys will select subjects and careers absolutely indiscriminately without regard to sex. Now in order to do this, they have been going after the textbook publishers thinking that if they reach the textbook publishers, they can very quickly change the educational system we have in this country . . . the guidelines for the illustrations are . . . funny. You must show a man in an apron every time you show a woman in an apron. You have to induce the role reversals by showing father washing the dishes while mother works at her desk. You should show little girls playing with snakes. You should show father using hair spray and on and on . . .

The second commandment of the women's liberation movement is that we must promote equality at the expense of justice. Now "equality" is a very beautiful word. We pride ourselves on being equal under the law, and in many aspects we are equal. We all have freedom of speech and press and religion, trial by jury, due process—in all those areas. But in other areas we do not treat people equally, and it would be grievously unfair to treat them equally. We treat people differently when, in fact, they are different. Look, for example, at the differences of treatment on the basis of age. You can vote when you're 18. If you could not discriminate on the basis of age, you would have to let children vote down into the cradle. You got your American citizenship the day you're born, but we think that it's good to have a cutoff age for people who vote ... If you could not treat people differently based on income level, you couldn't have any welfare, any housing benefits, any government scholarships—all of these aspects of our society in which we try to lend a helping hand to certain people when, in fact, they are different and need differences of treatment.

Now there are two basic differences between men and women—the women's liberation movement to the contrary notwithstanding—women have babies, and men don't have babies; and women simply do not have the same physical strength as men ... All the laws pertaining to the draft to the military and war must likewise be sex-equal. The laws today which exempt women from military combat are based on obvious sex differences between males and females. But in the Equal Rights Amendment, there are no exceptions. They defeated all exceptions. It says you must treat them equally on a basis of sex, and so women would have to be put into combat just like men ...

Now there are certain people who want that result, but I would suggest that most people don't want that result. We've been through nine wars over 200 years, and the American people have never felt that we wanted to put our young women into combat just like men. They don't want it, and yet this would be one of the inescapable facts that would result from the passage of the Equal Rights Amendment ...

The third commandment of the women's liberation movement is that you must give women the benefit of reverse discrimination. In other words, they want quotas, particularly in the job market. They want the less well-qualified woman to be hired in preference to the more qualified man in recognition of injustices or discriminations of past years ...

Now there are today 40 million wives who are being supported by their husbands. Do we want to induce any significant percentage of these 40 million wives to leave their homes and go into the job market? Several million of them have done that in the last few years, and we have the highest unemployment that we've had in many, many years. Do we want to induce the rest of them to go out of the homes? Do we want to tell all those husbands, "Maybe you've been supporting your wife up to now, but that's not your obligation anymore"? ...

The fourth commandment of the women's liberation movement is that we must promote uniformity rather than diversity. This is the federalization of every part of our society that hasn't already been federalized ... And this is not what American women want ...

The fifth commandment of the women's liberation movement is that we must be neutral as between morality and immorality. And you will find that this is a thread running through all of what they do. A major goal of their movement is to establish the homosexuals and the lesbians as just as respectable, just as entitled to rights and privileges under our system as husbands and wives ... They even got it into the regulations under Title IX, under the Education Amendments of 1972, that it is sex discrimination if you don't pay for an abortion for a teacher or a student, if your school or college has a medical plan. Now nobody but a women's liberationists could think that was sex discrimination, but they do, and it's part of this overall policy that we must be neutral as between morality and immorality.

I think this is breeding a new type of social disorder. I think it is promoting a new type of narcissism, and it is an attack on the family as the basic unit of our society. The women's liberation philosophy is basically terribly negative ...

You should wake up in the morning being glad and proud that you live in the greatest country in the world where you have such great opportunities where our unique combination of social and political and economic institutions has given us the greatest freedom that any country has ever had, the greatest prosperity that any country has ever had. Now if you go into marriage and the family, it is true you have to make certain social compromises in order to make that marriage work, but most people think it's worth those social compromises. A mother does have to be a self-sacrificing person, and if you're not willing to make those sacrifices, it's very difficult to bring up good children.

Really the very saddest thing I see as I go about the country is when I go to the college campuses, and the biggest thing that hits you on the college campuses today is that the young women are not planning on having any babies. They've taken some Women's Studies courses, and they've been fed the line that of all the goals and careers that women should look for in this life, being a wife and mother has got to be the last, that they should go into any other type of career. And the peer pressure for career fulfillment to the exclusion of marriage and homemaking is powerful on the college campuses today. All you have to do is look at the fall in the birthrate, and you see what has happened. And the more years that young women spend in college, the fewer babies they're having. Well, some of them may not find out how much fun it is to have a family. But at any rate unfortunately they have been fed so much of this from their Women's Studies courses that I think they are passing up great opportunities for fulfillment ...

The women's liberation movement is making a determined attack on the moral values, on the institution of the family, and I think those women who attended the conferences of International Women's Year have realized that the values you cherish, the world that you know, is threatened today. And you are needed to come and to defend those values and those institutions. You are needed to fight the battle in the schools, on the media, in your community, and the state capital, and in the Congress. You are needed because people have to speak up in defense of these values, in defense of things that a few years ago you would have not thought necessary that were needed to defend, but they do need you today . . .

So that is our task: to speak up! To speak up for the values that built our great country and that can build a future generation that can carry on the values we cherish.

Notes

1 Phyllis Schlafly, "Power of the Positive Woman," Eagle Forum, November 14, 1977, https://www.youtube.com/watch?v=IMoE0QXPjp0. Reprinted with permission from the Eagle Forum.

2 Donald T. Critchlow, *Phyllis Schlafly and Grassroots Conservatism: A Woman's Crusade* (Princeton, NJ: Princeton University Press, 2005), 23, 28–29.

3 Mary Kimbrough, "Housewife Who's Running for Congress," *St. Louis Post-Dispatch*, March 3, 1952, 30.

4 Critchlow, *Phyllis Schlafly*, 115.

5 Historians disagree about Schlafly's alleged alliance with the John Birch Society (JBS). After a review of STOP ERA funding records, biographer Donald Critchlow concludes that there is no evidence that Schlafly was a member of the JBS. Historian Marjorie Spruill, however, notes that both Fred and Phyllis Schlafly spoke at Birch rallies, and, at the very least, Phyllis Schlafly "shared many of its positions." Furthermore, Spruill underscores that many STOP ERA members were active members of the JBS. Most recently, historian Matthew Dallek states without equivocation that Schlafly was a "Bircher." See Critchlow, *Phyllis Schlafly*, 230; Marjorie J. Spruill, *Divided We Stand: The Battle Over Women's Rights and Family Values That Polarized American Politics* (New York: Bloomsbury, 2017), 77, 84; Terry Gross, "A Historian Details How a Secretive, Extremist Group Radicalized the American Right," *NPR*, May 17, 2023, https://www.npr.org/2023/05/17/1176662608/a-historian-details-how-a-secretive-extremist-group-radicalized-the-american-rig; Matthew Dallek, *Birchers: How the John Birch Society Radicalized The American Right* (New York: Basic Books, 2023).

6 Schlafly's endorsement of Trump over Texas Senator Ted Cruz proved controversial and fomented discord within the Eagle Forum's leadership. See Betsy Swan, "Ted Cruz's Coup Against Right-Wing Matriarch Phyllis Schlafly," *Daily Beast*, April 17, 2016, https://www.thedailybeast.com/ted-cruzs-coup-against-right-wing-matriarch-phyllis-schlafly.

7 Critchlow, *Phyllis Schlafly*, 219; Spruill, *Divided We Stand*, 83–84.

8 The 1973 advertisement continued to explain, "Job discrimination is against the law and is a waste. Think about your own daughter. She's handicapped too." See Patricia Agnew, "NOW Launching Ad Campaign," *Charlotte News*, March 2, 1973, 11.

9 "Women's Forum; Debate between Martha Griffiths and Phyllis Schlafly on the E.R.A.; F33," 1974-07-10, New England Public Radio, American Archive of Public Broadcasting (GBH and the Library of Congress), Boston, MA and Washington, D.C., August 4, 2021, http://americanarchive.org/catalog/cpb-aacip-305-1615dx01.

The Cause of Justice and Sisterhood Will Triumph at Last

Address at the Third Plenary Session of the First National Women's Conference

PATSY MINK
November 19, 1977[1]

Patsy Matsu Takemoto Mink (1927–2002) was born to Japanese-American parents in the town of Paia in Hawai'i.[2] After attending the University of Chicago Law School, Mink struggled to establish herself as a practicing attorney due to a sexist local statute and the prejudices surrounding her interracial marriage. She successfully fought the rule and later made history as the first Japanese-American woman to win seats in the Territorial House of Representatives, the Territorial Senate, and the State Senate—important precursors to her historic campaign for the lone seat to the U.S. House of Representatives Hawai'i gained upon achieving U.S. statehood in 1959. Mink became the first Asian American woman to serve in the U.S. Congress in 1964.[3]

Representative Mink made a name for herself as a devoted advocate for the rights of Asian Americans, women, and students during her Congressional tenures (1965–1977 and 1989–2003). She led the 1970 fight against Judge G. Harrold Carswell's failed nomination to the U.S. Supreme Court alongside Betty Friedan. Mink, Friedan, and others strongly objected to Carswell's record of promoting sexism, racial segregation, and white supremacy.[4] In many ways, Mink's greatest legacy is her co-authorship of the 1972 addition to the Education Amendments Act, which reads: "No person in the United States shall, on the basis of sex, be excluded from participation in, be denied the benefits of, or be subjected to discrimination under any education program or activity receiving Federal financial assistance."[5] For Mink, the ERA represented "Constitutional backing" for Title IX and other legislation ensuring women's equality. Mink helped plan the historic November 1977 National Women's Conference in Houston with her colleagues Bella Abzug and Shirley Chisholm. At that conference, Mink's keynote address firmly cast anti-ERA attitudes as a concerted attempt to keep women in subordinate roles.[6]

Your presence at this National Conference for Women attests to the importance you give to the changing role of women and the need to resolve a dynamic agenda for the future.

No matter who argues to the contrary, I believe there is a cross-section of America present here tonight and that your deliberations will reflect the major forces for change and reform in our society to the end that women shall be finally equal under the law.

Thousands of women who vied for your delegate's badges are not here but we are acutely aware they are vitally concerned that this event not only achieve a high place in history but that it record accurately the current attitudes and aspirations of women in our contemporary society.

Two hundred years have gone by to shape this nation, to give its institutions direction and purpose, to enable its citizens to flourish and enjoy the blessings of liberty and freedom. Each step of the way toward the building of our democracy has been hard fought.

The struggles of the blacks and of all minorities to be accepted and accorded the fullness of opportunity and recognition has been etched in blood and anguish and the struggle still continues.

This meeting of women is unique in that unlike the true minorities, you possess the numerical majority to make this country whatever you choose.

This is the obvious anomaly as well as the challenge of this historic convocation.

Our destiny is in our own creation. Do we want change? How shall we achieve it? How do we mobilize this numerical majority of women to act? How do we appeal to their self-interest and gain their support for issues which are so vital to our full birth as human beings?

How do we generate a common understanding that the mere denial to a single woman on account of sex of a job, of a promotion, of a scholarship, of a recognition, of an opportunity to be a self-supporting individual is an abrogation of the rights of all women for which we cannot remain silent, for silence is acquiescence to our own derogation[?]

There are some who would ridicule our efforts to improve the status of women here and elsewhere. They will try to radicalize simple efforts to state the fundamental principles of equality and our efforts to apply them to all persons, including women.

Anti-ERA attitudes are generated because equality is feared and the goal of status for women as persons under our Constitution to them threatens the basis of their preference for subordination.

So under the guise of "save the home," women are being told that equality will threaten their rights as homemakers. It is unproductive, it seems to me, to debate that issue with its advocates. What we need to do is take our cause affirmatively to the American woman. We need to dramatize the reality that you and I are homemakers too, that you and I have struggled separately for the most part of our entire adult lives to breathe life into equality, that we have pushed our way into the centers of business, of science, of government, of politics, despite the barriers that have only recently begun to be lifted because of our newly achieved collective strength.

This Conference, for me, is the culmination of a life's work—no small part of it being motivated by the intense wish that somehow all the personal affronts, put-downs, and outright discriminations which I endured to make my own way as a human being can be spared my daughter and yours.

I am therefore all the more incensed by those who would paint as anti-family, women who have lived hardships and out of their personal experiences are now committed to finding solutions for their children's future security and happiness.

We, each of us, have a great challenge to permit this Conference to express the will and determination of women who do desire equality before the law and who seek changes in status so that women can obtain positions of responsibility.

Women are needed as active participants in all institutions and forums of public policy. Women need to have a more direct voice in the formulation of policies and programs that vitally affect their lives and the lives of their family. Until we do, the maxim of our democracy "of the people and by the people" is diminished by half.

This is the high goal which this Conference must obtain. It must serve as a significant event of the coming together of women across this land, charged with a sense of importance and deeply committed as a group to achieve positive gains for women in all aspects of living. There can be no equivocation on this point.

No matter how vigorously we may disagree and debate procedures and strategies, the bottom line for this Conference must be a serious attempt to provoke meaningful change so that American women of the future can be assured justice, equal protection under the law, and full participation in their own government as proclaimed by our Constitution.

We know that we are at the most critical juncture of our Nation's history. The country is watching you tonight. What is the public verdict to be on this meeting? What we do here will determine whether we will be joined by the public in what could be this century's most significant policy platforms for the future.

I place my life, my future, and that of my family in the wise and effective deliberations which I have every expectation will highlight this Conference beyond all predictions.

With faith, perseverance, and personal commitment, the cause of justice and sisterhood will triumph at last.

Notes

1 Patsy Mink, "Speech by Honorable Patsy Mink, Assistant Secretary of State (Former Congresswoman and Co-sponsor PL 94–167)," Third Plenary Session, November 19, 1977, in *The Spirit of Houston: The First National Women's Conference*, An Official Report to the President, the Congress, and the People of the United States, March 1978, National Commission on the Observation of International Women's Year: 227–28. Public Domain.

2 We use the diacritical *'okina* in spelling Hawai'i. See *Guidelines for Hawaiian Geographic Names*, Developed by the State of Hawai'i Board on Geographic Names, https://files.hawaii.gov/dbedt/op/gis/bgn/Guidelines_for_Hawaiian_Geographic_Names_v1.1.pdf.

3 "Patsy Takemoto Mink," U.S. House of Representatives, History, Art & Archives, https://history.house.gov/People/detail/18329.

4 David M. Dismore, "Today in Feminist History: Women Oppose Supreme Court Nominee G. Harrold Carswell," *Ms. Magazine*, January 30, 2020, https://msmagazine.com/2020/01/30/today-in-feminist-history-women-oppose-nixon-supreme-court-nominee-g-harrold-carswell/.

5 Julie C. Suk, *We the Women: The Unstoppable Mothers of the Equal Rights Amendment* (New York: Skyhorse Publishing, 2020), 74, 78; Sherry Boschert, *37 Words: Title IX and Fifty Years of Fighting Sex Discrimination* (New York: The New Press, 2022).

6 Judy Tzu-Chun Wu, "Envisioning the National Women's Conference: Patsy Takemoto Mink and Pacific Feminism," in *Suffrage at 100: Women in American Politics Since 1920*, ed. Stacie Taranto and Leandra Zarnow (Baltimore: Johns Hopkins University Press, 2020), 259.

Declaration of Dependence

Address at STOP ERA Rally

Elisabeth Elliot
November 19, 1977[1]

Elisabeth "Betty" Howard Elliot Leitch Gren (1926–2015) was born to Presbyterian parents in Brussels, Belgium but spent her formative years in the Philadelphia suburbs. She graduated at the top of her high school class from a private Protestant boarding school with nine other students. Betty met her first husband Jim Elliot in their Greek class at Wheaton College, and thus began their unusual courtship where he pledged his undying love but was determined never to marry. Years later, he relented if she learned Quichua—the language of the isolated Ecuadorian indigenous tribe Jim had chosen to evangelize. Her parents announced the engagement in February 1953, and the next October, Jim and Betty had a civil ceremony in Ecuador.[2] In January 1956, Jim and four other male missionaries were killed by the Huaorani people with whom they had attempted contact for several months. The American press, both secular and evangelical, heavily publicized the modern-day martyr story of the white savior amid his dark assassins, with *Life Magazine* running multiple photo-essays.[3]

Their marriage only lasted 27 months, but Elisabeth Elliot's identity as a wife-of-a-martyr would propel her to fame as a popular Christian author and speaker until her death in 2015. For a woman first married in a civil ceremony who never took her second or third husband's names, her persona of the ideal submissive Christian wife made her an unusual, yet very effective anti-feminist spokesperson for conservative causes. In February 1971, Elliot delivered her first-ever public speech against "women's liberation" to an audience of students at Gordon College in Massachusetts. By this point, she had already been contemplating writing a book on marriage and womanhood. The product of her thinking was published in 1976 as *Let Me Be a Woman: Notes to My Daughter on the Meaning of Womanhood*, which firmly established her view that "the women's liberation movement has no place in the church or the home" since, she suggested, the Bible clearly establishes male headship and female submission as the correct order of things.[4]

Importantly, not all women who gathered in Houston in November 1977 participated in the National Women's Conference. An estimated 20 thousand anti-ERA women, men, and children—mostly white and representative of various Christian denominations—gathered in Houston for a STOP ERA Pro-Family Rally held at the Astro-Arena. Phyllis Schlafly, miffed that the International Women's Year Commission had only appointed a single anti-ERA member, headlined what Gloria Steinem called a "right-wing and religious counterconference."[5] Signs proclaiming "ERA is Anti-Bible" and "We Like Ladies Who Like Being Ladies" appeared at the rally, accusations that feminists were "perverts" flowed freely, and loud chants of "let me be a woman" arose from the audience.[6] Since her book of the same name had been published the year before, Elisabeth Elliot earned a coveted speaking spot as the token "Reformed" [read: Presbyterian] anti-feminist on the program. She delivered a short speech, less than four minutes, right after Lottie Beth Hobbs. Elliot issued a firm and feminine "declaration of dependence" on male leadership that required frequent pauses for audience applause.

I was speaking a few weeks ago on the subject of womanhood. And a girl came up to me and she said, "You know, I don't like some of the stuff you say about women." And I said, "Why?" And she said, "Well, I don't know. I mean, like you know, I just don't like to think of myself as a woman." I said, "What do you like to think of yourself as?" And she said, "As a person, just a person."

And it was very obvious to me when I looked at that girl that she did not think of herself as a woman, and my heart went out to her because she has been sold a bill of goods. She has been told that there is something reprehensible about the distinction between the sexes and that every effort must be made to obfuscate and to erase that distinction. I speak for thousands of Christian women who see sexuality as far deeper than a mere matter of biology. What we are told are mere stereotypes, socially conditioned which must be abolished, I see as more like archetypes. That is, that they have a far deeper origin than sociology or politics. They originate in a creator God. We see the world and the human body not as ends in themselves, not as possessions to be done with as we choose, but as temples of the Holy Spirit of God. We are bought with a price.

And so, I stand here today . . . I stand here to make my Declaration of Dependence, not as one who is incapable of what the world would call independence. I have been a missionary in the jungle. I went in in 1958 to live with a savage tribe that had murdered my husband and four other missionaries. I have been a writer and a speaker, and I've had to support myself having been twice widowed. But in those crises of my life, I have come to see the truth of Isaiah 43:1–2: "I, the Lord, have called thee. I created thee, formed thee, redeemed thee. Thou art mine." As Christian women, we ask for the right to be women, to live our lives in faithful obedience to the God who created us and who demonstrated the power of his love in the sacrifice of Jesus Christ who came to make us free.

Submission does not mean weakness. Sacrifice is not civility. Femininity is not frivolity.

Notes

1 Elizabeth Elliot, "Pro-Family Rally," Houston, November 19, 1977, www.youtube.com/watch?v=SpNa6BiSNFI. Reprinted with permission from the Elisabeth Elliot Foundation. A special thanks to Kathy Reeg for her assistance.

2 Lucy S. R. Austen, *Elisabeth Elliot: A Life* (Wheaton, IL: Crossway Books, 2023), 133–35, 139–46; Thomas S. Kidd, "Elisabeth Elliot Was a Flawed Figure God Used in Extraordinary Ways," *Christianity Today*, June 12, 2023, https://www.christianitytoday.com/ct/2023/july-august/elisabeth-elliot-biography-lucy-austen.html.

3 " 'Go Ye and Preach the Gospel': Five Do and Die," *Life Magazine*, January 30, 1956, 10–19; "The Martyr's Widows Return to Teach in Jungle," *Life Magazine*, May 20, 1956, 24–33; "Child Among Her Father's Killers: Missionaries Live with Aucas," *Life Magazine*, November 24, 1958, 22–29; Elisabeth Elliot, "Widow's Jungle Life amid Husband's Killers," *Life Magazine*, April 7, 1961, 118–33.

4 Austen, *Elisabeth Elliot*, 440, 471; Elisabeth Elliot, *Let Me Be a Woman: Notes to My Daughter on the Meaning of Womanhood* (Wheaton, IL: Tyndale House Publishers, Inc., 1976).

5 Gloria Steinem, *My Life on the Road* (New York: Random House, 2015), 58.

6 Donald Critchlow, *Phyllis Schlafly and Grassroots Conservatism: A Woman's Crusade* (Princeton, NJ: Princeton University Press, 2005), 246–47; Ann Gilbert, "Pro-Family Protests Convention," *Shreveport Journal*, November 25, 1977, 5B; "Solidarity Urged in Defeating ERA," *Terre Haute Tribune*, November 20, 1977, 2; "Feminists Called 'Perverts' at Counter Rally," *Press Democrat*, November 20, 1977, 8.

La Década de la Mujer

Article for Agenda: A Journal of Hispanic Issues

MARTA SOTOMAYOR
November/December 1977[1]

At the inception of the National Hispanic Council on Aging in the late 1970s, its first Executive Director served on a volunteer basis. Once Dr. Marta Sotomayor (1932–2013) formally accepted the position, she skillfully led the organization for 17 years between 1986 and 2003.[2] Sotomayor was the first Latina woman in the United States to earn a doctoral degree in social work. This Fulbright scholar and professor of social work at several institutions went on to work in the U.S. Department of Health and Human Services under Presidents Reagan, Bush, and Clinton. Sotomayor devoted her life to a number of public policy causes, particularly advocacy for aging members of the Hispanic community.[3]

The National Council of La Raza (NCLR)—today, UnidosUS—elected Sotomayor as its first woman president in February 1978. At the time, NCLR represented 108 organizations that lobbied for the rights of Mexican-Americans.[4] The year prior, while serving as Vice Chairperson of NCLR's Board of Directors, Sotomayor penned an essay for *Agenda: A Journal of Hispanic Issues*. Here, she placed the ERA within a constellation of issues vital to the progress of Hispanic women in the United States.

La Década de la Mujer—the specific meaning of this phrase is still uncertain to the majority of Hispanas. For involved women the meaning is as diverse as the various orientations and perspectives that characterize our communities. For some Hispanas, for example, the decade of women is best embodied in the Equal Rights Amendment, which clearly speaks of the legal framework for the exercise of some basic human rights. In the issue of abortion, that concept of human rights more often than not becomes diluted in the simplistic dichotomy of being either for or against abortion. For other Hispanas the feminist forum and agency (as varied as it is) provides one more arena to exercise their political skills regardless of the substance of the issues—the process, it is claimed, is what matters. For still another group of Hispanas the main issues revolve around a reevaluation of the roles, boundaries, and rules that have given a specific flavor to the transactional field between men and women.

The struggle becomes too easily translated into, and clouded by, the notion of *machos y hembras*[5] which is usually dealt with in the power arena.

One can go on to mention other perspectives of the feminist agenda, but the truth of the matter is that Hispana leadership has yet to identify carefully and systematically the issues that could be meaningful and useful to engage the majority of Hispanas in the *barrios* and *colonias*[6] in the process of self-change. While it is true that the majority of the issues being discussed by women in general are relevant to those Hispanas who have access to alternatives and choices, it is doubtful that those same issues, at this point, can be successfully utilized to organize the majority of average Hispanas and enable them to join that one other facet of the movement for liberation.

ERA, for example, as meaningful and important as it is, remains simply a legal strategy to guarantee certain rights to women; abortion, as crucial as it is in some instances, is merely a symptom of more severe and complex conditions that need to be understood, separated, and dealt with in a variety of approaches. While process is indeed important and political skills are indeed necessary to create change, process remains only the context and skills are only the tools to accomplish certain objectives. And while male and female relationships are quite basic and fundamental, and ascribed roles are often devastating for both sexes, a true reform movement must go beyond these sets of relationships.

It is true that certain principles are involved in the law, but the fact that a law exists does not necessarily mean that laws are enforced and that they will create basic attitudinal change. All of us, I am certain, are painfully aware that civil rights legislation of the last 25 years has not created the basic changes that are so needed in this society to increase the life chances and open more doors of opportunity to the minorities of color.

Available data does not indicate that more Hispanas are graduating from professional schools, or entering managerial positions, or becoming entrepreneurs; some do, but not enough to make a dent. However, available data, as crude as they are, indicate that Hispanas continue to show a greater incidence of uterine cancer and tuberculosis; have large unplanned families, and not enough money to make it from day to day; and live in unsanitary and dilapidated housing that breeds all types of disease, which does not help in significantly lowering the infant death rate.

Available data also show that while some Hispanas are beginning to venture into the work world, the most they will be able to find is inadequately paid menial or domestic jobs, and that the majority of Hispanas do not finish high school and thus do not acquire sufficient skills to allow them to enter a competitive labor market. There are many barriers that Hispanas face from day to day that seem to have been there from generation to generation. All are symptoms of the way that society is organized and structured, of the rules of the game that exclude others and provide special privileges to the few.

But those forces that oppose change seem to be gaining momentum, as evidenced by the events that have taken place in a number of state conferences sponsored as part of the International Women's Year. Those Hispanas who as delegates engaged in a process of change faced in Houston [National Chicana Conference, 1971] a series of disruptive tactics, well-organized caravans, and well-disciplined organizational machinery that includes husbands, brothers, sons, and anyone who can be mustered to openly attack the values and changes that all of us have been working for.

Those Hispanas who were elected as delegates, and who identify themselves as Hispanas for our cause, will not have an easy task in the future, for they will have to deal with overt expressions of bigotry and racism. They must, however, formulate a meaningful Hispana agenda based on the nature of their positions as leaders. They will have to identify those issues with which *la mujer en el barrio*[7] can identify, and develop strategies for change that are applicable and appropriate to the decades of the 1970s and 1980s.

But equally important is the fact that these women can provide role models for many young Hispanas that will follow in the years to come. It will not be an easy task, but it is a most crucial and necessary one.

Notes

1 Marta Sotomayor, "La Década de la Mujer," *Agenda: A Journal of Hispanic Issues* 7, no. 6 (November–December 1977): 2. Reprinted with permission from UnidosUS, formerly the National Council of La Raza.

2 "History: Almost 40 Years' Experience Improving Hispanic Older Adults' Quality of Life," National Council on Hispanic Aging," https://www.nhcoa.org/about-us/history/.

3 "Marta Sotomayor Papers," Texas Archival Resources Online, University of Texas-Austin, https://txarchives.org/utlac/finding_aids/00493.xml.
4 "The Nation," *Los Angeles Times*, February 26, 1978, 2; "Experts to Discuss 'Women at Risk,'" *Austin American-Statesman*, May 3, 1977, B7.
5 Men and women.
6 Neighborhoods and colonies.
7 The women in the neighborhood.

There Is No Time Limit

Address at the ERA March and Rally

Midge Costanza
July 9, 1978[1]

The fact that New Yorker Margaret "Midge" Costanza (1932–2010) found herself in the enviable position of being the first woman appointed as Assistant to the President for Public Liaison under Jimmy Carter is nothing short of remarkable. Costanza's role in the White House made her a bridge between the Executive Branch and disenfranchised collectives, especially women's rights and gay rights groups. With her partner Jean O'Leary, co-chair of the National Gay and Lesbian Task Force, Costanza coordinated the historic meeting between Carter and gay and lesbian leaders at the White House in March 1977.[2] Costanza was unafraid to push Carter in more progressive directions or even to disagree with him outright on issues such as abortion.[3] Her blunt style and fearless tactics made her several enemies in the White House and less than two years into the appointment, she resigned.[4] In her later years, she aided several political campaigns, ran a series of successful seminars for political campaigning, and consulted with various women's groups before dying of cancer in 2010.[5]

Costanza leveraged her political connections to boost the ERA from her platform. NOW organized a two-day July 1978 march and rally for the ERA in Washington, D.C. timed to coincide with the first anniversary of Alice Paul's death. As the ratification deadline rapidly approached with three states still needed, an estimated 50,000 to 100,000 women descended upon the nation's capital and walked the length of the Mall to the Capitol steps. Keynote speakers included Bella Abzug, Betty Friedan, Gloria Steinem, and Midge Costanza, whose speech garnered an ovation even though the crowd booed at the mention of Carter's name and shouted out questions about his absence from the rally.[6] As her remarks indicate, Costanza appeared not just in her capacity as a pro-ERA feminist but also as an official spokesperson for the president—even speaking about herself in the third person in "Carter's voice." And yet, Carter's support for the ERA by this point was "waning," and he had yet to voice support for extending the ratification deadline. Biographer Doreen Mattingly describes Costanza's speech as "directly going against Carter's position and the direction of other aides" (although Mattingly clarifies that if Carter was angered at Costanza going rogue, he did not show it).[7]

There is no time limit on human and civil rights.

There is no time limit on the full protection of the Constitution of the United States for every citizen.

And there is no time limit on this Administration's commitment to equal rights and equal opportunity.

This Administration supports the Equal Rights Amendment. We *support* extension of the legislative deadline for ratification.

We will continue together with you to support equal rights and equal opportunity *wherever* they are weak or lacking.

Together we will implement the Plan of Action adopted by the International Women's Year Conference in Houston.

Together we will assure that the voices of women are heard through the National Advisory Committee for Women, the Interagency Task Force for Women, and through my office—under the direction of Margaret "Midge" Costanza—to whom I have assigned the responsibility of women's issues, domestic human rights, and the ratification of the Equal Rights Amendment.

Together we will work to strengthen and broaden opportunities for women and minorities wherever needed—as we have already begun to do in our Civil Service Reform proposal which will increase employment opportunities for women and minorities.

And we need your help and support in this effort.

We see the Equal Rights Amendment as the foundation—the bedrock—for these efforts.

Today you make it clear . . .

You make it loud and clear . . .

That over half of the population of this nation will *not* be denied inclusion in the United States Constitution . . .

That over half of the population of this nation will *not* be denied or deprived of their rights because a minority of people do not want to exercise theirs . . .

And that the will of the majority of this country will *not* be delayed … will *not* be denied …

In the immediate and final ratification of the Equal Rights Amendment to the Constitution of the United States.

Notes

1 Midge Costanza, "Statement by the President of the United States to be Delivered by Margaret 'Midge' Costanza, Assistant to the President," ERA March and Rally, July 9, 1978, The White House, https://afeministinthewhitehouse.com/wp-content/uploads/2020/12/Statement_by_Pres_Carter_delivered_by_Midge_at_the_ERA_March_and_Rally_July_9_1978.pdf. Public Domain.
2 "Jean O'Leary—Part 2," *Making Gay History*, https://makinggayhistory.com/podcast/episode-15-jean-oleary-part-2/.
3 "Women in Administration Protest Carter Opposition to Abortion Aid," *New York Times*, July 16, 1977, 7.
4 Fred Barbash, "Midge Costanza Resigns: Colorful, Outspoken Presidential Aide," *Washington Post*, August 2, 1978, A1.
5 William Grimes, "Midge Costanza, 77, A Top Assistant to Carter, Dies," *New York Times*, March 25, 2010, A28.
6 Leslie Bennetts, "Supporters of the Equal Rights Amendment Gathering for March in Washington Sunday," *New York Times*, July 7, 1978, A10.
7 Doreen Mattingly, *A Feminist in the White House: Midge Costanza, the Carter Years, and America's Culture Wars* (New York: Oxford University Press, 2016), 179–80.

Black Women Have a Right to Be Properly Informed

Address to the Senate Judiciary Committee

DOROTHY HEIGHT
August 4, 1978[1]

Growing up in rural Pennsylvania, Dorothy Irene Height's (1912–2010) encounters with racism came early and often. A white playmate called her the n-word, another school's women's basketball team refused to play her school's team because three players (including Height) were Black, and a Pittsburgh Young Women's Christian Association (YWCA) turned her Girl Reserves Club away because the pool banned Black patrons. The list goes on. Height's oratorical achievements in a public speaking contest led to a four-year scholarship to attend New York University after Barnard College turned her away because of a school policy to not admit Black students. After postgraduate study at Columbia University and the New York School of Social Work, Height pursued a career as a social worker in Harlem.

In the early 1930s, she joined the United Christian Youth Movement and devoted her attention to anti-lynching initiatives and military desegregation efforts. For some 30 years, Height served on the staff of the national YWCA and helped de-segregate venues that had once turned her away. The mentorship of Mary McLeod Bethune in Height's formative years proved instrumental in recruiting her to the bourgeoning civil rights movement. The two women met in the late 1930s while Bethune led the National Council of Negro Women (NCNW), a post Height assumed in 1957 and held for more than 40 years.[2] The National Cathedral hosted Height's funeral in 2010 and President Barack Obama delivered the eulogy for the "Queen Esther to this Moses Generation."[3]

Dorothy Height came somewhat late to the ERA debate and did not publicly champion the amendment until the late 1970s. She was certainly no stranger to gender-based discrimination in a variety of explicit and implicit forms. In pivotal civil rights moments, she worked alongside luminaries such as James Farmer, Martin Luther King, Jr., John Lewis, and Roy Wilkins. Height was often one of the only women in the room, which was the case at the founding of the Council for the United Civil Rights leadership group. Even so, the path to Height's ERA endorsement was neither straightforward nor inevitable. Representing the NCNW, Height served as the only Black commissioner of Kennedy's Presidential Commission on the Status of Women, staffed by nearly all ERA opponents.[4] The NCNW opposed the amendment and as late as 1971, with its leaders and members voting against an ERA endorsement. But the NCNW changed course by 1977, largely out of a desire to set a global example for gender equality.[5] Bringing with her the full weight of the NCNW's reputation and organizational prowess, along with her own ethos as an eloquent civil rights activist, Height testified favorably for the ERA at the 1978 hearings for extending the ratification deadline. A point of particular concern for her had to do with the misinformation that women, particularly Black women, continually encountered about the amendment.

I am Dorothy I. Height, President of the National Council of Negro Women, a 43-year-old organization composed of a coalition of 27 national affiliated organizations and involved individuals, with an outreach to 4 million women throughout the country.

Since its founding by Mary McLeod Bethune, the National Council of Negro Women has worked to advance opportunities and the quality of life for Black women in every walk of life.

I am here today to speak in support of the proposed extension for ratification of the ERA. Of particular importance is the understanding of what the ERA will mean to our society. The public has been flooded with sensational misrepresentation of the effects of the amendment, financially backed by a consortium of interest groups who feel they have more at stake in the status quo than in moving our culture toward implementation of the spirit of this constitution, guaranteeing basic human rights to its citizens with every piece of social legislation, it has taken time for society to lessen its fears of the change and to understand the positive effects of the change on the society. The ERA does not take away rights, protection and guarantees of liberties. It extends basic rights and opportunity to both men and women. The ERA is not for white middle-class women only, it's for Black, Brown, Yellow, Red and White women and men from every economic level.

Although the opposing forces have worked to divide feminist and minority interest, major organizations that represent minority constituencies are fighting for ERA—understanding its particular importance to their specialized needs and concerns. The additional time period is crucial to allowing these organizations to help their constituencies unlearn the misinformation that went hand in hand with the scare tactics of the anti-ERA forces. In several of the states where ERA was not ratified, thousands of leaflets were passed out by anti-ERA forces using a quote from a former officer of the National Council of Negro Women saying that ERA would be detrimental to Black women—it would make them "lifters and toters." This quote was issued several years ago when the previously proposed ERA would have voided protective state legislation limiting the number of pounds a woman could be forced to lift. With Black women being in abundance in service trades, this was of concern to us. However, this state legislation has since been repealed making the present ERA necessary as a protection to both men and women. Even though [the] NCNW has taken a strong stand in support of the present ERA, this out-of-date literature was utilized to deliberately misinform Black women. Black women have a right to be properly informed. The public has a right to be informed. The three-year extension will give the public the necessary time to sort fact from fiction and truly understand that this is a universal civil rights issue.

I would like to feel that our legislators believe in the basic rights of people because ERA is a fundamental human rights issue, and it will not go away after March 1979. Can we afford to spend the time and energies of our Congress, our state legislators and the public by beginning the process once again when we have so many other crucial issues to address?

Notes

1 *Hearings Before the Subcommittee on the Constitution of the Committee on the Judiciary*, United States Senate, Day 2, 95th Congress, (1978) (Statement of Dorothy Height). Public Domain. We note that Height's oral testimony differs slightly from her prepared statement for the record, which is what we have included.

2 Marilyn Hoffman, "Dorothy Height—An Optimist With No Illusions," *Christian Science Monitor*, March 26, 1980, 19.

3 Barack Obama, "Remarks by the President at Funeral Service for Dr. Dorothy Height," White House, April 29, 2010, https://obamawhitehouse.archives.gov/the-press-office/remarks-president-funeral-service-dr-dorothy-height.

4 Elisabeth Griffith, *Formidable: American Women and the Fight for Equality 1920–2020* (New York: Pegasus Books, 2022), 136–37.

5 Rebecca Tuuri, *Strategic Sisterhood: The National Council of Negro Women in the Black Freedom Struggle* (Chapel Hill: University of North Carolina Press, 2018), 165, 192.

The Patriarchal Panic

Address at Mount Vernon College

SONIA JOHNSON
February 10, 1979[1]

Sonia Ann Harris Johnson (1936–present) was a faithful and fifth-generation member of the Church of Jesus Christ of Latter-day Saints until her political activism in favor of the Equal Rights Amendment prompted the LDS church to deem the "housewife" a "heretic." The mother of four, who played the organ and held an Ed.D. degree from Rutgers University, initially encountered the ERA in 1978 through disparaging church materials that objected to the proposed extension deadline for ratification. Johnson found herself utterly baffled at the opposition ("I loved it. I just loved it," she recalled, upon first reading the amendment).[2] With her friends Hazel Davis Rigby, Maida Rust Withers, and Teddie Wood, Johnson formed Mormons for ERA, with Johnson serving as president. The church excommunicated her in December 1979 since her politics were "not in harmony with church doctrine concerning the nature of God in the manner in which He directs His church on earth."[3] The excommunication thrust Johnson into the national limelight. She became associated with a small, but mighty and vocal group of LDS women who supported the ERA. Her testimony before a Senate Subcommittee on Constitutional Rights underscored how women in the church remained unequal. Male church leaders were horrified and Johnson became the "worst nightmare" of Utah Republican Orrin G. Hatch, an ERA opponent who tried to block the extension in the Senate.[4]

In May 1982, Johnson joined six other ERA supporters—including Sister Maureen Fiedler—in a hunger strike in Illinois to urge the state to pass the amendment. Under a banner proclaiming "Women Hunger for Justice," Johnson announced that "we hope the spiritual energy and enlightenment we generate will ultimately free both the oppressed and the oppressors from the cycle of injustice in which we have both been bound."[5] While one striker said, "I'd give my right arm for a Fresca," Johnson was craving scrambled eggs.[6] Eight days into the strike, a group of elderly women arrived and counter-protested by devouring chocolate candy bars in sight of the starving protesters. Two days later, a group of male politicians gleefully brought a full-fledged meal to eat in the rotunda, just a few feet away from Johnson and her fellow "feminist fasters."[7] Although she was hospitalized for low blood pressure and potassium levels at one point, Johnson considered the strike a success since participating proved "courage" to the nation. Certainly, the national coverage of the 37-day fast brought a lot of media attention to the ERA.[8]

Johnson delivered this speech at Mount Vernon College in Virginia four years before the hunger strike. She drew parallels between the furthest right organizations like the John Birch Society and Schlafly and the Mormon patriarchal fear of losing their white male supremacy—an allegation that Betty Friedan controversially advanced, minus the Mormon connection, earlier that decade.[9] Notice her term, "Schalflyeese." She's identifying that rhetorical habit among the anti-ERA crowd to merely replicate the same phrases and terms from a charismatic personality than to really engage with the issues. The confrontational style employed here reveals why the LDS church found Johnson so threatening and subversive.

On November 8, Robert Beers of Virginia Stop ERA, told 75 Mormon women assembled at the first Mormon anti-ERA organization meeting in Virginia—assembled by the men of the Church—that the prime objective in 1979 was to get the VA legislature to vote for a citizen's advisory referendum.[10]

Who is Bob Beers and how did the Mormons get mixed up with him and his group? I don't know the particulars, but the general pattern of seduction by the right wing of conservative groups for the purpose of extending the political power of the far right is clearly evident here (business interests vs. labor interests).

So, to understand the referendum strategy, we have to understand some important things about the opposition. Everyone here is, unfortunately, all too well aware of most of these facts: that the Antis are ultra-conservatives, so far to the right on the political continuum that they are almost crowding those on the far left. A good example, and one I know well, is the John Birch Society and all its front organizations: The Conservative Caucus, Freeman Institute, HOTDOG,[11] etc. But there are many more, probably different in name only and consisting of persons who are Birch members, or members of the American Party or Liberty lobbyists.

In April 1977, the Conservative Caucus met in Salt Lake City. Although this was just one of the 50 conferences being held in the various states of the nation, their National Director, Howard Phillips, was there—which, even if more direct ties were not known, would create some suspicion about the relationship of the Birch Society and the Mormon Church.[12] At the meeting, according to a *Salt Lake Tribune* article, plans were discussed for appointing 30 leaders in each congressional district in the United States, for publishing a newspaper in each of the 435 congressional districts, for taking over Congress by 1980 and the Senate by 1982.

Perhaps this is just megalomania or delusions of grandeur, but obviously there's serious and frightening political ambition here and lots of confidence. The Birch Society goes on record proudly as opposing civil rights for blacks, Indians, women, residents of Washington, D.C., etc. In short, they are opponents of human rights, non-trusting, manipulative, and hungry to tell others what to do and to have the power to enforce their wishes. Sounds like something out of Solzhenitsyn, doesn't it?[13]

But why have such groups chosen the referendum as part of their strategy? Because, for one thing, it is an excellent organizational tool. Like all of us, they have difficulty getting their people to come back time and time again to work against all the things they are against. It provides a rallying point for the far right—witness Florida and Nevada—bringing voters who haven't been to the polls for years out of the woodwork. And, of course, it is a delaying tactic until they can get their people elected to office.

But in the referendum the Antis have something undeniably positive (for a change): "let the people speak." Something undeniably democratic and patriotic, which seems to put them solidly on the side of freedom and the flag, right in tune with the "no taxation without representation" war cry of their ancestors. This issue is different in kind, in tone, and especially in defensibility, from the usual scare tactics.

For this reason, it is a difficult scheme to attack. Arguments against it are subtle and seem to be nitpicking. The opposition knows that these arguments make us look undemocratic, afraid of the truth, even like liars, since we have always said that the majority of American citizens want the ERA. "If you're right and they really want it," the opposition jeers, "what are you afraid of?" And they smile knowingly at their constituents, insinuating that we're frauds.

But they're quite right about one thing: we are afraid of several things. One of them is the habits of voters on the matter of referendums. The *Christian Science Monitor* disclosed that of the 4,000 referendums that have appeared on ballots in this nation, only 400 have ever passed, which means that people simply don't, as a rule, vote for referendums, no matter how innocuous or even how popular the issue may be. The leaders of the opposition know the predilections of voters as well as we do and see how it works right into their hands. They also know that it is easier to influence uninformed voters than it is to influence better informed legislators. In addition, they would, I think, like to establish an entirely different method of amending the Constitution than now exists: all controversial issues, such as abortion, going to referendum because they know that with the hysteria they can stir up combined with the natural disinclination of voters to vote for referendums, they can much more easily control politics. They distrust and dislike representative government because they cannot control it so easily (witness the extension). Then there are state legislators like Bob Thoburn in Virginia who told Jean Clark that even if 99 percent of his constituents voted for the ERA on a referendum, he would vote against it.[14] So, what's the use of it anyway?

But what has all this to do with Bob Beers and the Mormons? Everyone here is far too well acquainted with how the opposition stirs up hysteria: Mormons distributing gross pictures of aborted fetuses door-to-door in Las Vegas just before the election; Anita Bryant in Florida speaking against the ERA with the Gay Rights March in San Francisco projected in the background; the lies that mothers would be put in the front lines, that homosexual marriages would be legal, that we'd all share the same toilets, and so on, ad infinitum. What you might be more interested in is how they seduced the Mormon Church and got them to do their dirty work for them.

In 1975, Phyllis Schlafly met with some top officials of the Mormon Church. Church leaders had already expressed dissatisfaction with the Equal Rights Amendment but were not making any official pronouncements—encyclicals—about it. But shortly after Schlafly's visit, the First Presidency of the Church issued its first anti-ERA policy letter, which was accepted churchwide as revelation, though President Kimball has never personally referred to it as such.[15] And this letter which began the Church's openly anti-female campaign was couched in *Schlaflyeese*—her own words, much of it. I am pretty certain that Church leaders view Schlafly as inconsequential; perhaps if they're very shrewd, as a catalyst. But I doubt if they realize that they were clearly manipulated by her for her purposes and the purposes of the right wing, and that the right wing ALWAYS has the upper hand.

But why should Schlafly wish to seduce the Mormons and why were they so susceptible to her?

Schlafly, and people like her—Bob Beers, her disciple and trainee in Virginia—know a gold mine when they see it, and they definitely see it in the Mormon Church in several senses. In the most obvious one, the Church is one of the top 50 corporations in the United States, bringing in between 3 and 4 million dollars a day (which also says a great deal about why they fear equality—which costs big corporations lots of money). But perhaps just as important as the wealth in dollar terms, is the church's wealth in terms of person-power. The organization of the Church is marvelously tight and the obedience of the members marvelously thoroughgoing. As I have heard so often lately in meetings, "When the prophet speaks, the thinking has been done. The debate is ended." . . .

In addition, I believe the Mormon Church may be the last great Western patriarchy. I know Catholics and Jews may argue with that, but I'll put my patriarchs up against theirs any time. At least there are groups of Catholics and Jews—sizable groups—who favor priesthood for women and the Equal Rights Amendment. There is some evidence of the woman's movement in these churches. But the number of Mormons who would JOIN AN ORGANIZATION with the goal of securing the priesthood for women in the Church could be counted on a hand and a half, and those who would even dare think seriously of it at home in their private bathrooms with the doors locked and lights off could be counted on two. Women simply have no place in the church except as an admiring audience for the male superstars. To demand their rights is to hit their Mormon brethren where they live—in their delicate egos (Warenski and *Patriarchs and Politics: The Plight of the Mormon Woman*). We frighten church members by saying that the fight over the ERA in this country has provided the greatest political training ground for women since the world began, and by asking, "How you going to keep them down on the farm after they've seen Paree?" The Church has all unknowingly furthered the ends of the women by catapulting them out into the world of politics . . .

There is another dimension to the Mormon connection. We have a prophetic tradition in the Church that in the last days, which these are, the Constitution of the United States will hang by a thread and the Elders of the Mormon Church will save it. Because of this, Mormons fully expect to become top political and governmental leaders in this nation in the not-too-distant future. The Church sees this political power as its God-given right and destiny, and is reaching out, as one of the growing tentacles of the far right, to take it. At every training meeting of the Mormon women, male church leaders were in attendance, often reminding them of this prophecy and urging them to help save the nation (the "This is the Hour" paper from Nevada). Mormons see themselves as the stewards of this vineyard, the saviors of this country, which accounts for much of the incredible zeal and religious fervor they put into their politics. In Virginia, Mormons distributed, door-to-door, 80,000 anti-ERA brochures; there are only 25,000 Mormons in Virginia of all ages, which means no more than 10,000 adults at best. In the first organizational meeting, Bob Beers told the women that this was just the first of many such issues they would be expected to put their energies behind. In other words, the Church is just beginning.

Schlafly, Welch, Beers—the big as well as the little boogeymen—play upon the fears that fundamental religionists have acquired from study of the scriptures, the Old Testament in particular. The prophesies about the last days are filled with warnings of rampant sin, Satan's ruling the earth, moral dangers on every hand. This creates a panicky mindset which makes people susceptible to the tactics of the Schlafly's of the earth. Mormons—and Baptists and others—are already programmed with dread, conditioned to see the worst on every hand, and to go on record as fighting evil to the end . . .

All of which is so unchristian that it is in itself a contradiction—how a church named the Church of Jesus Christ of Latter-day Saints could be bogged down in the Old Testament, which the teachings of Christ came to update. The Mormon Church, and those other churches experiencing the Patriarchal Panic, are admitting that they are still 2,000 years behind times and have yet to enter the Christian era.

We would like to issue a call for pressure to be put on the Mormon Church at their large gatherings in this area: dignified but determined vigils and pickets. We think this can attract the press, and nothing daunts the Mormon Church quite so much, quite so successfully, as negative press. In addition, the people of this nation need to know that the Mormons are fighting women's rights with all their considerable might. Nothing but pressure from OUTSIDE the church will ever cause the patriarchs to pause and consider if perhaps the price isn't too high. Because the price of denying basic human rights in this age and in this country is too high for any group to pay. And will most certainly bankrupt religion.

Notes

1 Sonia Johnson, "The Patriarchal Panic," ERA Referendum Strategies, ACTION 1979 ERA-VA, Washington Institute for Women in Politics, Mt. Vernon College, Washington, D.C., February 10, 1979. Reprinted with permission from Sonia Johnson. A special thanks to Betsey Welland at the University of Utah's Special Collections, J. Willard Marriott Library.

2 Martha Sonntag Bradley, *Pedestals and Podiums: Utah Women, Religious Authority, and Equal Rights* (Salt Lake City: Signature Books, 2005), 332–35, quotation on 332.

3 Majorie Hyer, "Mormon Bishop Excommunicates Woman Who Is Supporting ERA: Feminist Is Excommunicated," *Washington Post*, December 6, 1979, A1.
4 Bradley, *Pedestals*, 332.
5 Stephanie Mansfield, "The Hunger for Equality: Seven Women in Springfield Fast for the ERA," *Washington Post*, June 11, 1982, D1.
6 " 'I'd Give My Right Arm for a Fresca' . . . We've Got to Stop Talking about Food," *Southern Illinoisan*, May 20, 1982, 8.
7 "Ex-Mormon Leads ERA Hunger Strikes," *Daily Herald*, Provo, UT, May 19, 1982, 13.
8 "ERA Hunger Strike Ends, Called 'Success,' " *Southern Illinoisian*, June 23, 1982, 1.
9 Rachel Shteir, *Betty Friedan: Magnificent Disrupter* (New Haven: Yale University Press, 2023), 184, 223. Friedan also contended that the Ku Klux Klan funded STOP ERA. Shteir emphasizes that scholars continue to debate these alleged connections among Schlafly, STOP ERA, the John Birch Society, and the Klan.
10 Robert Beers, a Mormon, worked as a political action coordinator for STOP ERA in Virginia. See Bradley, *Pedestals*, 348, 350–52.
11 HOTDOG, which stands for "Humanitarians Opposed to Degrading Our Girls," is an ad hoc group that stemmed from the Birch Society and worked against the ERA in Utah. See Jill Mulvay Derr, "Scholarship, Service, and Sisterhood: Women's Clubs and Associations, 1877-1977," in *Women in Utah History: Paradigm Or Paradox?*, Patricia Lyn Scott and Linda Thatcher, ed. (Logan: Utah State University Press, 2005), 281.
12 Endorsed by the Ku Klux Klan, Howard Phillips is also notorious for his Christian nationalist empire and his son, Doug Phillips of Moscow, Idaho. For additional context, see Simon J. Levien, "The Crimson Klan," *Crimson*, March 25, 2021, https://www.thecrimson.com/article/2021/3/25/harvard-klan-scrut/; Julie Ingersoll, "Doug Phillips' Biblical Patriarchy Scandal Moves to the Courts," *Huffington Post*, June 17, 2014, https://www.huffpost.com/entry/doug-phillips-biblical-patriarchy_b_5151442.
13 Russian writer and historian Aleksandr Solzhenitsyn faced imprisonment and exile for criticizing Joseph Stalin and Communism. See "Biography," Aleksandr Solzhenitsyn Center, https://www.solzhenitsyncenter.org/his-life-overview/biography.
14 Jean Marshall Clark, a NOW state coordinator in Virginia, was arrested with Marianne Fowler for protesting on the state capitol steps and charged with trespassing and civil disturbance. The images of police dragging Clark away made news and disclosed the dangers pro-ERA women faced for dissenting. See Paula Bernstein, "ERA Going a Long Way—Maybe," *Daily News (New York)*, March 19, 1978, 49.
15 Spencer W. Kimball served as the twelfth President of the LDS Church from 1973 to 1985. See "Spencer W. Kimball," Church of Jesus Christ of Latter-day Saints, https://history.churchofjesuschrist.org/landing/prophets-of-the-restoration/spencer-w-kimball?lang=eng.

I Am Not Threatened by ERA

Address to the Matrix Luncheon of New York Women in Communication

Rosalynn Carter
April 26, 1979[1]

Eleanor Rosalynn Smith Carter (1927–2023), known by many as the "Steel Magnolia," certainly lived up to the moniker during and beyond her tenure as U.S. first lady. Between 1977 and 1981, she expanded the scope and influence of her undefined position in the White House—best exemplified in her 1977 solo tour of Latin America, her meaningful advocacy on behalf of mental health, and her post-White House humanitarian work with her husband. Although she understood that many of her state's constituents were wary of the ERA and she thought that feminists like Gloria Steinem were too "strident" and "militant" in their approach, Rosalynn Carter publicly supported the amendment in interviews and speeches as Georgia's first lady.[2] In a rather unusual precedent, Carter got to work on supporting the amendment during the liminal period between Election Day and Inauguration Day. As ratification in Indiana came down to a single vote, Senator Birch Bayh (D-IN) attempted to reach the president-elect but got his wife on the phone instead. The incoming U.S. first lady personally called legislator Wayne Townsend (D-IN), who was on the fence, and persuaded him to endorse ratification. The gambit worked and Indiana became the 35th state to ratify the ERA on January 18, 1977.[3]

Once in the White House, Rosalynn Carter delivered speeches, wrote letters, made telephone calls, lobbied elected officials, and held fundraisers for the ERA. Like Betty Ford, her efforts attracted praise and censure. Anti-ERA legislators balked that an unelected political spouse intruded on the process.

Thousands of letters poured into the East Wing. Phyllis Schlafly organized protesters outside the gates of the White House carrying signs saying things such as "Please, Mrs. Carter, let us stay home and be mothers too."[4] Even so, Carter remained a polarizing ally among some feminists due to her antiabortion stance, perceptions that Jimmy Carter's record on women's issues left much to be desired, and concerns that the Carter "partnership" approach to the presidency rendered the first lady unwilling to publicly challenge her husband's views.[5]

Despite these obstacles, Rosalynn Carter's support for the ERA was both symbolically important and pragmatically valuable.[6] In this selection from her remarks to the New York Women in Communication, Carter closed with what the *New York Times* termed a "strong feminist appeal" for the ERA and for the women working at state levels to pursue further ratifications.[7] Upon her death in November 2023, Carter's obituary noted that the ninety-six-year-old former first lady felt that the ERA's "failure was the greatest disappointment of her White House years."[8] As the ERA's twenty-first century supporters reminded the American public at this moment, Carter "fervently support[ed]" the amendment. Realizing her dream to see "the ERA enshrined in our Constitution," the ERA Coalition advised, would be an apt way to honor Carter's legacy.[9]

In the past decade the number of female legislators has more than doubled. And in my view, this may be the key to the passage of the Equal Rights Amendment—an issue I feel I must address today. The Equal Rights Amendment must be ratified—and right now women at the state level are in the center of the action.

In North Carolina, for instance, for the first time, the women in the House agreed to block vote[s] on other key issues so that they could force male House members to vote with them on ERA. In Florida, all of the women in the State House went together as a unified group to the Governor to ask for a change in his timetable for consideration of the Amendment. In Oklahoma, two women legislators are keeping ERA alive. And in Kentucky, the woman Lt. Governor has successfully blocked efforts to rescind the ERA.

I think we should consider our own responsibility here. Millions of Americans still need to be educated about the positive benefits of ERA—not only the men who feel threatened, but the women who insist they are for women's rights—and against ERA. We must inform them that ERA will ensure that both women and men are guaranteed choice in all areas of their lives. And that ERA will not require changes for those who do not want changes.

I feel that it is especially important to explain that women like me support the ERA. I am a relatively traditional person. I enjoy my roles as wife, mother, partner and businesswoman. I care how I look—and what I think. I am not threatened by ERA. I feel freed by it.

You and I can try to make this controversial issue understandable. We can talk about the breadth of its support. We can be assertive in targeting our attention on key legislators in unratified states—and on those women in elected positions at the state level who are desperately working for all of us.

I think we are fortunate to be in the communications business—and I would like to include myself in your field today. We can choose our message. We can affect attitudes. We have influence. What we need is the self-confidence to use that influence to help ourselves. We can hold out for better jobs in our areas of employment. We can choose to take a sabbatical from professional life and offer ourselves for public service. We can insist on standards that call for the perspective of women in our governing bodies. We can refuse to accept anything less than the total equality and choice offered by ERA. I do not think that these are unrealistic goals.

I came here today hoping to wield some First Lady influence in urging you to join me—as communicators, as citizens, as examples for others—in encouraging women throughout our country to have the self-confidence to ask for nothing less than full equality.

All of us are responsible for building a more just and caring society—and certainly one in which we have more control over our own lives.

Notes

1 Rosalynn Carter, "Mrs. Carter's Remarks to the Matrix Luncheon of New York Women in Communication," Kathryn Cade's Project Files, Container 29, Jimmy Carter Presidential Library and Museum. Public Domain.

2 Rosalynn Carter, *First Lady from Plains* (Boston: Houghton Mifflin, 1984), 100; E. Stanly Godbold, Jr., *Jimmy & Rosalynn Carter: The Georgia Years, 1924–1974* (New York: Oxford University Press, 2010), 213–17.

3 Scott Kaufman, *Rosalynn Carter: Equal Partner in the White House* (Lawrence: University Press of Kansas, 2007), 55.

4 Robert L. Joiner, "Pickets Led by Mrs. Schlafly Urge Mrs. Carter to Quit ERA Drive," *St. Louis-Dispatch*, February 5, 1977, 2A.

5 Kaufman, *Rosalynn Carter*, 55–57.

6 After the release of *Mrs. America*, the Jimmy Carter Presidential Library and Museum curated a digital exhibit highlighting the first lady's work on behalf of the

ERA. See "Mrs. America: Rosalynn Carter and the ERA," https://artsandculture.google.com/story/mrs-america-rosalynn-carter-and-the-era-jimmy-carter-presidential-library-and-museum/6gVRfUOfkeb5Lw?hl=en.

7 Judy Klemesrud, "Rosalynn Carter, in Speech to Communicators, Makes Strong Feminist Appeal," *New York Times*, April 27, 1979, B4.

8 Valerie J. Nelson and Beverly Beyette, "Rosalynn Carter, Former First Lady Who Pushed for Mental Health Reform, Dies at 96," *Los Angeles Times*, November 19, 2023, https://www.latimes.com/obituaries/story/2023-11-19/rosalynn-carter-first-lady-jimmy-carter-dead.

9 "First Lady Rosalynn Carter, 1927–2023," ERA Coalition, post on X (formerly Twitter), November 20, 2023.

Reverence for Life Means Reverence for Equality

Brochure by Catholics Act for ERA

Maureen Fiedler
1980[1]

Sister Maureen Ellen Fiedler (1942–present) has been politically active for social justice for half a century. Her 1977 Georgetown University doctoral dissertation, "Sex and Political Participation in the United States: A Comparative Analysis of Masses and Elites," was just the beginning for this "feminist nun" who has fought for peace in Central America, religious pluralism on abortion, women's rights to ordination, and justice for sexual abuse victims.[2] Fiedler's interfaith approach to questions of gender and racial equality has been guided by her abiding belief that "Jesus was open to dialogue with anyone, including people with whom he vehemently disagreed." She credited the teachings of Virginia Ramey Mollenkott for helping her come to the realization that Jesus "was not a sexist" but rather "treated women equally."[3] For more than 25 years, she co-directed the Quixote Center, a Maryland-based international peace and justice organization. Fiedler also hosted *Interfaith Voices*, a syndicated public radio show which "explores how faith intersects with culture, public policy, ever mindful of the news of the day," until 2018.[4]

Fielder's most dramatic entry into American politics came in 1978 when she started Catholics Act for ERA. She was among the seven women, including Sonia Johnson, who participated in a "fast for justice" as the 1982 ratification loomed. Over 37 days at the Illinois Capitol, Fiedler diligently sat in the rotunda, survived on water and fruit juice, and became the group's unofficial spokesperson in interviews and at rallies.[5] As Phyllis Schlafly claimed the singular Catholic viewpoint, Fiedler interrupted to argue that supporting the ERA is more faithful to pro-life values of faith. The text below was a brochure distributed by Catholics Act for ERA throughout Iowa meant to bolster efforts for the federal ERA as well as an amendment to the Iowa state Constitution.

The Equal Rights Amendment is an Issue of Human Life

For Women Who Are Poor

Poverty is a daily issue of life for many women and children.

79% of the poor people in the United States are women and children.

More than 8 million American families are headed by women, yet 33% of those households are below the poverty level, compared to 6% of those headed by men.

In 1977, the median income of families headed by women was $7,765; the median income of families headed by men was $14,538.

Full-time working women today earn only 59 cents for every dollar earned by full-time working men.

Minority women are hardest hit, with black and Hispanic women at the bottom of the national wage scale.

Women work for the same reason as men: economic need. Yet they are still seen as a "marginal" workforce—those who earn the "second" salaries in families.

For every dollar earned by men, women in the same job category earn much less:

	Women	Men
Sales	$0.45	$1.00
Clerical	$0.64	$1.00
Service	$0.65	$1.00
Manufacturing	$0.59	$1.00

THE EQUAL RIGHTS AMENDMENT will provide a constitutional commitment to equal pay for equal work and equal employment opportunity. Discrimination today can be profitable. The Equal Rights Amendment will help take the profit out of discrimination.

"Choose life that you and your children may live." Deut. 30:19

Discrimination Is Anti-Life

Discrimination against women undermines their dignity, treats them as inferiors, denies them full and productive lives. Often, it deprives them of food, clothing, fuel, and shelter: the very necessities of life.

People who cherish life struggle to overcome discrimination because reverence for life is meaningless without reverence for equality.

For Widows

Widows are often victims of inequality in social security payments, pension plans, and inheritance taxes. In fact, two out of three poor persons over age 65 are women.

Mary Heath knew discrimination as a widow. Her husband died after 30 years in which they shared the hard work of a farm in Cody, Nebraska. The law required her to pay $25,000 in inheritance taxes in order to keep the land on which she had worked all her adult life! If she had died first, her husband would not have had to pay a cent!

For Homemakers

Many women choose to be full-time homemakers. Yet our laws do not protect their choice or livelihood.

Many states deny the homemaker equal ownership of home, savings account, and other household property.

Most states place no economic value on work in the home. As a result, many homemakers find themselves without money or resources if their husbands die or leave unexpectedly.

THE EQUAL RIGHTS AMENDMENT will mean legal recognition of the economic value of the homemaker's services. It will ensure that husband and wife have a right to joint ownership of household property. In Pennsylvania—thanks to its state E.R.A.—these provisions are already the law.

The Iowa Equal Rights Amendment

On November 4, 1980, the voters of Iowa will decide whether or not to add an equal rights amendment to the Iowa Constitution. This amendment will make Iowa a true state of equality.

The Iowa Equal Rights Amendment will appear on the top row, far righthand corner of the voting machine. The actual question is:

AMENDMENT TO THE CONSTITUTION OF IOWA

To ensure that the state shall not deny or restrict the equality of rights under the law on the basis of gender.

The Equal Rights Amendment has Nothing to do with Abortion

Here's why:

The legislative history of the Amendment makes clear that E.R.A. does not apply to physical characteristics (like pregnancy) which are unique to one sex (Senate Report 92–689).

It will have "no effect on any abortion law of any state" (Martha Griffiths, chief E.R.A. sponsor in the House, 117 Cong. Rec. 35302). The Supreme Court is obliged to follow the clearly stated legislative intent of Congress.

The E.R.A. is based on the legal doctrine of equal protection. The Supreme Court has never found abortion to be an issue of equal protection or sex discrimination. Abortion decisions of the Court (e.g., *Roe v. Wade*, *Doe v. Bolton*[6]) have been based on other legal grounds.

No state with a state-E.R.A. has been required to change its abortion laws because of its E.R.A.

Ratification of the E.R.A. would not prevent passage of a Human Life Amendment. Congress always has the right to propose later amendments (U.S. Constitution, Article V).

The Equal Rights Amendment guarantees equal rights for men and women. Laws must be able to be applied to both sexes for such a doctrine to operate. And the plain facts of life are these: men can't have babies—or abortions. There is no way any ERA can give—or deny—men an "equal right" to abortion with women!

The Equal Rights Amendment

All men and women are, by nature, free and equal and have certain inalienable rights—among which are those of enjoying and defending life and liberty, acquiring, possessing, and protecting property, and pursuing and obtaining safety and happiness. Neither the state nor any of its political subdivisions shall, on the basis of gender, deny or restrict the equality of rights under the law.

This is the entire amendment. These words will mean justice for us and for generations to come.

"As a pro-life, pro-family mother of three, I strongly support the ERA. In a democratic society, we should not have two standards of treatment. ERA will accelerate a standard of fairness for both sexes before the law."

—Representative Margaret Heckler, R-MA, U.S. House of Representatives

"We should celebrate life and equality. We should pass the ERA. When people hear I'm for the ERA, they think I'm for abortion. I separate the two, as they should be, and have no difficulty supporting the ERA."

—Father Theodore Hesburgh, CSC President, Notre Dame University

Organizations endorsing E.R.A. include: National Conference of Catholic Charities, Canon Law Society of America, Leadership Conference of Women Religious, National Coalition of American Nuns, National Assembly of Women Religious, Priests for Equality, Chicago Catholic Women, NETWORK, Las Hermanas, PADRES, Association of Chicago Priests, Quixote Center, Sisters of Loretto, Church Women United, Feminists for Life (a national pro-life group) and many others.

Notes

1 Catholics Act for ERA, "Reverence for Life Means Reverence for Equality," 1980. Folder: Printed Material—Produced by Supporting Groups, Box 8, Iowa ERA Coalition Collection, Iowa Women's Archives, University of Iowa. Public Domain.

2 Associated Press, "Catholic Group Petitioning Church for Change," *Daily Sentinel*, February 17, 1997, 11B; Maureen Fiedler, "Bishops, We Cannot Wait Centuries for Justice," *National Catholic Reporter*, November 13, 2018, https://www.ncronline.org/news/ncr-today/bishops-we-cannot-wait-centuries-justice.

3 Mary Segers, "Sister Maureen Fiedler: A Nun for Gender Equality in Church and Society," in *Religious Leaders and Faith-Based Politics*, ed. Jo Renee Formicola and Hubert Morken (Lanham, MD: Rowman & Littlefield, 2001), 175, 181; see also Maureen Fiedler, ed., *Breaking Through the Stained Glass Ceiling: Women Religious Leaders in Their Own Words* (New York: Seabury Books, 2010).

4 "Our Mission," *Interfaith Voices*, 2018, https://interfaithradio.org/About/Our_Mission.

5 "ERA Leader Refuses to Give Up Fasting," *St. Louis Post-Dispatch*, June 2, 1982, 3A; Bob Springer, "Faithful 7 Hunger For ERA Ratification As Deadline Nears," *Sacramento Bee*, June 20, 1982, A12.

6 *Doe v. Bolton* (1973) struck down a Georgia law making abortion unconstitutional. See "Doe v. Bolton, 410 U.S. 179 (1973)," *Justia*, U.S. Supreme Court, https://supreme.justia.com/cases/federal/us/410/179/.

The Legal Consequence of ERA on Indian Women

Address to the Ohoyo Resource Center Conference on Educational Equity Awareness

Ethel Krepps
April 3, 1981[1]

The obituary for Ethel C. Krepps (1937–1996) described her as "a mentor and a role model [who] always gave of herself and supported every right and just cause."[2] Krepps excelled at the University of Tulsa Law School, where she won a national award from the American Trial Lawyers Association in her third year for an essay about pollution problems on Navajo Indian Reservations.[3] After graduation, she applied her legal expertise fighting for the rights of her people. Krepps led the Kiowa Tribe as its secretary, directed the Oklahoma Indian Child Welfare Association, and served as legal counsel for the Kiowa Tribe, the Pawnee Tribe, the Native American Coalition, and the Tulsa Indian Youth Council. She spent her career shining a light on discrimination against Native Americans through written and spoken advocacy.[4]

At the 1981 regional Ohoyo Resource Center Conference on Educational Equity Awareness in Tahlequah, Oklahoma, speakers addressed the theme of "Indian Women at the Crossroads: Identifying Guideposts." Some three hundred Native American women gathered in the capital of Cherokee Nation to hear Krepps speak to how—and if—the federal Equal Rights Amendment constituted one such guidepost. Krepps rehearsed the winding history of the ERA and then narrowed in on any legal consequences that may arise for indigenous women if the amendment were passed. Krepps situated the ERA's implications within legal precedent about tribal sovereignty established by the Indian Civil Rights Act (IRCA) of 1968 and the Supreme Court case *Santa Clara Pueblo v. Martinez* (1978). The IRCA extended certain constitutional protections in the Bill of Rights to Native Americans, while *Pueblo v. Martinez* recognized the sovereignty of tribal courts over native civil rights claims—two decisions which, coupled together, walk the line "between assimilation and determination."[5] While supportive of the ERA, Krepps ultimately concluded that the amendment had little bearing on the status of her audience.

Equality of Rights Under the Law shall not be denied or abridged by the United States or by any State on account of sex.

This is the proposed 27th Amendment to the Constitution of the United States. And to quote Erma Bombeck, "No words have been so misunderstood since 'one size fits all.' "[6]

Brief Overview of the ERA

I want to share a brief overview of the ERA with you. This brief historical account of the ERA was taken from the 1975 Report of the Interdepartmental Task Force for International Women's Year. That report states that ERA was a natural outgrowth of the struggle for the women's suffrage amendment which was adopted in 1920. For 72 years women's efforts were directed at trying to get women's voting rights implemented on a state-by-state basis. This struggle demonstrates the impossibility of trying to gain equal rights for women utilizing a step-by-step approach. It is, therefore, evident that an overall constitutional amendment ensuring women equality under the law throughout the nation is necessary. Back in the year 1923, a lady by the name of Alice Paul, a member of the National [Woman's] Party, wrote the Equal Rights Amendment. The 24 words which I quoted to you. The ERA was subsequently introduced in Congress and finally, on October 12, 1971, the ERA was voted and passed in the House of Representatives by a vote of 354 to 23. The Senate vote, March 22, 1972, was 84–4.

Within hours of the final senate vote, Hawaii became the first state to ratify the Amendment. Twenty-one additional states ratified in 1972, with eight the following year (1973). Then three more states in 1974. Only one, North Dakota, was ratified in 1975, and in 1977 Indiana became the 35th state to ratify the Equal Rights Amendment. The 95th Congress extended the deadline for ratification of the Equal Rights Amendment to June 30, 1982. Thirty-five of the necessary 38 states have ratified. Those states not yet ratified are: Alabama, Arizona, Arkansas, Florida, Georgia, Illinois,

Louisiana, Mississippi, Missouri, Nevada, North Carolina, Oklahoma, South Carolina, Utah, and Virginia. Three of these states just named must ratify the ERA by the June 30, 1982, deadline if it is to become an amendment to the Constitution. Two states have attempted to rescind their ratification. Idaho rescinded by a vote of both Houses of the Legislature, declaring that state's ratification revoked. Another state, South Dakota, passed a null-and-void bill. However, an opinion issued by the Justice Department in February 1979, declared that both "rescission" and "null and void" resolutions are held to be unconstitutional.

Issues of ERA

Let's discuss the basic issues which ERA is all about. The basic intents of ERA are these:

- ERA will ensure that all states and the federal government review and revise any laws or practice to eliminate discrimination on the basis of sex.
- ERA will ensure that discrimination laws are not enacted in the future.
- ERA will enforce the principle that the homemaker's role in the marriage contract is given full economic value and full partnership states under the law.
- ERA will ensure equal opportunity, privileges and benefits in all aspects of government employment.
- ERA will ensure equal opportunity in public schools and colleges, in "manpower" training programs of all federal, state and local governments, and in governmental recreational programs.
- ERA will ensure that the families of women workers receive the same benefits as families of men, workers under the social security laws and under pension plans run by the government at any level, and also under worker's compensation laws.
- ERA will ensure that married women can engage in business as freely as married men and that they can dispose of separate or community property on the same basis as married men.
- ERA will require that married women be permitted to maintain a separate legal domicile from their husband's domicile.
- ERA will require that women prisoners be given the same opportunities and privileges as men prisoners and that sentences be arrived at and administered under the same law for both sexes.

While it is true that both Congress and state legislatures have passed specific laws prohibiting discrimination against women in the areas of employment, credit and education, there has to be a constitutional guarantee of equality or legislatures, both federal and state, will be free to revoke these laws they have passed. It is also true that most employment practices are already provided for under Title VII of the Civil Rights Act of 1964.

Another factor to consider with the passage of ERA will be within the judicial system—judges will be able to look at cases involving Fifth and Fourteenth Amendment cases which now only apply to race and religion. Women have attempted to use the Fourteenth Amendment to gain equality with men. That Amendment which prohibits any state action which denies to any person "the equal protection of the laws" was aimed at preventing states from passing laws against Blacks after the Civil War. Now the Supreme Court refuses to consider the status of women (sex) as it considers the status of race and religion. However, with the passage of the ERA "sex" status would become a suspect category for discrimination.

Basically, the intent of ERA is simply stated: passage of ERA requires that the federal government, and all state and local governments, treat each person, male or female, as an individual. The amendment applies only to governmental action, and it does not affect private actions or purely social relationships between men and women. Confusion about the difference between Right of Equality and Right of Privacy must be defined. The Right of Privacy is in no way affected by the Right of Equality. Private relationships and family matters remain protected by the Right of Privacy. Community privacy standards would also be protected. The laws would continue to permit separation of the sexes in such matters as public restrooms, sleeping quarters in public institutions, etc. Other laws that deal with physical characteristics or physical attributes of one sex or the other would not be prohibited as such laws could not by their very nature deny equal rights to the opposite sex.

Evidence shows that in those states that have passed their own Equal Rights Amendments women's experiences have all been positive. For example, Pennsylvania has an equal rights provision, and women there are now in a stronger position, particularly in the area of domestic relations, as a result. As to child custody and child support, in the state of Washington, Dan Evans, former Washington Governor, states: "I am aware of no classification privileges that a woman has lost because of adoption of the ERA . . . adoption of ERA and the implementation dissolution law merely make it clear that either spouse may sue for support. A woman has not lost her right to be supported by her husband; rather, she never had such a right. Support within marriage has been a matter of custom and has never been guaranteed by law. Child support and child custody would be determined on the individual parent capabilities rather than on the basis of sex."

The passage of [the] Equal Rights Amendment would be commitment to the right of equal treatment for all citizens.

The ERA and Indian Women

Indian women hold a unique position in relation to ERA because Indian women have two unique relationships which other non-Indian women do not have. Indian women are citizens of their respective states, as are other non-Indian women; however, they are also members of their respective tribes and they also have a trust responsibility or a guardian-ward relationship with the federal government. What is the legal consequence of ERA on Indian women? As members of tribes, Indian womens' lives are actually controlled by a three-tier governmental system. Her tribe has the authority to pass laws which would govern her actions. This power to pass laws by tribal governments comes from the inherent ability of tribal people to govern themselves. The ERA will have absolutely no effect on the ability of her tribe to pass laws and govern its own tribal members. The areas where ERA could affect the Indian woman is in the area where the federal government has a special relationship with Indian people. This is in the area of employment. The term "Indian preference" means that if two people apply for the job, everything else being equal, except that one of the applicants is Indian and the other non-Indian, the Indian applicant will get the job. Indian preference is practiced in two institutions that deal with Indian people. The IHS and the BIA.[7] Passage of the ERA would mean a stricter enforcement of equality of the sexes in these two federal agencies. Indian preference would be applied evenly to Indian men and Indian women alike. ERA would have no other effect on Indian preference.

The effect of ERA on trivial judicial systems would be nil. The Supreme Court has already determined in the Martinez decision that any alleged violations of the 1968 Indian Civil Rights Act must be heard and decided only in the tribal court. The Martinez decision is often misunderstood because the case began as an attempt by Mrs. Martinez to use the equal protection clause of the Indian Civil Rights Act to invalidate her tribal enrollment procedure which she contended discriminated against women. The Supreme Court didn't reach the issue, however, as they decided Indian tribes could not be sued in federal court under the Indian Civil Rights Act in the first place.

Notes

1 Ethel Krepps (Kiowa/Miami), "Equal Rights Amendment: How Does It Relate to Indians?" *Words of Today's American Indian Women, Ohoyo Makachi: A First Collection of Oratory by American Indian/Alaska Native Women*, ed. Owanah Anderson and Sedelta Verble (Wichita Falls, TX: 1981), 35–39. Reprinted with permission from George Krepps.

2 "Krepps," Deaths and Funerals, *Daily Oklahoman*, July 16, 1996, 24.

3 "TU Law Student Wins Essay Test," *Daily Oklahoman*, August 29, 1978, 7S.

4 Kurt M. Hochenauer, "Indian Girl in Middle of Controversy," *Daily Oklahoman*, April 10, 1983, 1A, 2A.

5 Christian M. Freitag, "Putting *Martinez* to the Test: Tribal Court Disposition of Due Process," *Indiana Law Journal* 72 (1997): 831–67.

6 Erma Bombeck, a longtime syndicated columnist and humorist, strongly supported the ERA, yet often disagreed with feminist tactics to promote the amendment. See "Political Involvement," *Erma Bombeck Collection* (Dayton, OH: University of Dayton, n.d.), https://ermabombeckcollection.com/life/political-involvement/.

7 Indian Health Services and the Bureau of Indian Affairs.

Section V The Debate Continues: 1983–2015

The Equal Rights Amendment's original ratification deadline was seven years after its acceptance in both houses of Congress—March 22, 1979. In 1978, approval from state legislatures remained stalled at just three short of ratification. Seeing the deadline looming and after much lobbying by pro-ERA women, Congress with President Jimmy Carter's approval extended the deadline to June 30, 1982. No new states joined the other 35 in those additional three years. The ERA, it seemed, was dead in the water. NOW president Eleanor Smeal proposed at least four reasons why ratification efforts failed: growing and coordinated Republican opposition to women's rights under Ronald Reagan's presidency; "lukewarm" support for the ERA by Democrats; "special corporate interests" that aligned with anti-ERA legislators and organizations; and persisting "sex bias" in state legislatures.[1]

Gloria Steinem's 1983 book *Outrageous Acts and Everyday Rebellions*, her postmortem, outlined a fifth reason. The ERA campaign failed, she argued, because of the press's irrational habit of both-sides-ism. By giving equal time to mere attention-seekers like Phyllis Schlafly, Steinem contended, the media was uncritically elevating anti-ERA arguments above their reasonableness and truthfulness.[2] To an extent, Steinem anticipated the third-wave feminist argument about media bias against women. In her 1991 book *Backlash: The Undeclared War Against American Women*, Susan Faludi claimed that American women experienced intense backlash against the feminist gains of the previous decades under the Reagan and Bush presidencies. This backlash proposed that the women's liberation movement caused all women's problems, insisting that women already *are* equal, and this equality has, in turn, made them *terribly unhappy*.[3]

As time stretched on beyond the close of the ratification period, some women forgot all the advantages for which their foremothers had fought. They soon presumed that attending college, owning property, opening a bank account, asserting their sexuality, and accessing safe medical care were always available. Some even sneered at the term "feminist" and found it, like the ERA, to be a useless relic of the past.[4] As a 1986 article in *Elle* declared, "all those ideals that were once held as absolute truths—sexual liberation, the women's movement, true equality—have been debunked or debased."[5] Many women in the late 1980s and 1990s did not want to be associated with the image of an angry, militant feminist—or with the Equal Rights Amendment.

As for the ERA, it was only buried and asleep. "We haven't lost. We just haven't won yet," actor Alan Alda—a longtime ERA ally—declared in the gloomy days after the ERA's defeat.[6] Slowly, all the suspicions that STOP ERA had brewed in the 1970s were coming to pass. Women in the military? When Professor Antonia Chayes was appointed to the upper echelons of the Air Force, the argument that women could not serve effectively and honorably in the armed forces seemed moot. Her persona and her argument made equality seem not merely possible but also necessary. Over 24,000 women subsequently served in the Gulf War.[7] Divorce law protections? The Supreme Court ruled that women and men are equal in the eyes of the court back in 1979.[8] Unisex bathrooms? By 2008, shopping malls had installed them under the name "family restrooms."[9] Same-sex marriages? The Supreme Court made it the law of the land in 2015.[10] Nonetheless, women were still consistently earning under 80 cents for every dollar a man earned—even less for women of color.[11] Women also continued to fight for maternity leave, management inclusion, clerical ordination, and elected office. Although "fragmented and wounded" in the aftermath of the ERA's defeat, the women's movement "remained immensely alive."[12]

Although NOW membership dropped following the ERA's defeat, members debated how—and whether—to keep the debate alive. Judy Goldsmith succeeded Ellie Smeal as NOW's president in 1982 and lamented that, in her view, NOW had become "a single-issue organization." Further pursuing the ERA, Goldsmith continued, was an "exercise in futility."[13] The statement ruffled many NOW members, especially in the wake of Ronald Reagan's reelection in 1984. As a consequence, Smeal announced she would run for another term and if elected, would move the ERA "out of the deep freeze and turn up the heat on those who profit from sex discrimination." Smeal's victory in 1985, following a contentious "Ellie" versus "Judy" contest, ensured that the ERA stayed firmly affixed at the top of NOW's agenda.[14]

Between the mid-1980s and early 2000s, NOW leaders and members pushed for Congressional briefings to keep the proposed amendment on the table, pursued individual bills to assure equality in state constitutions, supported pro-ERA feminist candidates for political office, registered women voters, and held an ERA Summit in 1995.[15] Members split over the ERA at both the 1995 and 2000 annual NOW conferences. Some hoped to revive the ERA campaign, while others proposed an alternate "Constitutional Equality Amendment" (CEA). The CEA used language that guaranteed reproductive rights and added language about race, sexual orientation, national origin, and indigenous status. Though divided in the proposed means of either backing the original ERA or pursuing a new CEA, these factions demonstrated unification in the overarching commitment to ensuring equality through a federal constitutional amendment past the ratification period.[16]

While still keeping the ERA in focus, NOW leaders and allies to the cause for women's equality pursued a new, more aggressive electoral strategy that aligned with and promoted Democratic candidates.[17] In a 1989 speech, Irene Natividad vowed to get more women elected despite the 1980s groundswell of political conservatism under Reagan's two terms. In some cases, women politicians during this period tried to shed the "feminist" label and distanced themselves from their NOW ties by seeking new alliances forged with those who opposed the ERA and abortion.[18] Reagan's reelection in 1984—over the pro-ERA Democratic ticket of Walter Mondale and Geraldine Ferraro—no doubt prompted some to seek ways to widen their appeal as the conservative ideologies of the New Right took hold in both religious and secular corners of the nation.

The political and cultural tides shifted when lawyer Anita Hill gave voice to credible allegations of workplace sexual harassment in 1991 against her former employer at the EEOC, George H.W. Bush's Supreme Court nominee Clarence Thomas. Sexist hostility from Hill's questioners on the Senate Judiciary Committee only amplified Hill's allegations. Outraged women joined their local NOW chapters.[19] Four thousand women alone joined NOW the week following Hill's testimony, though the organization struggled with its leadership, finances, infrastructure, and mobilization tactics throughout the 1990s.[20] Women's anger was not enough, however, and Thomas was confirmed. The Hill-Thomas hearings, historian Julie Berebitsky explains, "served as a touchstone, a moment in which the country's awareness of an issue suddenly changed, and it has remained in their consciousness ever since."[21] Over the next five years, the number of women who filed EEOC complaints about workplace sexual harassment "more than doubled after the public hearings, going from 6,127 in 1991 to 15,342 in 1996."[22] By the end of the decade, Ellie Smeal had articulated another persisting inequality that American women faced in the workplace—the "gender gap," which she attributed to losing the ERA fight a decade earlier. Simply defined, the gender gap refers to "the difference in the way all genders vote," which has been "popularized its usage in election and polling analyses to enhance women's voting clout" since first articulated.[23]

The tides shifted once again when, exactly 70 years past the ERA's introduction, a new political icon emerged. In his first year in office, Bill Clinton needed a Supreme Court nominee. First lady Hillary Rodham Clinton, herself a feminist lawyer, suggested another feminist lawyer whom she admired be added to the top of the list.[24] Utah Republican Orrin Hatch concurred and recommended the same lawyer, who he saw as a moderate, consensus-builder jurist from the D.C. circuit.[25] Ruth Bader Ginsburg would become a force for all generations of women. Ginsburg was a woman, Bill Clinton declared as he nominated her, who "cannot be called a liberal or a conservative, [for] she has proved herself too thoughtful for such labels."[26] Ginsburg stated in her Senate confirmation hearing, "I remain an advocate of the Equal Rights Amendment for this reason. I have a daughter and a granddaughter." Her simple affirmation was personal and assertive—and it anticipated the rising advocacy at the end of her SCOTUS tenure nearly 30 years later.[27] In the same hearings, antiabortion lobbyist Paige Comstock Cunningham reminded the world of the STOP ERA antagonism. Her testimony warned of the dual dangers posed by renewed conversation about the ERA and a so-called faux moderate Ginsburg on the Court.

Cunningham's critique appeared measured in comparison to some other post-1982 attacks on the ERA. The amendment stayed relevant in certain right-wing quarters, if only to take on the role of a catch-all condemnation of feminism. As just one example, in the early 1990s, Iowa legislators proposed adding an equal rights provision to the state constitution. Phyllis Schlafly intensely opposed the ballot initiative, and televangelist and 1988 presidential candidate Pat Robertson joined her in the crusade. The latter infamously circulated a fundraising letter claiming:

> Radical feminists have made Iowa a target. Their goal is simple: to resurrect the Equal Rights Amendment as the first step toward the radical feminist movement . . . The feminist agenda is not about equal rights for women. It is about a socialist, anti-family political movement that encourages women to leave their husbands, kill their children, practice witchcraft, destroy capitalism and become lesbians.[28]

The Iowa ERA was defeated by a slim margin. Local journalist Lynda Waddington astutely observed that "Robertson and his ilk were also handed a new national boogeyman to fuel their anti-feminist rants: Hillary Rodham Clinton."[29]

And yet, the ERA was never at the forefront of Clinton's progressive agenda as first lady, New York senator, two-time presidential candidate, or

Secretary of State—a national political career that spanned the early 1990s through the 2016 presidential election. There was no trace of a constitutional amendment for women's equality when Clinton declared on the world stage that "women's rights are human's rights" in 1995 at the Fourth World Conference on Women.[30] Barbara Bush similarly did not attempt to revive the ERA during her tenure between 1988 and 1992, even though she had controversially endorsed both the amendment and abortion rights when her husband ran for president in 1980.[31] By 1984, Bush stated that she still supported the ERA but was "not as excited about it as I once was."[32] As first lady, Bush toed the Republican Party line. She expressed a vague support of "equal rights for women" and refused to be lured into debating the defeated amendment. When a reporter asked her about the ERA in 1989, she cagily replied, "No. I'm not against it or for it. I'm not talking about it."[33] Bush's trajectory with the amendment mirrored that of many Republican women who eventually stopped backing the ERA during the Reagan years.

As support for the ERA waned in the Executive Branch, the women of the Legislative Branch continued to talk about the amendment's virtues and dangers well into the next decade. Activated by what they saw unfold in the Thomas confirmation hearings, some women decided their lack of representation in Congress yielded the disgraceful questioning of Anita Hill and the flippant dismissals of her lived experience. The 1992 election was deemed "The Year of the Woman" (a catchphrase some women bristled at) with 24 women elected to the House of Representatives and five women—all Democrats—elected to the Senate. Among the latter group was the first Black female U.S. senator, Carol Moseley Braun of Illinois. The names of these women—Braun, Barbara Boxer (D-CA), Dianne Feinstein (D-CA), Barbara Mikulski (D-MD), and Patty Murray (D-WA)—can be found in Congressional records throughout the 1990s and 2000s as co-sponsors who routinely introduced joint resolutions to propose the ERA be added to the U.S. Constitution. Ninety-year-old Feinstein and seventy-two-year-old Murray, the last women still in office from this cohort in January 2023, both signed on as co-sponsors of "S. J.Res.4—A Joint Resolution Removing the Deadline for the Ratification of the Equal Rights Amendment"—some 30 years after they first came to the Senate.[34] By September, Feinstein—the longest-serving woman senator in American history—had passed away without seeing the ERA finally added to the Constitution.[35]

House Democrat Carolyn Maloney (D-NY) also made the ERA a legislative priority ever since she entered Congress in 1992. After the September 11 attacks in 2001 threatened America's existence, the nation wondered if it could protect its citizens. That's what Maloney, in turn, questioned before Congress as she sought to re-elevate the ERA during wartime. Just months earlier, she had reintroduced the ERA to Congress with bipartisan co-sponsorships from Representative Stephen Horn (R-CA) and Senator Edward Kennedy (D-MA)—nearly 40 years after the Kennedy administration's Presidential Commission on the Status of Women concluded that the time for the ERA was "not now."[36] In contrast, Florida Republican Ileana Ros-Lehtinen took the position that the time for the ERA should be "not ever." Rather than claim it threatened the sanctity of life like Schlafly or Robertson insisted, Ros-Lehtinen asserted that Alice Paul would oppose linking the ERA with abortion.[37]

If the ERA's supporters thought the election of the first Black president would make a substantive difference in the amendment's prospects, they were mistaken. Barack Obama joined George H. W. Bush, Bill Clinton, and George W. Bush in issuing proclamations that easily invoked the language of equal rights and promoted legislative efforts to improve women's lives. "Yet none of these presidents after Jimmy Carter," Minnesota NOW member Beth Anderson observed in 2015, "specifically mention[ed] the Equal Rights Amendment."[38] What can be read as an exchange between NOW President Terry O'Neill and Obama administration staffer Tina Tchen underscored the unfinished business of the ERA in the early years of the new century. O'Neill asked why the ERA was still "not here," while Tchen countered that President Obama *did* support the ERA. Tchen pointed O'Neill and any other skeptics toward Obama's proven record in protecting women's rights under his presidency.

By the end of the two-term Obama administration, a question remained: what, if anything, would it take for the ERA to finally wake from its slumber? The answer would come soon enough.

Notes

1 Maryann Barakso, *Governing NOW: Grassroots Activism in the National Organization for Women* (Ithaca: Cornell University Press, 2004), 86.
2 Gloria Steinem, *Outrageous Acts and Everyday Rebellions* (New York: Holt, Rinehart and Winston, 1983).
3 Susan Faludi, *Backlash: The Undeclared War Against American Women* (New York: Crown Publishers, Inc., 1991).
4 Carol Horner, "NOW at 25: Girding for the Future," *Philadelphia Inquirer*, January 13, 1992, 1E, 5E.
5 Rory Dicker, *A History of U.S. Feminisms* (Berkeley, CA: Seal Press, 2016), 108.
6 Susan McNamara, "Push for an Equal Rights Amendment a Possibility," *Democrat and Chronicle*, July 8, 1998, 6A.

7 "Women in the Army," *Army.mil*, https://www.army.mil/women/history/.
8 *Orr v. Orr*, 440 U.S. 268, https://supreme.justia.com/cases/federal/us/440/268/1.
9 Levi Fishman, "Family Restrooms Ease Growing Safety Worries," *Chicago Tribune*, January 9, 2008, https://www.chicagotribune.com/news/ct-xpm-2008-01-09-0801070190-story.html.
10 *Obergefell v. Hodges*, 2015, https://www.law.cornell.edu/supremecourt/text/ 14-556.
11 "The Gender Wage Gap: 2015; Annual Earnings Differences by Gender, Race, and Ethnicity," *Institute for Women's Policy Research*, June 11, 2020.
12 Ruth Rosen, *The World Split Open: How the Modern Women's Movement Changed America* (New York: Viking, 2000), 264.
13 Brad Lemley, "Eleanor Smeal in Overdrive," *Washington Post*, November 24, 1985, SM12.
14 Katherine Turk, *The Women of NOW: How Feminists Built an Organization that Transformed America* (New York: Farrar, Straus and Giroux, 2023), 289–92.
15 "The Intertwining History of NOW and the ERA," National Organization for Women, https://now.org/the-intertwining-history-of-now-and-the-era/.
16 Barakso, *Governing NOW*, 131–32.
17 Barakso, *Governing NOW*, 90, 126.
18 Ellen Hume, "Some Women Politicians Are Backing Away from Feminist Label to Expand Base of Support," *Wall Street Journal*, April 3, 1985, 1.
19 Paula Cindric, "Women Outraged," *Pittsburgh Press*, October 20, 1991, B4.
20 Turk, *The Women of NOW*, 299, 305.
21 Julie Berebitsky, *Sex and the Office* (New Haven: Yale University Press, 2012), 273.
22 Dicker, *A History*, 117.
23 "Eleanor Smeal," National Women's Hall of Fame, https://www.womenofthehall.org/inductee/eleanor-smeal/; Eleanor Smeal, "Abortion and Affirmative Action," National Press Club Luncheon Address, February 13, 1997, C-SPAN, https://www.c-span.org/video/?78875-1/abortion-affirmative-action.
24 Ariane de Vogue, "Hillary Clinton Admits She Played a Role in RBG's Selection for Supreme Court," *CNN*, October 30, 2019, https://www.cnn.com/2019/10/30/politics/hillary-clinton-ruth-bader-ginsburg-supreme-court-pick/index.html.
25 Thomas Burr, "Sen. Orrin Hatch's Impact on the Supreme Court: How a One-Time Lawyer from Pittsburgh Shaped the Highest Court in the Land," *Salt Lake Tribune*, July 29, 2018, https://www.sltrib.com/news/politics/2018/07/29/sen-orrin-hatchs-impact/.
26 William J. Clinton, "Remarks Announcing the Nomination of Ruth Bader Ginsburg To Be a Supreme Court Associate Justice," June 14, 1993, *American Presidency Project*, https://www.presidency.ucsb.edu/documents/remarks-announcing-the-nomination-ruth-bader-ginsburg-be-supreme-court-associate-justice.
27 Jeffrey Rosen, *Conversations with RBG: Ruth Bader Ginsburg on Life, Love, Liberty, and the Law* (New York: Henry Holt and Company, 2019), 20–21, 150; Jane Sherron De Hart, *Ruth Bader Ginsburg: A Life* (New York: Vintage Books, 2020), 84–85, 106.
28 Maralee Schwartz and Kenneth J. Cooper, "Equal Rights Initiative in Iowa Attacked," *Washington Post*, August 23, 1992, A15.

29 Lynda Waddington, "1992 Iowa and the Rebirth of Feminism," *Iowa Gazette*, December 17, 2017, https://www.thegazette.com/staff-columnists/1992-iowa-and-the-rebirth-of-feminism/.
30 Hillary Rodham Clinton, "Remarks to the U.N. Fourth World Conference on Women Plenary Session," Beijing, China, September 5, 1995, https://www.americanrhetoric.com/speeches/hillaryclintonbeijingspeech.htm.
31 Susan Page, *The Matriarch: Barbara Bush and the Making of an American Dynasty* (New York: Hachette Book Group, 2019), 209.
32 "The Active Life of Barbara Bush," *New York Times*, April 8, 1984, A68.
33 Donnie Radcliffe, "Barbara Bush, Beginning Herself," *Washington Post*, January 15, 1989, F1.
34 S.J.Res.4—A Joint Resolution Removing the Deadline for the Ratification of the Equal Rights Amendment, 118th Congress (2023–2024), January 24, 2023, https://www.congress.gov/bill/118th-congress/senate-joint-resolution/4/cosponsors?s=1&r=1.
35 Clare Foran and Paul LeBlanc, "Dianne Feinstein, Longest-Serving Female US Senator in History, Dies at 90," *CNN Politics*, September 29, 2023, https://www.cnn.com/2023/09/29/politics/dianne-feinstein-death/index.html.
36 "Equal Rights Amendment Re-Introduced in Congress; ACLU Says Measure Necessary to Protect Women," *ACLU Press Release*, March 22, 2001, https://www.aclu.org/press-releases/equal-rights-amendment-re-introduced-congress-aclu-says-measure-necessary-protect.
37 Ileana Ros-Lehtinen, "To Be a Feminist Means To Be Pro-Life," Address to the House of Representatives," Congressional Record—House, 4213, June 14, 1999.
38 Beth Anderson, "Consider Equal Rights Amendment this Women's Equality Day," Minnesota NOW, August 18, 2015, https://mnnow.org/consider-equal-rights-amendment-this-womens-equality-day/.

We Must Ask Them

Excerpt from Outrageous Acts and Everyday Rebellions

GLORIA STEINEM
September 1, 1983[1]

No person from second-wave feminism is more iconic than Gloria Marie Steinem (1934–present), the granddaughter of Jewish suffragist Pauline Perlmutter Steinem.[2] Gloria Steinem's youthful persona and distinctive glasses epitomized the mid-century feminist movement. After graduating from Smith College in 1956, Steinem began her career in journalism writing for *Esquire*, *Show*, *New York Magazine*, and *Cosmopolitan*—all before she co-founded the feminist periodical *Ms. Magazine* in 1972. Perhaps Steinem's best-known article was her 1963 exposé "A Bunny's Tale," which documented her undercover investigation of working conditions at Hugh Hefner's Playboy Club (Steinem described the atmosphere as "profoundly tacky").[3] The energetic, accessible, and at times biting tone Steinem mastered in those early years has persisted across a long and illustrious rhetorical career that began with a self-described "aversion" to public speaking.[4] For six decades, as evidenced by the frequency in which her name is mentioned in the biographies of other contributors to this anthology, Steinem has tirelessly advocated for women and children around the world.

In 1970, Steinem testified before the Senate explaining that the goals of the feminist movement were best achieved through the Equal Rights Amendment. She argued that "women are not more moral than men. We are only uncorrupted by power. But we do not want to imitate men, to join this country as it is, and I think our very participation will change it."[5] When the amendment failed to pass in 1982, Steinem openly reflected on its defeat in her 1983 essay collection, *Outrageous Acts and Everyday Rebellions*. In this statement from that collection, she blamed the both-sides-ism of journalistic coverage surrounding the amendment. She contended the media indulged STOP ERA fear-mongering and, in turn, manipulated the American people to vote against their own interests. Steinem's pointed critiques about the role of media framing remain timely 40 years on, as the ERA debate continues today.

The Equal Rights Amendment began its long ratification process in 1972, yet to my knowledge, not one major newspaper or radio station, not one network news department or national television show, has ever done an independent investigative report on what the ERA will and will not do.

Instead, the major media have been content to present occasional interviews, debates, and contradictory reports from those who are for or against. One expert is quoted as saying that the ERA will strengthen the legal rights of women in general and homemakers in particular by causing the courts to view marriage as a partnership, and the next one says the ERA will force wives to work outside the home and eliminate alimony. One political leader explains on camera that the ERA protects women and men from discriminatory federal laws; then another politician calls the ERA a federal power grab that will reduce individual rights. One activist says that the ERA is a simple guarantee of democracy that should have been part of the Bill of Rights, had the Constitution not been written by and for property-owning white males, and the next one insists it will destroy the family, eliminate heterosexuality, and integrate bathrooms.

Understandably, the audience is confused. We thought the sky was blue to begin with, but equal time and prestige given to an insistence that it's really green may finally cause us to doubt our perceptions. It's true that the majority of women and men have continued to support the ERA (by a margin that has increased since the Reagan administration demonstrated that existing progress could be reversed without it), but I'm not sure the media can take much credit for that fact. There is some evidence that 50-50, so-called objective reporting has actually *impeded* the building of a larger majority.

For instance, reading or hearing the actual 24 words of the ERA is the most reliable path to its support. Many people are still surprised to learn that there's no mention of *unisex* or *abortion* or *combat* in its text; such is the confusion created by anti-ERA arguments. Yet most ERA news coverage never quotes its text at all.

Among reporters and news executives, however, there is great self-righteousness. They have followed the so-called fairness doctrine. They have presented "both sides of the issue" by devoting the same number of minutes or amount of space to the "pro" and the "con." This has remained true, even though majority support for the ERA means a "con" is often tough to find. I've frequently been called by an interviewer and asked, "Would you bring an 'anti' with you?"

One result of this prizefight school of journalism is that Phyllis Schlafly, who was not a nationally famous person pre-ERA, has become the only name that most Americans can think of when asked what women oppose it. In a real sense, she is an artificial creation of the fairness doctrine. Another result is the idea that *women* voted against the ERA; not the two dozen or so aging white male state legislators, plus economic and religious interests, who are the actual culprits. A third result is the notion that black Americans don't support the ERA, though black state legislators have voted overwhelmingly for it. If black women and men had been represented in legislatures in proportion to their present numbers in the population, especially in southern states, the ERA would have passed long ago.

In the early days of the civil rights movement, most journalists followed the same "equal time" formula. When they reported on black voter registration in the South, for instance, they quoted civil rights workers saying they had been beaten up in jail. Then they quoted the sheriff saying that these young people had attacked the police or had beaten up each other. Readers were left with either their confusion or their original biases intact.

Eventually, however, most serious media assumed responsibility for doing their own investigations. They reported, to the best of their ability, what the facts really were.

Unfortunately, that has yet to be done for the ERA. It isn't that such independent reporting would be difficult. More than 50 years of legislative history is available to explain the impact intended by Congress. An issue of *The Yale Law Journal* and many authoritative books have been devoted to projecting its impact in scholarly detail. Finally, there are a few states that have already begun to enforce statewide ERAs with the same or similar wording proposed federally. Pennsylvania, for instance, adopted its ERA more than a decade ago. Bathrooms have not been integrated, abortion and homosexual rights have not been affected, for better or worse, but women's economic rights have been strengthened; equality in education, employment, and insurance benefits has advanced; and sex-based discriminatory laws against men also have been struck down.

So why haven't independent, in-depth reports been done? Why don't the media of your town (and mine) take this historic issue seriously? Why do they allow legislators to vote against the majority opinion in their own districts, as reflected in independent polls, without fearing a journalistic exposé of the special interests they are responding to?

We must ask them. A future with or without the ERA is at stake. And so is good or lousy journalism.

Notes

1 Gloria Steinem, *Outrageous Acts and Everyday Rebellions* (New York: Holt, Rinehart, and Winston, 1983), 328–31. Excerpt from OUTRAGEOUS ACTS AND EVERYDAY REBELLIONS Copyright © 1983 by Gloria Steinem; © 1984 by East Toledo Productions; © 1995 by Gloria Steinem. Reprinted in the United States and territories by permission of Henry Holt and Company. Reprinted in the UK/the British Commonwealth by permission of Levine Plotkin, LLP. All Rights Reserved.

2 Gloria Steinem, "Pauline Perlmutter Steinem 1866–1940," *Shalvi/Hyman Encyclopedia of Jewish Women*, Jewish Women's Archive, December 31, 1999, https://jwa.org/encyclopedia/article/steinem-pauline-perlmutter.

3 "Gloria Steinem Reflects on Her Playboy Bunny Days," *CBS News*, August 10, 2011, https://www.cbsnews.com/news/gloria-steinem-reflects-on-her-playboy-bunny-days/.

4 Gloria Steinem, *My Life on the Road* (New York: Random House, 2015), xviii.

5 *Committee on the Judiciary, Subcommittee on Constitutional Amendments. Hearings to Amend the Constitution So As to Provide Equal Rights for Men and Women*, Day 2, 91st Cong. (1970) (Statement of Gloria Steinem).

The ERA Will Strengthen National Defense

Testimony to the Subcommittee on the Constitution of the Committee on the Senate Judiciary

ANTONIA HANDLER CHAYES
February 21, 1984[1]

A lifelong champion of equal opportunity for women's service, employment, and leadership in the military, Antonia Handler Chayes (1929–present) grew up in New York and graduated with honors from Radcliffe College. Chayes took coursework at Yale Law School before earning a Juris Doctorate from George Washington University in 1953. After graduation, she practiced law in Boston and later joined Tufts University as Dean of the Jackson College for Women.[2] From 1962 to 1963, she served on the Committee on Education for President Kennedy's Commission on the Status of Women. She also worked as Director of Education and Urban Development in the Action for Boston Community Development Agency and was among the planning staff for the National Institute of Mental Health in the late 1960s.[3]

President Jimmy Carter nominated Chayes to serve as Assistant Secretary of the Air Force in May 1977—a remarkable feat considering women were only allowed to enter all-male military colleges beginning in 1975, and the Air Force only began accepting women on an "equal basis with men" in 1976.[4] The Senate confirmed the appointment and she held the position for two years before becoming Under Secretary of the Air Force. As Assistant Secretary, Chayes fought for equal participation in the military on issues spanning women serving in underground missile silos to women in combat.[5] Not until 2013 did the military finally lift the ban on women in combat.[6] Nearly 30 years earlier, Chayes appeared before Congress to further express her support for women's equal opportunity in the military within the context of the ERA. The ratification deadline had passed, but Chayes offered a nuanced and lengthy policy argument about the ERA's potential to bolster the nation's line of defense amid the prospect of nuclear war. We include the second half of her statement below.

The purpose of this hearing, it seems to me, is to illuminate one question: Whether the passage of the equal rights amendment would have an impact on our Nation's ability to sustain and field combat-ready forces in any emergency . . .

What concerns me is that this history of discrimination against women and the restrictions in effect today have seriously damaged women's career progress in the Armed Forces, and in fact, it damages our national security. Women are denied opportunities, not on the basis of their skills or capability, but solely because of their sex. I saw this in the whole pilot training issue. I worked on the WASP legislation in order to bring recognition of the fact that more than a generation earlier, women had flown every aircraft in the inventory, and yet, in the late 1970s the women were kept in test status until it became embarrassingly obvious that they could fly any aircraft to which they were assigned.

It is hard to expect the Air Force to invest time and money to train women to operate fighter aircraft or bombers if they are unable to use the women as pilots during a crisis. So therefore fewer women are rated than aspire to pilot training. I think this use of quotas interferes with career advancement. The same is true with Army and Navy career lines where combat restrictions limit opportunities for training, education, assignment, and promotion. But more important, perhaps, I think than the effect on women's careers, is that restrictive policies deprive us of needed military strength.

In my view, gender-based restrictions serve very little purpose. Administrative convenience has never been an argument that persuaded the courts, and with respect to the military, the administrative argument is not generally persuasive at all. Gender-based restrictions permit unexamined prejudices to everyone's detriment. The example that I often cite is the restriction of the missile career field to men officers. We made the change in 1978 so that women were introduced into the Titan system. This was not a combat exclusion. Nor was it capability that excluded women from the Minuteman II and III.[7] It was the fear of wives' resentment over two-person silo manning. Other professions have overcome these problems with little disruption to family life and no interference with professionalism. I was glad to learn that women will be assigned to the GLCM deployments in Europe but I really cannot find the military rationale for that distinction.[8]

The ERA will secure for military women the fair professional treatment that they have not fully gained to date. The ERA will offer consistency of treatment for military planners and for women who want to plan lifelong career commitments.

The ERA would eliminate gender-based restrictions in the statutes, relations, and practices. The statutes that limit the utilization of women by the Air Force and Navy, 10 U.S.C. 8549 and 6015 have served to restrain that advancement without serving military purpose.[9] These provisions have been the source of policy confusion and fluctuation. There are inconsistencies within services and across service lines. For example, in the Air Force, women pilots may not be assigned to duty in [an] aircraft engaged in combat missions. They can fly long-range transports, the C-141, but not intratheater aircraft, but the C-141's sometimes land in the theater.[10]

The "risk of hostile fire" is not a criterion that translates easily to military assignments. Women in traditional roles, nursing, for example, have not only faced hostile enemy action but have died and been prisoners of war in the service of their country.

The Navy's restriction, up to 1978, expressed no restriction about aircraft. 10 U.S.C. 6015 restricts permanent assignment to combat vessels.[11] Since few ships are likely to remain unengaged in war, these are few permanent billets. Thus, career advancement is hampered because shore billets must be kept open for rotation.

The Coast Guard, by contrast, has no statutory restrictions, and women serve well in a wide range of shipboard roles. The Army also free from these legislative restrictions has imposed its own combat exclusion and has gone through a number of iterations in the definition of combat, increasing the exclusion from 38 to 61 specialties and back down again to 49.

We worked hard during the Carter administration to eliminate the combat restrictions. On several occasions we sought repeal of those provisions so as to release the services from a burden of difficult legal construction and to leave military assignments to the discretion of military experts. I am convinced now that it will take the ERA to accomplish this goal.

The implications of such a change are frightening to many people. The shibboleths of women wounded and tortured, failing in courage and destroying unit morale are not easy to overcome, but it is important to remember that almost any war in which we can contemplate extensive U.S. military involvement is a war that is likely to involve our Nation's soil. It will not be possible to protect women from the scourge of war, if, in fact, we have been unable to deter war from the beginning.

Under ERA, the sex-specific barriers in the selective services laws and its assignment policies would have to be replaced with gender-neutral criteria. The military will not be required to utilize soldiers who are unfit or untrainable, will not be able to exclude women from positions on the grounds of assumed lack of qualifications. By enlarging the pool of qualified applicants for positions requiring specialized skills, ERA will strengthen, not weaken, national defense.

Up to now, under present constitutional tests, the deference given to the military has obscured decisions rooted in prejudice and unexamined stereotypes. With the adoption of the ERA, explicit gender-based exclusions would fail. Tests of strength and aptitude will have to bear proper relation to the tests whose qualifications they purport to describe. The entire history of litigation under Title VII has illuminated the importance of such validation. While it is costly to construct validated tests, it is a process already well begun and well worth that cost and effort. It will match personnel to task based on performance criteria and help assure greater productivity and effectiveness.

In my view, should we move to a draft, I would expect women to be included even without the ERA as a matter of military exigency.

But in my view, however difficult it would be to make a case for excluding women from the draft today, I do not think it will be possible to do so after the passage of the ERA. Its incorporation in the Constitution will mean that any classification based on sex, just as race, will be unacceptable.

The obvious and explicit gender-based exclusions will be eliminated by the services, probably without resort to the courts. Civilian and military leadership have already urged the end of major statutory restrictions in order to enhance the flexibility and to promote national security.

Yet I do not believe the courts would construe the ERA to preclude legitimate transitions or cause the courts to be deaf to all evidence explaining disparate impacts in military assignments. Strength differences remain, and the impact of long-term vocational tracking on job selection may continue for some time to come. There may be reasons to provide transition to ameliorate sociological problems. It will be necessary to develop understanding of the impact of larger numbers of women generally and in the fields presently closed to them. While the burden of justifying neutral standards that may effectively exclude women will be increased, congressionally examined and approved policies of the military which have been carefully designed are not apt to meet court disapproval. They will not place a crushing burden on national security. Indeed, the requirement of providing an objective rationale for policies with a disparate impact is not an impediment to national security at all. Our military services bear a burden of strict scrutiny on budget items every year before Congress. They are well-equipped to make their case when they have strong factual evidence.

No one is proposing social experiments that endanger national security, but the time has come to accept the contributions that women have made to our Armed Forces. Despite all the evidence of a job well done, the resistance keeps cropping up. Despite tests and studies designed to prove the negative, as I said, the results are positive. The ERA is needed because the current legal framework is inadequate to sustain progress.

For all women, discrimination in the military has a profound effect on their status as citizens. Women's exemption from full military service interferes with their access to national leadership roles. Military service is often seen as a political credential. It has been credited with legitimizing the citizenship status of other groups, particularly racial minorities. Nearly all men are subject to the military call if they are needed in a national emergency. It is seen as a basic responsibility of citizenship, one that is currently denied to half the citizens of the country.

I urge this committee to support the equal rights amendment not despite its consequences for national security, but because it will strengthen our ability to meet all military requirements and still eradicate a remaining bastion of inequality in our society.

Thank you.

Notes

1 *Hearings before the Subcommittee on the Constitution of the Committee on the Senate Judiciary*, Day 1 and 2, 98th Congress (1984) (Statement from Antonia Chayes). Public Domain.
2 "Biographical Sketch of Antonia Handler Chayes," Hearing Before the Committee on Armed Services, United States Senate, 96th Congress (1988), 6–7.
3 Cynthia Harrison, *On Account of Sex: The Politics of Women's Issues, 1945–1968* (Berkeley: University of California Press, 1989), see Appendix 3.
4 Terri Moon Cronk, "Women in the Military Academies: 40 Years Later," *Department of Defense News*, October 2, 2020, https://www.defense.gov/Explore/Features/Story/Article/ 2369469/women-in-the-military-academies-40-years-later/; Martha Lockwood, "Women's Legacy Parallels Air Force History," *Air Force News Service*, September 18, 2014, https://www.af.mil/News/Article-Display/Article/497548/womens-legacy-parallels-air-force-history/.
5 Bernard Weinraub, "Air Force Plans to Assign Women to Titan Missile-Launching Crews," *New York Times*, September 24, 1977, 49.
6 Bernard Weinraub, "Pentagon Asks Congress to End Ban on Women in Combat Units," *New York Times*, March 4, 1978, 1; Ernesto Londoño, "Pentagon Removes Ban

on Women in Combat," *Washington Post*, January 24, 2013, https://www.washingtonpost.com/world/national-security/pentagon-to-remove-ban-on-women-in-combat/2013/01/23/6cba86f6-659e-11e2-85f5-a8a9228e55e7_story.html.

7 "Missile Jobs for Women?" *Atlanta Constitution*, September 24, 1977, 3A.

8 See Peter Grier, "The Short, Happy Life of the Glick-Em," *Air Force Magazine*, July 2022, 70–74.

9 These statutes "prohibit assignment of Air Force and Navy women to aircraft or naval vessels engaged in combat missions." See "Women in the Military: Impact of Proposed Legislation to Open More Combat Support Positions and Units to Women," Briefing Report to Congressional Requesters, United States General Accounting Office, National Security and International Affairs Division, July 15, 1988, 1–16.

10 Intratheater aircraft refers to "operations exclusively within one geographic combatant command." See "Air Force Doctrine," Curtis E. Lemay Center for Doctrine, Development, and Education, June 28, 2019, https://www.doctrine.af.mil/Portals/61/documents/AFDP_3-36/3-36-D04-Mobility-Inter-Intra.pdf.

11 Under Bill Clinton, Congress repealed 10 U.S.C. 6015 in 1993 and women first served on the combatant vessel *Dwight D. Eisenhower*. See "Twenty-Five Years of Women Aboard Combatant Vessels," *Naval History and Heritage Command*, April 27, 2021, https://www.history.navy.mil/content/history/nhhc/browse-by-topic/diversity/women-in-the-navy/women-in-combat.html.

We Want to Create an All-Girls Network

Remarks at the New Campaign for an Equal Rights Amendment

Irene Natividad
January 3, 1989[1]

Irene Natividad (1948–present) was born in the Philippines but grew up in the United States. She graduated as valedictorian from Long Island University's Brooklyn Center, where she was the first student to graduate with a degree in comparative literature.[2] Natividad decided to become an activist after handing out leaflets in Boston to support Senator Eugene McCarthy (D-MN), the anti-war candidate who ran for president in 1968. In 1985, Natividad prevailed in the race to lead the NWPC, which sought to encourage more women to run for office.[3] As the caucus's first Asian American president, Natividad called for members to "not be discouraged or deterred by the nation's current conservatism."[4] She vowed to promote four key issues during her tenure: affirmative action, pay equity, reproductive choice, and the Equal Rights Amendment. Natividad chaired the National Commission on Working Women in the 1990s and, in more recent years, has turned her attention to promoting women's leadership around the world. She currently chairs the GlobeWomen Research Institute and is President of the Global Summit of Women.[5]

Natividad spent the late 1980s calling for the ERA's passage in the next decade. She appeared outside Congress in 1989 with several ERA supporters—including Congresswoman Nancy Pelosi, NWP President Elizabeth Chittick, and NOW President Molly Yard—to reintroduce the amendment to the 101st Congress. Among other things, Natividad's pithy remarks forecasted the political strategy of the next decade: passing the ERA by electing more women to office. Her speech was prescient indeed. More women were elected to Congress in 1992—the "Year of the Woman"—than ever before. Not long after, key legislation that advanced women's rights passed with their help during the Clinton administration, including the Family and Medical Leave Act (1993) and the Violence Against Women Act (1994).[6]

Good morning. When people ask me, "do we still need the Equal Rights Amendment?" I point to the Bork Nomination Hearings as the reason for why.[7] Do you remember? During those hearings we discovered that women had equal rights because of some judge's expanding reading of the Equal Protection Clause of the Fourteenth Amendment of the Constitution. And should you have a judge nominated with very conservative limited readings of the Constitution, we would not be there. That, in fact, I, as an Asian American, would be there in the Constitution and protected, but not I as a woman.

Now Congress passed the ERA before, and I'm hoping that the 101st Congress will do that again. But Congress is not our stumbling block. It is the state legislatures. That is why the strategy of the National Women's Political Caucus to fight for the ERA is the state legislative one. We want to create an all-girls network. So, we want to elect more women to public office but especially in the state legislatures.

When the ERA first passed Congress in '72, there were only 362 women in state legislative positions. In 1988, 1,079 won, and if you were to add to that the holdovers, I believe we will have well over 1,200. That is, 17% roughly. Not bad. We are getting there. But I am convinced that the only way to win this in the states is to have more women in elected office. Thank you very much.

Notes

1 Irene Natividad, Remarks at New Campaign for an Equal Rights Amendment, January 3, 1989, *C-SPAN*, https://www.c-span.org/video/?5571-1/campaign-equal-rights-amendment. Public Domain.
2 "Commencement Stars at LIU," *New York Daily News*, June 24, 1971, 417.
3 "Woman's Caucus Elects New Yorker," *New York Times*, July 1, 1985, B6.
4 "Educator Will Head Caucus," *Sioux City Journal*, July 1, 1985, 5.
5 Irene Natividad, Globe Women Directors International, https://globewomen.org/globalsummit/irene-natividad-2/.
6 Margaret Wolf Freivogel, "Women's Groups Unite on Legislative Issues," *St. Louis Post-Dispatch*, January 18, 1987, 4B.

7 Under the leadership of its new president Molly Yard, NOW led the campaign against Ronald Reagan's unsuccessful nomination of Robert Bork to the Supreme Court. Yard referred to Bork, an ERA opponent, as a "Neanderthal" for his stance on women's issues and brash communication style. See "NOW Plans Bork Battle, New President Calls Him 'A Neanderthal,'" *Chicago Tribune*, July 21, 1987, 4.

I Remain an Advocate of the Equal Rights Amendment

Nomination to Be Associate Justice of the Supreme Court of the United States

RUTH BADER GINSBURG
July 21, 1993[1]

Before she joined the Supreme Court as only its second female justice, attorney Joan Ruth Bader Ginsburg (1933–2020) enjoyed a long and distinguished legal career fighting against sex discrimination. The self-proclaimed "Brooklynite" met her husband Martin at Cornell University and the two proceeded to Harvard Law School together. She finished her legal education at Columbia University in 1959, tied for first in her class. Like so many of the women in this collection, Ginsburg confronted sex-based discrimination when seeking employment as a lawyer who also happened to be a wife and mother.[2] In 1963, Rutgers School of Law hired Ginsburg, who pioneered the earliest law courses in sex discrimination and the law. Ginsburg's *alma mater* hired her away in 1972, and she became the first tenured woman law professor at Columbia.[3] At Rutgers and Columbia, Ginsburg continued to develop a "minimalist" judicial perspective. She believed that the best way to change the law was incrementally and methodically through narrowly decided cases that located, debunked, and overturned discriminatory laws that hurt both women *and* men—along with exposing the sex-based stereotypes undergirding those laws.[4]

Outside of the classroom, Ginsburg enacted this legal perspective in several landmark cases for women's rights argued before the Supreme Court throughout the 1970s and 1980s. *Reed v. Reed* (1971) successfully invoked the Equal Protection Clause of the Fourteenth Amendment to nullify sex-based discrimination when appointing estate administers, while *Frontiero v. Richardson* (1973) established that the spouses of services members should be treated equally when it came to benefits regardless of sex.[5] On the brief for *Reed*, Ginsburg cited as co-authors two feminist lawyers whom she credited with inspiring her arguments: Dorothy Kenyon and Pauli Murray.[6] Ginsburg co-founded the American Civil Liberties Union's Women's Rights Project in 1973 with pro-ERA attorney Brenda Feigen. Jimmy Carter, who dramatically updated the federal judiciary to include more women, appointed Ginsburg to the Washington D.C. Court of Appeals in 1980. And when Byron White retired from the Supreme Court in 1993, Bill Clinton nominated Ginsburg to replace him.[7]

The nomination drew some critics from both sides of the political aisle. Antiabortion advocates found Ginsburg's support of a woman's right to choose indefensible, while her belief that *Roe v. Wade* should have been decided more narrowly based on the Equal Protection Clause rather than the broader right to privacy angered pro-choice advocates. Equally controversial, though less publicized at the time, was how Ginsburg's record on the ERA factored into the discourse surrounding her nomination. Prior to joining the Supreme Court, she authored law articles defending the ERA, testified before Congress to extend the ratification period, and served on the NWP Board from 1977 to 1980.[8] As she wrote in a 1973 *American Bar Association Journal* article, the ERA "firmly rejects sharp legislative lines between the sexes as constitutionally tolerable."[9]

Twenty years later, Ginsburg fielded questions about her positive stance on the amendment from Senator Arlen Specter (R-PA), as she had expressed in a 1979 article for the *Washington University Law Quarterly*, before the Senate confirmed her in a smooth 96 to 3 vote. Ginsburg's brief, though powerful reaffirmation inspired many women's rights activists to suggest that 1993 was the year to reintroduce the ERA—approximately 60 years since its first introduction in Congress.[10] The "Notorious RBG," as a younger twenty-first-century generation came to know her, lived long enough to see the ERA's revival during the Trump presidency. Ginsburg cautioned that the ratification process should "start anew" since several states had rescinded their ratifications—a strategy some other ERA supporters, as well as opponents, have contemporarily embraced.[11] But she still believed, as ever, that "equal citizenship stature for men and women belongs in any fundamental instrument of government."[12]

It is part of our history—a sad part of our history, Senator Specter, but undeniably part of our history—that the 14th amendment, that great amendment that changed so much in this Nation, was not intended by its framers immediately to change the status of women. And it is part of history that the leading feminists of the day—Susan B. Anthony, Elizabeth Cady Stanton, Lucretia

Mott—campaigned against ratification of the 14th amendment because it allowed a system to persist in the United States where women couldn't vote, they couldn't hold office, if they married they couldn't hold property in their own name, they couldn't contract for themselves. That is what life was like for women in the middle of the nineteenth century.

Times changed, and eventually, after nearly a century of struggle, women achieved the vote. They became full citizens. And many people thought that when women became full citizens, entitled to the vote, they had achieved equality. The vote should have qualified women as full and equal citizens with men, entitled to the same equal protection before the laws.

The position was that, yes, it took bold and dynamic interpretation in view of what the framers of the 14th amendment intended. The framers of the 14th amendment meant no change, they intended no change at all in the status of women before the law. But in 1920, when women achieved the vote, they became full citizens, and you have to read the Constitution as a whole, changed, as Thurgood Marshall said, over the years by amendment and by judicial construction. So it was certainly a bold change from the middle of the nineteenth century until the 1970s when women's equal citizenship was recognized before the law.

I remain an advocate of the Equal Rights Amendment for this reason. I have a daughter and a granddaughter. I know what the history was. I would like the legislators of this country and of all the states to stand up and say we know what that history was in the nineteenth century; we want to make a clarion announcement that women and men are equal before the law, just as every modern human rights document in the world does, at least since 1970. I would like to see that statement made just that way in the U.S. Constitution. But that women are equal citizens and have been ever since the 19th amendment was passed, I think that is the case. And that is what the *Washington University Law Quarterly* article is about.[13] That is what the second circuit debate was about. And I do not think my statements should be applied out of context. This was a precisely focused article about women's entitlement to equal citizenship before the law.

Notes

1 *Nomination of Ruth Bader Ginsburg, to Be Associate Justice of the Supreme Court of the United States: Hearings Before the Committee on the Judiciary*, United States Senate, Day 2, 103rd Congress (1993) (Statement from Ruth Bader Ginsburg). Public Domain.

2 Ruth Bader Ginsburg and Amanda L. Tyler, *Justice, Justice Thou Shalt Pursue: My Life's Work Fighting for a More Perfect Union* (New York: Simon & Schuster, 2021), 3.

3 The 2018 film *On the Basis of Sex*, written by her nephew, depicts the years of Ginsburg's life and career prior to her term on the Supreme Court.
4 Jeffrey Rosen, *Conversations with RBG: Ruth Bader Ginsburg on Life, Love, Liberty, and the Law* (New York: Henry Holt and Company, 2019), 166; Jane Sherron De Hart, *Ruth Bader Ginsburg: A Life* (New York: Vintage Books, 2018).
5 Ruth Bader Ginsburg, "The *Frontiero* Reply Brief," reprinted in *My Own Words*, ed. Ruth Bader Ginsburg, Mary Hartnett, and Wendy W. Williams (New York: Simon & Schuster, 2016), 131–38.
6 Melvin L. Wulf, Ruth Bader Ginsburg, Allen R. Derr, Pauli Murray, and Dorothy Kenyon, Brief for the Appellant, *Reed v. Reed*, No. 70–4 (1971), https://documents.alexanderstreet.com/d/1000675826.
7 Jill Lepore, "Ruth Bader Ginsburg's Unlikely Path to the Supreme Court," *The New Yorker*, October 1, 2018, https://www.newyorker.com/magazine/2018/10/08/ruth-bader-ginsburgs-unlikely-path-to-the-supreme-court.
8 This information comes from the resumé Ginsburg submitted for the transcript of her Supreme Confirmation hearings.
9 Ruth Bader Ginsburg, "The Need for the Equal Rights Amendment," reprinted in *My Own Words*, ed. Ruth Bader Ginsburg, Mary Hartnett, and Wendy W. Williams (New York: Simon & Schuster, 2016), 148.
10 Cynthia Terrell, "Time to Reconsider ERA," *Christian Science Monitor*, August 17, 1993, https://www.csmonitor.com/1993/0817/17191.html.
11 Ginsburg cited an ongoing strategy for which other ERA supporters advocated. See "In Congress," 117th Congress, Equalrightsamendment.org, https://www.equalrightsamendment.org/incongress.
12 Rosen, *Conversations*, 227; see also Julie C. Suk, "Justice Ginsburg's Cautious Legacy for the Equal Rights Amendment," *Georgetown Law Journal* 110, no. 6 (September 2022): 1391–1436.
13 Ruth Bader Ginsburg, "Sexual Equality Under the Fourteenth and Equal Rights Amendments," *Washington University Law Quarterly* (1979): 161–78.

The Grand and General Language of ERA

Testimony at the Confirmation Hearings of Ruth Bader Ginsburg

PAIGE COMSTOCK CUNNINGHAM
July 23, 1993[1]

In her opening statement opposing Ruth Bader Ginsburg's nomination to the Supreme Court, Paige Comstock Cunningham (1955–present) admitted that her ability to appear at all likely grew "from the seeds sown by Judge Ginsburg in her efforts to abolish sex-based discrimination in the law."[2] Cunningham's résumé is impressive and varied. She holds a law degree from Northwestern University, a Master's degree in bioethics from Evangelical Trinity International University, and a doctorate in education from Trinity's seminary.[3]

From January 1993 to May 1995, Cunningham served as president of Americans United for Life (AUL), a nonprofit antiabortion lobbying group based in Washington D.C. and founded in 1971 by theologians, academics, and attorneys seeking secular means to protect the unborn. AUL has achieved a number of anti-choice legislative victories that range from abortion bans to heartbeat bills to fetal cremation laws through grassroots lobbying and with the financial support of unnamed investors.[4] Since her time with AUL, Cunningham has widely published on topics related to the intersection of bioethics and the law, taught courses in abortion and law at Wheaton College, and expressed public opposition to in vitro fertilization.[5] Most recently, she served as interim president of her undergraduate *alma mater* Taylor University, an evangelical Christian college in Indiana, and chaired Donald Trump's controversial Human Fetal Tissue Research Ethics Advisory Board.[6]

Cunningham's testimony represented some of the (few) opposing arguments presented at Ginsburg's confirmation hearings.[7] Cunningham had testified against the ERA before the Subcommittee on Civil and Constitutional Rights of the House of Representatives in 1983. At the time, she claimed to be "neutral" on the ERA itself but opposed its legal implications on the question of abortion. A decade later, Cunningham submitted Ginsburg's support of the ERA as proof for her disqualification to serve on the Supreme Court. Although Cunningham focused much of her testimony on abortion and *Roe v. Wade*, she expressed concerns about Ginsburg's judicial activism, her status as a "radical feminist," and her record on the ERA. Cunningham's view is plain in this selection from the written supplement that appeared as an appendix following her oral statement in the transcript of Ginsburg's confirmation hearings. For Cunningham, the ERA may not have been ratified, but those who—like Ginsburg—still supported the amendment presented an imminent danger to their own conservative views about womanhood in the early 1990s.

Judge Ginsburg's lack of appreciation for the traditional roles of women appears in her statement that some feminists argue forcibly that women, at least as childbearers, perform a service for society that nature did not equip men to perform, a service essential to the survival of the human race, one that should attract special recognition and rewards. (People concerned with population growth, one might note, have doubts about encouraging such service.)

Her view of traditional roles may be colored by her apparent belief that those roles were inferior and that dependency allowed or encouraged considerable suffering and legal disadvantage for women.

It is possible to recognize the historical problems women have faced without denigrating traditional roles, or assuming that only through wholesale restructuring of family life can women have equal "stature" with men. As an advocate for the ERA, Judge Ginsburg argued that the Constitution had excluded women, and that gender cases prior to 1971 demonstrated social and legal hostility toward women. She supported the "grand" and general language of the ERA as giving a textual basis for equal rights for women, which would strip away any laws which demeaned women, but extend genuine protection to all. In fact, Judge Ginsburg was either telling only part of the story or was just plain wrong on all points.

Most of the Constitution deals with the structure of our government; the bill of rights protecting individuals did not trump states' rights of legislating matters related to the family, employment and voting, even after the incorporation of the Civil War Amendments—not really until the last three decades of this century. To present cases such as *Bradwell* (1873)[8] (challenging a law barring women from practicing law) or *Happersett* (1873)[9] (challenging a state law barring women from voting) as evidence of the law's inherent devaluation of women is to misrepresent those cases, which were decided on the basis of the states' right to set policy in these matters, not on a fundamental hostility toward women. The High Court's attitude to many gender rights cases prior to the middle of this century echoes that of the *Happersett* court: "If the law is wrong, it ought to be changed; but the power for that is not with us." Feminist revisionist readings of cases regarding women's rights can produce a powerful emotional response from an audience, but does not encourage careful, thoughtful analysis of our constitutional principles.

Seeking to ground rights on a constitutional test is laudable, but for Judge Ginsburg to insist that the "grand" language of the ERA is still a workable approach to equity for women requires her to ignore some social changes of the past two hundred years. At the time the Constitution was ratified, it was not intended to embody the whole of our law; state law was taken seriously, and the family and the church were strong social institutions which provided a guide for individual and familial behavior. With the growth of the welfare state, and the increasing reliance on the Constitution as a guarantor of unenumerated fundamental rights, the family and church appear to be weaker, and the absolute language of the amendment could be interpreted in ways that may not help women.

Our recent history suggests that while it may be theoretically possible to envision an ERA that would preserve genuinely protective laws and expand them to include all persons, courts more frequently strip away protective laws than extend them because striking down legislation as unconstitutional is clearly within the power of the judiciary, while extending benefits of the law to persons not included by legislative mandate edges toward judicial overreaching.

Notes

1 *Hearings Before the Committee on the Senate Judiciary*, Day 1, 103rd Congress (1993) (Testimony of Paige Comstock Cunningham Concerning the Nomination of Ruth Bader Ginsburg to Be an Associate Justice of the United States Supreme Court). Public Domain.

2 *Hearings Before the Committee on the Senate Judiciary*, Day 1, 103rd Congress (1993) (Statement from Paige Comstock Cunningham).

3 Paige Comstock Cunningham, Center for Bioethics & Human Dignity, Trinity International University, https://www.cbhd.org/people/paige-cunningham.

4 Susan Roberts, "Surprised By All These Abortion Bans? Meet Americans United for Life—The Most Significant Antiabortion Group You've Never Heard Of," *Washington Post*, May 31, 2019, https://www.washingtonpost.com/politics/2019/05/31/surprised-by-all-these-abortion-bans-meet-americans-united-life-most-significant-pro-life-group-youve-never-heard/.

5 Sarah Pulliam Bailey and Ariana Eunjung Cha, "Lawmaker's Resignation Raises Questions of 'Pro-Life Approach' to IVF, Surrogacy," *Washington Post*, December 8, 2017, https://www.washingtonpost.com/lifestyle/lawmakers-resignation-raises-questions-of-pro-life-approach-to-ivf-surrogacy/2017/12/08/ab720d7c-dc5b-11e7-8e5f-ccc94e22b133_story.html; see further Elizabeth Dias, "What Christian Traditions Say About I.V.F. Treatments," *New York Times*, February 24, 2024, https://www.nytimes.com/2024/02/24/us/christian-tradition-ivf.html.

6 "Paige Comstock Cunningham Named Interim President of Taylor University," *Taylor University*, August 1, 2019, https://www.taylor.edu/news/paige-comstock-cunningham-named-interim-president-of-taylor-university; Meredith Wadman and Jocelyn Kaiser, "Antiabortion Ethicists and Scientists Dominate Trump's Fetal Tissue Advisory Board," *Science.org*, July 13, 2020, https://www.science.org/content/article/antiabortion-ethicists-and-scientists-dominate-trump-s-fetal-tissue-review-board; Michelle Onello, "Limiting Scientific Research Is Another Front in the War on Abortion," *Ms. Magazine*, October 6, 2020, https://msmagazine.com/2020/10/06/reproductive-freedom-hft-human-fetal-tissue-abortion-trump-hhs-alex-azar/.

7 "Ginsburg Draws Little Criticism as Confirmation Hearings End," *St. Louis Post-Dispatch*, July 24, 1993, 16B.

8 *Bradwell v. Illinois* (1873). See "Myra Bradwell," U.S. Supreme Court, n.d., https://www.supremecourt.gov/visiting/exhibitions/LadyLawyers/section1.aspx.

9 Here, Cunningham refers to *Minor v. Happersett* (1875), not 1873. See "Minor v. Happersett (1875)," National Constitution Center, https://constitutioncenter.org/the-constitution/supreme-court-case-library/minor-v-happersett.

To Be a Feminist Means To Be Pro-Life

Address to the House of Representatives

ILEANA ROS-LEHTINEN
June 14, 1999[1]

Ileana Ros-Lehtinen (1952–present) and her family fled Cuba when she was eight years old, just as Fidel Castro seized control of the country.[2] The Cuban-American Republican and former teacher began her legislative career in the Florida House of Representatives then moved to the Florida Senate before winning a seat in the U.S. House of Representatives in 1989 representing Miami, Coral Gables, and the Florida Keys. Ros-Lehtinen held on to her seat for nearly 30 years and made history as both the first Latina elected to Congress and the first woman to chair the House Foreign Affairs Committee. During her lengthy tenure, Ros-Lehtinen was not afraid to break ranks and often won the respect of colleagues across the aisle for her positions. In 2012, she became the first in her party to publicly support marriage equality in Congress and she opposed Donald Trump's positions on immigration, health care, and transgender rights. For Ros-Lehtinen's outspoken advocacy against his communist regime, Fidel Castro called her "loba feroz" (ferocious wolf), a moniker she bore proudly.[3] Ros-Lehtinen did not seek reelection in 2018 and now works as a senior adviser to an international lobbying firm.[4]

Ros-Lehtinen won her House seat by supporting the National Rifle Association and opposing abortion rights. As a Congresswoman, she voted against providing abortion counseling at federally-funded family planning clinics and sponsored legislation criminalizing a non-parent taking a minor over state lines to get an abortion. This 1999 floor speech argued that feminism and pro-life politics are not incompatible by claiming that Alice Paul would have opposed coupling abortion and the ERA. While Ros-Lehtinen did not take an explicit position on the ERA itself, she did advance a common narrative promoted by the amendment's opponents: that early women's rights activists opposed abortion.[5] Some contemporary legal experts and women's historians assert that this narrative has no basis in fact.[6] As Faye E. Dudden argues, "most early feminists [including Susan B. Anthony and Elizabeth Cady Stanton] expressed decided skepticism about outlawing abortion."[7] But Alice Paul went on the record in 1972 to affirm that, in her view, "the ratification of the Equal Rights Amendment has been made a bit harder by these people who run around advocating, for instance, abortion. As far as I can see, ERA has nothing whatsoever to do with abortion."[8] Many of the ERA's conservative opponents, like Ros-Lehtinen does here, have attempted to rhetorically sever the connection between the amendment and abortion as a part of their opposition campaign.

Mr. Speaker, at one time or another we have all seen the bumper sticker which reads: "Pro-Women = Pro-Choice," and it is presumed that feminists and defenders of equity and rights for women are defenders of abortion.

But in fact, what most feminists do not wish to acknowledge is that the early suffragists who are responsible for today's women's movement actually were staunchly pro-life.

Over a century ago, Susan B. Anthony tirelessly campaigned for suffrage, for women's employment rights, and for the abolition of slavery. She voted illegally, took part in the underground railroad, and yes, Susan B. Anthony, a mother of the feminist movement, opposed abortion.

In *The Revolution*, the radical women's paper which she published, along with Elizabeth Cady Stanton, Anthony strongly editorialized against abortion. She referred to the bloody act as child murder and infanticide and addressed its root causes in women's oppression and in the abdication of family planning. She argued that laws pertaining to abortion victimized women while absolving men of all responsibility.

Susan B. Anthony was not alone in her thinking. Other early feminists also opposed abortion. For example, Elizabeth Cady Stanton proclaimed that "If it is degrading to treat a woman as property, it is no better for a woman to treat her own child as property."[9] Suffragist Margaret Sanger stated that abortion was the disowning of feminine values.

The first female presidential candidate, Victoria Woodhull, was likewise strongly against abortion. She stated that every woman knows that if she were free, she would never bear an unwished-for child nor think of murdering one before its birth.[10]

Astonishingly enough, most feminists prefer to ignore that Alice Paul, the original author of the Equal Rights Amendment, the ERA, of 1923, said: "Abortion is the ultimate exploitation of women."[11] Naturally, Paul opposed the later trend of linking abortion with the ERA movement.

Like the early suffragists who fought to give women's rights, a feminist should believe in the right to protect her own body, and in the likeness of Susan B. Anthony, the feminist should stand up to defend the poor, oppressed, and rejected. She should fight for all human beings, whether they are black or white, born or unborn.

The phrase, "It's a man's world'" is often used to describe today's society, a society which tends to view unplanned pregnancy and motherhood as an inconvenience. But many of today's feminists, rather than focusing on a woman's financial distress, the problems she may be facing at school, work, or at home, choose to give in to the pressures of a man's world.

Rather than fight for acceptance and protection for women facing unexpected pregnancies, many feminists suggest a dangerous, potentially fatal abortion as the remedy to all conditions. What would the suffragists have to say about giving in to this cruel society? Early feminist Susan Norton said, "Perhaps there will come a time when an unmarried mother will not be despised because of her motherhood, when the right of the unborn to be born will not be denied or interfered with."

As one of six pro-life women in Congress and a mother of two daughters, I believe that abortion is not a sign that women are free to choose. On the contrary, it is a sign that women incorrectly feel desperate and feel that they have no choice. Susan B. Anthony and the early defenders of the women's rights would agree that the slogan "pro-choice" is by no means to be equated with being pro-women. Perhaps if the early feminists were alive today, they would be fighting to amend those bumper stickers to instead read, "Pro-Women = Pro-Life."

Notes

1 Ileana Ros-Lehtinen, "To Be a Feminist Means To Be Pro-Life," Address to the House of Representatives," Congressional Record—House, 4213, June 14, 1999. Public Domain.

2 Ileana Ros-Lehtinen, United States House of Representatives, https://history.house.gov/People/detail/20624.

3 Lizette Alvarez, "Public Lives: Fight Over Boy Is Latest in Lawmaker's War with Castro," *New York Times*, January 10, 2000, A12.

4 Miles Parks, "U.S. Rep. Ros-Lehtinen, First Cuban-American Elected to Congress, Retiring Next Year," *NPR*, April 30, 2017, https://www.npr.org/sections/thetwo-way/2017/04/30/526291214/u-s-rep-ros-lehtinen-first-cuban-american-elected-to-congress-retiring-next-year.

5 Jeanne DeQuine and Bob Minzesheimer, "GOP Candidate Wins in Miami," *USA Today*, August 30, 1989, 04A; "Poor Need Counseling on Abortion," *Sun Sentinel*, November 10, 1991, 6G; "Parental OK on Abortion Again Clears House," *Los Angeles Times*, April 18, 2002, A13.

6 Tracy A. Thomas, "Misappropriating Women's History in the Law and Politics of Abortion," *Seattle University Law Review* 36, no. 1 (2012): 1–68; Lynn Sherr and Ann D. Gordon, "No, Susan B. Anthony and Elizabeth Cady Stanton Were Not Antiabortionists," *Time*, November 10, 2015, https://time.com/4106547/susan-b-anthony-elizabeth-cady-stanton-abortion/.

7 Faye E. Dudden, "Women's Rights Advocates and Abortion Laws," *Journal of Women's History* 31, no. 3 (2019): 102–23.

8 Susan Ware, "The Book I Couldn't Write: Alice Paul and the Challenge of the Feminist Biography," *Journal of Women's History* 24, no. 2 (2012): 13–36, quotation on 14.

9 This quotation, which differs from Ros-Lehtinen's phrasing in her speech, allegedly originates from a letter Stanton sent to Julia Ward Howe dated October 16, 1873. It reads: "When we consider that women are treated as property, it is degrading to women that we should treat our children as property to be disposed of as we see fit." The letter is quoted in Hunter Baker, "Storming the Gates of a Massive Cultural Investment: Reconsidering *Roe* in Light of Its Flawed Foundation and Undesirable Consequences," *Regent University Law Review* 14 (2001): 35–65, quotation on 42. And yet, *ABC News* broadcaster Lynn Sherr and historian Ann D. Gordon counter that no such letter exists because Stanton and Howe were in fact together on that very day listening to speeches on the subject of "Enlightened Motherhood." See further Sherr and Gordon, "No, Susan B. Anthony and Elizabeth Cady Stanton."

10 For a deeper understanding of Woodhull's views on abortion in her own words, see Victoria Woodhull, "When Is It Not Murder to Take Life?" *Woodhull & Claflin's Weekly* 1, no. 21 (October 8, 1870): 11, http://iapsop.com/archive/materials/woodhull_and_claflins_weekly/woodhull_and_claflins_weekly_v1_n21_oct_8_1870.pdf.

11 This quotation is frequently attributed to Paul in pro-life materials, yet typically comes with no citation. According to one source, Paul allegedly said this "to a colleague" who remains unnamed. See further John Hunt, "The Abortion and Eugenics Policies of Nazi Germany," *Association for Interdisciplinary Research in Values and Social Change Research Bulletin* 16, no. 1 (2001): 1–8, quotation on 8.

Memo on the Equal Rights Amendment 2000

Article from the Eagle Forum

EAGLE FORUM
January 2000[1]

After the Equal Rights Amendment failed to tally enough states for ratification, its critics relished their victory. Phyllis Schlafly's STOP ERA—which transitioned into the Eagle Forum—crowed the loudest, for there was much to celebrate. On June 30, 1982, Schlafly stood in the Senate Caucus Room and took credit for what she described as "the gift we give America today."[2] Schlafly and her breadmakers had successfully stirred the nation's fears and wooed enough conservatives into political activism. After 1982, Schlafly maintained a rigorous schedule. She continued writing books, kept *The Phyllis Schlafly Report* alive, hosted syndicated weekly radio shows, and appeared on television. The ERA never left her purview, but she honed a socially conservative, anti-feminist platform that sought to strengthen the GOP's pro-life commitment, to defend traditional "pro-family values," to involve parents more deeply in children's education (specifically, sex education), to ban pornography, to reject same-sex marriage, and to push for a stronger military defense. State and local Eagle Forum chapters took their cues from Schlafly and continue to exercise influence on GOP politics today.[3] In more recent years, some Eagle Forum state chapters and members have led book-banning initiatives against diversity, equity, and inclusion (DEI) literature, supported legislation that criminalizes gender-affirming medical treatment for transgender youth, and opposed mandated COVID-19 vaccinations.[4]

By the turn of the twenty-first century, the Eagle Forum's confidence surrounding the ERA seemed to wane but not fully dissipate. They insisted that the ERA was "dead," yet they continued to talk about its "carcass," implying that its heart was still beating, albeit faintly. The "dead" and still-not-ratified ERA still threatened Eagle Forum supporters because tax dollars might go to fund abortions and same-sex couples might still be legally married. Was the ERA—and its implications for abortion and homosexuality—really a threat for Schlafly's white, middle-class, heterosexual audience or was it a convenient scapegoat to boost her subscriber list after the contentious battles of the 1970s and 1980s? The turn-of-the-century memo below signals that both goals need not be mutually exclusive.

The original Equal Rights Amendment (ERA) resolution, which passed Congress on March 22, 1972, set this time limit for the ratification period: "seven years from the date of its submission by the Congress." When the end of the seven years approached and it became clear that three-fourths of the states would *not* ratify the ERA, Congress passed the ERA Time Extension resolution. This act purported to change "seven years" to 10 years, three months, and eight days, extending the time to June 30, 1982.

This Extension resolution was greeted with widespread public condemnation. The cartoonists and editorialists had a field day, comparing it to adding three more innings to a baseball game, or a fifth quarter to a football or basketball game, even though the game was not tied. Public reaction was so adverse that not a single additional state ratified ERA after the Time Extension was passed.

After a two-and-a-half-year lawsuit, the U.S. District Court ruled on December 23, 1981, in *Idaho v. Freeman* that the ERA Time Extension was unconstitutional. When the Idaho case was appealed to the U.S. Supreme Court, it was dismissed as "moot" on October 4, 1982 (*NOW v. Idaho*, 459 U.S. 809). In support of its ruling, the Supreme Court cited as controlling the memorandum of the U.S. Administrator of General Services, who had argued that "the Amendment has failed of adoption no matter what the resolution of the legal issues presented here."[5]

Thus, the Supreme Court held that ERA was dead whether ERA expired on March 22, 1979, or on June 30, 1982. The Supreme Court and all the parties to the case agreed that ERA was dead.

For State Legislators to presume to breathe life into this carcass, having been proclaimed legally dead 18 years ago by the U.S. Supreme Court, would make them the laughingstock of the nation.

Much additional evidence has surfaced to validate the decision of the American people in the 1970s to reject ERA.

1. **ERA would give those who perform abortions a constitutional right to be paid by our tax dollars.** This is proved by the unanimous decision of the Supreme Court of New Mexico on November 25, 1998, that New Mexico's state Equal Rights Amendment requires the state to pay for elective abortions under the Medicaid program. The decision adopted the feminist argument that to deny funding for abortions would be sex discrimination under the meaning of ERA. The decision said that the law against abortion funding "undoubtedly singles out for less favorable treatment a gender-linked condition that is unique to women." New Mexico is one of the few states whose state constitutions contain an ERA in practically the same language as the defeated federal ERA. (*N.M. Right to Choose/NARAL v. Johnson*, 975 P.2d 841, 1998).

   Likewise, the Connecticut Superior Court previously ruled that the state ERA requires Connecticut taxpayers to pay for abortions, stating: "Since only women become pregnant, discrimination against pregnancy by not funding abortions ... is sex-oriented discrimination ... The court concludes that the regulation that restricts the funding for abortions ... violates Connecticut's Equal Rights Amendment" (*Doe v. Maher*, April 9, 1986).

   The argument that *to deny taxpayer funding of abortions is "sex discrimination"* was developed by the American Civil Liberties Union when Ruth Bader Ginsburg was one of their lawyers. The ACLU has argued this position in abortion cases in several different states. There's no doubt that the ACLU's former colleague, now Justice Ginsburg, would vote for this reinterpretation of our basic law. We must see to it that she never gets the chance.

2. **ERA would put new homosexual rights into the Constitution, particularly the right of same-sex couples to get marriage licenses.** Hawaii is one of the few states that have a state Equal Rights Amendment in the same language as the proposed federal ERA. In 1993, the Hawaii Supreme Court ruled in *Baehr v. Lewin* (852 P.2d 44, 1993) that the denial of marriage licenses to same-sex couples

was sex discrimination and unconstitutional under the Equal Rights Amendment of Hawaii's state constitution. The court remanded the case for trial. On December 3, 1996, the Hawaii trial court in *Baehr v. Miike* (Haw. Cir. Ct., Civ. No. 91–1394) enjoined the denial of marriage licenses to same-sex couples, ruling that the state statute allowing only heterosexual marriage was unconstitutional.

In order to undo the damage done by adding ERA to the Hawaii constitution, Hawaii voters had to pass a new constitutional amendment. On November 3, 1998, Hawaii voters passed a constitutional amendment stating that "the legislature shall have the power to reserve marriage to opposite-sex couples."

Legitimizing same-sex marriages has been on the ACLU agenda for many years, and it is obvious that there is a nationwide campaign to achieve this goal. It is clear that one of the mischievous results of ERA would be to give [a] green light to same-sex marriages.

Notes

1 "Memo on the Equal Rights Amendment 2000," *Eagle Forum*, January 1, 2000, https://eagleforum.org/memo-on-the-equal-rights-amendment-2000.html. Reprinted with permission from the Eagle Forum.

2 Lyle Denniston, "No Eulogy for ERA: Foes Clapping, Pros Mapping Comeback," *Baltimore Sun*, July 1, 1982, A3.

3 Donald Critchlow, *Phyllis Schlafly and Grassroots Conservatism: A Woman's Crusade* (Princeton: Princeton University Press, 2005), 270–83; Marjorie J. Spruill, *Divided We Stand: The Battle Over Women's Rights and Family Values That Polarized America* (New York: Bloomsbury, 2017), 326–27.

4 Jemma Stephenson, "How Does Alabama Choose Textbooks? Slowly," *Alabama Reflector*, May 23, 2023, https://alabamareflector.com/2023/05/23/how-does-alabama-choose-textbooks-slowly/; Jacob Holmes, "Eagle Forum Fighting DOJ Subpoena Over Bill Targeting Trans Medical Treatment Ban," *Alabama Political Reporter*, September 8, 2022, https://www.alreporter.com/2022/09/08/eagle-forum-fighting-doj-subpoena-over-bill-targeting-trans-medical-treatment-ban/; Ashley Bowerman, "Speakers at Conservative Forum Oppose Vaccine Mandates," *WSFA 12*, October 27, 2021, https://www.wsfa.com/2021/10/27/speakers-conservative-forum-oppose-vaccine-mandates/.

5 Lawrence G. Wallace, "Memorandum," Washington, D.C., July 1982, https://eagleforum.org/era/now-v-idaho-memo.html.

Equal Justice Under the Law

Address to the House of Representatives

Carolyn Maloney
March 12, 2003[1]

Fifty-eight years after Elizabeth Cady Stanton's granddaughter appeared before the House Judiciary to endorse the ERA, Democrat Carolyn Jane Bosher Maloney (1946–present)—Alice Paul's relative through marriage—stood before her House colleagues to reintroduce the ERA as a bipartisan effort.[2] Maloney represented the New York 12th District covering parts of Manhattan and Queens since 1992, when she was elected in the sweeping "Year of the Woman" that put more women in Congress than ever before. Maloney has made women's and children's issues a priority throughout her political career. She sponsored legislation to reduce the backlog of rape kits, pushed for reform in childcare affordability, and promoted paid family leave for federal employees.[3] "Where are the women?" she famously asked at a 2012 all-male panel on the Obama administration's healthcare plan and contraception.[4] As chief sponsor of the Smithsonian Women's History Museum Act, Maloney saw her bill passed in January 2021, guaranteeing that women's history will at long last have a place on the National Mall.[5] In 2022, she lost her seat to redistricting and subsequently accepted a position to lead NOW's New York chapter, where she continues fighting for women's rights.[6]

Maloney has been a tireless advocate for the ERA ever since arriving to Washington, D.C. She has taken her case from the halls of Congress and the pages of newspapers and magazines to social media and the 2021 Met Gala, where she accessorized a colorful suffrage-inspired gown with a green purse inscribed with "ERA YES."[7] As America faced the prospect of a long and deadly war in the Middle East after the horrific September 11 attacks in her home state, Maloney insisted that women's rights were under threat and that the ERA was still relevant and necessary in the aftermath.

Mr. Speaker, this is a difficult time. We're worried about the possibility of war and concerned about the men and women in our armed forces, but the best way to honor democracy is to ensure equality and justice for all. That's why we're leading this bipartisan movement for the Equality Amendment for women and men. We intend to do all we can to see that it becomes part of the Constitution, which is where it belongs.

I am proud to be joined by my Republican colleagues, Jim Leach [R-IA] and Judy Biggert [R-IL]. I am also grateful to the dean of the House, John Dingell [D-MI], for his leadership on so many issues important to women; to leading pollster Mark Penn of the firm Penn, Schoen, and Berland; and to the noted economist, Dr. Heidi Hartman. I'd also like to acknowledge the representatives of so many organizations dedicated to improving the lives of women and families.

Women have achieved a great deal, but the statutory route has not been as successful as we hoped. The Glass Ceiling, the Pink Ghetto,[8] the wage gap, the occupation gap, and sexual harassment are real problems. We're reintroducing the Equality Amendment because the only guarantee that American women will never again be subject to inferior treatment is to engrave the principle of women's equality into the Constitution.

We've seen over the years that laws can change, judicial attitudes can shift, and the gains we've won can slip from our grasp. The need for a constitutional guarantee of equal rights for women is compelling. We must do more, much more, to guarantee fair treatment in the workplace. Existing laws can't get the job done and could be rolled back.

Title IX, which for three decades guaranteed equality in education and in academic sports programs, is being eroded.

Enforcement measures on discrimination laws are backlogged and badly underfunded.

Women continue to be treated differently than men in pensions, insurance, and judicial awards.

Women still have trouble gaining access to housing and equal pay for equal work. The wage gap persists. In fact, the Dingell-Maloney study that we released last year showed the gap in managerial salaries is actually widening.[9]

Women still earn 76 cents for each dollar earned by a man. After a full day's work, no woman should be forced to take home only three-quarters of a paycheck.

Too many women continue to be victims of sexual harassment.

Over 9 out of 10 Americans support equal rights for men and women, as Mark Penn can discuss. In fact, polling data shows that most Americans think the Constitution already guarantees gender equality—and they don't want it repealed. The ERA would establish that as a reality once and for all. It is time to ensure that the legal right to equality regardless of sex is subject to the same level of judicial review as race or other classes.

With 187 co-sponsors so far, the Equality Amendment has strong support in the House. And it enjoys strong backing in the Senate. Ours is a bipartisan grassroots effort. With the help of organizations represented here and over 140 groups that have already endorsed it, I hope we'll be able to move the ERA to a vote.

It is time for women to have an equal place in the Constitution. It is time for the Equal Rights Amendment to become law. Inscribed over the Supreme Court is the statement "Equal Justice Under the Law" and it means ALL people. And in 2003, we intend to SEE that equal justice under the law happens ... and making the ERA part of the Constitution is the right way to do it.

Notes

1 Hon. Carolyn B. Maloney of New York, "The Reintroduction of the Equal Rights Amendment," Congressional Record—Extension of Remarks," March 12, 2003, E443. Public Domain.

2 Martha F. Davis, "The Equal Rights Amendment: Then and Now," *Columbia Journal of Gender and Law* 17, no. 3 (2008): 419–59.

3 Jordan Lancaster, "House Passes Bill Aimed at Reducing Rape Kit Backlog," *The Hill*, October 24, 2019, https://thehill.com/blogs/blog-briefing-room/467365-house-passes-bill-aimed-at-reducing-rape-kit-backlog; Ralph R. Ortega, "Rep. Carolyn Maloney Wants More Paid Leave for Federal Employees," *City & State*, July 9, 2021, https://www.cityandstateny.com/personality/2021/07/rep-carolyn-maloney-wants-more-paid-leave-federal-employees/183670/.

4 Martha Stewart, "Angry Lawmakers Challenge Lineup at Hearing: 'Where Are the Women?'" *CNN*, February 17, 2012, https://www.cnn.com/2012/02/16/politics/women-lawmakers-hearing/.

5 Michael Rock, "Maloney's Women's History Museum Bill Passes Congress," *New York County Politics*, January 4, 2021, https://politicsny.com/2021/01/04/maloneys-womens-history-museum-bill-passes-congress/.

6 Nancy Vu, "Outgoing Rep. Carolyn Maloney Will Be the Next President of the New York Chapter of the National Organization for Women," *Politico*, December 23, 2022, https://www.politico.com/minutes/congress/12-23-2022/maloney-president-now-ny/.

7 Virginia Chamlee, "Congresswoman Carolyn Maloney Calls for 'Equal Rights for Women' with Suffragette-Themed Met Gala Dress," *People*, September 14, 2021, https://people.com/style/congresswoman-carolyn-maloney-wears-suffragette-themed-met-gala-dress/.

8 "Pink ghetto" is a term that signifies jobs customarily held by women (i.e., "women's work"). See Renee Nicole Allen, Alicia Jackson, and DeShun Harris, "The 'Pink Ghetto' Pipeline: Challenges and Opportunities for Women in Legal Education," *University of Detroit Mercy Law Review* 96 (Summer 2019): 525–55.

9 Shannon Henry, "Male-Female Salary Gap Growing, Study Says," *Washington Post*, January 24, 2002, https://www.washingtonpost.com/archive/politics/2002/01/24/male-female-salary-gap-growing-study-says/081e9dc5-83e7-4573-9939-b289b4564c49/.

It's Not Here

Speech on the U.S. Capitol Steps

TERRY O'NEILL
January 5, 2011[1]

When law professor Terry O'Neill (1953–present) was teaching feminist legal theory at Louisiana's Tulane University, she entered the political fray by joining the resistance to Grand Wizard of the Ku Klux Klan David Duke's 1991 run for governor. She went door-to-door in her neighborhood to get the word out, likely aided by the fact that she studied speech at Northwestern University in the 1970s.[2] That political activism against violent white nationalism, in part, prompted her to join NOW the next year. Domestic violence fueled her activism as well. O'Neill left an abusive marriage in her twenties and consequently pursued a legal education to fight for women's rights. "My experience with domestic violence as an abused wife left me humiliated and embarrassed. I only began to talk about this publicly five years ago as I realized to keep quiet was to continue the abuse. I want to empower women and telling my story does just that," she said upon her election as NOW's president in 2009.[3]

O'Neill worked on both Hillary Clinton and Barack Obama's 2008 presidential campaigns but also worried that the Democratic Party was losing credibility with women voters.[4] As to the ERA, in March 2011, the Obama-era White House Council on Women and Girls released "the first comprehensive federal report on women" since the 1963 PCSW report. Unlike the 1963 report which took the position of "not now" on the ERA, the 2011 report made no mention of it all.[5] And so, when the 112th Congress opened its session and read the Constitution aloud, O'Neill and three congresspersons—including Carolyn Maloney—stood outside on the U.S. Capitol steps and confronted the fact that women had not yet been included in the supreme law of the land. O'Neill's short speech was folksy and even comical as she flipped through Representative Moore's

Constitution looking for any reference to women. And yet, no newspaper or media outlet covered it whatsoever.

When I heard that John Boehner[6] had decided to read the Constitution of the United States on the House floor, I thought to myself, "Oh! So, I wonder what he'll do when they get to the part of the Constitution that guarantees equal rights for all women?" So, I borrowed Congresswoman Moore's[7] Constitution book. Let me see, let's see, where is it ... Here's Article 1, Article 2 ... Hmmm. It's not here.

Let's flip to the amendments. Oh! Oh wait, Amendment 19! Oh, Amendment 19 is just about the vote. It was very important, and it does talk about women, but it just guarantees the vote.

Oh! Amendment 14! Maybe that says something. What does it say? "Nor shall any state deprive any person of equal rights under the law." But gee, a man in power like Antonin Scalia insists that the word "person" in the Fourteenth Amendment doesn't apply to half the population of the United States. A man in power like Speaker of the House of Representatives John Boehner last year led the fight to stop the passage of the Paycheck Fairness Act, which would have made it possible finally for women to start closing that wage gap.

As long as there are men in power in this country that keep women down, we have to have an explicit guarantee of equality in the Constitution. That's why we need a constitutional equality amendment. That's why we need Representative Maloney. That's why we need Senator Menendez[8] and Representative Moore and all the other brave legislators that are supporting us. Thank you.

Notes

1 Terry O'Neill, "It's Not here," *NOW Rally*, Washington, D.C., January 6, 2011. https://www.youtube.com/watch?v=Ulm2M6J_oTc&ab_channel=NationalOrganizationforWomen%28NOW%29. Reprinted with permission from Terry O'Neill.

2 "Fmr. NOW Chief Terry O'Neill Is Tulane Law Graduation Speaker," Tulane University, January 10, 2018, https://law.tulane.edu/news/fmr-now-chief-terry-oneill-tulane-law-graduation-speaker; Courtney Vaughn, "NOW and Then: Feminist Leader Terry O'Neill Lands in Portland," *Portland Tribune*, July 7, 2022, https://www.portlandtribune.com/news/now-and-then-feminist-leader-terry-oneill-lands-in-portland/article_e812891a-87e3-5770-92a8-1e89ca7a2180.html; "Terry O'Neill '74 on NOW: Past, Present, and Future," Northwestern University Giving, July 7, 2016,

https://giving.northwestern.edu/s/1479/282-giving/basic-page-nonav-campaign.aspx?sid=1479&gid=282&calcid=14699&calpgid=8420&pgid=19680&crid=0.

3 Associated Press, "NOW Elects MD. Woman President," *El Paso Times*, June 22, 2009, 3A.

4 "Terry O'Neill," Equal Means Equal, https://equalmeansequal.com/terry-oneill/; Matea Gold and Jordan Steffen, "Female Voters Desert Democrats," *Los Angeles Times*, November 9, 2010, 5.

5 "White House Releases First Comprehensive Federal Report on the Status of American Women in Almost 50 Years," White House, Office of the Press Secretary, March 1, 2011, https://obamawhitehouse.archives.gov/the-press-office/2011/03/01/white-house-releases-first-comprehensive-federal-report-status-american-; *Women in America: Indicators of Social and Economic Well-Being*, U.S. Department of Commerce Economics and Statistics Administration and Executive Office of the President Office of Management and Budget, March 2011, https://obamawhitehouse.archives.gov/sites/default/files/rss_viewer/Women_in_America.pdf.

6 John Boehner (R-OH) served in the House of Representatives from 1991 to 2015, and served as Speaker of the House from 2011 to 2015.

7 Gwendolynne "Gwen" Moore (D-WI) has served in the House of Representatives since 2005.

8 Robert Menendez (D-NJ) served in the House of Representatives from 1993 to 2006 and has served in the Senate since 2006.

Supporting the Equal Rights Amendment

Blog Post for the Obama White House Website

TINA TCHEN
June 22, 2011[1]

Christina "Tina" Tchen (1956–present) grew up in Columbus, Ohio, the daughter of Chinese immigrants. After graduating from Harvard University, she relocated to Springfield, Illinois to work for the Department of Child and Family Services and became a chapter president for NOW as the ERA debate waged on. The recent college graduate worked the phone banks and lobbied for the ERA in Phyllis Schlafly's home state before departing to attend law school at Northwestern University.[2] Tchen practiced as an attorney for much of her career before joining forces with an up-and-coming Chicago politician named Barack Obama. Tchen held a number of positions in the Obama White House including Deputy Assistant to the President, Executive Director of the White House Council on Women and Girls, and Chief of Staff to the First Lady. With Michelle Obama, Tchen took on issues such as championing girls' education around the world and fighting sexual assault on college campuses.[3] Since her time in the White House, Tchen has consulted on workplace culture for women and minority staff with the Southern Poverty Law Center and served as President and CEO of *TIME'S UP* to fight against victims of sexual assault and harassment from 2019 to 2021.[4]

During the 2012 presidential election, the Democratic Party platform reaffirmed support for the Equal Rights Amendment while the Republican Party platform did not, as it had not since 1980. Republican Mitt Romney's campaign remained silent about the ERA, while the incumbent Barack Obama's campaign stressed that he was a longtime supporter of the amendment (even though it just simply was not a legislative priority of his presidency).[5] Tchen's blog post for the White House website shared her own ERA story, reiterated the president's support for the amendment, and emphasized the legislative victories for gender equality achieved under Obama's tenure. More broadly, Tchen's post can be read as a response to critiques—like Terry O'Neill's speech—that Obama and Democrats had not done enough to propel the ERA forward since 2008. While Tchen expressed a vague Democratic "reaffirmation of support" for the ERA, she offered no specifics about its ratification status and provided no specific plan for moving it forward should Obama be re-elected in 2012. Women's advances, she underscored, were nonetheless progressing under Obama's leadership.

Earlier today, Senator Robert Menendez and Representative Carolyn Maloney reintroduced the Equal Rights Amendment (ERA). I am proud to serve in the Obama Administration, as this is one of so many policies important to women that the President strongly supports.

When I lived in Springfield, Illinois in 1978, I was transfixed by the ERA debate in the General Assembly. It amazes me that the ERA has been painted as a radical idea, not only upon its introduction in 1923, but even when it passed both houses of Congress in 1972. Its premise is quite simple: men and women shall have equal rights under the law. It is hard to imagine an argument against this basic concept. I remember wearing a 59-cent pin to represent the wage gap at the time—and to show my support for ratification. It was the first time I learned about the importance of public engagement and saw firsthand some of the frustrations of the political process. In 1982, the ERA ultimately failed when it fell three states short of the 38 states required for ratification before the deadline. Since then, women have broken countless barriers, and we have taken huge strides to strengthen our position in society. But the fact remains: women are still underpaid and underrepresented in our country.

It is a source of pride for me and my colleagues that President Obama has a proven track record of supporting the ERA. As an Illinois State Senator, he was a sponsor of a joint resolution ratifying the Equal Rights Amendment, and as a United States Senator he was a cosponsor of the Women's Equality Amendment. Under then-Senator Obama's leadership, the 2008 Democratic Party Platform also reaffirmed support for the Equal Rights Amendment and laid out a strong stance to ensure women's rights.[6]

It is no secret that President Obama has placed an emphasis on supporting women and girls throughout his career and, in particular, since the day he took office. The first bill he signed into law was the Lilly Ledbetter Fair Pay Act,[7] and he created the White House Council on Women and Girls,[8] whose aim is to ensure that the Federal Government takes the interests of women and girls into account, particularly as we consider and amend public policy.

Recently, President Obama said, "History shows that countries are more prosperous and more peaceful when women are empowered." This principle rings true in every country and every era. Of note, that recent quote originates from a speech he was making about the Middle East and North Africa. This basic truth resonates just as strongly at home. That is why this Administration is committed to protecting and advancing the role of women and girls in every aspect of society. From protecting women's health to helping women realize their full economic potential; and from ending violence against women to promoting international women's rights, I am gratified to know and report that this Administration is working each day to improve the lives of women and girls in the United States and around the world.

Notes

1 Tina Tchen, "Supporting the Equal Rights Amendment," White House, June 22, 2011, https://obamawhitehouse.archives.gov/blog/2011/06/22/supporting-equal-rights-amendment. Public Domain.

2 Carrie N. Baker, "My ERA Story: Time's Up CEO Got Her Feminist Start Working for the ERA," *Ms. Magazine*, March 16, 2021, https://msmagazine.com/2021/03/16/my-era-story-times-up-ceo-feminist-equal-rights-amendment-tina-tchen-illinois/; Kerri Lee Alexander, "Tina Tchen," National Women's History Museum, https://www.womenshistory.org/education-resources/biographies/tina-tchen.

3 Amelia Lester, "Tina Tchen on Time's Up and Working for the Obamas," *Sydney Morning Herald*, February 9, 2019, https://www.smh.com.au/world/north-america/tina-tchen-on-time-s-up-and-working-for-the-obamas-20190205-p50vq2.html.

4 Matt Pearce, "Southern Poverty Law Center Picks Michelle Obama's Former Chief of Staff Tina Tchen to Investigate Workplace Complaints," *Chicago Tribune*, March 18, 2019, https://www.chicagotribune.com/nation-world/ct-southern-poverty-law-center-tina-tchen-20190318-story.html.

5 Roberta Francis, "Obama, Romney, and the Equal Rights Amendment," *Huffington Post*, December 31, 2012, https://www.huffpost.com/entry/women-equal-rights-_b_2044309.

6 The platform simply states "we reaffirm our support for the Equal Rights Amendment." See "2008 Democratic Party Platform," *American Presidency Project*, https://www.presidency.ucsb.edu/documents/2008-democratic-party-platform.

7 The Lilly Ledbetter Fair Pay Act (2009) establishes that "an unlawful employment practice occurs when: (1) a discriminatory compensation decision or other practice is adopted; (2) an individual becomes subject to the decision or practice; or (3) an individual is affected by application of the decision or practice, including each time wages, benefits, or other compensation is paid." See "S. 181—Lilly Ledbetter Fair Pay Act of 2009," United States Congress, https://www.congress.gov/bill/111th-congress/senate-bill/181.

8 President Obama created the Council by Executive Order and in an advisory capacity to "be responsible for providing recommendations to the President on the effects of pending legislation and executive branch policy proposals; for suggesting changes to Federal programs or policies to address issues of special importance to women and girls; for reviewing and recommending changes to policies that have a distinct impact on women in the Federal workforce; and for assisting in the development of legislative and policy proposals of special importance to women and girls." See "Executive Order 13506—Creating the White House Council on Women and Girls," White House, March 11, 2009, https://obamawhitehouse.archives.gov/the-press-office/executive-order-creating-white-house-council-women-and-girls; "The White House Council on Women and Girls," White House, Washington, D.C., https://obamawhitehouse.archives.gov/administration/eop/cwg.

Section VI The Debate Persists: 2016–2023

When the *Washington Post* received a 2005 recording of then-presidential candidate Donald Trump's crass entitlement to non-consensually grabbing women's bodies during the 2016 election, the nation really believed his dabbling in national politics was over.[1] Both sides of the political aisle were aghast, especially Trump's Republican running mate, fundamentalist Christian, Mike Pence. But Trump survived the controversy to win the presidency against Hillary Clinton, a formidable opponent and the first female candidate to reach the general election. Countless American women were appalled. They saw what their safety and sanctity were now worth to many of their fellow citizens. To let their voices be heard clearly, on the day after Trump's inauguration in 2017, between 3 and 5 million people around the country marched in solidarity with half a million people marching on Washington, D.C. These dissenters wore "pussy hats"—a play on Trump's crass brag—and "pussycats"—knitted and crocheted in hot pink by crafters nationwide. Cisgender men and women wore them. Black, brown, and white people wore them. Muslim, Jewish, and Christian people wore them. Transgender people donned variations.[2] All gathered to demand equality and to organize their voices ahead of what would be four years of political chaos where women systematically saw their rights rolled back.

Donald Trump's first move was to nominate Jeff Sessions for Attorney General. Anti-Trump feminist senator and ERA supporter Elizabeth Warren (D-MA) read a letter from her predecessor Edward Kennedy calling Sessions "a disgrace." Warren continued with another opposing letter from Coretta Scott King, and that's when Republican Steve Daines (R-MT) interrupted her for deriding Sessions' character. Warren responded that she was citing Kennedy and King, whose words were already a part of the Senate record, and so Daines permitted her to continue. As Warren got to the part in King's letter stating, "Mr. Sessions has used the awesome power of his office to chill the free exercise of the vote by Black citizens," Senate Majority Leader Mitch McConnell (R-KY) objected. Daines, then, called for a vote, and the Republican-majority Senate voted for Warren to be silent for the remainder of the hearing. McConnell went on to explain, "Senator Warren was giving a lengthy speech. She had appeared to violate the rule. She was warned. She was given an explanation. Nevertheless, she persisted."[3]

Now clad in their pussyhats and with a new slogan to "persist," American women seized the moment. Nevada State Senator Pat Spearman capitalized on the verb "persist" and challenged her audience to join feminists from the last century to get women's equality enshrined in America's most sacred political text. Her state ratified the Equal Rights Amendment in March 2017, exactly 35 years after the 1982 deadline passed. Seven months later, after shocking revelations of Hollywood producer Harvey Weinstein's Trump-like misogyny and entitlement, actress Alyssa Milano built on the ideas and labor of longtime activist Tarana Burke[4] and wrote on Twitter, "If you've been sexually harassed or assaulted write 'me too' as a reply to this tweet."[5] A new hashtag and movement had arrived: #MeToo. By the 2018 midterm elections, women were fully awake—and so was the ERA. A record number of 117 women were sent to Congress that year.[6]

Human rights lawyer Jessica Neuwirth concurrently started the ERA Coalition in 2018 as an umbrella organization to some one-hundred national and local groups pursuing the ERA's ratification through lobbying, campaigning, educating, and protesting.[7] The coalition's numerous partners reflect a diverse combination of longtime ERA supporters, previous ERA opponents, and new groups on the political scene. Among them are the AFL-CIO, the Alice Paul Institute, the American Association of University Women, the Coalition of Labor Union Women, the Feminist Majority Foundation, the General Federation of Women's Club, the Gay and Lesbian Alliance Against Defamation (GLAAD), the League of Women Voters (and several state LWV chapters), Mormons for ERA, Ms. Foundation for Women and *Ms. Magazine*, the National Association of Women Lawyers, the National Congress of Black Women, the National Council of Jewish Women, the National Council of Negro Women, NOW (and several NOW state chapters), the National Woman's Party, the National Women's Political Caucus, the Women's Law Project, and the YWCA.[8] In January 2021, Columbia Law School's Center for Gender and Sexuality Law launched "The ERA Project" as a resource for generating ERA-related research, publishing policy papers, holding workshops, and partnering with other groups to make the ERA the 28th Amendment to the U.S. Constitution.[9]

Quantitative research in the twenty-first century proved that Americans overwhelmingly support the ERA as well. A 2020 Pew Research Poll found that 78% of American adults, including those who do not identify as feminists, endorsed adding the Equal Rights Amendment to the Constitution.[10] Ironically, a different 2020 poll concluded that 72% of Americans erroneously believed the ERA is *already* in the Constitution—underscoring the fact that vast misinformation about the ERA endures.[11]

The ERA was, once again, on the move.

As in the 1970s, Utah's LDS women have been among the vocal supporters and opponents during the ERA's renewal. Never-Trumper and lawyer Michelle Quist renewed the old Republican support for the ERA with some familiar arguments, while Professor Valerie M. Hudson wondered what the new "rush" to pass the amendment is about. Hudson urged readers to consider carefully both the motives of the ERA's supporters and the multifaceted ramifications of the amendment if passed. Texas Congresswoman Sylvia Garcia coalesced the Latina support by asserting that the amendment would benefit women of color who are paid less than men and face sexual harassment and assault. The ERA would, she believed, go a long way in addressing these societal ills.

In Virginia, an unprecedented rhetor added new layers of meaning to what passing the ERA might accomplish. The first openly transgender state-elected official, Danica Roem, joined the ERA debate with excommunicated Mormon feminist Kate Kelly and gave voice to what the amendment would mean for LGBTQIA+ rights amid contentious cultural debates about gender identity, roles, expression, discrimination, and inclusion. With Roem and Congresswoman Jennifer Carroll Foy leading the way, Virginia became the 38th state to ratify the Equal Rights Amendment in January 2020 which, many have strenuously argued, *already* makes it the 28th Amendment to the Constitution—97 years after its proposal and 48 years after its Congressional approval.[12]

The ERA's opponents responded swiftly and, in some cases, with now-familiar unconventional creativity. The Eagle Forum has retained a steady flow of anti-ERA articles on its website, such as a May 27, 2023 article capitalizing on Betty Friedan's assertion to Phyllis Schlafly that she would like to "burn you at the stake!" to advance familiar opposing arguments in the twenty-first century.[13] In a similar vein, Doreen Denny of the Concerned Women for America renamed the ERA as the "Every Right to Abortion" amendment.[14] Denny's argument reflected a much broader rhetorical trend by various right-wing, antiabortion groups that—alongside the Eagle Forum and CWA—have in recent years lobbied against the ERA on the basis of that it might strengthen access to abortion services. Three of those groups are Susan B. Anthony Pro-Life America, the National Right to Life Committee, and Students for Life America—all groups that, some critics have asserted, accept unknown amounts of dark money to "undermine the amendment."[15]

In Congress, women have stayed divided as well, yet have still found opportunities for bipartisan cooperation reminiscent of decades past. Republican Senators Susan Collins (R-ME) and Lisa Murkowski (R-AK) departed from their party's line and have been vocal ERA advocates. "It has been nearly 50 years since Congress passed the ERA with overwhelming support from both sides of the aisle ... Congress should remove this roadblock that could impede the full ratification of the ERA," Collins observed as cosponsor (along with Murkowski) of a resolution to remove the ratification deadline.[16] And yet, some women in the House—led by Representatives Vicky Hartzler (R-MO) and Marjorie Taylor Greene (R-GA)—have used their platform to advance Denny's line of argument and to express additional concerns about both gender identity and procedure surrounding the ratification deadline.

Nancy Pelosi (D-CA) disagreed with those concerns. As the first female Speaker of the House, she was the first woman to ever be third in line for the Presidency and, thus, broke a political glass ceiling. In 2021, she vowed that America will keep its promise of equality to women. On March 22, 2022—the fiftieth anniversary of Congress passing the ERA—Representative Carolyn Maloney wrote to the National Archives (an executive agency her committee oversaw) explaining that "women and people of all marginalized genders across the United States continue to experience discrimination on the basis of sex. The only way to ensure true and equal protection under the law is to cement the ERA into the U.S. Constitution."[17] A year later, exactly one hundred years after the ERA's first introduction to Congress, Representative Ayanna Pressley (D-MA) stood on the steps of the Capitol surrounded by her sisters in Congress to announce the formation of a new twenty-first-century Caucus for the ERA.

Despite this reinvigorated interest, the three new state ratifications, and the joint resolution that removed the original ratification deadline passed by the House of Representatives in 2021, the ERA's future remained legally and politically uncertain at the close of 2023. Passing the ERA inspired a heated exchange between two Democratic candidates in Election 2020: then-Senator Kamala Harris (D-CA) and former Vice President Joe Biden. Harris distinguished herself from Biden by claiming that the ERA was necessary "to preserve the civil rights of all people."[18] After the two teamed up into a single ticket, the Biden/Harris campaign website promised that, if elected, "Biden will work with advocates across the country to pass the Equal Rights

Amendment so women's rights are once and for all explicitly enshrined in our Constitution."[19] Harris even pledged to help get the ERA passed within her first 100 days in office.[20] As recently as Women's Equality Day in August 2023, the Biden/Harris administration issued a proclamation assuring that "this year, we also mark the 100th anniversary of the introduction of the Equal Rights Amendment. It is long past time to definitively enshrine the principle of gender equality in the Constitution, and I will continue to fight for the Equal Rights Amendment as I have throughout my career."[21] And yet, Democratic inaction from the Biden/Harris administration thus far continues to disappoint pro-ERA women's groups and advocates. As *Chicago Tribune* columnist Michele Thorne put it in 2022, the administration (including Attorney General Merrick Garland) has done little more than "offer thoughts and prayers" for the ERA.[22]

Moreover, the current senate bill for ratification removal does not have support from 60 senators—the amount needed to bypass a filibuster. The stalemate was even more plain on April 27, 2023, when the ERA failed to generate the needed votes to move forward, despite bipartisan votes from Senators Collins and Murkowski. Should the ERA manage to pass in the Senate, it is unclear as to whether the amendment's status would reach the Supreme Court and if it would be rendered unconstitutional by the conservative-leaning majority on a bench stacked with three deeply conservative Trump appointees.[23]

The ERA's conservative challengers in the Senate voted down the measure on at least four familiar grounds that have constituted the twenty-first-century opposition.[24] First, some suggested that the Fourteenth Amendment already protects women and, therefore, the ERA is superfluous. Second, critics cited the expired ratification deadline and insisted that passing the ERA now would be procedurally flawed, a view in keeping with the 2021 U.S. District Court ruling that the newest state ratifications "came too late to count."[25] ERA supporters countered that Article V of the Constitution authorizes Congress to decide the "mode of ratification" and, therefore, allows Congress to impose and rescind ratification deadlines.[26] Third, many contended that revival of the ERA was a blatant attempt to counter the Supreme Court ruling in *Dobbs v. Jackson*. "Why bring back the ERA now?" asked Emma Waters of the conservative Heritage Foundation. Because, she maintained, "the radical Left have worked tirelessly to enshrine abortion in federal regulations and state law."[27] Senator Lindsey Graham (R-SC), who openly fist-bumped GOP colleagues when delivering his "no" vote on the Senate joint resolution, gave voice to a fourth reservation anticipated by Danica Roem and Kate Kelly's arguments in this section. Graham suggested that Senate Republicans should oppose the ERA not only because ratification would threaten antiabortion measures but also because it could allow transgender athletes to compete in sports that align with their gender identity.[28] A week before the Senate vote on the ERA ratification deadline, the House of Representatives divulged its majority position on this particular issue by passing legislation banning transgender women and girls from participating in women's sports.[29]

The ERA's twenty-first-century supporters struggled to hide their disappointment and frustration. In an appearance at the Boston Public Library after the vote, Ayanna Pressley took issue not only with the fact that there were opposing votes but also with the visibly cavalier way in which those votes were expressed: "It was very demoralizing to see Republicans in the Senate defiantly putting a thumbs down. I mean, they were just so defiant and indignant and proud to be putting a thumbs down as if they don't have mothers or women in their family or raising daughters. Nothing should be controversial about this."[30] On July 13, 2023, Representative Cori Bush (D-MO) and Senator Kristen Gillibrand (D-NY) introduced a joint resolution stating that the ERA has already met its ratification threshold and that the United States archivist must finalize the amendment. Pressley, Bush, Gillibrand, and others have vowed to keep the ERA alive.[31]

A new generation of activists is also keeping the ERA alive. Following the 2022 *Dobbs* decision, high school seniors Rosie Couture and Belan Yeshigeta took a small group from Arlington, Virginia into the national spotlight to form "Generation Ratify," a "youth-led movement to ratify the Equal Rights Amendment and advance gender equality in the United States of America."[32] The young people of Generation Ratify have partnered with ERA-supporting politicians in Congress and the ERA Coalition to raise up their voices in favor of the amendment through rallies, protests, workshops, blogs, and webinars.

On July 21, 2023, ERA supporters in Congress, Generation Ratify, the ERA Coalition, and the ERA Project held an historic three-day meeting in Seneca Falls, New York, to mark the centennial anniversary of when Alice Paul unveiled the ERA. Nearly three hundred ERA supporters gathered for an "interfaith ERA revival," a march and rally, and breakout sessions "on organizing for equality, intergenerational and cross movement coalition building, state and local ERA organizing and faith organizing." Many of the women in this volume—Sylvia Garcia, Carolyn Maloney, Kate Kelly, Ayanna Pressley, Ellie Smeal, and Pat Spearman—participated that weekend. Generation Ratify's Rosie Couture aptly summed up the significance of the meeting: "The contemporary movement for the Equal Rights Amendment truly is inclusive, expansive and intersectional, and centers the people that stand to gain the most from the ERA."[33]

As this next generation forges ahead to keep the ERA alive, we are left to wonder: Are we there? Are womankind and sisterhood united for the good of America writ large? Will women remain divided on the ERA? Will it take another century to see it enshrined in the U.S. Constitution? The ERA debate, nevertheless, persists.

Notes

1 David A. Fahrenthold, "Trump Recorded Having Extremely Lewd Conversation about Women in 2005," *Washington Post*, October 7, 2016, www.washingtonpost.com/politics/trump-recorded-having-extremely-lewd-conversation-about-women-in-2005/2016/10/07/3b9ce776-8cb4-11e6-bf8a-3d26847eeed4_story.html.

2 I, Camille, personally knitted five hot-pink hats for march attendees as well as one hot-pink-and-electric-blue variation for a transgender friend.

3 "Congressional Record—Senate," *Congress.gov*, February 7, 2017, S853.

4 Sandra E. Garcia, "The Woman Who Created #MeToo Long Before Hashtags," *New York Times*, October 20, 2017, www.nytimes.com/2017/10/20/us/me-too-movement-tarana-burke.html.

5 Alyssa Milano, *Twitter.com*, October 15, 2017, twitter.com/Alyssa_Milano/status/919659438700670976.

6 Maya Salam, "A Record 117 Women Won Office, Reshaping America's Leadership," *New York Times*, November 7, 2018, www.nytimes.com/2018/11/07/us/elections/women-elected-midterm-elections.html.

7 Jessica Neuwirth, *Equal Means Equal: Why the Time for an Equal Rights Amendment Is Now* (New York: The New Press, 2015).

8 "Our Partners," ERA Coalition, eracoalition.org/partners/.

9 "Team & Mission," The ERA Project, Center for Gender and Sexuality Law, Columbia Law School, https://gender-sexuality.law.columbia.edu/content/team-mission; "The Intertwining History of NOW and the ERA," National Organization for Women, https://now.org/the-intertwining-history-of-now-and-the-era/.

10 Rachel Minkin, "Most Americans Support Gender Equality, Even If They Don't Identify as Feminists," *Pew Research Center*, July 14, 2020, www.pewresearch.org/short-reads/2020/07/14/most-americans-support-gender-equality-even-if-they-dont-identify-as-feminists/.

11 "The Equal Rights Amendment and Discrimination against Women," AP-NORC, University of Chicago, January 16–21, 2020, https://apnorc.org/projects/the-equal-rights-amendment-and-discrimination-against-women/?doing_wp_cron=1678463939.1467111110687255859375.

12 "Pressley, Cardin, Colleagues Unveil Resolution Affirming Ratification of the Equal Rights Amendment," *House.gov*, January 31, 2023, https://pressley.house.gov/2023/01/31/pressley-cardin-murkowski-dean-garcia-spanberger-bush-kamlager-dove-unveil-resolution-affirming-ratification-of-the-equal-rights-amendment/; Carrie N. Baker, " 'The Equal Rights Amendment Has Been Ratified. It Is the Law': U.S. House Resolution Declares ERA 28th Amendment," *Ms. Magazine*, January 27, 2022, https://msmagazine.com/2022/01/27/equal-rights-amendment-resolution-us-house-28th-amendment-constitution/.

13 Shia Kapos, "Betty Friedan's Most Famous Quote Is an Attack on a Woman," *Eagle Forum*, May 27, 2023, https://eagleforum.org/publications/cori-commentary/id-like-to-burn-you-at-the-stake.html; see further https://eagleforum.org/topics/era.html.
14 Doreen Denny, "How the Battle for the ERA Became Every Right to Abortion," *Concerned Women for America*, February 10, 2020, https://concernedwomen.org/how-the-battle-for-the-era-became-every-right-to-abortion/.
15 Ansev Demirhan, "The Same Groups That Helped Overturn Roe and Attack Abortion Pills Are Also Lobbying Against the ERA," *Ms. Magazine*, April 11, 2023, https://msmagazine.com/2023/04/11/anti-abortion-groups-era-equal-rights-amendment/.
16 "Senator Collins Co-Sponsors Bipartisan Legislation to Remove the ERA Deadline, Finalize Ratification," May 7, 2021, www.collins.senate.gov/newsroom/senator-collins-co-sponsors-bipartisan-resolution-remove-era-deadline-finalize-ratification.
17 Carolyn Maloney, "Letter from Chairwoman Maloney to Archivist David Ferriero," *Records Related to the Equal Rights Amendment*, March 22, 2022, www.archives.gov/foia/records-related-equal-rights-amendment.
18 "Kamala Harris Attacks Joe Biden's Record on Race in Democratic Debate," *Guardian News*, June 28, 2019, www.youtube.com/watch?v=S6-UC8yr0Aw.
19 Lloyd Grove, " 'This Is Some Bullshit': Women's Group Rails Against Biden Inaction on Equal Rights Amendment," *Daily Beast*, June 10, 2021, www.thedailybeast.com/this-is-some-bullshit-womens-group-rails-against-biden-inaction-on-the-equal-rights-amendment.
20 Chloe Angyal, "Kamala Harris Says It's Time To Make Women Full Citizens at Last," *Marie Claire*, February 28, 2019, www.marieclaire.com/politics/a26551159/kamala-harris-equal-rights-amendment/.
21 "A Proclamation on Women's Equality Day, 2023," White House, August 25, 2023, www.whitehouse.gov/briefing-room/presidential-actions/2023/08/25/a-proclamation-on-womens-equality-day-2023/.
22 Michele Thorne, "The Biden Administration Offers Thoughts and Prayers on the ERA. Can It Do More?" *Chicago Tribune*, September 26, 2022, www.chicagotribune.com/2022/09/26/michele-thorne-the-biden-administration-offers-thoughts-and-prayers-on-the-era-can-it-do-more/.
23 H. J. Res. 17—Removing the Deadline for the Ratification of the Equal Rights Amendment, 117th Congress (2021–2022), www.congress.gov/bill/117th-congress/house-joint-resolution/17; Alexandra Hutzler, "Senate Fails to Extend Deadline to Ratify Equal Rights Amendment as Most Republicans Vote No," *ABC News*, April 27, 2023, https://abcnews.go.com/Politics/senate-fails-extend-deadline-ratify-equal-rights-amendment/story?id=98908318; Julie C. Suk, *After Misogyny: How the Law Fails Women and What to Do about It* (Oakland: University of California Press, 2023), 230.
24 "Editorial: Failure to Move the Equal Rights Amendment Says It All About Today's GOP," *St. Louis Post-Dispatch*, May 4, 2023, www.stltoday.com/opinion/editorial/editorial-failure-to-move-the-equal-rights-amendment-says-it-all-about-todays-gop/article_d3c29676-e5e6-11ed-9b5d-232defae47d8.html.

25 Katharine Jackson, "U.S. Equal Rights Amendment Blocked Again, A Century After Introduction," *Reuters*, April 27, 2023, www.reuters.com/legal/government/us-equal-rights-amendment-blocked-again-century-after-introduction-2023-04-27/.

26 Kate Shaw and Julie C. Suk, "It's Time to Reacquaint Americans With the Possibility of Changing the Constitution. Here's Where to Begin," *New York Times*, May 2, 2023, www.nytimes.com/2023/05/02/opinion/equal-rights-amendment-constitution.html.

27 Emma Waters, "Want to Protect Life? Oppose Revival of the Equal Rights Amendment," *Heritage Foundation*, March 1, 2023, www.heritage.org/life/commentary/want-protect-life-oppose-revival-the-equal-rights-amendment.

28 Emily Jacobs, "Schumer's Equal Rights Amendment Vote Fails 51-47 in Senate," *Washington Examiner*, April 27, 2023, www.washingtonexaminer.com/news/senate/schumer-equal-rights-amendment-vote-failure.

29 Annie Karni, "House Passes Bill to Bar Transgender Athletes from Female Sports Teams," *New York Times*, April 20, 2023, www.nytimes.com/2023/04/20/us/politics/transgender-athlete-ban-bill.html.

30 Alvin Buyinza, "Ayanna Pressley Promises To 'Take the Mantle' of Equal Rights Amendment Fight," *Mass Live*, May 3, 2023, www.masslive.com/news/2023/05/ayanna-pressley-promises-to-take-the-mantle-of-equal-rights-amendment-fight.html.

31 Alexandra Hutzler, "Democrats Unveil New Effort to Rescue the Equal Rights Amendment," *ABC News*, July 13, 2023, https://abcnews.go.com/Politics/democrats-unveil-new-effort-enforce-equal-rights-amendment/story?id=101220031.

32 "Rosie Couture and Belan Yeshigeta, Executive Directors of Generation Ratify at Rally for ERA," September 29, 2021, www.youtube.com/watch?v=xkkHUWvNQr0; "About," Generation Ratify, www.generationratify.org/about.

33 Carrie N. Baker, "ERA Centennial Convention in Seneca Falls: Intergenerational, Diverse and Determined," *Ms. Magazine*, July 26, 2023, https://msmagazine.com/2023/07/26/seneca-falls-equal-rights-amendment/.

We All Must Persist

Address to the Nevada Assembly Committee on Legislative Operations and Elections

Pat Spearman
March 7, 2017[1]

Since her election to the state senate, Dr. Patricia "Pat" Ann Spearman (1955–present) relentlessly pursued ERA ratification in Nevada. Spearman endured racial slurs and physical violence as a student of color when she integrated her Alabama high school, and confronted sexism as the first woman to earn a Military Police Corps "Regular Army" commission. She worked up to the rank of Lieutenant Colonel and, along the way, studied at the Episcopal Theological Seminary of the Southwest to become an ordained Methodist minister. Her foray into politics started with volunteering for Barack Obama's presidential campaign in 2008 and culminated in her achievement as the first lesbian elected to the Nevada legislature in 2012.[2]

Thirty-five years after the ERA's ratification deadline passed, the state of Nevada astonishingly passed the amendment on March 22, 2017, making it the 36th state to ratify. Spearman shepherded the ERA along beginning in 2015.[3] Detractors accused her of mounting a "publicity stunt," but Spearman persevered as the ERA's chief sponsor.[4] "We have delayed passage long enough," she countered: "Now is the time to show the country, and the global neighborhood, we as Nevadans lead when it comes to equality for all."[5] Spearman's impassioned speech before her colleagues and some 40 visitors earlier that month foregrounded an hour-long debate about Senate Joint Resolution 2 to ratify the ERA. As Spearman delivered a speech that honored those who came before her—from Ruth Bader Ginsburg to Shirley Chisholm—several of her fellow senators dressed in white, echoing a strategy reminiscent of the suffragists a century earlier. In so doing, Spearman and her colleagues paved the way for other states—like Illinois and Virginia—to soon follow suit.[6]

I represent Senate District No. 1. It is an honor to be here today to introduce Senate Joint Resolution 2, which, in my opinion, is one of the most historic pieces of legislation that the Nevada Legislature has considered in many years. This legislation brings years of remarkable history to the forefront. It recognizes the decades-long plight of women and men who have fought for equal rights, fairness in the workplace, gender equality, and safeguards against sex discrimination. To put it succinctly, this resolution is about equality under the law for all people regardless of their gender. There is no hidden agenda or Trojan horse to allow people to marry the Eiffel Tower or lose Social Security benefits when a spouse dies. It is not about subversive activity to ignore physical differences. It is about equality.

In many respects, given the social and political challenges seen in recent years, the continuing debate to ratify the Equal Rights Amendment (ERA) baffles the mind and perpetuates the myth of patriarchal superiority. It normalizes misogyny and moderates the collective cognitive dissonance related to universal equality. Frankly, I am surprised this resolution has not already been adopted. Now is the time for S.J.R. 2, which calls for Nevada's ratification of the Equal Rights Amendment to the U.S. Constitution, to become a reality.

By way of a bit of history, Congress passed the Equal Rights Amendment in 1972 and sent it to the states for ratification. At that time, Congress set a seven-year time limit for ratification in the resolving clause of the amendment. This was later extended to June 1982. Thirty-five of the necessary thirty-eight states ratified the ERA between 1972 and 1977. While some would argue that the time for ratifying the ERA has long passed, I would respectfully disagree and argue just the opposite.

As noted in S.J.R. 2, Congress adopted the Twenty-Seventh Amendment to the U.S. Constitution in 1992. The Twenty-Seventh Amendment prohibits any law that increases or decreases the salary of members of Congress from taking effect until the start of the next set of terms of the offices for those representatives. This amendment was proposed in 1789 by our first Congress, but not ratified by three-fourths of the states until May 7, 1992, over 200 years later. The restricting time limit for ratification of the Equal Rights Amendment can be found in the resolving clause, and it is not part of the amendment that was proposed by Congress. Moreover, having passed a time extension for the Equal Rights Amendment on October 20, 1978,

Congress demonstrated that a time limit in the resolving clause may be disregarded if it is part of the proposed amendment. If an amendment to the U.S. Constitution has been proposed by a two-thirds vote of both houses of Congress and ratified by three-fourths of the state legislatures, Congress determines the validity of the state ratifications occurring after the time limit in the resolving clause but not in the amendment itself.

We continue to see evidence of the need for passage of the ERA every day. Pay equity, or should I say pay inequity, is still a significant concern. Women earn 80 percent of what men earn. African American women earn 68 percent of what men earn. Latinas earn 60 percent of what their male counterparts earn (Exhibit C). This year, April 4, 2017, marks equal pay date. This date symbolizes how far into 2017 women must work to earn what men earned during the previous year. This body even considered legislation last session to require paycheck fairness with tangible consequences for companies perpetuating economic discrimination based on gender. When there is a question of sports funding, why is it that sports programs at all levels, from the United States Women's Soccer Team to the girls' softball team at the local high school, continue to struggle to obtain adequate and equal funding when compared to male sports? Moreover, when it comes to crimes against women, women still suffer from victim blaming, shame, stigma, and the engraining of guilt upon the female victim. All of that still occurs today. Clearly, we struggle with equality under the law, and the ratification of the ERA is a step in the right direction.

A 1997 article in the *William & Mary Journal of Women and the Law* (Exhibit D) concludes that while women enjoy more rights today than they did when the ERA was first introduced in 1923, or when it was passed out of Congress in 1972, hard-won laws against sex discrimination do not rest on an unequivocal constitutional foundation. Laws can be inconsistently enforced or repealed. The article further concludes that the need for a federal equal rights amendment remains as compelling as it was in 1978.[7] In that year, Ruth Bader Ginsburg wrote in the *Harvard Women's Law Journal*: "With the Equal Rights Amendment, we may expect Congress and the state legislatures to undertake in earnest, systematically and pervasively, the law revision so long deferred. And in the event of legislative default, the courts will have an unassailable basis for applying the bedrock principle: All men and all women are created equal."[8]

These words were spoken on the floor of Congress regarding the Equal Rights Amendment: "This is what it comes down to: Artificial distinctions between persons must be wiped out of the law. Legal discrimination between the sexes is, in almost every instance, founded on outmoded views of society and the prescientific beliefs about psychology and physiology. It is time to sweep away these relics of the past and set further generations free of them." Congresswoman Shirley Chisholm spoke these words in her August 10, 1970, testimony for House Joint Resolution 264. The original bill advocated for full equality of women. In her speech, she proclaimed the need for the ERA with the words: "It provides a legal basis for attack on the most subtle, most pervasive, and most institutionalized form of prejudice that exists. Discrimination against women, solely on the basis of their sex, is so widespread that it seems to many persons normal, natural, and right."[9]

When the Equal Rights Amendment first gained popularity in the late 1960s and 1970s, it was heard as a cry for change, just as the cry for change continues for racial equality, fairness, and justice 152 years after the adoption of the Thirteenth Amendment. This cry has not diminished for the Equal Rights Amendment. I urge you to support this critical resolution, ratifying the ERA to the U.S. Constitution. The cry for change today has become a clarion call to act in a responsible manner that ensures equality for all citizens.

In the 1880s, sisters Sarah Moore Grimké and Angelina Grimké Weld used similar language advocating equal rights for women. "... whatever it is morally right for a man to do, it is morally right for a woman to do. I recognize no rights but human rights."[10] Fifty years ago, as the equal rights movement gained momentum, President Lyndon B. Johnson said these words: "We have talked long enough in this country about equal rights. It is time now to write the next chapter and to write it in the books of law."[11] In 1995, during her speech at the United Nations Fourth World Conference on Women held in Beijing, then-First Lady Hillary Rodham Clinton said, "Human rights are women's rights, and women's rights are human rights."[12]

I know there are some citizens, and perhaps even policymakers, who oppose this measure with the belief that the ERA will weaken the family. I challenge them to look at the inequity in pay and the number of women heads of household in this country. If they are concerned about the strength and viability of the family, then I say give your passionate, political voice and unwavering support for pay equity.

Some believe the ERA will put women at risk for the draft. It is important for those opponents to know that conscription, or what is normally called the draft, ended in 1973. Therefore, the historic facts render that argument moot. The military has been an all-volunteer force since January 27, 1973. That is 44 years of the all-volunteer military. There is the argument about children with two parent military members. The service requires them to have a family emergency plan in the event of mobilization. By practice, the military goes to great lengths to ensure both parents are not deployed at the same time. Last session, I sponsored a bill that would give priority placement to Gold Star children, or children who had lost a parent in combat. Even though the bill passed out of Committee, it was put on the Secretary of the Senate's desk without passage. Although I tried several times to get it off the desk, my request failed along party lines. If opponents are truly concerned about the welfare of military children, they might lobby their federal representative to pass bills to increase pay, housing allowance, health care, and benefits. In other words, we cannot just talk about supporting military families; we must be about supporting military families.

Madam Chairwoman and members of the Committee, I am before you today because I believe from the bottom of my heart in the foundations of the ERA and what it stands for, for all people.

Recently, a Senate colleague silenced Senator Elizabeth Warren on the floor of the United States Senate for giving a lengthy speech, including a letter written by Coretta Scott King. Senator Warren fought hard to be heard. One of her Senate colleagues noted, "She was warned. She was given an explanation. Nevertheless, she persisted." When it comes to ratification of the ERA, we all must persist. We have delayed Nevada's ratification of the ERA long enough, and now is the time to show the country and our global neighborhood that we, as Nevadans, lead when it comes to equality for all.

At every decision point in history, the quest for equality has been met with stiff and recalcitrant opposition. Equal justice has never been given. During antebellum times, abolitionists persisted to end the heinous practice of slavery. Negroes in the South persisted to end Jim Crow laws, and African Americans persisted to get the Civil Rights Act of 1964 passed. In addition, César Chávez and migrant workers persisted to improve working conditions. Vietnam veterans persisted to get health care recognition for their service and appreciation for their sacrifice, and HIV/AIDS activists persisted to ensure that human dignity was not diminished for those infected and affected by this terrible disease. Members of the lesbian, gay, bisexual, transgender, and queer (LGBTQ) community persisted to gain marriage equality, and Hillary Rodham Clinton persisted to put more than 60 million cracks in the political glass ceiling. Persistence, faith, and hope fuel the indomitable spirit of this movement.

At this moment in history, the legislation to ratify the ERA is before the Committee for consideration because millions of women, boys, and girls, have persisted. We must honor the sacrifice of our mothers and grandmothers, and we must commit to the preservation of justice and equality for our posterity. Galatians 6:9 says, "Be not weary in well doing. You will reap the harvest if you do not faint." Madam Chairwoman and members of the Committee, we got tired, but we did not faint. We became weary, but we did not faint. Pass this resolution as we persist in the name of all that is good. It has been a long road. It is worth noting that the Women's March in Washington, D.C., crossed all ethnic, social, economic, educational, and gender barriers.

I will end with the words spoken by Fannie Lou Hamer. Ms. Hamer was an African American voting rights activist, civil rights leader, daughter of a Mississippi sharecropper, and philanthropist. In 1964, someone asked her why she continued to fight for civil rights even in the face of unyielding opposition. I believe her words punctuate the persistence of all those testifying in support of this resolution. She said, "I am sick and tired of being sick and tired."[13]

That concludes my opening remarks, and I will yield to questions or for other people who would like to testify on behalf of this resolution.

Notes

1 "Minutes of the Meeting of the Assembly Committee on Legislative Operations and Elections," 79th Session, March 7, 2017, https://www.leg.state.nv.us/Session/79th2017/Minutes/Assembly/LOE/Final/428.pdf. Public Domain.
2 Frank Bruni, "Voters Love Lesbians," *New York Times*, July 30, 2017, SR3.
3 David Montero, "'It's Never Too Late to Support Equality': Nevada Assembly Votes to Ratify Equal Rights Amendment—35 Years Past Deadline," *Los Angeles Times*, March 21, 2017, A5.
4 Marsha Mercer, "#MeToo Fuels a Comeback for the Equal Rights Amendment," *USA Today (Online)*, March 1, 2018.
5 Colin Dwyer, "Nevada Ratifies the Equal Rights Amendment ... 35 Years After the Deadline," *NPR*, March 21, 2017, https://www.npr.org /sections/thetwo-way/2017/03/21/520962541/nevada-on-cusp-of-ratifying-equal-rights-amendment-35-years-after-deadline.
6 Julie C. Suk, *We the Women: The Unstoppable Mothers of the Equal Rights Amendment* (New York: Skyhorse Publishing, 2020), 131.
7 Allison L. Held, Sheryl L. Herndon, and Danielle M. Stager, "The Equal Rights Amendment: Why the ERA Remains Legally Viable and Properly Before the States," *William & Mary Journal of Women and the Law* 3, no. 1 (1997): 113–36.
8 Ruth Bader Ginsburg, "The Equal Rights Amendment Is the Way," *Harvard Women's Law Journal* 1 (1978): 19–26.
9 Shirley Chisholm, "For the Equal Rights Amendment," August 10, 1970, Archives of Women's Political Communication, Iowa State University, https://awpc.cattcenter.iastate.edu/2017/03/21/for-the-equal-rights-amendment-aug-10-1970/.
10 The Grimké sisters, two white Southerners who migrated North, were rhetorically active earlier than 1880. Both took great risks to write and speak in public on behalf of abolition and women's rights, primarily throughout the 1830s. Angelina Grimké Weld wrote the words Spearman quotes in a letter to Catherine Beecher in 1838. See Ellen Carol DuBois, "American Women Won the Right to Vote After the Suffrage

Movement Became More Diverse. That's No Coincidence," *Time*, February 20, 2020, https://time.com/5787130/suffrage-history-diversity/.

11 See Lyndon B. Johnson, "Address Before a Joint Session of the Congress," November 27, 1963, *American Presidency Project*, https://www.presidency.ucsb.edu/documents/address-before-joint-session-the-congress-0.

12 See Hillary Rodham Clinton, "Remarks to the United Nations Fourth Conference on Women," Beijing, China, September 5, 1995, White House, https://clintonwhitehouse3.archives.gov/WH/EOP/First_Lady/html/China/plenary.html.

13 See Maegan Parker Brooks and Davis W. Houck, *The Speeches of Fannie Lou Hamer: To Tell It Like It Is* (Jackson: University Press of Mississippi, 2013), 57–64.

The Conservative Case for the Equal Rights Amendment

Editorial for the Salt Lake Tribune

MICHELLE QUIST
October 3, 2019[1]

Michelle Quist (1975–present) is part of the long tradition of politically active Mormon women. After Wyoming, Utah was the second territory to grant (white) women suffrage and the first to see women actually exercise the right to vote. Because the LDS early practice of polygamy led many Americans to look askance at faithful Mormons, East Coast politicians and suffragists such as Susan B. Anthony and Elizabeth Cady Stanton proposed woman suffrage in the Western territories as a strategy to end polygamy. Subsequently, Utah politicians argued that suffrage would improve LDS credibility. Within this controversy, Utah's women rose to prominence as assertive but conservative political actors.[2] And Michelle Quist continues that tradition. She currently practices law in Salt Lake City and writes daily editorials for the *Salt Lake Tribune*. She's a registered Republican and a vocal critic of the GOP move away from its conservative roots during the Trump administration.[3]

In recent years, Quist has used her journalistic platform to advocate for the ERA and to counter what she describes as "old, stale and nefariously misleading arguments" against the amendment.[4] Quist's 2019 argument for conservative support of the ERA was reminiscent of white middle-class women's arguments before World War II. She cited the founding Utah documents and the potential economic and domestic benefits. She also neutralized those fears stirred up by the anti-ERA folks in the mid-century. Her conservative case for the ERA, in turn, countered the surging conservative and right-wing opposition to the ERA after Trump's election.

"Both male and female citizens of this State shall enjoy equally all civil, political and religious rights and privileges."

No, that's not the language of the Equal Rights Amendment. That's the language that has been in the Utah Constitution since 1895, Article IV, Section 1. In other words, Utah passed its own statewide ERA a long time ago.

Utah has the chance to be the 38th state—the deciding state—to ratify the federal Equal Rights Amendment.

"*Equality of rights under the law shall not be denied or abridged by the United States or by any State on account of sex.*"

In 1972 Congress passed the ERA and sent it to the states to ratify. Only 35 states had ratified the amendment; we needed 38.

In March 2017 Nevada became the 36th state; Illinois became the 37th in 2018 (championed by a Republican legislator named Steven Andersson[5]).

There is one spot left.

Eighty percent of Americans are surprised to learn that the Constitution does not already guarantee equal rights for women, and 94% support ratifying the amendment now.

The U.S. Constitution does not currently guarantee equal rights for women.

Let me say that again.

The U.S. Constitution does not currently guarantee equal rights for women. Even Justice Antonin Scalia has admitted the Constitution does not protect women from discrimination, saying, "Certainly the Constitution does not require discrimination on the basis of sex. The only issue is whether it prohibits it. It doesn't."[6]

Utah's state Constitution does, though.

The nation is celebrating 100 years of women's suffrage. Utah is celebrating 150 years since the first woman's vote, which was cast here in Utah by Seraph Young.[7] Utah has always been at the forefront of the fight for women's rights.

But why is it even a fight?

The ERA is good for families. It recognizes women as equal in home and civic economies. It could aid in ensuring women receive equal pay, including single mothers supporting children.

The ERA is good for business. Most women work and deserve protections in the workplace. Even more, many companies now require that businesses who work for them use a diverse workforce. The ERA supports that effort. It also encourages millennials to come and work in Utah. By passing the ERA, Utah would be communicating that we value equality. That matters to the younger generations.

Finally, conservative support for the ERA is an opportunity to rehabilitate and revive a party known to be led by old, white, men. We're losing the popular vote. We lack a strong moral compass. This effort could help bring back women and younger voters.

The parade of horribles that were trotted out in the 1970s as arguments against the ERA have mostly come to pass—same-gender bathrooms, gay marriage, women in the military. The doomsday prophecies are now moot. And contrary to arguments otherwise, this simple language will not open the floodgates to federally-funded abortion.

If the ERA will result in federally-funded abortion, then why haven't we seen state-funded abortion in Utah resulting from the language already included in Utah's Constitution? The answer is that the ERA won't affect abortion laws.

If the greatest argument against passing the ERA is that women are already equal and we don't really need it, well, that's just not good enough. The scriptures are filled with symbols used to communicate meaning and value. This could be a symbol worth the story behind it.

Just this week The Church of Jesus Christ of Latter-day Saints announced a huge policy change to allow women to act as witnesses in baptism and sealing ordinances.[8] Last week, many would have said we didn't need such a change to prove women are valued and equal in the church. And maybe we didn't. Maybe it's just symbolic. But it sure feels meaningful.

Today, those same people that would have balked last week at a request for women to act as witnesses embrace the notion this week that of course women should act as witnesses. Why not?

Well, of course, Utah should pass the ERA. Why not? Why shouldn't we stand for equality for women? Why shouldn't we send a message to the nation that, just like 150 years ago, we value, honor, and respect women enough to stand up and put it in writing.

Speaking of the elephant in the room (see what I did there?)–The Church of Jesus Christ of Latter-day Saints' position on the ERA is currently unknown. They have remained neutral during efforts in other states to pass the ERA. We can't afford the negative publicity a stance against the amendment would create. The church should stay neutral and focus on spreading Christ's message of love and forgiveness.

This isn't just the conservative case for the ERA. This is the case. If you're offended that liberals may also agree that passing the ERA is a good thing, then you're blinded by a partisanship that doesn't belong in a conversation about equality for women.

Legislators: Don't let this issue wait until March. And don't let it die in a committee. Decide to do the right thing now.

Conservatives: Let's vote for women. Join them. Speak up. Contact your legislator and tell them you support the ERA.

Women: Stand up and use your voice. And don't be gaslighted into thinking we don't need it because we're already equal. If we're already equal, then this amendment will just confirm the obvious.

They say we're equal. Let's see it in writing.

Notes

1 Michelle Quist, "The Conservative Case for the Equal Rights Amendment," *Salt Lake Tribune*, October 3, 2019, https://www.sltrib.com/opinion/commentary/2019/10/03/michelle-quist/. Reprinted with permission from Michelle Quist.

2 Katherine Kitterman, "Utah Women Had the Right to Vote Long Before Others—And Then Had It Taken Away," *Washington Post*, February 14, 2020, https://www.washingtonpost.com/outlook/2020/02/14/utah-women-had-right-vote-long-before-others-and-then-had-it-taken-away/.

3 "Michelle Quist: Columnist," *Salt Lake Tribune*, https://www.sltrib.com/staff/mquist/.

4 Michelle Quist, "LDS Church and Its Newspaper Dredge Up Tired Old Arguments Against the ERA," *Salt Lake Tribune*, December 9, 2019, https://www.sltrib.com/opinion/commentary/2019/12/04/michelle-quist-lds-church/.

5 Representative Steven A. Andersson (R-IL) played a significant role in passing the ERA in Illinois. See Rachel Otwell, "Steve Goes to Washington," *Illinois Times*, March 19, 2020, https://www.illinoistimes.com/springfield/steve-goes-to-washington-for-era/Content?oid=11952031.

6 See Stephanie Condon, "Scalia: Constitution Doesn't Protect Women or Gays from Discrimination," *CBS News*, January 4, 2011, https://www.cbsnews.com/news/scalia-constitution-doesnt-protect-women-or-gays-from-discrimination/.

7 See Dianna Douglas, "Meet America's First Voting Woman: Utah's Seraph Young," *Deseret News*, January 20, 2020, https://www.deseret.com/utah/2020/1/19/21071219/seraph-young-utah-first-woman-to-vote-america-suffrage.

8 See "Women Can Serve as Witnesses for Baptisms, Temple Sealings, First Presidency Announces," Church of Jesus Christ of Latter-day Saints, October 2, 2019, https://www.churchofjesuschrist.org/church/news/women-can-serve-as-witnesses-for-baptisms-temple-sealings-first-presidency-announces?lang=eng.

Feminists Should Ask Tough Questions about ERA

Article for Public Square Magazine

VALERIE M. HUDSON
November 18, 2019[1]

Valerie M. Hudson (1958–present) is a University Distinguished Professor and holds the George H.W. Bush Chair in the Department of International Affairs of the Bush School of Government and Public Service at Texas A&M University. A trained political scientist, Hudson taught for 25 years at Brigham Young University and her area of expertise is women, peace, and security. Since 2001, her WomanStats database has tracked the status of women around the globe and informed both academic research and policy development. *Foreign Policy* magazine included Hudson on its 2009 list of the "Top 100 Global Thinkers."[2] She is the coauthor of several books such as *Sex and World Peace*, *The Hillary Doctrine: Sex and American Foreign Policy*, and *The First Political Order: How Sex Shapes Governance and National Security Worldwide*. All of this is to say that Professor Hudson's contributions to the study of women and gender on the world stage are remarkable.[3]

Hudson has been open about converting to Mormonism from Roman Catholicism and has described how her faith informs her identity as a feminist. "I believe that one of the most profoundly feminist acts one can commit is to share the Restored Gospel of Jesus Christ with others," she wrote in a 2010 testimony.[4] Yet the twenty-first-century renaissance of the Equal Rights Amendment gave her pause. She touted her personal alliance with the LDS religion as foregrounding nuance in all her political decisions, and, thus, she argued for "healthy skepticism" rather than bandwagon enthusiasm or outright dismissal at this moment.

With the recent change in control of the Virginia legislature, it's almost certain that the state will ratify the Equal Rights Amendment. Meanwhile, in Utah, some are eager to have the Beehive State follow suit.

As a dyed-in-the-wool feminist, I have spent my scholarly career asserting that equality between men and women is the foundation of national security, prosperity, and stability. As a member of the Church of Jesus Christ, I am filled with admiration and gratitude for the pioneering strides made by the state of Utah in its early days, so ably chronicled by the BetterDays2020 project.[5] The Utah Territory granted women the right to vote in 1870, and the new State of Utah did the same in 1896, making it only the third state to do so. In that same year, the Utah State Constitution was adopted, which stipulated, "Both male and female citizens of this State shall enjoy all civil, political and religious rights and privileges."

So the Equal Rights Amendment (ERA) should be a slam dunk for me, right?

I'm still open-minded, but all of us who have lived through two decades of the twenty-first century now have a much healthier skepticism concerning the simple and seemingly straightforward solutions of earlier years being applied to the complex problems of today.

The simple solution of financial industry deregulation in the 1980s was obscenely gamed, setting our country up for the Great Recession of 2008. The straightforward HIPAA legislation intended to safeguard our privacy did not anticipate the day that it would be used as legal cover for Google to hoover up the personal health histories of hundreds of millions of Americans. We're hopefully savvier now at the beginning of the 2020s; we understand that the simple solutions of earlier decades may not anticipate the complexities of later decades.

As a woman, I'm hypervigilant about those questions because across the sweep of human history, the one group that has most often seen its rights thrown under the bus is women. For example, as an international relations scholar, I was not surprised at all that the "Arab Spring" of 2011 turned out to be wintertime specifically for women, who found their rights and their safety rolled back in nearly every nation that rose up against its dictators (with the possible exception of Tunisia).[6] And as a person who concurs with The Church of Jesus Christ of Latter-day Saints' more nuanced view on abortion (i.e., there are some circumstances under which women should have access to abortion services, but that these circumstances are limited in scope), I have witnessed the attempted abolition of all abortion services in my state of residence, Texas, on the grounds of "safeguarding women's health."

So count me as one of those women who—when told that a nearly century-old, one-line solution will solve the complex problems facing American women today—feels [the need] to raise an eyebrow and inquire, how might this be gamed, and who will get the short end of the stick when it is?

I'd like the sentence that the ERA proposes to add to the Bill of Rights– "Equality of rights under the law shall not be denied or abridged by the United States or by any state on account of sex"—comprehensively vetted by legal scholars across the political spectrum, with a full public discussion of their opinions.

When it's suggested that "we" can legally disregard the ERA's sunset clause, ignore the several un-ratifications by states that rescinded theirs, and call it one and done with the new ERA-friendly Virginia legislature, my female hypervigilance kicks in.

Why the rush? And who's being given the rush? Is it women?

I'm no lawyer, so I'm not going to attempt that vetting here. But there are at least two aspects of how the ERA could be gamed that trouble me. I'm happy to be reassured on those points by those who have the expertise to address them, but please don't tell me I'm somehow ignorant or anti-feminist for having concerns; I'm a feminist political scientist, after all.

First of those two points: what does "sex" mean in the ERA amendment in 2019? I am sure Alice Paul wasn't thinking about that question in 1923 when she first proposed the amendment, and I am sure Richard Nixon wasn't thinking about that question when he publicly endorsed the ERA in 1968 as a presidential candidate. But it's a timely question today, because now—according to the proposed Equality Act—the word "sex" in every piece of federal legislation must be replaced with the phrase "sex (including sexual orientation and gender identity)."[7]

So if we amended the Constitution using the word "sex," and the Equality Act were to one day pass the Senate (the House has already approved it) and become law, would we legally interpret the ERA to say "Equality of rights under the law shall not be denied or abridged by the United States or by any state on account of sex (including sexual orientation and gender identity)"?

To say that there is vibrant disagreement in the United States today over whether that legal interpretation would help or utterly decimate the cause of biological women is an understatement. We women have already discovered that if our sex-based rights are in conflict with the rights of others based on gender identity, we are too often thrown under the bus. Does the Equality Act turn the ERA into a Trojan horse for women, actually serving to erase them completely within the U.S. Constitution itself?

Second, it is widely agreed that the ERA would make any future imposition of a military draft impossible. That may or may not be a good thing—there are persuasive arguments on both sides. But if there is no appetite for drafting women aged 18–24 into the infantry—and indeed, I would argue that would actually represent a deepened form of misogyny and discrimination because women already give their lives for their country in a way men do not—then with the ERA amendment there is no longer any possible legal grounds for a male-only draft in wartime. I'd like to see a full public discussion of whether that is what the United States desires and intends, and that discussion should include military professionals.

At the end of the day, when you pick up one end of the stick, you pick up the other. So let's study what we're proposing to pick up, in its entirety.

The state of Utah is a unique place for such study to take place, in great measure because the values of the Church of Jesus Christ still carry weight among many voters. This dialogue has already produced non-simplistic solutions to today's complex problems, such as we saw with the Utah Compromise which holds forth a nuanced approach to competing foundational principles—equal protection and religious freedom. We've also seen the Church of Jesus Christ helpfully ask for a balanced approach on legislative issues such as immigration, medical marijuana and restrictions on psychological practice.

Now is the time, I argue, for the Utah Clarification of the ERA. Now is the time for persons of good will in the state of Utah to ask the hard questions about the ERA, about how its terms are to be defined and about its probable consequences for a wide variety of issues. Utah is the place that could happen—the state that proudly claims Emmeline B. Wells[8] and Martha Hughes Cannon[9] as its foremothers.

Notes

1 Valerie M. Hudson, "Feminists should ask tough questions about ERA," *Public Square Magazine*, November 18, 2019, https://publicsquaremag.org/sexuality-family/era-feminists-passage/. Reprinted with permission from Valerie M. Hudson.

2 Shelby Smith, "Valerie Hudson Named One of the World's 100 Most Influential Thinkers," *Battalion*, March 5, 2020, https://www.thebatt.com/life-arts/valerie-hudson-named-one-of-the-world-s-100-most-influential-thinkers/article_4f45d538-5f3a-11ea-96f0-3b29313c6431.html.

3 "Valerie Hudson," Faculty Bio, Texas A&M University, https://bush.tamu.edu/faculty/vhudson/.

4 Valerie Hudson Cassler, "I Am a Mormon Because I Am a Feminist," *FAIR: Faithful Answers, Informed Response*, September 2010, https://www.fairlatterdaysaints.org/testimonies/scholars/valerie-hudson-cassler.

5 See Katherine Kitterman, "Better Days," Salt Lake City, 2002, https://www.betterdays2020.com/.
6 See Rita Stephan and Mounira M. Charrad, ed., *Women Rising: In and Beyond the Arab Spring* (New York: New York University Press, 2020).
7 See H.R.5 "Equality Act," 117th Congress, 1st Session, March 1, 2021, https://www.congress.gov/117/bills/hr5/BILLS-117hr5pcs.pdf.
8 Among other accomplishments, Mormon journalist and poet Emmeline B. Wells worked alongside Susan B. Anthony and Elizabeth Cady Stanton for the suffrage cause. See "Emmeline B. Wells," Church of Jesus Christ of Latter-day Saints, https://www.churchofjesuschrist.org/study/history/topics/emmeline-b-wells?lang=eng.
9 Dr. Martha Cannon Hughes, a physician and suffragist, served as Utah's first female state senator. See Mari Graña, *Pioneer, Polygamist, Politician: The Life of Dr. Martha Cannon Hughes* (Guilford, CT: TwoDot, 2009).

It's Time, Finally, to Adopt the Equal Rights Amendment

Op-Ed for the Houston Chronicle

Sylvia Garcia
November 21, 2019[1]

Congresswoman Sylvia Rodriguez Garcia (1950–present) made history in November 2018 when she was elected as the first Latina to represent the Texas 29th district encompassing much of Houston. Garcia was among the attendees at the 1977 National Women's Conference in Houston and participated in the Chicana caucus.[2] She studied law at Texas Southern University and worked in local government before her election to the Texas State Senate in 2013. During the impeachment proceedings against Donald Trump in 2020, Garcia was front and center as one of seven House impeachment managers appointed by Speaker Nancy Pelosi—a somewhat unusual appointment for a freshman Congressperson, but a capacity in which Garcia served with distinction.[3]

Texas ratified the ERA in March 1972, but that did not stop Garcia from pushing for other states to follow suit in the new century. Forty-five years after the National Women's Conference, Garcia joined a panel about the conference's impact and told her audience, "Regretfully, we still haven't gotten it done. It's amazing to me that I was fighting that fight back in '77 and here I am, as a member of Congress sitting on the Judiciary Committee and we had a hearing on the same thing again."[4] In this op-ed for the *Houston Chronicle*, Garcia used her platform to argue that the ERA would be especially beneficial to Latinas and to lend her support to ratification efforts in Virginia. On January 15, 2020, the Virginia Senate passed the ERA on a 28 to 12 vote, while the House of Delegates voted 59 to 41; thus, making Virginia the 38th state to ratify the amendment.[5]

Leading up to the early 1970s, women (and some men) fought for the "radical idea" that women and men should be equal under the Constitution—"that all men and women are created equal, that they are endowed by their Creator with certain unalienable Rights, that among these are Life, Liberty, and the Pursuit of Happiness."

Years of activism in favor of full equality culminated with the passage of the Equal Rights Amendment (ERA) in the U.S. House of Representatives on Oct. 12, 1971, and in the Senate on March 22, 1972.

I vividly remember this time because I was just starting to get involved in politics. At the time, I felt hopeful. It seemed like our country was starting to change its views about women.

Just days after Congress passed the ERA, I was in Austin when Texas became the eighth state to pass it. I thought we were on the verge of real change in America.

History would prove me wrong.

By 1977, 35 states had ratified the ERA in state legislatures across the country. During this time, however, we also saw four states rescind those ratifications and advocates were increasingly worried that we would not meet the 1979 deadline for ratification of the ERA. These concerns became a reality and America did not codify equality for women in our Constitution.

It turned out that change is not as easy if you are a woman in America. Throughout my life and career, despite women consistently fighting for their rights, we have not seen women achieve full equality. This is even more true if you are an African American or Latina woman.

In the late 1980s, by the time I became presiding judge of the Houston municipal courts, it seemed that full equality for women was no longer a priority in our national dialogue. Our country was more interested in maintaining the status quo than helping women achieve full equality.

In 2002, I became the first Hispanic and the first woman elected in her own right to the Harris County Commissioner's Court. Even then, we were still talking about equal pay for equal work and fighting to recognize men and women as equal. African American and Latina women were still making significantly less than white, non-Hispanic men.

Fast forward to 2019, as we mark Latina Equal Pay Day, there is now a newfound jolt of energy in the march toward full equality for women that has reverberated across the country.

As a country, we have seen women stand up against the rape culture that has made them the target of sexual assault.

As a country, we have seen women fight for their right to choose and push back against men who want to control our bodies.

As a country, we have seen women raise their voices against the gender pay gap that allows African American women to make 63 cents and Latinas to make 54 cents for every dollar earned by a white, non-Hispanic man.

As a country, we have seen women run for office and break glass ceilings at every level of government, such as when I became one of the first two Latinas ever elected to Congress from Texas.

And most recently, we have seen a renewed call for the ratification of the ERA, the unfinished work of the women's liberation movement and a response to the sexism that has come to define the Trump administration.

The United States has a long way to go if we are to achieve full equality for women. My hope is that every little girl in this country will one day live in an America that embraces their full humanity and guarantees full equality to them.

We can achieve this by ensuring all women, and especially African American and Latina women, are no longer paid less than men. We can achieve this by reauthorizing the Violence Against Women's Act that protects women from domestic violence and sexual assault. We can achieve this by supporting Virginia in becoming the 38th state to ratify the ERA and lifting the 7-year ratification deadline, which will pave the way for the United States to finally live up to its values of equality and justice for all.

This is about the more than 1.16 million women and girls that live in Houston. This is about the more than 166.2 million women and girls across the country. We have the power to guarantee full equality under the Constitution for every woman and little girl in America. The question is whether the United States will embrace equality for women or leave it up to the next generation?

I'm hopeful we will live up to our ideals as Americans by choosing equality.

Notes

1 Sylvia Garcia, "It's Time, Finally, To Adopt the Equal Rights Amendment," *Houston Chronicle*, November 21, 2019, https://sylviagarcia.house.gov/media/in-the-news/it-s-time-finally-adopt-equal-rights-amendment-opinion. Public Domain.

2 "Daily Breakthrough: Where Women Are News: In Celebration of Women," *Associates in Growth, Inc.*, Houston, TX, November 18, 1977, 27.

3 Abby Livingston, "How U.S. Rep. Sylvia Garcia of Houston Landed in the Middle of Donald Trump's Impeachment," *Texas Tribune*, January 29, 2020,

https://www.texastribune.org/2020/01/29/how-us-rep-sylvia-garcia-houston-landed-middle-impeachment/; "About," Congresswoman Sylvia Garcia, https://sylviagarcia.house.gov/about.

4 Errin Haines, "What's Left Undone 45 Years After the National Women's Conference," *19th News*, March 25, 2022, https://19thnews.org/2022/03/national-womens-conference-1977-undone/.

5 Bill Chappell, "Virginia Ratifies the Equal Rights Amendment, Decades After the Deadline," *NPR*, January 15, 2020, https://www.npr.org/2020/01/15/796754345/virginia-ratifies-the-equal-rights-amendment-decades-after-deadline.

Bring It On

Article for Marie Claire

Jennifer Carroll Foy
January 16, 2020[1]

The 1996 Supreme Court ruling in *United States v. Virginia*, or the VMI case as it came to be called, decided against the Virginia Military Institute's long-standing policy to only admit males. Justice Ruth Bader Ginsburg's bench announcement summed up the meaning of the ruling, which effectively struck down the "law or official policy that denies to women, simply because they are women, equal opportunity to aspire, achieve, participate in, and contribute to society based upon what they can do."[2] Of all the cases she heard on the Supreme Court, Ginsburg cited VMI as the one she believed did the most to advance civil liberties in the United States.[3] The career of Congresswoman Jennifer Denise Carroll Foy (1981–present), among the earliest female graduates of VMI, supports Ginsburg's sense of the case's importance. Foy holds a law degree from the Thomas Jefferson School of Law and has worked as a magistrate judge and public defender. She represented the 2nd District in Virginia's House of Delegates from 2017 to 2020, when she launched an unsuccessful yet historic bid to become the state's first female governor. On November 7, 2023, Foy successfully won a state senate seat in the 33rd district of Virginia.[4]

With one state left to meet the ratification requirements, Foy led the fight to make Virginia the last crucial piece of the puzzle. She served as the chief sponsor of the bill that, on January 15, 2020, helped Virginia become the 38th state to ratify the ERA. Foy strategically capitalized on the Democratic majority in the House of Delegates and the state senate to propel the ERA forward.[5] Nearly 25 years after VMI opened its doors to women, Foy took her case to the court of public opinion by publishing an article in the popular magazine *Marie Claire*. Foy's appeal was deeply personal and anchored her arguments in her experiences as a woman attending VMI—an opportunity that other woman may not have in the future, she contended, without the security guaranteed by the ERA.

I grew up in Petersburg, VA, a town where many people were not set up to thrive. In a community with one of the highest child poverty rates, and one of the highest teen pregnancy rates, my friends and I faced a number of challenges. Many of my friends and neighbors struggled to get by and women had even fewer opportunities than men. Luckily, my grandmother, who raised me, taught me to be determined, persistent, and service-oriented—values that continue to define my life. It was those values that piqued my interest in public service, starting with my time in JROTC [Junior Reserve Officers' Training Corps] in high school. As one of the few women in the program, I constantly had to prove myself, understanding that there were still too few opportunities for women in this field.

But then, something big happened for me and Virginia women: the United States Supreme Court issued a decision compelling the Virginia Military Institute, a legendary institution in a Commonwealth that only admitted men, to admit women as well. For so long, women had been shut out of this institution. But even when the decision came down, the men in my JROTC classroom sided with the efforts to exclude women. I watched the Supreme Court take this tremendous step for women while surrounded by people who doubted me as a woman, and truly thought of me as a second-class citizen.

My classmates doubted a woman's ability to succeed at VMI, but I didn't let that stand in my way. I knew VMI would be the perfect training ground for people like me, who were committed to a lifetime of services, so I immediately applied. Years later, I graduated from VMI, and in fact, was the only one to walk across the stage at graduation—the men in my JROTC program did not. I did it thanks to the determination instilled in me by my grandmother, and a consequential United States Supreme Court decision to open up opportunities for women. From there, I went on to become a magistrate judge, public defender, and in 2017, was elected to represent my community in the Virginia House of Delegates.

As a new delegate, my goal was, and still is, to serve as many people the best I can. And it became clear to me that I could do that very thing by introducing a resolution to ratify the Equal Rights Amendment in Virginia—opening new doors for women in my state and across the country. Growing up in Virginia as a young woman of color, it was very clear to me that our Commonwealth was on the wrong side of history for so many reasons, so many times. Unfortunately, the Commonwealth does not have a great history when it comes to matters of equality. But by passing the Equal Rights Amendment, we'd finally be able to get it right, not only in our state, but for the rest of the country, too. If Virginia becomes the 38th state to ratify the Equal Rights Amendment, this amendment will be eligible to be added to the United States Constitution, providing protections from gender discrimination that women currently don't have.

Today, preventing gender discrimination is the responsibility of elected officials. I knew that laws and Supreme Court decisions, like the one that allowed me to go to VMI, can always be reversed, and laws can always be changed as often as legislators change their minds which of course means those officials must believe in gender equality in the first place. Clearly, that doesn't cut it. We currently have a president who does not see women as equals and has enacted an agenda to match. And in many states, it's just the same, which has led to policies that quite literally threaten women's lives and livelihoods. If we pass the Equal Rights Amendment, and add it to the Constitution, we'll be shoring up protections for women's rights, and in many cases, establishing those protections for the first time.

When I think about passing the Equal Rights Amendment, I think of a world where women are truly equal to men. A world where we're paid equally, where getting pregnant won't lead to discrimination in the workplace, and where a woman can make the best choices for her and her future. For too long, women have not had the protections from discrimination we deserve in the U.S. Constitution, and with passage of the Equal Rights Amendment, we'll be that much closer to living in a world where women and girls have the same opportunities as men.

I was proud to do my part in Virginia and introduce the Equal Rights Amendment, and it's been an honor to work alongside trailblazers like Ellie Smeal to ratify it. It's no surprise that the Trump administration is attempting to throw roadblocks on the path toward adding the Equal Rights Amendment to the Constitution, despite how wildly popular it is with the vast majority of Americans. But I'm a woman, like so many others, who refuses to back down from a challenge, and from fighting for what's right. I graduated from VMI when no one thought I could, and I was elected to the House when people doubted me. To anyone challenging the Equal Rights Amendment, I say: bring it on.

Notes

1 Jennifer Carroll Foy, "Women Are Not Granted Equality Anywhere in the Constitution: Virginia Could Finally Change That," *Marie Claire*, January 16, 2020, https://www.marieclaire.com/politics/a30534962/jennifer-carroll-foy-virginia-equal-rights-amendment/. Reprinted with permission from Jennifer Carroll Foy.

2 Ruth Bader Ginsburg, "Bench Announcement, June 26, 1996, *United States v. Virginia*," in *My Own Words*, ed. Ruth Bader Ginsburg, Mary Hartnett, and Wendy W. Williams (New York: Simon & Schuster, 2016), 153.

3 Jeffrey Rosen, *Conversations with RBG: Ruth Bader Ginsburg on Life, Love, Liberty, and the Law* (New York: Henry Holt and Company, 2019), 73.

4 "Jennifer Carroll Foy Wins 33rd District Senate Seat," *Prince William Times*, November 7, 2023, https://www.princewilliamtimes.com/elections/jennifer-carroll-foy-wins-33rd-district-senate-seat/article_50fa6880-7c41-11ee-b953-4bd308f88c75.html.

5 Maureen Groppe and Ledyard King, "Virginia Becomes 38th State to Pass ERA for Women, Likely Setting Up Issue for Courts," *USA Today*, January 15, 2020, https://www.usatoday.com/story/news/politics/2020/01/15/virginia-passes-era-38th-state-amendment-women/4477813002/; Daniel Berti, "Del. Jennifer Carroll Foy Re-Introduces Measure to Endorse Equal Rights Amendment," *Prince William Times*, November 19, 2019, https://www.princewilliamtimes.com/news/del-jennifer-carroll-foy-re-introduces-measure-to-endorse-equal-rights-amendment/article_08669d92-0b06-11ea-a5a6-f7b26861e37a.html.

The ERA Can't Be Defeated by Anti-Trans Scare Tactics

Editorial for Teen Vogue

DANICA ROEM AND KATE KELLY
January 16, 2020[1]

Danica Roem (1984–present) studied journalism and mass communication at St. Bonaventure University in New York, completing 13 years of Catholic schooling. After graduation in 2006, she returned to her home state of Virginia and reported for the *Gainesville Times*, the *Prince William Times*, and later the *Montgomery County Sentinel*. But she soon set her sights on public office. She became the first openly transgender delegate for the Virginia state house in 2018 and for the Virginia senate in 2024.[2] While in office, Roem authored a bill that made Virginia the 12th state to ban the "gay/trans panic" defense, which abolished lower sentences for those accused of committing a homicide who claim they "panicked after finding out the victim's sexual orientation or gender identity."[3]

Thus, Roem was a new kind of voice for support within the century of women debating the Equal Rights Amendment. She wrote in a so-called fashion magazine for young people on political policy with coauthor Kate Kelly (1980–present), a human rights attorney and law graduate of American University. Like Sonia Johnson before her, Kelly was excommunicated after three male Mormon leaders accused her of apostasy for shining a light on gender inequality in the LDS church. Her organization "Ordain Women" calls for the ordination of Mormon women and her podcast "Ordinary Equality" inspired the book *Ordinary Equality: The Fearless Women and Queer People Who Shaped the U.S. Constitution and the Equal Rights Amendment.*[4]

Together, Roem and Kelly expressed the persistent independence for the state Roem serves in celebration of Virginia's ratification of the ERA. They cited early suffragists, Alice Paul and Matilda Joslyn Gage. And in all that, they forcefully refuted the skepticism and prejudice of "gender critical" feminists (sometimes called "trans-exclusionary radical feminists," or "TERFs") who question the inclusion of transgender women in the fight for women's rights. Finally, Roem and Kelly wondered, after a century, if we can imagine a truly diverse and inclusive human rights movement that remedies the mistakes of the past.

Virginia just made history as the 38th state to ratify the long-overdue Equal Rights Amendment, and it did so with me, Danica Roem, the first out-and-seated transgender state legislator in American history taking a lead.

In the former waves of feminism, white leaders of the movement sacrificed certain groups of women when they thought it would help them make gains. Alice Paul herself, who wrote the original Equal Rights Amendment (ERA) in 1923, felt it was necessary to racially segregate the 1913 Woman Suffrage Parade. Paul feared that some white women would not support a suffrage movement that included black women.

[Ida B.] Wells courageously defied the concerns about racism and marched with her delegation at the front of the parade anyway. Yet, when the 19th Amendment was ratified in 1920, it primarily benefited white women as racist politicians and election workers still found ways to block women of color from casting ballots.

Suffrage leaders made choices that left many women behind. They also marginalized people in the movement who wanted to take a more inclusive path, like suffragist Matilda Joslyn Gage, who fought for Indigenous rights as a white woman. They didn't want inclusion to get in the way of their rights.

Almost a century later, we are more committed than ever to ratify the ERA and complete the unfinished business of former feminist movements. Yet we are determined not to repeat the mistakes of the past.

This past April, the House Judiciary Subcommittee on the Constitution, Civil Rights and Civil Liberties held the first official congressional hearing on the ERA in almost 40 years. Extraordinary progress at the state level during the last two years prompted this historic move, with two more states voting for ratification: Nevada in March 2017 and Illinois in May 2018.

On the heels of its recent election, Virginia has become the 38th and final state needed to ratify the ERA, so gender equality can become part of the U.S. Constitution. Just as the movement for the ERA is surging again, the tired arguments against it are also resurfacing. Many of these arguments center on excluding certain groups from constitutional protection, with particular hostility being shown toward trans women.

Back in April, three witnesses testified in favor of the ERA before the House Judiciary Committee: Oscar-winning actress Patricia Arquette, Nevada State Senator Pat Spearman, and former dean of Stanford law school Kathleen Sullivan. All three witnesses defended trans women and stated unequivocally that the ERA should cover all people, regardless of what we look like, who we love, or who we are.

Sullivan, a noted constitutional scholar who has argued cases before the Supreme Court, went through the legal arguments. "The ERA will prohibit discrimination on the basis of sex," she said. "If there's discrimination against LGBTQ people on the basis of sex, then it'll be covered. I believe the textual reading of the amendment does apply to sexual orientation and gender identity."

Arquette spoke of growing up with her sister, who is trans, saying, "The only scary thing about sharing a bathroom with her was fighting about who was going to replace the toilet paper roll." She deftly humanized the issue of trans inclusion in the realm of public accommodations for the committee members.[5]

In order to oppose the ERA, contemporary groups are using the classic tactic of pitting different groups of women against each other. There's just one catch: While this tactic helped stymie ratification of the ERA in the past, we're not falling for it this time. Modern feminists know we can't win our rights by throwing the most vulnerable people under the bus. We won't repeat the mistakes of the white suffragists who left out many women in the name of "strategy."

The word "women" is conspicuously absent from the ERA, which instead forbids discrimination on the basis of "sex." This simple, straightforward version of the language is what passed in Congress in 1972 and what Virginia has now ratified. It holds ample potential to protect all marginalized genders—binary and non-binary alike—and sexual minorities. This also includes people of color, who, like Delegate Jennifer Carroll Foy, are leading the way on the ERA. And, yes, ERA advocates do want the amendment to apply to everyone: trans women and non-binary people included. This is not a minus; it's a major plus. Equal means equal. Period.

The LGBTQIA+ rights movement has won tremendous victories and successfully made moot some of the original anti-ERA arguments, like the fear it would legalize marriage equality. Americans today are rethinking gender norms in new and exciting ways and looking beyond strict gender binaries. Thanks to the overarching language used by the original drafters of the ERA, it can serve as a large tent of constitutional protection today.

The ERA is an amendment for our times and we will not let those whose ideals are steeped in the prejudices of the past divide us.

We stood together to ratify the ERA in Virginia and will continue until we all get the equal rights and recognition more than 50 percent of the population deserves but lacks—for women, girls, non-binary people and all marginalized genders. The ERA isn't about who we're against; it's an affirmative statement about who we're for—everybody. This is about making our United States of America a more inclusive country, one where you're protected because of who you are, not despite it.

We ratified the ERA not by throwing trans women under the bus, but by having them play a key role in finally ratifying the amendment. Women—cis and trans alike—stand together to demand our fundamental constitutional rights.

Notes

1 Danica Roem and Kate Kelly, "The Equal Rights Amendment Can't Be Defeated by Anti-Trans Scare Tactics," *Teen Vogue*, January 16, 2020, https://www.teenvogue.com/story/equal-rights-amendment-anti-trans-scare-tactics-op-ed. Reprinted with permission from Kate Kelly.

2 Danica Roem, *Burn the Page: A True Story of Torching Doubts, Blazing Trails, and Igniting Change* (New York: Viking, 2022); Danica Roem, "Focusing on What Really Matters to Virginians," *DelegateDanicaRoem.com*, https://www.delegatedanicaroem.com/our-vision.

3 Jo Yurcaba, "Virginia Becomes 12th State to Ban Gay/Trans Panic Defense," *NBC News*, April 2, 2021, https://www.nbcnews.com/feature/nbc-out/virginia-becomes-12th-state-ban-gay-trans-panic-defense-n1262933.

4 Kate Kelly, "Ordain Women," *OrdainWomen.org*, Washington, D.C.; Kate Kelly, *Ordinary Equality: The Fearless Women and Queer People Who Shaped the U.S. Constitution and the Equal Rights Amendment* (Layton, UT: Gibbs Smith, 2022).

5 A full transcript of the hearings, including the testimony of Arquette, Spearman, and Sullivan, can be found here: https://www.govinfo.gov/content/pkg/CHRG-116hhrg41176/html/CHRG-116hhrg41176.htm.

I Urge My Colleagues to Vote "No"

Address to the U.S. House of Representatives

VICKY HARTZLER
March 17, 2021[1]

Republican Vicky Jo Hartzler (1960–present) began her political career as a representative in the Missouri State House from 1995 to 2000 before moving to the U.S. House of Representatives, where she represented the 4th Congressional District from 2010 to 2023. With backing from the deeply conservative Tea Party, Hartzler strongly opposed abortion, same-sex marriage, and the Violence Against Women Act (VAWA).[2] Hartzler wrote of the latter in 2019 that the VAWA has "been hijacked by liberals with a political agenda who seek to elevate transgender politics over the safety and well-being of women," even though she previously voted to reauthorize it.[3] In 2012, Hartzler aligned herself with the "birther movement" that questioned whether Barack Obama was truly born in the United States.[4] She later sided with Donald Trump's charges of voter fraud and irregularities, even as she simultaneously condemned Trump's irresponsible remarks following the horrifying January 6, 2021 attack on the U.S. Capitol.[5]

Hartzler vocally opposed the ERA as it remerged during the Trump and Biden administrations. Amid a sea of masked colleagues at the height of the coronavirus pandemic, Hartzler advised against passing H.J. Res. 17, a resolution to remove the ERA ratification deadline sponsored by her colleague Jackie Speier (D-CA). Hartzler's March 2021 speech appropriated and reimagined the anti-ERA appeals crafted by earlier labor advocates as protectionist arguments of a different sort—arguments that insisted women are *already* equal. She was not alone in voicing anti-ERA, pro-life, and anti-LGBTQIA+ contentions at these hearings. Trump loyalists Marjorie Taylor Greene (R-GA), Debbie Lesko (R-AZ), and Victoria Spartz (R-IN) echoed Hartzler's insistence that the ratification deadline had already passed and that their Democratic colleagues were quite obviously trying to push a nefarious political agenda through. "The reviving of the deadline and ratifying of this amendment would destroy all distinctions between men and women, enshrine abortion, and empower the woke feminist mob," Greene warned while donning an "America First" face mask.[6]

But with a Democratic majority, Hartzler and her cohort faced strong opposing arguments for ratification at this hearing from ERA supporters Sylvia Garcia, Carolyn Maloney, Nancy Pelosi, Jackie Speier, and others. Thanks to the Democrats' united efforts, the House voted 222–204—mostly along party lines, but with a handful of Republican defectors—that same day to remove the deadline.[7]

Thank you, Madam Speaker. I rise today to celebrate the achievements women have made and reaffirm that we are already equal under current law.

Women represent 51 percent of the population, comprise over half of college students, make up the majority of medical and law school students, and run 12.3 million women-owned businesses while generating 1.8 trillion dollars each year. Little girls can be whatever they want to be, whether that be an astronaut, a doctor, a full-time mom working at home, or a member of Congress.

The ERA would not add to the rights already guaranteed by the Fourteenth Amendment Equal Protection Clause. But it could jeopardize them. How? Two ways.

First, by making it discriminatory to offer benefits to women not offered to men: women's scholarships, women's colleges, job protection for pregnant women, and safe spaces may all be on the chopping block. When the Equal Rights Amendment was first proposed a century ago, many women's rights advocates recognized the negative ramifications it would bring. In fact, future first lady Eleanor Roosevelt expressed concerns that legislation protecting women in the workplace could be eliminated should the ERA become part of the U.S. Constitution.

Secondly, because the 1972 definition of "sex" as "male" and "female" is no longer accepted by many today, and instead will require new protections for sexual orientation and gender identity. This is a path that has already proven to be a threat to women's privacy, safety, and equality. Don't take it from me. Talk to the nine women in California who were sexually harassed in a women's shelter by a biological male identifying as a woman.

The Equal Rights Amendment would not only codify inequality for women but also destroy the rights of the unborn. ERA advocates have been unequivocal about their support for abortion and for using the ERA to overturn pro-life laws. Courts have already used state versions of the ERA to force taxpayers to fund abortions. A federal ERA would threaten state pro-life laws, federal protections like the Hyde Amendment, and conscience protections for American medical professionals who may otherwise be forced to perform an abortion.

Fortunately, the time limit to pass the ERA expired decades ago and there is agreement that Congress cannot go back and remove a deadline from a previous constitutional amendment initiative. For example, the Supreme Court has already recognized that the 1972 ERA expired and the Department of Justice issued a ruling saying, "Congress may not revive a proposed amendment after a deadline for its ratification has expired." Just over a week ago, a federal district court ruled that the deadline to ratify the ERA "expired long ago." And the recent ratifications of the amendment "arrived too late to count."[8] Pretending we can remove the deadline for passage is both futile and deceptive.

The ERA is a threat to the historical strides women have made. It will eradicate state and federal pro-life laws and policies. And the process is blatantly unconstitutional.

I urge my colleagues to vote "no" on this resolution and instead uphold the Constitution, promote life, and protect women's rights.

Notes

1 Vicky Hartzler, *Removing Deadline for Ratification of Equal Rights Amendment; U.S. House of Representatives,* H.J. Res. 17, March 17, 2021, https://www.c-span.org/video/?509880-1/house-session&start=1300. Public Domain.

2 "Biography," Vicky Hartzler, Missouri's Fourth Congressional District, https://hartzler.house.gov/about/biography; "Marriage and Life," Vicky Hartzler, Missouri's Fourth Congressional District, https://hartzler.house.gov/legislative-work/issues/marriage-and-life.

3 Vicky Hartzler, "The Violence Against Women's Act: No Longer About Protecting Women," Press Release, April 5, 2019, https://hartzler.house.gov/media-center/press-releases/violence-against-womens-act-no-longer-about-protecting-women; "Hartzler Votes to Reauthorize Violence Against Women Act," Press Release, May 16, 2012, https://www.legistorm.com/stormfeed/view_rss/44502/member/2769/title/hartzler-votes-to-reauthorize-violence-against-women-act.html.

4 Mackenzie Weinger, "Pol Moves Off Birther Comments," *Politico*, April 9, 2012, https://www.politico.com/story/2012/04/rep-moves-off-birther-comments-074954.

5 Vicky Hartzler, "Hartzler Statement on House Certification of 2020 Election Results," Press Release, January 7, 2021, https://hartzler.house.gov/media-center/press-releases/hartzler-statement-house-certification-2020-election-results; Rudi

Keller, "Vicky Hartzler Battles Headwinds of Trump Anti-Endorsement as Senate Race Reaches Climax," *Missouri Independent*, July 20, 2022, https://missouriindependent.com/2022/07/20/vicky-hartzler-battles-headwinds-of-trump-anti-endorsement-as-senate-race-reaches-climax/.

6 Marjorie Taylor Greene, *Removing Deadline for Ratification of Equal Rights Amendment; U.S. House of Representatives*, H.J. Res. 17, March 17, 2021, https://www.c-span.org/video/?509880-1/house-session&start=1300.

7 "House Debates Resolution Removing Deadline to Ratify Equal Rights Amendment," March 17, 2021, *C-SPAN*, https://www.c-span.org/video/?c4952344/house-debates-resolution-removing-deadline-ratify-equal-rights-amendment; Susan Cornwell, "U.S. House Passes Resolution Aimed at Advancing Equal Rights Amendment," *Reuters*, March 17, 2021, https://www.reuters.com/world/us/us-house-passes-resolution-aimed-advancing-equal-rights-amendment-2021-03-17/.

8 "Ratification of the Equal Rights Amendment," U.S. Department of Justice, Office of Legal Counsel, January 6, 2020, https://www.justice.gov/d9/opinions/attachments/2020/01/16/2020-01-06-ratif-era.pdf.

The Unfulfilled Promise

Remarks on the Floor of the U.S. House of Representatives

Nancy Pelosi
March 17, 2021[1]

Politics are in Nancy Patricia D'Alesandro Pelosi's (1940–present) blood, so it should be no surprise that this Italian Catholic girl from Maryland made history as the first woman Speaker of the U.S. House of Representatives. Her father Thomas D'Alesandro Jr. served in the House of Representatives and later as mayor of Baltimore.[2] Nancy Pelosi's entrance into politics began with answering phones in the office of Senator Daniel Brewster (D-MD). As a thirty-five-year-old housewife in San Francisco, she accepted a four-year appointment to the San Francisco Public Library Commission.[3] In 1987, she successfully ran for Representative Sala Burton's California seat and became the first daughter of a congressman to succeed her father in the House.[4] Representative Nancy Pelosi has proven to be a deft legislator, a resilient party leader, and a formidable champion of women's rights. Throughout her political career, she has consistently promoted issues such as equal pay, parental leave, access to day care, improved preschools, increased funding for breast cancer research, access to birth control, reproductive rights, and fighting violence against women. During the tumultuous four years of Donald Trump's presidency, Pelosi stood toe-to-toe with the brash commander-in-chief as his most powerful check and balance.[5]

Pelosi joined her colleagues in announcing that the ERA would be reintroduced to the 101st Congress shortly after arriving to Washington, D.C. She argued in 1989 that "as great as our Constitution is, it can be better, and we must have the standard of equality for women in the highest law of the land so that we truly do have the freest country in the world with the greatest document."[6] More than 30 years later, Pelosi still led the fight for the ERA and consistently leveraged her position as Speaker (between 2007–2011 and 2019–2023) to draw support for the amendment in the House. Under Pelosi's leadership, the House voted in favor of H.J. Res 17 to remove the time limit for the ERA on March 17, 2021, hoping to further pave the way for activating the "three-state strategy" (Nevada, Illinois, and Virginia) to reach the final threshold of required states.[7]

Thank you, Madam Speaker. I thank the gentleman for yielding. And it's wonderful to see Members of Congress wearing white today to observe the fact that we are making history by passing legislation about equality in our country.

I thank Congresswoman Jackie Speier for her relentless championing of this Equal Rights Amendment in terms of the date that distinguished Chair of the Judiciary Committee referenced. And I also thank Carolyn Maloney for her long-term advocacy of the Equal Rights Amendment. Thank you, Mr. Chairman Nadler, for bringing—for enabling us to have this legislation on the Floor today and for your leadership on this issue over time.[8]

Madam Speaker, 100 years ago, 1921, a solemn promise was made to the women of our country, one honoring our most fundamental truth as a nation, as the Equal Rights Amendment was first introduced.[9] When it was first introduced it said, "Men and women shall have equal rights throughout the United States and every place subject to its jurisdiction." Simple, clear, fair, and just.

Yet, a century later, that promise remains unfulfilled. The Equal Rights Amendment still has not been enshrined in the Constitution, and American women still face inequality under the law and, therefore, in their lives.

In recent years, American women have renewed the legal fight for the Equal Rights Amendment. Women of all backgrounds, students, mothers, seniors, women of color, indigenous women, et cetera, have taken up the mantle of the suffragists before them, standing on suffragists' shoulders as they marched and mobilized, protested and picketed for their rights. And because of their courage and commitment, 38 states have now ratified the Equal Rights Amendment. But one final barrier remains, removing the artificial, arbitrary time limit for ratification. As the distinguished Chairman pointed out, that deadline is not in the–timetable is not in the Constitution. Until we remove that arbitrary time limit, the ERA cannot become part of our Constitution. Last year, the House passed legislation to remove this arbitrary time limit, but unfortunately, the Senate failed to do so.

So, today, the House will once again pass this legislation and send it to the Senate for a vote and we are proud to be doing it in Women's History Month. We salute, again, Congresswoman Jackie Speier, our champion on this legislation on the Floor today, and Congresswoman Carolyn Maloney, who has been our lead sponsor of the ERA for 25 years now. And I thank Members on both sides of the aisle, including Cosponsor, Representative Tom Reed of New York, for their bipartisan support in the Congress, which reflects the overwhelming bipartisan support in the country. A full 94 percent of the public supports the Equal Rights Amendment, including 99 percent, nearly unanimous support, among Millennials and Generation Z.

Let us not forget that in 1972, the Equal Rights Amendment was passed with bipartisan super-majorities in both houses–Chambers of Congress and it enjoyed the strong support of President Nixon, who wrote in 1968 that "[t]he task of achieving Constitutional equality between the sexes is still not completed," and pointed out that all Republican National Conventions since 1940 have supported the longtime movement for equality.

There is no reason why, today, after 80 years of Republican support, the ERA should not have full bipartisan support in the Congress. The resolution on the Floor today will pave the way to passage of the Equal Rights Amendment, which is one of the most important steps that we can take to affirm and ensure women's equality in America.

The text of the Equal Rights Amendment states, "Equality of rights under the law shall not be denied or abridged by the United States or by any State on account of sex." On the account of sex. It recalls to mind the beautiful documentary about Ruth Bader Ginsburg.

Passing the Equal Rights Amendment will create essential avenues of legal recourse for people who face discrimination under the laws on the basis of sex. It will ensure that the Supreme Court applies the same standard of review for sex discrimination cases as it applies to cases of discrimination based on race and national origin. It will help Congress pass laws for better legal protections against injustice, including those related to sexual assault, domestic violence and paycheck fairness, or unfairness. And it will confirm the rightful place of gender equality in all aspects of life.

There are some who say the Equal Rights Amendment is not needed. To them, I quote the late Justice Antonin Scalia who said—Justice Scalia said, "Certainly the Constitution does not require discrimination on the basis of sex. The only issue is whether it prohibits it. It does not." There are not—these are not just words. This is the daily reality. "It does not." This is the daily reality for American women who face inequality and injustice for so many arenas of life, from a massive wage gap, to pregnancy discrimination, to sexual harassment in the workplace, to economic disparities that have worsened during the coronavirus.

Passing this resolution and then the ERA will not only help women. By unleashing the full economic potential of women—doing so will help families and boost our economy, all the while advancing justice and equality in America for everyone.

With that, I urge a strong bipartisan vote on this strong step toward equality for women, progress for families and a stronger America, affirming the truth, Madam Speaker, that you have espoused: When women succeed, America succeeds. With that, I, again, commend the leadership on this issue: the distinguished Chairman, the sponsor of the resolution, Jackie Speier, Carolyn Maloney, and yield back the balance of my time.

Notes

1 Nancy Pelosi, "Floor Speech in Support of Resolution to Remove the Time Limit for ERA Ratification," U.S. House of Representatives, Office of the Speaker of the House, March 17, 2021, https://pelosi.house.gov/news/press-releases/pelosi-floor-speech-in-support-of-resolution-to-remove-the-time-limit-for-era. Public Domain.

2 Vincent Bzdek, *Woman of the House: The Rise of Nancy Pelosi* (New York: Palgrave Macmillan, 2008), 17, 69.

3 Molly Ball, *Pelosi* (New York: Picador, 2020), 16–17.

4 Ball, *Pelosi*, 28–32, 37.

5 For an in-depth discussion of Pelosi's leadership during the Trump administration, see Ball, *Pelosi*, 236–322.

6 Nancy Pelosi, "New Campaign for an Equal Rights Amendment," *C-SPAN*, January 3, 1989, https://www.c-span.org/video/?5571-1/campaign-equal-rights-amendment.

7 Carrie N. Baker, "House Votes to Clear the Way for ERA in the Constitution: Feminists React," *Ms. Magazine*, March 18, 2021, https://msmagazine.com/2021/03/18/era-equal-rights-amendment-house-representatives-feminist-women/; Hannah Hayes, "100 Years On, the ERA Rises from the Ashes," American Bar Association, March 25, 2020, https://www.americanbar.org/groups/diversity/women/publications/perspectives/2020/march/100-years-the-era-rises-the-ashes/.

8 Congressman Jerrold Nadler (D-NY) has served in the U.S. House of Representatives since 1992.

9 Although the ERA was not formally introduced to Congress until December 1923, Alice Paul, Crystal Eastman, and others were in the process of drafting the amendment by 1921.

We Follow in Their Footsteps

Address to the U.S. House of Representatives for Women's History Month

AYANNA PRESSLEY
March 23, 2023[1]

As a founding member of the Trump-resisting "Squad" alongside Alexandria Ocasio-Cortez (D-NY), Ilhan Omar (D-MN), and Rashida Tlaib (D-MI), Ayanna Soyini Pressley (1974–present) was the first woman of color elected to represent Massachusetts in the House of Representatives, where she has served since 2019. The Chicago native spent her early years cultivating leadership skills in student government and competitive debate. She attended Boston University in the early 1990s but left before graduating to take care of her single mother. Undeterred by this change in her trajectory, Pressley found work as an aide under Representative Joseph Kennedy II (D-MA) and served as a longtime staffer for Senator John Kerry (D-MA). By 2009, Pressley had made history as the first woman of color elected to serve on the Boston City Council.[2]

In Congress, Pressley has used her position to advocate for the rights of women. She has pushed for reproductive justice, supported paid leave, served on the Pro-Choice Caucus, and co-sponsored the Women's Health Protection Act (WHPA), federal legislation that seeks to guarantee women have access to abortion care in the wake of the Supreme Court's anti-choice ruling on *Dobbs v. Jackson Women's Health Organization* in 2022.[3] Pressley has also been a vocal opponent of the Hyde Amendment, which inhibits Medicaid coverage for abortion services.[4] Perhaps Pressley is best known for living with alopecia, an autoimmune condition that causes hair loss. Through foregoing her wig in public and talking openly about her experiences, Pressley has helped demystify alopecia through consciousness-raising and advocacy.[5]

In early 2023, Pressley joined forces with several colleagues to create the first-ever Congressional Caucus for the Equal Rights Amendment. Among its leaders were Representatives Cori Bush (D-MO), Judy Chu (D-CA), Sydney Kamlager-Dove (D-CA), Summer Lee (D-PA), and Jennifer McClellan (D-VA). On March 28, these members gathered on the steps of the U.S. Capitol to publicly launch the caucus. In her remarks at the press conference, Congresswoman Bush contextualized the formation of the caucus within the legacy of "those who came before us, who's example we now carry—we're talking about Mary Church Terrell, Pauli Murray, Barbara Jordan, Shirley Chisholm, Aileen Hernandez, and Flo Kennedy." These women, Bush highlighted, not only have yet to get their due credit as ERA advocates but also struggled to be included in the conversation in the first place.[6] Just five days earlier, Pressley made a similar point in a ceremonial tribute to Shirley Chisholm on the floor of the House of Representatives for Women's History Month. The women of color in Congress, Pressley argued, were poised to pick up the torch and fight for the next generation's rights to equality under the Constitution.

As we enter this next century of women debating the addition of gender equality to the law of the land, do women have the rhetorical resources to make it official? Have the state constitutions and smaller statutes put the matter to rest? Or will the opposition continue to prevail? With a new multiracial and intergenerational coalition leading the way, Pressley and her allies remain hopeful that the ERA campaign begun in 1923 will at long last triumph.

Mr. Speaker, neither my mother Sandy nor my father Martin raised me to ask permission to lead. I do believe that a parent is a child's first and best teacher. Instead of traditional bedtime stories of princes and knights in shining armor, my mother read me the powerful speeches of Black congresswomen like Barbara Jordan and Shirley Chisholm. Since my formative years, I have felt this soul tie to Shirley Chisholm—long before my work led me to this chamber. In fact, my first office here as a freshman of the 116th Congress was formerly Shirley Chisholm's office.

Not only was Shirley—and I don't say that to be in any way disrespectful by not referring to her as a congresswoman—but she is in fact so iconic that you can just say her first name and it is clear who you are talking about. Not only was Shirley a "first" as the first Black woman elected to the House of Representatives. She was disruptive, she was brave, she was a trailblazer. In fighting injustice, she was an inspiration.

Very often, iconic leaders can be singularly defined by one great speech and some powerful quotes. I think it is tempting to do that with Congresswoman

Shirley Chisholm. But it would be a disservice to do so. While certainly she was the first Black woman elected to Congress [and] the first Black woman to pursue the U.S. presidency, let the record reflect that Shirley Chisholm was an effective legislator in her own right serving here for seven terms. The daughter of immigrants from Barbados and Guyana, she has blazed the trail for every Black woman in this body, including myself today as the first person of color and the first Black woman to ever represent the commonwealth of Massachusetts in the U.S. House of Representatives. Everyone, including Vice President Kamala Harris, owes her a debt of gratitude.

But her contributions go well beyond that. During her time in these sacred halls of power, Shirley played a critical role in advancing policies that support our most vulnerable and marginalized communities. As a member of the Agricultural Committee, Shirley was pivotal in enacting the SNAP Program, which helps feed over 42 million people each year. She was also one of 13 founding members in 1971 of the Congressional Black Caucus, which today boasts its largest membership in history. And she was also a founding member of the National Women's Political Caucus. Everyone wants to be a part of something when it's already established. But it takes a certain kind of grit, vision, and determination to be the founder of something. Shirley was both a visionary and a doer and tenacious in the actualization of these caucuses which live on today.

And Shirley Chisholm was a forceful champion for the Equal Rights Amendment, a cause I'm honored to lead in partnership with my colleagues and movement allies in the House today. In her words, in the words of Congresswoman Shirley Chisholm, spoken right here in the People's House, she said the ERA "provides a legal basis for attack on the most subtle, most pervasive, and most institutionalized forms of prejudice that exist. Discrimination against women solely on the basis of their sex is so widespread that it seems to many persons normal, natural, and right."

Mr. Speaker, Black women like Shirley Chisholm have done the work of preserving and defending our democracy for centuries. But for far too often, our contributions are ignored, erased, or rendered a footnote in history. And it's not lost on me that the first time the ERA was put forward, women of color were not even a part of the conversation.

Today, there will be no erasure. We stand on the shoulders of folks like Shirley Chisholm leading a multiracial, intergenerational coalition to advance this priority.

Mr. Speaker, when asked how she wanted to be remembered, Shirley Chisholm said that she wanted to be remembered as a Black woman who lived in the twentieth century and dared to be herself—a catalyst for change.

Today, during Women's History month, and every month, we honor women like Shirley, we follow in their footsteps, and we continue running, winning, leading, legislating, and taking up all the space with our full, authentic selves just as Shirley taught us. May she rest in peace and power. Happy Women's History Month. Thank you.

Notes

1 "Ayanna Pressley Hails Shirley Chisholm's Legislative Prowess, Leadership on Equal Rights Amendment," Rep. Ayanna Pressley, U.S. House of Representatives, March 23, 2023, https://www.youtube.com/watch?v=SQIeT1KgKfo. Public Domain.

2 "U.S. Representative Ayanna Pressley," National Urban League, https://nul.org/events-ayanna-pressley.

3 Abigail Tracy, "'They Don't See Us': Ayanna Pressley Won't Let Women Be Ignored by the Republican Majority," *Vanity Fair*, December 13, 2022, https://www.vanityfair.com/news/2022/12/ayanna-pressley-congress-republican-majority.

4 "Hyde Amendment," Planned Parenthood, https://www.plannedparenthoodaction.org/issues/abortion/federal-and-state-bans-and-restrictions-abortion/hyde-amendment.

5 Merrit Kennedy, "'Freed from the Secret': Rep. Ayanna Pressley Opens Up about Living with Alopecia," *NPR*, January 17, 2020, https://www.npr.org/2020/01/17/797295985/freed-from-the-secret-rep-ayanna-pressley-opens-up-about-living-with-alopecia.

6 "Rep. Cori Bush Leading New Push for ERA Passage," *St. Louis American*, March 30, 2023, https://www.stlamerican.com/news/cori-bush-leading-new-push-for-era-passage/article_b84ee7bc-ce7d-11ed-988f-f7c8a9df1f21.html; "Reps. Ayanna Pressley & Cori Bush Launch the First-Ever Congressional Equal Rights Amendment Caucus," Rep. Ayanna Pressley, U.S. Capitol, March 28, 2023, YouTube, https://www.youtube.com/watch?v=WQ29TZEqWwk.

Index

www.ingramcontent.com/pod-product-compliance
Ingram Content Group UK Ltd.
Pitfield, Milton Keynes, MK11 3LW, UK
UKHW020201290926
15471UKWH00005B/1010

9 781636 675046